CLAIMING UNION WIDOWHOOD

F in the case of

Harry Whitney for

nt of County,

Office address:

DECLARATION AND ...

PROOF

Enrolled Feb. 20, 1864

Genl. U.S.A. as follows;

7 ... July 20th 1865

No record. Proved by

Clergyman who married

CLAIMING UNION WIDOWHOOD

Race, Respectability, and Poverty in the Post-Emancipation South

BRANDI CLAY BRIMMER

Duke University Press *Durham and London* 2020

Designed by Aimee C. Harrison
Typeset in Minino Pro by Westchester

Library of Congress Cataloging-in-Publication Data

Names: Brimmer, Brandi Clay, [dates].
Title: Claiming Union Widowhood : race, respectability, and poverty in the post-emancipation South / Brandi Clay Brimmer.
Description: Durham : Duke University Press, 2020. | Includes bibliographical references and index.
Identifiers: LCCN 2020018449 (print) | LCCN 2020018450 (ebook) | ISBN 9781478010258 (hardcover) | ISBN 9781478011323 (paperback) | ISBN 9781478012832 (ebook) | ISBN 9781478090403 (ebook other)
Subjects: LCSH: United States. Army—Minorities—History—19th century. | Military pensions—United States—Civil War, 1861-1865. | Military pensions—North Carolina. | Widows—North Carolina—History—19th century. | African American women—North Carolina—History—19th century. | Women's rights—United States—History—19th century. | Racism—United States—History—19th century. | United States—History—Civil War, 1861-1865—Pensions.
Classification: LCC UB374.N8 B756 2020 (print) | LCC UB374.N8 (ebook) | DDC 331.25/291355008996073—dc23
LC record available at https://lccn.loc.gov/2020018449
LC ebook record available at https://lccn.loc.gov/2020018450

COVER ART: Adapted from Fanny Whitney's claim for pension, with minor children, 1867. From pension file of Fanny Whitney, widow of Harry Whitney (WC 130403), Civil War Pension Index: General Index to Pension Files, 1861–1934, Records of the Department of Veterans Affairs, 1773–2007, RG 15, National Archives and Records Administration, Washington, DC.

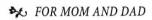

FOR MOM AND DAD

Contents

Cast of Principal Characters ~ ix
Acknowledgments ~ xi
Introduction ~ 1

PART I A PEOPLE AND A PLACE

1. Black Life and Labor in New Bern, North Carolina, 1850–1865 ~ 23

2. The Black Community in New Bern, 1865–1920 ~ 46

PART II ENCOUNTERING THE STATE

3. Her Claim Is Lawful and Just: Black Women's Petitions for Survivors' Benefits ~ 77

4. Black Women, Claims Agents, and the Pension Network ~ 101

5. Encounters with the State: Black Women and Special Examiners ~ 123

6. Marriage and the Expansion of the Pension System in 1890 ~ 144

7. Black Women and Suspensions for "Open and Notorious Cohabitation" ~ 163

8. The Personal Consequences of Union Widowhood ~ 184

Conclusion ~ 205
Notes ~ 217
Bibliography ~ 277
Index ~ 299

Contents

Cast of Principal Characters

BLACK UNION WIDOWS

Charlotte Banks (freedwoman, washerwoman)
Mary Lee (freedwoman, washerwoman, cook, and farm laborer)
Louisa Powers (freedwoman [?], farm laborer, domestic)
Fanny Whitney (freedwoman, domestic)

WHITE CLAIMS AGENTS

Augustus Sherrill Seymour (attorney, state senator, judge)
Edward W. Carpenter (attorney, journalist, probate judge)
William L. Palmer (U.S. commissioner, mayor, notary public)
Henry Hall (Confederate veteran, bookseller)
Ethelbert Hubbs (veteran, notary public)

BLACK CLAIMS AGENTS

James D. Barfield (grocer, merchant)
Charles Cox (office worker)
Frederick C. Douglass (teacher, minister, justice of the peace)
Phillip Lee (veteran, grocer, merchant, teacher, minister, justice of the peace, community leader)
Andrew J. Marshall (veteran, county coroner, minister)
Emanuel Merrick (grocer)
Alfred Small (veteran, minister)

BLACK PROPRIETORS AND MUNICIPAL LEADERS

James Harrison (justice of the peace)
Julia Jackson (officer, National Ex-Slave Mutual Relief, Bounty and Pension Association)
Robert G. Mosley (grocer, real estate agent, merchant)

Washington Spivey (postmaster, James City)
Merritt Whitely (undertaker)

BLACK ELECTED OFFICIALS

Henry P. Cheatham (Republican, congressman, attorney)
James O'Hara (Republican, congressman, attorney)
George H. White (Republican, congressman, attorney)

WHITE ELECTED OFFICIALS

Charles B. Aycock (Democrat, governor of North Carolina, 1901–5)
Furnifold Simmons (Democrat, U.S. senator, attorney)
Charles Thomas (Democrat, U.S. senator, congressman, attorney)

SPECIAL EXAMINERS FROM WASHINGTON, DC

Emmett D. Gallion (Pennsylvania)
Charles Gilpin (Kentucky)
Thomas Goethe (South Carolina)
W. L. Harris (New York)
C. D. McSorley (New York)
H. P. Maxwell (Tennessee)
William Porter (Massachusetts)
G. H. Ragsdale (?, special agent)
J. O'C. Roberts (Alabama)
I. C. Stockton (Illinois)
Grafton Tyler (West Virginia)

COMMISSIONERS OF THE U.S. PENSION BUREAU, WASHINGTON, DC

John H. Baker (1871–75)
Dr. Henry Van Aernam (1878–82)
J. A. Bentley (1876–1881)
William W. Dudley (1881–84)
John C. Black (1885–89)
Green B. Raum (1889–93)
Julius Lincoln, acting commissioner (1890)
William Lochren (1893–96)
H. Clay Evans (1897–1903)

Acknowledgments

This book is the result of the support, generosity, and intellectual rigor of a lot of different people who believed in me from beginning to end. The unwavering support from Laura F. Edwards, an extraordinary mentor and generous scholar, taught me the art of asking "big questions" and investing time in thinking through the answers. A mentor and friend, Laura's commitment to my development as a historian continues to humble me. She has commented on numerous drafts of this project, advised, supported, and directed with kindness and generosity. At the University of California, Los Angeles, where this project began, I had the great fortune of also working with Naomi Lamoreaux, Jan Reiff, Brenda Stevenson, Robert Hill, Cheryl Harris, Ellen DuBois, and Richard Yarborough in the Departments of History and African American Studies. Foundational courses on the history of enslaved women taught by Stevenson deepened my resolve to center the voices of newly freed black women in my work.

Initial funding from the North Caroliniana Society and a kind note from the founding director, H. G. Jones, led me to Frederick C. Douglass's papers at Eastern Carolina University. There I had the good fortune of meeting and learning from Don Lennon, the longtime director of the East Carolina Manuscript Collection. Lennon generously guided me in my early days of research. Once the project picked up steam, Kate Collins helped me navigate the Rubenstein Library and University Archives at Duke. Collins is nothing short of a miracle worker, whose keen knowledge helped me locate a hard-to-find collection of correspondence. Writing about New Bern is one thing; the opportunity to visit is quite another. Both Sharon Bryant (Tryon Palace) and

Ben Watford (James City Historical Society) took days out of their schedules to walk the neighborhoods and business district shortly before the hurricane of 2018 hit.

This project is based on years of archival research, and I am particularly grateful to the staff at the National Archives in Washington, DC, who worked tirelessly behind the scenes helping me locate pension files and a range of bureaucratic records. I am indebted to Leslie S. Rowland and Steven F. Miller at the Freedmen and Southern Society Project, part of the History Department at the University of Maryland, College Park, who taught me how to navigate the records of the U.S. military and honed my understanding of the complexities of wartime bureaucracy. Working at the project gave me the opportunity to study Reconstruction from the bottom up and simultaneously forge a friendship with the late Ira Berlin.

An early opportunity to participate in a conference at New York University, convened by Michele Mitchell, Jennifer Brier, and Jennifer Morgan, helped me think through critical questions surrounding racialized gender and political claims. I met Jim Downs there, who encouraged me to do this work unapologetically. Feedback from Eileen Boris, Nancy Bercaw, Grey Osterud, Elsa Barkley Brown, Noralee Frankel, Sonya Michel, Stephanie Shaw, Jeff Kerr-Ritchie, Mia Bay, Rhonda Williams, Joan Kosics, and James F. Best resulted in a full reorganization of the project and new interrogations of black women's claims making. Rhonda Williams believed in the work, supported the vision, read and reread, and—perhaps most importantly—provided a space for me to do so at Case Western Reserve. Research assistance from Jeanette Lugo proved instrumental in the early stages of this work.

When I joined the History Department at Morgan State University, I had the benefit of working with a talented and dedicated group of teacher scholars who welcomed me into one of the most collegial and supportive academic communities I've ever known. Their brilliance and dedication to teaching made me a better scholar, teacher, and intellectual. I am particularly grateful to Takkara Brunson, Herbert Brewer, Jewel Debnam, Frances Dube, Felicia Thomas, Bob Morrow, David Terry, Linda Noel, Larry Peskin, Annette Palmer, and Brett Berliner. Brett is simply the best kind of colleague. He read and reread final drafts of the introduction, giving up his time off during the holiday season and spring break. Cynthia Spence, Beverly Guy-Sheftall, Dalila de Sousa, Margery Ganz, Kathleen Phillips-Lewis (KPL), Jackie Mercadal, Catherine Odari, and Yan Xu welcomed me into their intellectual community at Spelman College as I put the finishing touches on various chapters.

Mentorship, guidance, and intellectual inspiration have come from Eileen Boris, Dennis C. Dickerson, Rosanne Adderley, Thavolia Glymph, Tera Hunter, Stanley Harrold, Randall Miller, Mia Bay, Heidi Ardizonne, Nancy Bercaw, Noralee Frankel, and Rhonda Williams. I simply could not have produced this work without early guidance from Grey Osterud and later input from the anonymous readers of this manuscript. Several people across the profession took me under their wing and contributed to this book in particular ways. Though I never had the opportunity to meet the late Megan McClintock, her scholarly work has guided and inspired me throughout the research and writing process. Anthony Kaye was instrumental in helping me organize, think through, and theorize the professional work of black claims agents. Kaye, along with William Blair, was also instrumental in the completion of my first peer-reviewed article. Gregory Downs, Matt Karp, Dylan Penningroth, Kate Masur, Emily Osborn, Anastasia Curwood, Lou and Freida Outlaw, Gary Gerstle, Elizabeth Lunbeck, Jane Landers, Farrell Evans, Richard Pierce, Gail Bederman, Heidi Ardizzone, Sharon Romeo, Paul Finkelman, and Jessica Millward provided constructive feedback and advice on various iterations of the work. Karen Cook-Bell, Natanya Duncan, Sharita Jacobs Thompson, Sherie M. Randolph, Furaha Norton, Arlisha Norwood, Dierdre Cooper Owens, my fellow writers in the Women Who Write Working Group, and Trevor Muñoz kept me sane and intellectually inspired by and through their own scholarly productions. The teaching from and spiritual friendships with Claybourne "Clay" Earle, Tonya Frazier, Stephanie Brown, Delores Orduna, Sister Dr. Jenna, and Santosh have been life-changing. I have had the privilege of teaching some truly brilliant students while honing the arguments for this book. A special thanks goes Jeanette Lugo, Paulé Elizabeth Jackson, Candace Jackson-Gray, Dalia Kijakazi, and Rachel Nelson for sharing their critical insights with me in the classroom.

Generous financial support over the years has come from the North Caroliniana Society, the Institute for American Cultures (UCLA), the Erskine Peters Predoctoral Program at the University of Notre Dame, the Provost Office at Vanderbilt University, the Ford Foundation Postdoctoral Fellowship, the College of Arts and Science at Case Western Reserve University, and the College of Liberal Arts and the Benjamin Quarles Humanities and Social Science Institute at Morgan State University. The stars aligned when I met Gisela Fosado, who believed in this project and walked me through the final phases of completion with patience and grace. Without question, the dedicated assistance of Alejandra Mejía, Aimee Harrison, Melanie Mallon, Ellen Goldlust, Sandy Sadow, and Bill Nelson's mapmaking got me over the finish line.

This has been a long journey for me, and I've learned many lessons along the way. The women who animate the pages of this book have taught me so much about political struggle and humanity. Anika Hunter, Kimberly Williamson, and Aisha Sterling have all been willing listeners and a constant source of joy and laughter. I am deeply humbled and forever grateful for the love, patience, and kindness my family has extended to me over the years. Edward Brimmer Sr., Hallie Brimmer, Gertrude Jacke, Hurdle Clay Jacke, Minnie Reyes, and Lura B. Smith laid the foundation for this work by pouring their love, time, and resources into me. Profound gratitude is reserved for my godparents, Michelé and Zelber Minnix, and my brother, Erik, for their encouragement as I labored through this study. As the research and writing for this *Claiming Union Widowhood* was coming to a close, I had the good fortune of meeting James Fitzgerald "Gerald" Best Jr. as the writing and revision process unfolded. Simply put: James has been my rock through the ups and the downs. We always find a way to see the light in the struggle, and I am grateful for our friendship, partnership, and spiritual walk. My parents, Marilyn and Edward Brimmer, have loved and supported me through it all. With the support of my parents and the love of God, all things are possible; it is for this reason that I dedicate this book to them.

Introduction

This book tells the story of how black women asserted their views of citizenship, rights, and worthy widowhood to the U.S. Pension Bureau during the late nineteenth and early twentieth centuries. They qualified for entitlements based on their standing as soldiers' widows, but black women whose husbands had served in the military had to contend constantly with racial prejudice and sexual scrutiny to claim their pensions. As beneficiaries of monies apportioned for the wives, mothers, and children of dead black soldiers, these women laid bare the social and economic concerns of poor and working-class black women, who had historically been excluded from notions of womanly respectability and worthiness. In their struggle to claim Union widowhood, these women negotiated and challenged the intersectional race, class, and gender assumptions that hitherto defined not only the pension system, but also the very boundaries of U.S. citizenship.

Fanny Whitney, a newly freed black woman born in Craven County, North Carolina, around 1828, was one such woman, and the concerns she tenaciously articulated were not merely private matters but public ones to be debated in the pension system and in her community. Fanny Whitney and thousands of other newly freed black women engaged in protracted battles with the U.S. Pension Bureau to claim their benefits and maintain their position on the pension roster; their actions inspired this study of black women's claims for survivors' benefits. It is written from the perspective of newly freed black women and thus depicts how a complex interweaving of family and kin relationships forged over the course of the nineteenth century sustained their struggle for recognition within the pension system, and, by extension, the nation-state.

Black women's petitions for survivors' benefits were a crucial dimension of freedpeople's demands for full citizenship. As the largest group of Union widows in the South, these women asserted their rights and established a direct relationship to the federal government. Throughout the war, the promise of survivors' benefits was an effective incentive for white male enlistment. Black men, by contrast, volunteered to fight for freedom without any promise of survivors' benefits. In 1864, however, Congress extended the federal pension system to the formerly enslaved on a limited basis. Not until 1866 would black survivors file petitions with great frequency.

Extending benefits to the formerly enslaved constituted a powerful commitment at a crucial time in U.S. history. Emboldened by the end of slavery and the ratification of the Thirteenth Amendment, black people flooded public spaces to celebrate the destruction of slavery. When the federal pension system was initially opened to black women, black citizenship remained an open question, and the idea of black women making claims and obtaining government resources represented a threat to the evolving racial and gender order. Petitions for survivors' benefits signaled black women's vision of themselves as worthy citizens before the 1868 enactment of the Fourteenth Amendment.

The expansion of the pension system proved controversial as the years wore on, and its implementation was problematic because only the Bureau of Refugees, Freedmen, and Abandoned Lands, conceived as a temporary agency, distributed aid to blacks at this scale. Established in early March 1865, under the direction of General Oliver Otis Howard, the Freedmen's Bureau assisted ex-slaves in the transition to the free labor system. It was often criticized for undermining the South's social and economic order by supporting freedpeople's rights in disputes with white employers and landlords.[1] The Freedmen's Bureau's belief in the fidelity of the contract was ineffective, as freedpeople preferred systems of work that afforded them control of their families and their own labor. Unlike the Freedmen's Bureau, whose social welfare activities were effectively ended in 1868, the Pension Bureau expanded its commitment to disabled soldiers and their families through the early twentieth century.

Claiming Union Widowhood probes the multidimensional facets of working-class black women's lives through the lens of social and political history. Foundational insights set down in W. E. B. Du Bois's *Black Reconstruction* (1935), Thomas Holt's conceptualization of the problems of freedom, and nearly two decades of scholarship focusing on gender and the long emancipation illustrate freedwomen's central participation, as Leslie Schwalm asserts, "in the interrelated struggles to define freedom and free labor."[2] By centering the experiences of black women and their roles within their households, historians of gender and emancipation untangle the vital connections between working-class black women's pursuit of family life, personal autonomy, and the evolution of free labor in the post-emancipation South.[3] Freedwomen expanded the consequences of their freedom by laying claim to family life: caring for spouses, children, and extended families in the roles of full-time wife and mother, roles that were denied to them under slavery.

This book is conceptually indebted to Leslie Schwalm's and Noralee Frankel's scholarly analyses of freedwomen's encounters with military administrators and federal agencies during the Civil War and Reconstruction years. Black women's prioritization of their own family needs proved disruptive to the new order northern proponents of free labor had envisioned. Conflicts arose as military administrators and Freedmen's Bureau agents attempted both to dictate what constituted legitimate marital relations and to mediate black women's assertions of free womanhood by compelling them to prioritize wage labor over their own families. Ideas about gender and racial difference, Schwalm explained, informed "the articulation of power, the development of postbellum social and economic policy . . . and the material consequences of such policies."[4] Frankel's analysis of African American intimate relations and gender constructions in Civil War–era Mississippi showed the extent to which blacks continued to embrace prewar community standards and norms, rather than legal institutions, in defining their marital lives. Frankel's intervention is critical to this book's conceptual framing because she, like Schwalm, shows the difficulties freedwomen had expressing the "terms and conditions" of their marital relations in federal agencies and legal institutions. Adherence to alternative notions of marriage and womanhood, Frankel showed, severely limited black women's economic claims in the Freedmen's Bureau and the pension system.[5]

Claiming Union Widowhood outlines the meaning, construction, and contested nature of federal entitlements from the grassroots perspective.[6] It explores and highlights two aspects of black women's pension case files that informed the women's concept of Union widowhood: (1) the conditions and experiences of their lives before, during, and after the war; and (2) the boundaries and norms of Union widowhood that circulated among black people. The claims-making process became a terrain of debate within the black community and between black people and the federal government. Tensions existed between women's desire to live by their own designs, their community's standards, and the Pension Bureau's rules.

Women's claims for survivors' benefits hinged on the bureau's construct of marriage. Bureau administrators required that petitioners reconstruct their intimate histories leading up to, during, and after the war, as well as their marital relation to the soldier. This application requirement revealed the degree to which black people defined their married and family lives on their own terms and outside legal institutions. Agents of the Pension Bureau scrutinized the private realm of marriage to determine who should have access to the designation of "legal widow." This status was significant within the pension system because it officially legitimated a woman's relation to the soldier on which she based her claim. To maintain this designation, these women would have to abide by the bureau's construct of womanly respectability.

Tera Hunter's landmark study of slave and free black marriages in the United States over the course of the nineteenth century is vital to this work because it fundamentally alters long-standing assumptions about the meaning, definition, and purpose of heterosexual marital relations among African Americans. African Americans viewed marriage as fundamental to their conception of citizenship rights in the United States, but they continued to embrace marital fluidity to mitigate the impact of poverty and deprivation in their transition to free labor. Understanding how marriage operated in the lives of poor and working-class black women is central to interpreting the political meanings of black women's claims for pension.[7]

Black women's battles for pensions constitute an underappreciated dimension of black women's protest politics during the late nineteenth century. At the heart of these struggles lay freedwomen's competing definitions of marriage, worthy womanhood, family, and by extension citizenship. Black women's complex understanding of marriage and Union widowhood is prominent in their petitions for survivors' benefits. Their dreams for the future grew out of the darkest days of slavery, the horrors of family separation and sexual violation. Efforts to realize full freedom for themselves and their children are evident in the case files of petitioners like freedwoman Charlotte Banks, who waged a decades-long—albeit unsuccessful—battle to secure benefits and to have bureau officials recognize her "slave marriage," even after it was documented that she had remarried.

The stories recounted in this book unfold in New Bern, North Carolina, where thousands of black refugees and white military administrators mixed with a preexisting community of politically savvy blacks, many of whom had been enslaved. With the end of federal intervention in the South after 1877, blacks then focused on strengthening the black community to take care of its own interests. Blacks had to because the Democrats who took over North Carolina's state legislature began chipping away at Republican-sponsored initiatives that had, during Reconstruction, protected black rights. Black citizens thus developed multiprong initiatives to chart the future direction of their communities. Black men pushed back against efforts to limit their power in the electoral arena, securing elected office in their communities and congressional districts.[8]

Throughout this study, I devote considerable attention to theorizing and analyzing what I refer to as the "grassroots pension network." This network grew out of the development and maturation of black institutions and political achievements in the electoral arena during the Reconstruction era. W. E. B. Du Bois credited black leadership with the installation of democratic governments, public schools, and new social legislation, while Eric Foner's seminal study *Reconstruction* unveiled the political significance, consolidation, and expansion of black institution building across the South. "Blacks during Reconstruction," Foner insisted, "laid the foundation for the modern black community, whose roots lay deep in slavery, but whose structures and values reflected the consequences of emancipation."[9] Fanny Whitney, Charlotte Banks, and others in New Bern's black neighborhoods breathed life into the very institutions that empowered black women to challenge racialized gender constructions of Union widowhood, which regularly excluded them from the pension roster.

By placing the social ties and associational life in black neighborhoods at the center of the claims process, *Claiming Union Widowhood* deepens historians' understanding of the relationship between working-class black women and federal authorities in the decades leading up to the twentieth century. Poor black women initiated these petitions with the assistance of their neighbors and members of the grassroots pension network. After Reconstruction, by 1880, black women, with the assistance of professional black men, forged a grassroots regional infrastructure that facilitated black women's claims on the government. The specific and localized protocols and exchanges that occurred within women's homes, places of worship, grocery stores, and banks, as well as on street corners, constituted important aspects of this network. Grassroots in its nature, this network existed apart from the Pension Bureau's formal structure. Building on Anthony Kaye's groundbreaking analysis of neighborhoods and black social ties, this study shows how black working-class women used their own social networks and the grassroots pension apparatuses to sustain their relationship with the federal government over long spans of time.[10]

By placing black female petitioners' battles for survivors' benefits at the center of struggles for citizenship and economic justice, *Claiming Union Widowhood* rescripts late nineteenth-century African American political history by offering a longer periodization, new definitions of social welfare, and a more capacious definition of political acts. It draws extensively on scholarly work that examines the social and political consciousness of poor black women in the urban South. Incorporating Elsa Barkley Brown's insights about the black public sphere, I argue that the factors leading to black women's years-long battle for survivors' benefits sprung from sources of empowerment cultivated in their households, neighborhoods, and community institutions.[11] Without black women's demonstrated self-assertion and consciousness of themselves as worthy, New Bern's grassroots pension network—which proved to be a valuable income stream for black and white professional men—simply would not have been possible.[12]

In analyzing the political dimensions of New Bern's grassroots pension network, this study builds on Steven Hahn's contention that familial and kin networks formed the basis of black people's political communities in the late nineteenth century. Such communities, Hahn argued, "continually made and remade their politics and political history in complex relation to shifting events; they did not have their history made for them."[13] New Bern's grassroots pension network was not necessarily exceptional. Rather, the community component of this study provides the specific context necessary to understand the nature of poor black women's claims and the contours of the tortuous claims process. Local analysis allows for the study of a tenacious group of people whose ties to old plantations, farm neighborhoods, settlement camps, and new neighborhoods, such as the Fifth Ward and James City, anchored blacks through periods of chaotic upheaval, dislocation, and death. New Bern's postwar neighborhoods, reconstituted after the chaos of war, brought together these old and new social networks. Succinctly stated, black women's battles for survivors' benefits cannot be understood apart from the neighborhoods in which they were rooted or how they lived their lives.[14] Fanny Whitney, Charlotte Banks, and a host of other people who make their appearances in these pages attest to this claim.

Black women often hired claims agents to navigate the time-consuming, protracted, and difficult-to-understand claims process. Claims agents, as the Pension Bureau called them, both helped women assemble witnesses, affidavits, and other evidence and corresponded directly with the bureau or acted as go-betweens with the national firms that represented claimants, the largest of which were in Washington, DC. Claims agents were not required to have formal legal training to represent a claimant before the Department of the Interior or one of its bureaus, but they had to be able to read and write and have a basic understanding of the pension laws.

Authenticated by the panoply of institutions rooted at the center of black civil life, a cadre of black professional men who had distinguished themselves as socially responsible leaders would eventually serve as claims agents—oftentimes at the behest of African American war widows. The ambitious black men who assumed these roles were farmers, barbers, teachers, ministers, grocers, and retailers; most combined two or three of these occupations. Some were veterans themselves. Of the sixteen blacks identified as claims agents in this study, more than half had been enslaved.[15] Working on behalf of formerly enslaved women meant providing services that went well beyond filling out paperwork. At times, claims agents took on responsibilities that mirrored those of benevolent societies, providing shelter and financial assistance to disabled veterans and needy widows before their quarterly stipends arrived. These men translated black women's experiences into terms the federal government recognized, a feat that the previous generation of white claims agents had not been able to accomplish.[16] They became the conduit through which black women interacted with the federal government.

Claims agents helped widows use various institutional mechanisms, such as appeals, petitions, and letters, to engage with the federal government for survivors' benefits. They sought to instigate special examinations, draw authorities' attention to a woman's case, or secure a woman's position on the pension roster. The special examination phase of the application process, in which a bureau agent, typically a white man who came from outside the community, scrutinized a woman's life to ascertain whether she met the strict criteria for eligibility, was conducted with much of the formality of a court trial, with claimants speaking for themselves. These examinations opened a discursive space for black women, as well as for their friends, family members, and neighbors, to set forth their own definitions of both Union widowhood and worthiness.

Black women experienced the surveillance of the agents of the Pension Bureau, which at minimum amounted to paternalistic scrutiny. The special examination process, which took place in women's neighborhoods, probably felt overwhelming to most, but it did not prevent the claimants and their witnesses from telling stories that challenged the sensibilities of the examiners. Notably, women spoke of sexual exploitation and abuse when discussing the range of skin colors and hair textures among their children, some of whom white men had fathered. The localized nature of special examinations enabled black women to present themselves as individuals and community members whose understandings of marriage, citizenship, and service to the country others validated.

Union widows occupy a complex place in U.S. history and culture. The meaning of Union widowhood was constructed in congressional debates, in editorials, and, as this book demonstrates, in women's neighborhoods, churches, and households. Family, kinship networks, bonds among neighbors and congregation members, childcare, and the work women performed in support of their ailing loved ones all shaped black women's understanding of themselves as soldiers' wives and Union widows. As a result, their formulation of Union widowhood differed in both content and symbolism from that of the Pension Bureau's.

An ethos of collective autonomy and mutuality proved instrumental to the rebirth of black neighborhoods across the South and guided working-class black women's approach to the pension system. This "collectivist ethos," Thomas Holt has observed, governed social, economic, and political relations within post-emancipation black communities across the South. This ethos further instilled a sense of autonomy and the ability to make life choices about one's personal destiny. The sense of autonomy was not "purely personal"; rather, it embraced "familial and community relationships."[17] Tensions erupted between black Union widows and their neighbors over how they dispensed their resources and lived their lives, revealing anxieties about a group of women who conformed (or not) to behavior patterns the federal government dictated. Moreover, many of New Bern's black residents understood survivors' benefits as an economic resource the community mediated, not the federal government. This understanding of the pension system regularly placed black women at odds with government officials, the black middle class, black veterans, friends, and other Union widows.

THE FEDERAL PENSION SYSTEM AND BLACK WOMEN

The U.S. Bureau of Pensions was initially set up in 1815 as an office under the War Department; Congress created the position of the commissioner of pensions.[18] Sixteen years later, the bureau was moved to the Interior Department, where the secretary could review and undo decisions the commissioner of pensions rendered.[19] The primary responsibility of the commissioner and bureau agents was to determine who was "entitled to receive pensions as provided by existing law."[20] The office expanded during the Civil War, when widows of black Union soldiers were deemed eligible to collect survivors' benefits. Newly freed black women faced enormous challenges petitioning, much less securing, benefits; most notably, they were unable to provide the necessary legal evidence of their marriages; in fact, the legal institution of marriage was not even available to the enslaved.

Soldiers' widows were eligible to file claims under two basic systems: the general law and the Dependent Pension Law of 1890 (referred to as the service law of 1890). In February 1862, the Republican-dominated Congress passed the first of a series of bills that addressed support for families of the injured and dead. The Act of July 14, 1862, which set up the "general law pension system," provided for disabled veterans, widows, children, and other dependent relatives of soldiers through a legal structure that required proof of legal marriage and evidence of war-related death or disease. Since slave marriages were neither authorized nor effectuated through legal routes, and therefore not "valid," black soldiers' widows were initially excluded from the system.

Wartime protests from black soldiers' wives and widows and the Confederate massacre of black soldiers at Fort Pillow, Tennessee, in April 1864 prompted lawmakers to address this injustice. Congress revised the pension bill, ostensibly to include the families of all dead black soldiers. To accommodate formerly enslaved women, the Supplemental Act of July 1864 accepted eyewitness testimony, in the form of affidavits, to prove that a couple "habitually" recognized each other as husband and wife for a period of two years. Two years later, in June 1866, lawmakers recognized African American's emancipated status by eliminating references to their formerly enslaved status. All black petitioners for widows' pension could now submit proof of cohabitation without legal documentation, as required for white claimants. Federal lawmakers now recognized "slave marriages" retroactively. Worded in nondiscriminatory terms, the act sought to eliminate the evidentiary obstacles, especially for marriages, that impeded the families of formerly enslaved soldiers from claiming benefits. The law, implemented by the Pension Bureau, qualitatively altered black women's relationship to the federal government, even as it preserved and institutionalized inequality in new ways.

Bureau policy, with its universalizing language of marriage, seemingly embraced all women, but these policies were derived from the standpoint of middle-class whites. In fact, the acts of 1864 and 1866 carried implicit racial and class-based content that became powerful in the identification of beneficiaries. Moreover, at the center of the construction of Union widowhood rested ideas about white feminine virtue. Consequently, definitions of marriage, sexual morality, respectability, and notions of proper family relationships became central points of contention in the dialogue between black women and bureau administrators. Moreover, bureau officials' ideas about racial inferiority and black women's sexuality informed their repetitive scrutiny of the private lives of claimants. Ultimately, the law of 1882, which used sexual morality as a basis for determining Union widows' eligibility to collect government aid and terminated a widow's pension if she was found to be involved in a sexual relationship with a man, undermined the rules introduced in 1866.

The greatest expansion of the pension system came with the introduction of the service law in 1890. As one historian described it, the law allowed "any veteran who had honorably served ninety days in the military, even if never injured or a noncombatant, [to] apply for a pension, if he could find a physician to affirm his unfitness for manual labor."[21] Under this law, soldiers' widows no longer had to establish a causal connection between their late husband's military service and his death. Widows of veterans who died of old age became eligible for survivors' benefits, provided that they were "dependent on their own labor for support."[22] The service law ostensibly expanded access to pensions to all widows of former soldiers, yet questions of marriage and notions of worthy womanhood still limited black women's ability to obtain recognition as deserving. No matter under which law a woman filed a claim, the bureau's formulation of marriage affected her. As Hunter observed and this study will demonstrate, newly freed black women struggled to configure their marital relations in the discourses of U.S. law and policy.[23]

The federal pension system, which was crafted for male veterans and for women whose husbands had fought for the Union, was not designed for the far different life circumstances of black women, especially the many who had been enslaved. Black women who came forward to stake their claim to survivors' benefits interpreted the definition of marriage, family, and womanhood in radically different terms than how the white men who devised and administered the pension system imagined that Union widows would act. Their life experiences and the arguments that they advanced within the pension system did not conform to the narrow ideological construction of Union widowhood, while their socioeconomic position as working poor led them into living situations that whites regarded as highly problematic. Indeed, gender ideology posed a particular set of problems for black women trying to navigate the pension system.

This book interrogates both the intersections of ideas about racial difference, gender constructs, and class in the making of Union widowhood and the workings of military entitlements. Historian Evelyn Brooks Higginbotham's insistence on theoretical frameworks that analyze how racism structures other social relations and the role of race in determining the meaning of gender undergird the conceptualization of Union widowhood and the "racialized gender state" detailed in this study.[24] Racism, alongside the need to secure competent representation, medical evidence, and other forms of legal documentation, compromised poor blacks' ability to file a claim, much less secure admittance to the pension roster.[25] Thus, while lawmakers did away with explicit references to racial difference in the Pension Bureau's eligibility rules by June 1866, race and racism remained alive and well in the bureau. Black women's struggle for survivors' benefits, therefore, cannot be fully explained without unveiling the racialized gender imperatives at the center of the pension system's rules concerning so-called "colored claimants."[26]

Studies of women and the welfare state and black feminist insights about how laws and government policies function in black women's lives have led to the development of theoretical constructs that question the ideological boundaries between the public and private realms, underscoring the politicization of black women's encounters with federal agencies. Scholars such as Linda Gordon, Gwendolyn Mink, Alice Kessler-Harris, and Eileen Boris have analyzed social welfare policies and the different racial and gender ideologies underlying such policies.[27] This study excavates ideologies of racial difference from the pension records to highlight how notions of racialized gender inscribed black women's unworthiness in federal agencies.[28] Special examiners projected their ideas about race and gender differences onto the bodies of black female applicants. Examiners effectively, then, institutionalized their biases, categorizing many black women as criminally unworthy; pension officials could then remove black female claimants from the pension roster.

Claiming Union Widowhood thus charts the surveillance features of the pension apparatus and interrogates the discourses special examiners deployed to justify the policing of black women's bodies. By highlighting black women's contentious relations with special examiners—which involved household visits and intrusive questioning—neighbors, and other claimants, this study invites readers to contemplate the consequences of the expansion of the federal government's surveillance powers in the realm of social welfare.

To recognize a woman as a Union widow, pension authorities had to acknowledge the existence of legitimate marital relations, families, and, by extension, black people's humanity. As the widows of Union soldiers, black women forged a special relationship to the nation-state and took a step toward citizenship for black people.[29] Indeed, the significance of black women's petitions to the Pension Bureau during and immediately following the Civil War cannot be overstated.[30] At the war's end, freedpeople's legal standing remained an open question at the state level, and federal officials had not yet extended civil rights to blacks. Against this backdrop, the possibility of survivors' benefits and designation "Union widow" meant a great deal. Four years after federal lawmakers crafted a pathway to ensure provision for the dependents of black soldiers, the Fourteenth Amendment recognized all native-born black Americans as U.S. citizens on the same basis as native-born white Americans. The Pension Bureau, then, was a rare legal site where black women could make a claim for equal treatment under the law.[31]

Though impoverished, thousands of black women, like Fanny Whitney, petitioned for survivors' benefits not based on their financial need, but because the men in their lives had earned them based on their military service. Survivors' benefits were entitlements. When black women—especially the formerly enslaved—claimed the same pension benefits as white women, they directly challenged antebellum legal codes and popular constructions of black women as unworthy dependents devoid of virtue.[32] At stake in the battles over Union widowhood was gender ideology, the maintenance of white respectability, and the meaning of citizenship in the wake of black women's freedom. Definitions of marriage, sexual respectability, and domesticity were central to the project. References to nonmonogamous marital forms and hypersexuality helped to maintain lines of racial difference and justify additional layers of scrutiny.[33] The rights talk of ordinary black women, then, attempted to confront and unravel notions about racial inferiority, dependency, and inequality all bound up and deeply ingrained in the bureau's construction of Union widowhood.[34]

Black women laying claim to Union widowhood made the claims process a significant political arena in which poor black women challenged the bureau's use of racialized gendered criteria for determining their benefits.[35] Black women confronted examiners with revelations about their experiences of sexual abuse and rape, domestic violence, abandonment, and social and economic injustice. They also wanted it known that the vulnerability of their marriages resulted from past injustice and continuing racial prejudice, and they defined Union widowhood in their own terms, centering on worthy womanhood, labor, and motherhood. In the midst of war and in the interstitial spaces leading up to Reconstruction, black women cultivated conceptions of worthy widowhood based on the identities they forged, the work they performed inside and outside their households, and the communal virtues, values, and survival mechanisms they carried over from slavery. For these women, Union widowhood was a malleable and an inclusive construct. In their petitions, they confidently based their cases on the benefits promised to their loved ones during the war. In so doing, they articulated a distinctive set of claims that was at odds with the Pension Bureau's construct of marriage and respectable womanhood. The refusal of many black women to relinquish their diverse family forms and fluid definition of marriage—even after the bureau's policy on cohabitation became more transparent—resulted in a dialogue with the bureau about the meaning of marriage and worthy widowhood that continued into the early twentieth century.

CONCEPTUAL FRAMING AND SOURCES

Claiming Union Widowhood joins a dynamic body of scholarly works that explore the process by which black people "imagined, claimed, and enacted their relationship to law" and governmental institutions in the United States during the nineteenth century.[36] Martha Jones's analysis of former slaves and their descendants in antebellum Baltimore illuminates "how people with limited access to legal authority" won rights and recognition by presenting themselves as rights-bearing people.[37] Free blacks frequently raised their voice in official arenas of redress before and after the Supreme Court's *Dred Scott v. Sandford* decision (1857), which excluded African Americans from the status of "citizen." In the aftermath of the *Dred Scott* decision, Jones notes, free blacks "kept a steady presence in the local courthouse."[38] In Sharon Romeo's study of wartime St. Louis, she examined the process by which African American women removed the bonds of slavery to claim freedom and citizenship rights. Taking seriously the contending meanings of municipal citizenship, state citizenship, and federal citizenship, Romeo showed how black women made claims outside legal frameworks and government agencies. Hannah Rosen's analysis of black women's testimony before the Joint Select Committee on Klan Violence in 1872 revealed how black women produced alternative constructions of citizenship. In these public hearings, black women represented themselves as citizens and characterized their sexual assaults as rape. The act of coming forward and testifying, Rosen contended, challenged whites' authority to represent themselves as all powerful.[39] Jones, Romeo, and Rosen's interventions are critical to this study's interpretation of how black women carved out space for themselves to claim worthy widowhood in the bureau and beyond the authorized application chain.

The scholarship of Megan McClintock and Theda Skocpol, both of whom view the pension system as a social welfare system, laid important groundwork for this study. For Skocpol, the construction of social welfare policies happened from the top down and derived principally from middle-class white women's reform efforts. Importantly, Skocpol charted middle-class women's influence on the development of social policy from outside the federal system—namely the introduction and implementation of mothers' pensions—but had little to say about the beneficiaries (both black and white) who operated from within. These critical omissions have obscured how poor black women are represented in the larger story of the expansion of the U.S. pension system.[40] McClintock's research convincingly highlighted the linkage between wartime mobilization and "family need" in the expansion of social welfare policy during the Civil War and the following decades.[41]

While the pension system functioned like a social welfare program in many respects, the benefits women claimed were not charitable assistance to the poor. *Claiming Union Widowhood* shows that the benefits were circumscribed by ideas about what types of women did or did not deserve remuneration. This book thus challenges existing interpretations of the origins of social assistance in the modern United States that neglect racial anchoring and centers the experience of poor black women. The Reconstruction era through the early twentieth century constituted a critical period in the full integration of ideologies of racial difference and class-based gender constructions into the Pension Bureau's policies. Moreover, black women's ongoing interaction with the Pension Bureau by way of the special examination process made them central to the larger project of state making during the late nineteenth century.

This study analyzes the repertoire of strategies that black women used to publicize their cases and the traditions and ideas on which they based their claims. To interpret women's petitions and the claim-making process, I employ a framework of politics inspired by political theorist Nancy Fraser and exemplified in the scholarly works of historians such as Linda Gordon and Lisa Levenstein, who reimagine the political nature of negotiations and exchange.[42] According to Fraser, "needs talk appears as a site of struggle where groups with unequal discursive resources compete to establish as hegemonic their respective interpretations of legitimate social needs." "Needs talk" carries a political dimension if it is contested across a spectrum of different discursive arenas and a range of different publics. Authoritative groups articulate needs interpretations that are intended to limit, while oppositional groups assert needs interpretations that are intended "to challenge, displace, or modify dominant ones." By drawing attention to African American widows' negotiations with local pension officials, this study illuminates how and why these women rejected the Pension Bureau's construction of widowhood and dependency.[43]

Black women's struggle to maintain their benefits was just as intense as their battles to gain admission to the pension roster. Scholars generally point out that bureau officials awarded African Americans and their families a small portion of their pension benefits. Historian Donald Shaffer studied a random sample of the index cards of 545 black Civil War soldiers; of this group, 350 filed application for disability benefits, and 298 women filed petitions for benefits under the names of these same men. Shaffer found that nearly 61 percent of black Union widows "made at least one successful application, while nearly eighty-four percent of the white widows managed to receive benefits after one application."[44] When examined under the lens of the racialized gender state, Shaffer's findings about black women's success rate is somewhat deceptive. Black women rarely collected benefits without disruption and multiple intrusive investigations that resulted in suspensions. For this reason, this study differentiates between petitioning for benefits, securing benefits, and the ability to maintain standing on the pension roster over the course of a lifetime.

Claiming Union Widowhood's purpose is not simply to chart the names of those who successfully garnered survivors' benefits from the government; nor is it the intention of this study to merely point out that newly freed black women made claims on the government.[45] Rather, it interprets poor black women's perspective of social and economic justice and political freedoms through an analysis of their petitions for survivors' benefits. Cheryl Hicks's examination of black women, justice, and reform in New York illuminates the extent to which working-class blacks upheld their own ideas about respectable and moral womanhood in the late nineteenth century.[46] Importantly, Hicks shows how ordinary women used the language of respectability to reconfigure their relationship to the legal arm of the state.[47]

Poor black women produced a model of good womanhood and "rights talk" in the years leading up to the twentieth century that upheld their own version of womanhood and challenged black middle-class notions of respectability, while simultaneously casting themselves as worthy citizens.[48] In their claims, these soldiers' mothers and widows expressed subaltern understandings of worthiness that prioritized personal autonomy and freedom. Their assertions of themselves as respectable women derived from a long history of resistance to the slave system, forced breeding, and rape.

To understand the political appeals of black women within the pension system and how their petitions changed over time, I trace the broad patterns of ideas and conflicts that repeatedly emerge in their case files between 1866 and 1920. Not surprisingly, contestations over the definition and meaning of marriage (before and after the war) and ideas about black female sexuality and worthiness form two of the most prominent themes throughout the years under study. While this research attempts to unearth and draw attention to new political actors, I am keenly aware that the focus on black Union widows obscures the experiences of other groups of women—namely those who never married and those who never had any desire to enter into heterosexual marital relationships.[49]

Well over 1,500 pension files form the basis of this study.[50] All these women's case files have shaped my general analysis of black women's interactions with the Pension Bureau and my selection of themes. The case files of these women highlight the centrality of issues of marriage, family, and sexual morality to black women's understanding and experience of citizenship and justice. In-depth life histories of four women—Fanny Fonville (Whitney), Charlotte Cartwright (Banks), Louisa Jackson (Powers), and Mary Williams (Lee)—illustrate how black women's ideas, strategies, and life circumstances changed over long stretches of time from the experience of enslavement to one of living in a society based on free labor. The stories of those who never successfully garnered benefits from the bureau are examined as well as case files government officials deemed purely criminal and fraudulent. All these stories deserve deep study and attention. While I draw on pension records to reconstruct and trace the personal stories of a wide array of individuals, I simultaneously use them to reflect on the constructed and contested nature of the application process itself.[51] Though bureau officials regularly rejected women's petitions or suspended them from the pension roster, black women's unrelenting efforts allow for scholars to explore the interiority of their lives and the development of their political consciousness.

The events chronicled in this book took shape mostly in and around New Bern, North Carolina. Located in Craven County, at the confluence of the Neuse and Trent Rivers, the town was a significant center for the families of black soldiers. Scholars such as Eric Anderson, Catherine Bisher, Judkin Browning, David Cecelski, Glenda Gilmore, and Joe A. Mobley have written extensively about the social and political lives of blacks living in this region before and after the Civil War.[52] Black working women's struggle for pensions offers new insight into the complexity of New Bern's political landscape.

New Bern's Fifth Ward and the Trent settlement camp, later James City, emerge as distinct sites of political collaboration in the testimonies of black women seeking remuneration based on their husbands' military status. The constant flow of newcomers with an earnest desire to enact freedom on terms that made sense to them enriched New Bern's landscape during the Civil War. Local leaders such as Frederick C. Douglass, a black claims agent, emerged from the ranks of the black refugee population that settled in New Bern during the wartime years. These newcomers breathed new life into preexisting communal institutions and mobilized resources to establish new institutions. These institutions became increasingly important to the sustenance of the black community's political ambitions and outlets for social interaction.

The grassroots pension network also sheds light on poor black women's interactions with the professional class, namely claims agents. Pension records show how business relationships between working-class black women and black claims agents developed over time. The social status of black claims agents, and the result of their work on behalf of black soldiers' widows, was mediated first and foremost through black institutions and then by the Pension Bureau. This study, thus, complicates how historians conceptualize intercommunal class relations among blacks at the turn of the century. In other words, black middle-class efforts to reform the working classes do not fully represent the complexity of intraracial class interactions during the late nineteenth century.

This book traces patterns of ideas and conflicts that repeatedly emerge in the pension files of black Union widows and pays close attention to discursive processes by which black female claimants were constructed as inferior and, therefore, unworthy of the nation's bounty. The possibility of gaining lifelong economic benefits as soldiers' widows led some to express sentiments that put them in the best possible light to government examiners. Repeated phrases, figures of speech, and reference points in their testimonies suggest that advice on how to testify had spread among prospective claimants and their supporters.[53]

Despite the large number of black women who initiated claims for survivors' benefits in the pension system, the records are extraordinarily uneven. Reconstructing the lives of black Union widows thus presents numerous challenges. Alongside pension records, this study also draws on a multitude of archival sources to reconstruct black women's stories as well as the grassroots pension network. Records of the Freedmen's Bureau, national and local cemetery records, federal census records (including the 1890 veterans' census), newspapers, manuscript papers, tax records, bank records, wills and probate records, business directories, apprenticeship records, marriage certificates, birth certificates, the legal case files of claims agents, and the personal papers of agent Frederick C. Douglass enabled me to piece together key changes in these women's lives before and after they obtained pensions, which facilitated the reconstruction of black neighborhoods.

THE STORY

Claiming Union Widowhood begins by exploring the conditions of daily life for black soldiers' wives and widows by vividly re-creating the process of community formation in Civil War–era eastern North Carolina. Using personal stories, the first chapter charts the community's antebellum economy, demography, polity, and society, especially along the lines of race, gender, and class. Chapter 2 traces the transformations the war brought as wartime emancipation stimulated significant migration and destabilized social relations.

The remainder of the book is organized both thematically and chronologically; it draws extensively on pension case files to describe how poor black women actively engaged the federal government over the issue of survivors' benefits, thereby advancing their vision of citizenship and justice. Black women's testimonies in the pension case files offer insight into how working-class black women affirmed their identities foremost as human beings and as Union widows. Their sense of themselves as worthy stemmed from their desire to re-create their lives in freedom on their own terms.

Chapter 3 charts black women's petitions for pensions within overlapping and intersecting federal and state policies, alongside the social and economic realities of their lives in the postwar era. This chapter draws heavily on the experiences of women who filed claims shortly after the act of 1866, and it follows a host of northern-born white men, entrepreneurs, and military administrators who went into pension work, along with some of the first bureau examiners who conducted investigations in New Bern.

Chapter 4 reconstructs the pension application process in eastern North Carolina. By tracing women's activities through the case files over time and researching their past and later lives, I reveal how women built a pension network through their relationships to one another and through their actions on one another's behalf in the application and examination process. This chapter foregrounds the life experiences of black soldiers' wives and widows and interrogates the concepts of marriage, family, and womanhood that ultimately informed their interpretation of the meaning of widowhood. It then turns to the pension network, centered in New Bern, and the professional men and black women associated with it, who effectively addressed the concerns of women in responding to the demands of the government.

Chapter 5 examines black women's interactions with special examiners by returning to the case files of Louisa Powers and Mary Lee, among others. Analyzing these women's relationship to the Pension Bureau on the grassroots level builds on and revises the history of black women's struggle for citizenship at the turn of the century. No longer is the application process seen merely as a debate among bureau officials, examiners, and claims agents; rather, it began in the neighborhoods where working-class black women dealt directly with claims agents and special examiners. The maneuverings of women like Louisa Powers, Mary Lee, Charlotte Banks, Fanny Whitney, and many others have previously gone unrecognized by historians. Extending our understanding of black political culture to include poor and working-class black women's navigation of the pension system reveals new dimensions of citizenship debates.

By the 1890s, many women who had married before, during, or even after the war had become widowed. This aging group of soldiers' widows approached local claims agents and the bureau with a great sense of urgency. Chapter 6 examines both how black women filed claims under the Dependent Pension Law of 1890 (referred to here as the service law of 1890) and the debate that ensued between Pension Bureau officials about the meaning of marriage and worthy widowhood. The rise of white supremacy and new programs in the bureau brought new manifestations of racial and gender inequality. Chapter 7 examines the claims of prospective widows and black Union widows and analyzes how those claims changed in response to the 1882 law and to local social and political shifts in the aftermath of Reconstruction. It argues that sexual regulation counterbalanced the racially neutral rules initiated in 1866. It traces Louisa Powers, Mary Lee, and several other black Union widows' dealings with examiners from the U.S. Pension Bureau and with municipal leaders, both black and white. Chapter 8 examines how black soldiers' widows and pension beneficiaries made the case for Union widowhood in the wake of disfranchisement and at the cost of their status in their communities. In sum, *Claiming Union Widowhood* tells the story of how poor black women asserted their rights as citizens individually and collectively to make claims on the state and to define themselves and their community with the dignity and respect they knew they deserved.

A PEOPLE AND A PLACE

PART I

1

Black Life and Labor in New Bern, North Carolina, 1850–1865

Located at the confluence of the Neuse and Trent Rivers, approximately thirty miles from the Atlantic, New Bern was founded by European settler colonists in 1710 and grew into an important trading center.[1] Over the course of the colonial and antebellum periods, New Bern became the largest town in Craven County, which is situated on North Carolina's south-central coast between Jones and Carteret Counties to the south and Beaufort County to the north. It incorporated as a city in 1723 and served as the colony's capital until the British occupied it during the Revolutionary War.[2] Farmers came to New Bern to conduct business and to purchase and sell commodities. Ships loaded with tar, turpentine, lumber, and corn traveled between North Carolina and the West Indies; the port played a limited role in the transatlantic slave trade, as slave traders had difficulty navigating large vessels around the islands of the Outer Banks. Large slaveholders formed a small fraction of the state's white population, with the majority of enslavers owning between five and nine black people in 1860. This chapter chronicles the social, economic, and political developments that shaped the lives of New Bern's black residents—many of whom would later join the war effort as military workers, soldiers, or in unofficial capacities.

ENSLAVED AND FREE BLACKS BEFORE THE CIVIL WAR

Although relatively small compared to other port cities on the East Coast of the United States, New Bern was the state's second largest city on the eve of the Civil War. Urbanization and industrialization began around 1835, when the state launched a program of railroad building.[3] With the construction of a railroad line leading to the interior during the 1840s and 1850s, New Bern became one of the state's primary commercial hubs. The Atlantic and North Carolina Railroad, with Beaufort Harbor as its terminal, stimulated the growth of New Bern's population, which was surpassed only by that of Wilmington—a port city about ninety-two miles south of New Bern.[4] In later years it was sometimes called the Athens of North Carolina because of its cultural institutions, including a theater and an academy.[5] New Bern had two main streets, one running from the Neuse River and the other parallel to it; the city was planned so that a church would sit at the city center.[6]

New Bern was a significant trading center for the naval stores industry in the 1850s. Longleaf pine trees were plentiful in Craven County, and their resin supplied the raw material for the production of turpentine. When combined with alcohol, turpentine provided a less expensive form of lighting used for homes, public buildings, and streets from about 1800 to 1860. The alcohol-turpentine mixture was known as camphene, teveline, or palmetto oil, and demand for turpentine exploded between 1840 and 1860.[7] By 1840, North Carolina produced 95.9 percent of the naval stores in the country, and railroads encouraged the industry's expansion. New Bern was second only to Wilmington in the number of turpentine distillers. For swampers (enslaved lumbermen) and shinglers who worked in the turpentine industry, the pay was roughly two dollars per month, a pair of pants, a shirt, and food.[8]

Slavery formed a prominent feature of North Carolina's economy and society, although enslaved labor was not as central as it was in other southern states. In the mid-eighteenth century, the slave population in the eastern counties grew more rapidly than the slave population in the interior.[9] The greatest increase in the state's slave population occurred from 1790 to 1800, before the international slave trade ended.[10] The majority of North Carolina's enslaved population lived out there lives in holdings between two and four persons. In 1850, for example, less than 2.2 percent of enslaved blacks lived on large plantations.[11] By 1860, there were 661,563 whites and just over 331,000 enslaved persons in the state. Just over a quarter of the white population owned slaves, and only a small proportion of them owned twenty or more people and could be called planters. Historians surmise that the state would have had considerably more slaves were it not for the westward migration of tens of thousands of North Carolinians and the thriving interstate slave trade, which relocated thousands of North Carolina slaves west and farther south.[12]

Racial slavery proved central to Craven County's economic output. Enslaved men and women cultivated cotton, tended rice and corn, and collected pine sap, which was distilled into tar. Between 1790 and 1820, the free black population in Craven County rose from 337 to 1,744, most of whom were concentrated in New Bern.[13] By 1850, this primarily agricultural county on the coastal plain had 14,709 residents, half of whom were black. The numbers of free blacks in North Carolina grew as a result of migration, manumission (by will, deed, or legislative enactment), miscegenation, and self-liberation by purchasing their freedom or running away.[14]

Judge John R. Donnell, one of North Carolina's leading enslavers, called New Bern home. The Donnell family held a collection of farms in Hyde County near Lake Mattamuskeet, a few miles inland from Pamlico Sound. Relying mostly on their overseers, William Simmons and Henry Jones, to manage their properties, the Donnell family enslaved Fanny Fonville (Whitney) and her family, along with an estimated three hundred persons in Hyde County in the years leading up to the Civil War.[15] After Judge Donnell purchased a farm in Craven County in 1840, he appears to have transferred a group of enslaved men, women, and children to his property in Hyde.[16] Young Fanny, around twelve years old at the time, may have been part of this group.[17] Around 1851, she married Harry Whitney, an enslaved man who also belonged to Donnell. Donnell acquired and hired skilled artisans to work on building projects around New Bern and reportedly did business with John C. Stanly.[18] Stanly was a former slave who had become one of the most prosperous slaveholders in New Bern, owning an estimated 127 black slaves on his Cedar Grove and Hope plantations.[19]

Before his death in the mid-1840s, Stanly became one of the wealthiest men in New Bern and the largest slaveholder of color in the South. John was born in 1774 to an enslaved Igbo woman who was brought to America on a vessel captained by Alexander Stewart.[20] Contemporaries believed that the enslaved Stanly was the son of John Wright Stanly, a wealthy merchant and shipper who resided in New Bern.[21] Stanly's owners, Captain Stewart and his wife, Lydia, took steps to secure his education and a trade. As a trained barber, known as Barber Jack throughout the city, Stanly shaved the faces of white merchants and municipal leaders. In March 1795, he gained his freedom, after the Stewarts petitioned the Craven County courts.[22] Then, through a series of savvy business deals with local whites, Stanly earned enough money to purchase and free his wife, Kitty, and their three children. As documented by historian Catherine Bishir, Stanly helped many free black men secure freedom for their families.[23]

By hiring out their enslaved property, a widespread practice in New Bern, enslavers adapted their mastery to an economic system closely tied to maritime life in this port city.[24] Mary Norman of Terrell County hired out Turner Norman, an enslaved man, to Joseph L. Rhem, a wealthy farmer who held property on the outskirts of New Bern before the war. Turner labored as a farmer and a shingle maker and likely had to surrender the majority (if not all) of his wages to his mistress.[25] Julia Ann Foy, an enslaved woman born around 1806, was owned by Enoch Foy, a prominent Jones County slaveholder. When the patriarch died, Julia Ann "fell to his son [Charles] Henry Foy and then to his grandson." One of the Foy men hired Julia Ann out to work on other farms before the war. She recalled, "I was a field hand just like a man . . . and was sometimes hired out 30 miles away."[26]

The mother of at least eleven children, Julia Ann did not liberate herself while hired out (though she may have tried). Perhaps she was able to keep some of the money she earned, as some slaveholders allowed men and women to hire themselves out for wages and pay a set fee to their owners. An 1820 Craven County grand jury complained about the number of enslaved men and women hiring themselves out, which was estimated to be at least one hundred.[27] Thus, before the Civil War, some enslaved men and women in eastern North Carolina's urban centers experienced wage earning and a sense of personal autonomy.

Black women, free and enslaved, were integral to New Bern's social, economic, and political development. Free black women probably favored living in New Bern because of its wage-earning opportunities; their wages were low, but they struggled mightily to provide for themselves and their children. They had access to a limited number of public services, including a county poorhouse on Neuse Road, which on at least one occasion housed an indigent enslaved man.[28] They earned their living as laundresses, dressmakers, seamstresses, waitresses, and domestic servants in the city, and a few managed stalls, small shops, and stores. They bought, sold, and traded garden crops, rice, cotton, corn, tobacco, sugar, hogs, cattle, horses, sheep, poultry, eggs, honey, fish, fruit, and meats and prepared pies, bread, and cakes for sale.[29] A small cohort managed to become property owners or establish businesses. John Stanly's daughter, Catherine, who inherited four thousand dollars in property from her father, established a thriving dressmaking business that catered to New Bern's elite white women.[30]

Death in slaveholding families had devastating effects on enslaved families. Jane Richardson, who was born and raised in Craven County, was enslaved by the Reverend William P. Biddle, a prominent religious leader who owned eighty-six slaves valued at $40,585 when he died in 1853. In his final will, Biddle divided enslaved families among his children, and Jane may have been allotted to Biddle's daughter, Ann, and her husband, William "Bud" Pope.[31] The transfer disrupted Jane's family life, as she was married to Henry Richardson, whose name was not listed among the enslaved apportioned to the Popes. During the war, Pope impregnated Jane, who would have been nearing her early twenties and probably working as a domestic within his household. Jane gave birth to a girl she named Mary in 1865; Mary later identified her father as "Bud Pope." [32] New Bern's courthouse was also the site of family separations for many enslaved families. Just as the new year began, Lafayette Riggs's executor determined to sell off "a negro woman Margaret" as "she runs in the woods."[33] A trust sale scheduled to take place in November 1849 mentioned "two likely negro girls," along with household and kitchen furniture.[34]

Though the enslaved always outnumbered free blacks in New Bern, free blacks were a substantial part of the city's population and were central to the black community. By 1850, New Bern had 4,681 inhabitants, and its 800 free blacks composed one-sixth of its population.[35] On the eve of the Civil War, Craven County's population was 16,268, including 6,189 bondsmen and women. New Bern had grown, but the number of blacks living there had declined.[36] Still black residents outnumbered whites in New Bern, as they continued to do throughout the late nineteenth century. In 1860, 57 percent of the city's 5,432 residents were blacks—44 percent (2,383) enslaved, 13 percent (689) free.[37]

Because of the large size of New Bern's black population, runaways could remain somewhat anonymous in the city. Advertisements placed by enslavers offer tantalizing hints into the world of black fugitivity in the city. A reward of five cents was offered for the recovery of Edny Manor, a sixteen-year-old apprentice of light complexion, who had been on the run for at least twelve months. A slaveholder offered a reward of ten dollars for the recovery of "a negro man named Shade," who was suspected of "lurking" in a New Bern neighborhood "where he has a wife." Arch, a "well-spoken" man with a scar on his left leg, secreted himself in the city for at least four years before the city sheriff jailed him.[38] A reward of twenty-five dollars was offered for the capture of Sukey, who was believed to be in New Bern in search of her sister, "the property of Judge Donnell." A Lenoir County slaveholder offered a reward for Jerry, formerly owned by Judge Donnell, in the *North Carolina Sentinel* (New Bern), believing that he may have returned to New Bern in search of his family.[39]

Slave patrols monitored the streets of New Bern in search of black fugitives who were out and about without their owners' permission. Controlling black movement was essential to preventing escapes, and a curfew system, introduced in most North Carolina cities in the early nineteenth century, required blacks to be off the streets by a designated time.[40] Patrollers stopped everyone who was not recognized as residents of a street; passes were scrutinized and questions asked. They authenticated slaves' passes, verified the dates and signatures, and searched for weapons. Patrollers had the authority to detain slaves forcibly if they wandered off a main road, stayed out after curfew, or behaved in a manner they considered suspicious. Still on the eve of the Civil War, black fugitives continued to defy these tactics and hid in North Carolina's swampy areas.

Paul Heinegg's genealogical research demonstrated that an unusually large number of free blacks with mixed raced lineage settled in Craven County during the colonial period.[41] Many of these families migrated to the state from Virginia and Maryland. They forged a close-knit community that extended throughout the city, with small concentrations residing in the Fifth and Sixth Wards. Free black inhabitants included Mary Elizabeth Dove and Hezekiah Richardson, who lived in the Fifth Ward. Mary Elizabeth descended from the Dove family, which had arrived in Craven County from Anne Arundel County, Maryland, in the early eighteenth century. She married Henry Kent, a free black man, who earned his living as a wheelwright. Henry arrived in the city about 1856 from Hyde County, where he had been married to an enslaved woman. Mary and Henry wed at her father's home in 1860, but the couple lived apart before the war. The next year Kent enlisted in the Fourteenth Regiment of the U.S. Colored Heavy Artillery (USCHA).[42]

Despite the illegality of slaves' marriages and marriages between enslaved and free blacks in North Carolina's antebellum legal code, a complex body of customs—a set of unwritten rules concerning marital practices and intimate relationships—governed their relationships.[43] Sarah Copes, a free black woman living in New Bern's Sixth Ward, married Abner Williams, an enslaved man belonging to Isaac W. Hughes, who practiced medicine in New Bern with his sons.[44] Sarah and Abner had their first child, Mary, around 1842. Sarah surrendered custody of her Mary to Cloie Oliver, an enslaved woman who belonged to a "John Dumus."[45] While the arrangement between Sarah Williams and Cloie's owner is not clear from the records, it is hard to imagine that a slave owner would contract with a free black woman for the custody of a free black girl unless the arrangement took the form of an apprenticeship.[46]

Sarah's decision to place her daughter in the care of an enslaved woman at age five offers alluring details about relations between free black and enslaved women in this community. Sarah was probably well aware that she would have to apprentice her daughter, for the state law required that "the children of free negroes, where the parents with whom such children may live, do not habitually employ their time in some honest, industrious occupation," must be sent to live and work in another household.[47] The General Assembly also made it legal to enslave free blacks who could not pay their taxes. Sarah was most likely trying to earn wages to protect her and her daughter's free status. She might also have been attempting to earn enough money to purchase her husband from his owner. By 1850, Sarah had reclaimed custody of her daughter and moved into a house in the Fifth Ward valued at $160. Although the census identifies Sarah by her family name in 1850, her daughter Mary later explained that her mother went by her married name, indicating that Sarah self-identified as the wife of Abner Williams, and her peers recognized their union.[48] Sarah lived with her daughter until she died in New Bern sometime after 1900. As these examples demonstrate, North Carolina's General Assembly failed to prevent the formation of social and familial bonds between free and enslaved blacks.

The city's white residents championed the Democratic Party and began calling for secession shortly after Abraham Lincoln was elected. Historian Judkin Browning remarked that secessionist sentiment was brewing in Craven County as early as 1861, when white citizens voted in support of secession and elected delegates to support their views. A recent study of military occupation in North Carolina found that whites in Craven County, rather than turning on one another as some did elsewhere, unified around their opposition to the imposition of federal policies in the state.[49] By the time the Union Army reached New Bern in 1862, the majority of the white population, except those without the resources to move inland, had fled the city.[50] Leading members of New Bern's black artisan class fled too, relinquishing their hopes of expanding their freedom in the city and instead establishing themselves in urban centers in nonslave states such as Cleveland, Ohio.[51]

WHEN NEW BERN FELL

Wartime upheavals disrupted every aspect of life in New Bern. Its capture by the Union Army in March 1862 precipitated sweeping social, economic, political, and demographic changes in the city, as it did in all the areas it occupied in the South. As Union forces began to establish their presence in North Carolina's coastal region, word spread among the enslaved, prompting blacks throughout the region to liberate themselves and seek shelter behind Union lines. Ten thousand men, women, and children took refuge in the occupied areas of eastern North Carolina, with the greatest number settling in New Bern. The influx of blacks fleeing slavery and seeking freedom in military encampments behind Union lines transformed North Carolina's eastern seaboard. By 1865, the number of black refugees in Union-occupied areas of the state had grown to eighteen thousand, with the largest concentrations in New Bern, Beaufort (a city in Carteret County), and Roanoke Island (see map 1.1).[52] A substantial number of the new arrivals depended on federal agencies for housing and food.

As the days and weeks turned to months, military personnel submitted reports documenting the rising numbers of black refugees surrounding military outposts and labor camps. Women and children garnered special attention in these reports because of their perceived drain on the military's resources. Encounters between white military officials, white Northern missionaries, resident blacks, and black refugees occurred regularly. New Bern's black population doubled within a few months of the outbreak of the war, altering the city's racial demography.

General Benjamin F. Butler's "contraband" policy, implemented at Fort Monroe, Virginia, set the terms for fugitive blacks' legal standing in eastern North Carolina.[53] After May 1861, the federal government used the term *contraband of war* to describe fugitive slaves who had absconded to the Union-occupied zones, which allowed military personnel to establish the freedom of black runaways, use their labor, and uphold Lincoln's stance toward border states while sidestepping the question of emancipation altogether.[54]

With the appointment of Vincent Colyer as superintendent of the poor in the Department of North Carolina in late March 1862, General Ambrose E. Burnside, commander of volunteers, hoped to transform black people's desire for liberation into a reliable source of labor. General Burnside instructed Colyer to "employ as many negro men . . . up to the number of five thousand" and pay them eight dollars a month and a ration of clothes to work on fortifications. Colyer was unable to meet the labor quota, but he noted that during the four months he served in the position, "the men built three first class earth work forts; Fort Totten at Newbern . . . Fort Burnside on the upper end of Roanok & at Washington, N.C." Colyer also set up the first public schools for freedpeople in the city.[55]

The flood of black runaways forced military administrators to devise plans to handle the looming humanitarian crisis. As of April 1862, six hundred blacks in need of support resided in New Bern. Herman Biggs, the chief quartermaster of the Department of North Carolina, described the chaotic scene: "They are continually coming. . . . The number will soon be very large."[56] Brigadier General M. C. Meigs, the quartermaster general, agreed that employing able-bodied black men at "fair rates" to do public work was important but stressed that government appropriations were for work not charity.[57] Meigs then offered a compromise: "It is probably necessary in some cases . . .

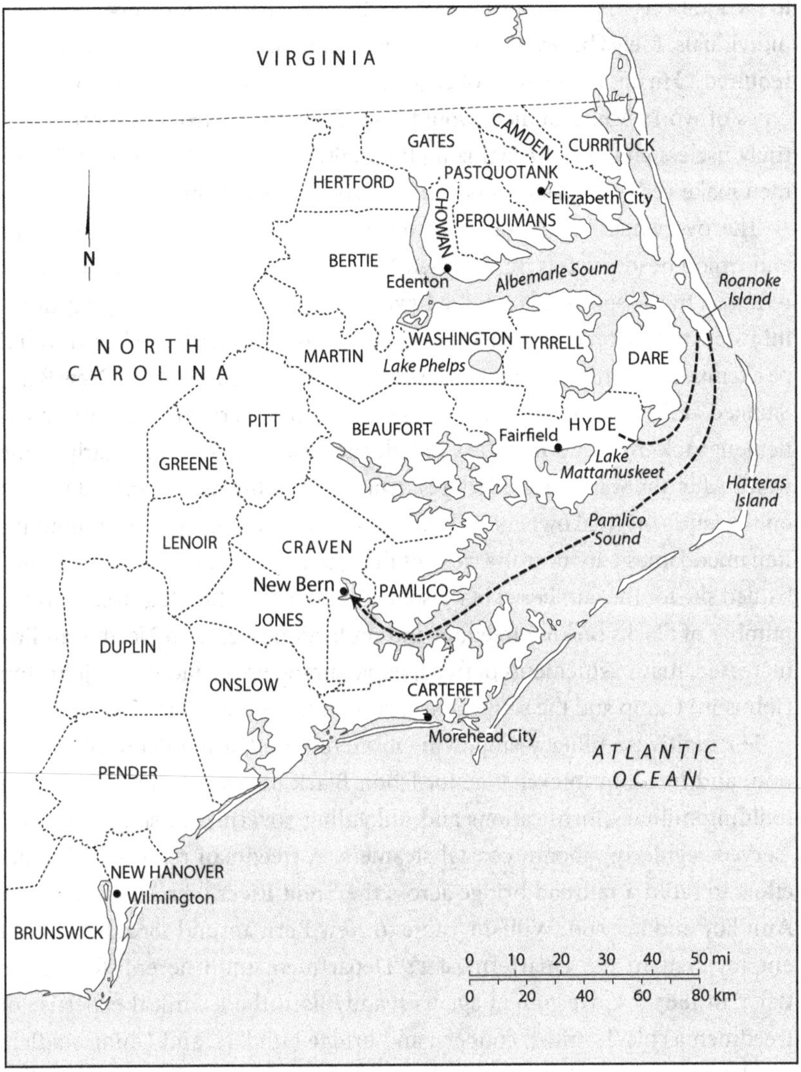

Map 1.1. Eastern North Carolina counties and Roanoke Island during the Civil War era. Map created by William L. Nelson.

to issue rations to persons, who may not be really needed for work." For such individuals, Meigs believed, "some equivalent in occasional labor—should be required." Hiring blacks to "police a city, or the Camps," and perform other types of work, Meigs opined, would keep the refugees from becoming "entirely useless charges." Recognizing the fugitives' skills, Meigs stated: "Black men make very good teamsters and hostlers for the general train."[58]

The overwhelming presence of federal troops, military administrators, and Union headquarters transformed New Bern into a major center for black refugees. In the spring of 1863, the Reverend Horace James, a Congregational minister from Worcester, Massachusetts, established what he believed would be a temporary settlement for black runaways about a mile south of New Bern. Situated at the confluence of the Neuse and Trent Rivers, the Trent River settlement took over land that the Confederate Army had occupied early in the war.[59] After the war ended, black residents of the settlement managed to fend off the land's original owners and transform it into a long-lasting community. Renamed James City near the close of the war, the settlement became an embattled site for the families of black soldiers and many other fugitives.[60] As the number of blacks seeking freedom and protection in eastern North Carolina increased, many settlements of freedpeople sprang up, including the Johnston (Johnson) Camp and the settlement surrounding Fort Macon.

For fugitives, military employment offered food, a modicum of protection, and freedom in exchange for labor. Black men worked as laborers in building military fortifications and unloading government ships, and they "served regularly" aboard coastal steamers. A freedman reportedly led the effort to build a railroad bridge across the Trent River.[61] Freedwoman Julia Ann Foy and her son, William, came to New Bern around 1862; he secured employment in the Quartermaster's Department until he enlisted in the USCT in 1863.[62] Government agents readily used the technical expertise of freedmen as blacksmiths, coopers, and bridge builders, and Union soldiers employed no fewer than fifty black refugees to help infiltrate the Confederate strongholds in eastern North Carolina.[63]

Early in the war black women and children earned wages washing and ironing, cooking, and baking pies and cakes for soldiers in Union Army camps. Ann Stamp, a midwife and displaced freedwoman who made it to the Trent River settlement after first stopping in Hatteras, "cooked the bread that the Northern soldiers eat when they came to take New Bern."[64] Mary Ann Starkey, a black community leader, ran a boardinghouse and fed low-ranking Union officers.[65] Women employed in the government hospitals earned four dollars a month for their service. Black women treated ailing

Figure 1.1. *Industry of the Women and Children*. From Vincent Colyer, *Report of the Services Rendered by the Freed People to the United States Army, in North Carolina, in the Spring of 1862, after the Battle of Newbern*. New York: Colyer, 1864.

soldiers in New Bern's special smallpox hospital. One scholar estimated that forty-four black women who served as nurses in the smallpox hospital lived in the settlement camps near New Bern (figure 1.1).[66] Other women earned wages from the Quartermaster's Department for mending army uniforms. Some sold produce and cooked food for soldiers.

Leadership changes, as well as new lines of military command and political authority, complicated blacks' wartime experiences in North Carolina. President Lincoln appointed Edward Stanly, a Beaufort County native who had been a powerful Whig politician, state legislator, and U.S. congressional representative, as the military governor of North Carolina. The new governor arrived in New Bern roughly two and a half months after Union forces took over the city. Lincoln hoped that Stanly would galvanize a surge of Unionist sentiment in the state, and he instructed the governor to enforce existing state laws.[67] Stanly, then, promptly announced his intention to return fugitive slaves to their owners.[68] This overture to slaveholders underscored the fragility of black people's freedom. Threats of re-enslavement led many blacks to take refuge in the surrounding swamp areas, and some quit their labor at military fortifications.[69]

Governor Stanly further opposed the military employment of black fugitives and threatened to enforce the state's "antiliteracy" act. Superintendent Colyer responded by abruptly shutting down the government-sponsored schools and reporting the matter to leading Republicans in Washington, key among them the fiery abolitionist senator from Massachusetts, Charles Sumner.[70] With little hesitation, Sumner personally reported the matter to Lincoln, but the president remained unconcerned. Colyer and Stanly never resolved their differences, but schools for freedpeople and poor whites reopened in June of the same year. Ultimately, Colyer's defiant stance toward Stanly led to his departure in the summer of 1862.[71] After Colyer left the post, Rev. Horace James assumed responsibility for black refugees across the state.

Before taking up his position in New Bern, James had been responsible for facilitating operations for the Roanoke Colony. Located inside the Outer Banks, between the Albemarle and Pamlico Sounds, Roanoke Island sits about twelve miles off the coast of North Carolina. During the war, black fugitives and, later, the families of black soldiers recruited in North Carolina and tidewater Virginia inhabited the island.[72] Before the arrival of Union forces on the mainland in 1862, black runaway slaves (called "contraband" because they were the property of the enemy but under the control of Union forces) flocked to the island much as they did to other Union outposts throughout the South. Increasing numbers of black refugees forced the Union Army to take action, which ultimately led to the establishment of the freedmen's colony on the island's northern end.[73] Roanoke was overcrowded and could furnish only modest means of self-sufficiency in the form of gardening. An 1864 census reported that 2,212 freedpeople had settled on the island, and by 1865, the number had increased to nearly 4,000, even after black men enlisted in the Union Army. The optimistic James envisioned Roanoke as a permanent, self-sustaining black settlement.

Freedpeople's desire to live beyond the site of their enslavement led some two hundred men, women, and children from Judge Donnell's Hyde County plantation to flee in hopes of resettling at the freedmen's colony at Roanoke

Island. "The Union troops . . . took a whole boat load of us from Hyde Co," Fanny Whitney recalled.[74] Whitney and her family envisioned a future in which they would determine the boundaries of their households and control the allocation of resources within them. The movement away from Donnell's land shows in compelling fashion how enslaved families transitioned to freedom as a diverse and complex community.[75] On more than one occasion, overseer Jones reported to Donnell that the formerly enslaved people were insolent and refused to work. Possibly fearing an uprising, Jones callously and cold-bloodedly shot one freedman.[76] Jones appeared to interpret black self-assertion and the expanding presence of northern soldiers as signaling the dawn of a new social order.

The surge of runaways to North Carolina's Union-occupied encampments coincided with Congress's enactment of the Second Confiscation Act on July 17, 1862, which freed all blacks who entered Union-occupied zones and authorized the president to compel formerly enslaved men and women to suppress the rebellion.[77] The Militia Act of 1862, which was passed at the same time, authorized the president to "receive into the service of the United States, for the purpose of constructing intrenchments, or performing camp service or any other labor, or any military or naval service for which they may be found competent, persons of African descent." Military officials were supposed to pay freedmen and freedwomen wages in exchange for their labor. Although this policy allowed for the hiring of women as well as men, black women were largely confined to improvised service positions.[78]

EMANCIPATION, ENLISTMENT, AND LABOR

President Lincoln issued the preliminary Emancipation Proclamation on September 22, 1862; when it came into force on January 1, 1863, the entire state of North Carolina was under Union control. Governor Stanly resigned his position in protest, believing that the proclamation went too far.[79] The new provisions allowing the enlistment of black soldiers and the guarantee of freedom to the enslaved who had fled to Union-occupied regions further stimulated the influx in eastern North Carolina, especially in New Bern.

National calls for black enlistment came from prominent blacks, such as the formidable abolitionist leader Frederick Douglass. Douglass believed that serving in the army would set blacks on the path to legal equality. President Lincoln had been reluctant to enlist black soldiers, seeking to appease the border slave states. Prospective black soldiers believed the government should guarantee them indemnity for their service and protection for their families. Military officers encouraged enslaved men to enlist and enslaved women to marry them.

In an effort to inspire black enlistment in Virginia and North Carolina, General Butler issued General Order 46 on December 5, 1863. Butler's order acknowledged that "colored soldiers have none of the machinery of 'State aid' for the support of their families while fighting our battles, so liberally provided for the white soldiers, nor the generous bounties given by the state and National Governments in the loyal states." Asking black men to leave their families, join the military, and risk their lives to preserve the Union required more than lofty promises. Butler authorized the distribution of bounty money for black enlistees who served a three-year term of service. On enlistment, each was to receive an immediate payout of ten dollars to "to supply his immediate wants."[80] The order went further, extending "suitable subsistence" to each soldier who remained in service no less than three years. If a soldier died, subsistence was to be continued "for at least six months to the family of any colored soldier who shall die in service by disease, wound, or battle."[81] Importantly, black soldiers' widows were not eligible to initiate claims within the pension system.

In the months leading up to the enforcement of the Emancipation Proclamation, William Henry Singleton recalled seeing scores of black men around New Bern organizing and drilling on their own in anticipation of serving in the Union Army.[82] Black enlistment was not a forgone conclusion, and black men made their concerns known to Union military administrators. New Bern's Mary Ann Starkey opened her boardinghouse as the meeting place for Abraham Galloway, the formerly enslaved black political leader who had worked as a Union spy, and Edward Kinsley, a New England abolitionist and government recruiting agent.[83] Freedmen insisted that they receive the same compensation as black soldiers in Massachusetts—who had demanded the same pay as white soldiers and refused pay at all until they were granted it—and that their families be provided for in the freedmen's camps.[84]

After Galloway was assured that the federal government would meet their demands, black men began enlisting in the Union's black regiments. Of the estimated 185,000 blacks who fought for the Union, 5,035 were recruited from North Carolina.[85] These men constituted roughly 8 percent of the state's black male population between the ages of eighteen to forty-five.[86] In addition to Galloway, a free black resident of New Bern, Philip Wiggins, recruited black men for the First North Carolina Volunteers.[87]

One recruit, Samuel Powers, lived among a group of runaway slaves between Duplin and Pender Counties before enlisting. He had escaped a one hundred-year indenture agreement a German merchant held. Samuel and the other runaways pilfered food from local stores to survive until local authorities apprehended them and placed them in the Duplin County jail. When the war broke out, the Union Army released Samuel, and shortly thereafter, on July 10, 1863, he enlisted in the Thirty-Fifth Regiment of the U.S. Colored Troops Volunteer Infantry (USCTVI) in New Bern, under the surname of the man who had apprenticed him when he was a small boy.[88] When Samuel's regiment moved through Richmond, Virginia, he met sixteen-year-old Louisa Jackson, who accompanied him for the entirety of his service.

The authorization of black enlistment prompted another wave of migration to eastern North Carolina, and black refugees flooding into Union-occupied zones forced military administrators to erect emergency settlements in and around New Bern.[89] Edward W. Carpenter, a white journalist who arrived in New Bern in March 1862, recalled the chaotic scene at New Bern's recruiting station:

> I took an active part in urging the recruits to enlist white and colored. I observed that in recruiting colored troops that when they asked them their ages and they were unable to give them their ages they would mark them down as 18 years old . . . as the regulations required a soldier to be that old and they would further state that it was a very difficult matter to discover the age of a colored person.[90]

Enlistees included Judy Blackwell, a nurse in the Union Navy, and Elizabeth Dempsey, a black woman who enrolled in the USCT as an army nurse under the direction of Captain Henry Orlando Marcy, a surgeon assigned to the Thirty-Fifth Regiment.[91] Yet racial discrimination persisted. "White privates received $13 per month plus a $3 clothing allowance; soldiers with higher ranks received more pay. Black Soldiers, regardless of rank, received $10 per month with $3 deducted for clothing."[92]

Black soldiers' strong communal and family attachments shaped the enlistment process. The pattern of enlistment of a group of black men enslaved on Judge Donnell's Hyde County plantation illuminates their priorities and concerns.[93] Men without families went directly to an enlistment station, but for Harry Whitney, ensuring the safety of his wife and children was a central priority. Harry's great-nephew, Nathan Whitney, recalled: "I went to Plymouth N.C. to enlist but having a family to look after Harry could not go . . . but later on through the assistance of the Union Soldiers he got his family to Roanoke Island and he enlisted."[94] The record is silent about whether the Whitney family carried personal items, as wartime observers frequently described of refugees, such as blankets, clothing, shoes, or cooking utensils, when they boarded the boat to Roanoke. Once they completed their medical examinations, the men often returned to say goodbye to their loved ones, as did Harry, who "came with his uniform on, gun, [and] haver sack" to say goodbye to Fanny and his children.[95]

The path to the Union lines and subsequent enlistment was a communal one for many black men. Charles Oats reflected on his journey to the lines with James Flowers: "We grew up boys together in Wayne Co., and we came to this town together from that county while the war was going on and later both of us enlisted in 37th U.S.C. Inf., and after discharge we both lived here in this city till he died."[96] In 1864, Mathew Walden and a large group of men from Hertford County crossed into the Union-occupied zones together: "29 of us runaway from Hertford Co, N.C. to get to the Union Lines. It was in February 1864 . . . we were about 3 weeks getting to Plymouth, NC about 60 miles from Hertford Co., N.C. I remember we came on a boat called the 'bombshell' from Catherine Creek on the Chowan River to Plymouth N.C. and went to Newbern . . . by boat."[97] At the military stations, the men were "stripped naked at enlistment and thoroughly examined physically" before they received their clothing and took their military oath.[98]

The confiscation acts of 1861 and 1862 and the Militia Act of 1862, Glymph argues, all but abandoned black women's struggles to realize their wartime freedom.[99] Lanner Jones remained on her owner's South River plantation as the war got underway and Union forces occupied North Carolina's eastern seaboard. "About a year afterwards" Lanner took off and then "left going from one house to another" until she made it to New Bern, where she settled in the Trent River camp. At the time of her "self-emancipation," marriage was not a route to citizenship. Nor was it a possibility for Mary Williams, who made her way to New Bern with her mother when New Bern fell.[100]

Freedom within the Union lines was gendered, and women who were unable to secure military employment pointed to the value of their labor as mothers and wives in the midst of war. Some women experienced pregnancy and childbirth while traveling with their husband's regiment. Mary Ann Starkey, president of the Colored Ladies' Relief Association, raised money and collected supplies for black refugees. The group broadened its efforts with black enlistment, supporting the black men who served in the Union Army by assisting the wounded soldiers and their families. In June 1863, the organization presented a flag to the First Regiment of the North Carolina Colored Volunteers (later the Thirty-Fifth USCT).[101] A statement circulated during the war read as follows: "We, the colored women of Newbern, North Carolina, desire to give to the world our object, plans, constitution, and our officers, for the purpose of ameliorating the miseries of our colored soldiers in their struggle for freedom, whatever may be the occasion against oppression."[102] The activities of Starkey and the Colored Ladies' Relief Association exemplify the crucial role black women played in addressing the concerns of New Bern's black community and government officials. Sarah Oxly, also a freedwoman, established a thriving bakery in the city, but a fire destroyed it and several other businesses in 1864. Referred to as "a colored Quakeress," Sarah earned respect among soldiers from Confederate and Union forces alike for the "attentive" care she rendered to the sick and needy.[103]

Threats of conscription haunted able-bodied men who remained wary of enlistment and military work. In the summer of 1864, rumors spread among local blacks that federal soldiers intended to recruit a large number of able-bodied black men, relocate them to Virginia battlegrounds, and force them to labor for the Army of the Potomac. The prospect of being coerced and working under conditions that resembled slavery led many to flee the city. Federal soldiers eventually captured large groups of black men who hid outside New Bern's boundaries and relocated them. According to David Cecelski, the men "found themselves digging trenches in Virginia."[104]

Military recruitment of black men transformed settlement camps across the South. Military employers and army recruiters now competed for the labor of healthy young black men, which resulted in black families' growing dependence on government assistance. Married women whose husbands had enlisted, single women with children, the elderly, and disabled people increasingly inhabited the camps.[105] Moreover, wages from men's army service were unpredictable, and women had no guarantees of whether, or when, they would receive compensation from the government. The mothers and wives of enlisted soldiers became responsible for the full support of their children while their husbands fought or until the government issued rations.[106]

Soldiers policed camps, which proved dangerous for unaccompanied women. The brutal rape of Rebecca Ann Cradle, a black girl working in the hospital at New Bern, surely stirred fear among women working among the military.[107] Easter Brown confided that she asked a man to stay with her during the war years—for protection.[108] Though it is not specified in her testimony, the protection Easter sought may have been associated with fears that Union Army soldiers would sexually violate her.[109] Few women could depend on black men, however, because there were fewer and fewer of them as enlistments intensified.

The status, legal standing, and experiences of black soldiers' wives differed depending on where they resided. The Emancipation Proclamation freed black soldiers' wives living in Union-occupied territories but not those in Union border states—Missouri, Kentucky, and Maryland—where the institution of slavery was legally protected. As historian Sharon Romeo reminds us, the transformation of an enslaved man into a U.S. soldier in St. Louis, Missouri, did not pave the way for citizenship for the soldier's wife. Left to their own devices, black women used their access to military policy and provost courts to press a wide range of claims and subvert their owners' power.[110] In Kentucky, Lorenzo Thomas, the superintendent in charge of camps there, ordered blacks unfit for military service to leave the camps and urged them to stay with their masters.[111] Frustrated superintendents at Kentucky's Union Camp Nelson repeatedly drove women and children away from the site. Administrators feared women would not only spread venereal diseases among the soldiers but become a burden on the government. Eventually a refuge was opened at the behest of the secretary of war to house the women and children at the controversial army camp. By January 1865, Camp Nelson housed some 3,065 people, mostly women and children with familial ties to enlisted soldiers.[112]

Settlement camps across the South provided opportunities for young girls and older women to build intergenerational relationships with one another while beginning their lives as free persons.[113] These networks were created in part by familial connections, through their previous neighborhoods, and based on personal friendships formed in the freedpeople's camps.[114] Women's kinship and communal ties proved invaluable, especially after the death of a male family member. When the recently widowed Charlotte Banks arrived in the Trent River settlement, she joined a network of women whose husbands had enlisted. Many of the freedpeople she encountered had come from Elizabeth City, where she had also lived before the war. Matilda Wells was only twelve years old when she met Charlotte in the Trent River settlement. "We all got here around the same time," Matilda recalled.[115] Young girls like Matilda, who came of age in settlements in eastern North Carolina, leaned on older black women for guidance as they formed new ideas and took new directions in their own lives.

Communication between the camps and the battlefield kept wives, mothers, and children informed about their loved ones. News of injuries and illness shuttled back and forth between soldiers and their families. These channels gave black families crucial information about men whom they cherished, even increasing their patriotic fervor. When a black soldier returned to Roanoke, Fanny Whitney learned that her husband, Harry, had died in a Wilmington hospital. "I remember the time I heard it," one young woman from the Donnell ex-slave community recalled, "there was a right smart sorrow about it."[116] The sorrow to which she bore witness appears to have been communal, as several of the men from the Donnell plantation died around the same time as Fanny's husband.[117]

Wartime movement was deeply gendered. A woman's ability to travel with her soldier-husband or intimate partner depended on her childcare responsibilities. Women without children often traveled with black and white regiments, doing laundry, preparing food, and applying their "lay" knowledge of healthcare for the soldiers' welfare. As Louisa Jackson traveled with Samuel Powers, she cooked, washed, and attended to his injuries.[118] The couple married in Charleston, South Carolina, on June 8, 1865.[119] Chaplain James Beecher, son of the prominent minister Lyman Beecher and half-brother of Harriet Beecher Stowe, officiated.[120]

During Louisa's time traveling with Samuel's regiment, she probably relied heavily on the relationships she built with other women living among the black regiments. Lucy Crocker vividly described her experiences in the field. She "went right into camp" the day her husband, Henry Crocker, enlisted in the USCT and did the "washing and ironing" for the captain of her husband's company.[121] When her husband's regiment moved to Richmond, Lucy and a group of soldiers' wives stayed behind. They supported themselves by taking in work and obtaining rations from the commissary at Fort Monroe. After a few months, Lucy's husband sent for her, and the couple traveled to Brazos, Texas.

Military officials and camp superintendents expressed fears about the dangers that women traveling with the regiments posed to the soldiers' morale and health. Black women, they believed, might spread venereal diseases among the soldiers, and ultimately their presence would become a "great expense to the government."[122] In reality, black soldiers and military officers benefited greatly from the presence of black women in the field. Professionally trained nurses were in short supply, and doctors rarely served black units, so medical care fell on the shoulders of black women. Three out of five men who died during the war succumbed to disease unrelated to combat, and black soldiers' rate of death as a result of disease was double that of white troops.[123] The lack of proper medical attention explains this disparity.

The unpaid labor black women performed on behalf of their husbands and other black and white soldiers was but one of many ways they contributed to the destruction of slavery and chipped away at the power of the Confederacy. Samuel Powers was injured in a battle at Olustee, Florida, on February 20, 1864. He was admitted to the general hospital at Jacksonville two months later and struggled with ill health for the duration of his military service, entering the hospital once again in Beaufort, South Carolina, in November 1864. At his discharge in June 1866, Samuel had not been paid since the previous December. After deductions for food and clothing, the military owed Powers $17.69 in wages and an enlistment bounty of $100. Louisa did not receive any pay for the nursing services she had provided for her husband.[124]

After several years of occupation, the port city of New Bern had turned into a cesspool of contagious diseases. During an inspection tour of the city, General Butler found conditions shocking. He complained of an "awful stench" near one of the soldiers' camps, within two miles of the city's edge.[125] Rotten beef set aside for the army and the horse manure used to cover it surely contributed to the odor.[126] Not surprisingly, a yellow fever epidemic broke out in New Bern during the summer of 1864. Freedpeople, refugees, native inhabitants, members of the military, and Northern migrants all succumbed to the disease.[127] Among the ill was William L. Palmer, who first served as captain and headed the U.S. Commissary of Subsistence in New Bern in 1864 and, after the war, as mayor of New Bern and a notary public.[128] According to historians Thomas J. Farnham and Francis P. King, the virus had appeared in coastal areas such as Charleston, South Carolina, and Brownsville, Texas. Transmitted by mosquitoes and passed easily from person to person, the disease had a high fatality rate.[129]

Smallpox, too, wreaked havoc on the inhabitants of settlement camps in Union-occupied zones. William O. Harris's mother, Sarah (born Richardson), died of smallpox. Nearly a year later William's father, Nathaniel, who had served in the Fourteenth USCHA, died from "hemorrhage of the lungs," most likely a result of tuberculosis.[130] One black soldier exposed the severe mistreatment of blacks infected with smallpox in the New Bern vicinity, saying they were buried in a hole without a coffin and received inferior treatment to that provided for whites. The medical inspector of North Carolina simply denied that these conditions existed.[131] Military administrators put the total number of deaths from the disease at one thousand, though it is not clear whether the official count included black civilians. Popular opinion held that inhabitants of settlement camps died at higher rates than those who lived in the city's established neighborhoods because living conditions were unsanitary and mosquitoes bred in the stagnant pools of water.[132]

Those with medical expertise, including black women, treated the injured and infected at New Bern's academy building, which was converted into a military hospital to treat victims of spinal meningitis, smallpox, yellow fever, and battle wounds.[133] In the absence of sufficient medical staff, the wives, intimate companions, and relatives of black soldiers provided essential care. Flora Lucas recalled a particularly trying moment in wartime New Bern when "the town was alive with [disease] and they died the same as sheep—we could not get boxes fast enough to bury them in."[134] Lucas and other black women applied their expertise to the care of ailing soldiers. As she recalled, "I was a kind of small pox nurse and took care of a number of cases about that time. . . . I understand the treatment of the disease. . . . I anointed his sores with lemon juice and was[hed] his face in chamber lye."[135] Needless to say, Flora Lucas and other black women performed much of this work without any compensation.[136] Elizabeth Dempsey was one of the few who managed to secure a regular paid nursing position in the army.[137]

Amid the turmoil of military enlistment, disease, death, and constant movement in and out of the region, military administrators insisted that freedpeople formalize their intimate relations. Recognizing that many couples in the freedpeople's camps had not been allowed to marry because they had been enslaved, Northern military officials moved to ameliorate what they deemed a moral problem. U.S. authorities required soldiers' wives and children to be recognized as their dependents; all marriages had to be solemnized by an army chaplain on authority granted by the provost marshal.[138] Freedwoman Harriet Barlow remembered that "a man by the name of Chaplain Green married us, he was a Chaplain in the Army."[139] Shortly after John Jackson escorted his wife and child from his owner's plantation in Jones County, he went to the provost marshal's office and secured a marriage license by paying twenty-five cents.[140] With marriage came new legal standing and privileges for the families of enlisted soldiers in Union-occupied territories.

The legal position of black soldiers' wives depended greatly on the state where they resided. Soldiers' wives were formally emancipated in March 1865, when Congress passed a joint resolution offering freedom to the wives and children of currently serving black soldiers.[141] This policy was especially important for those who resided in border slave states and, as Herbert Gutman has shown, served as a recruiting tool in states such as Kentucky, where black enlistment and subsequent marriages "bankrupted slavery."[142] As recognized dependents, wives and children were entitled to rations, a demand that black soldiers had made before agreeing to enlist.[143] Freedwomen whose husbands were serving in the USCT drew limited food rations. Freedwoman Charlotte Banks, whose soldier-husband had died, recalled, "I was furnished rations during the war as his widow by the Union Army stationed" in New Bern.[144] For those like Matilda Wells, who had no connection to an enlisted soldier, kin groups and intergenerational networks of women proved vital to their survival.

The money black soldiers sent home provided crucial support for their families living in the freedpeople's camps. A neighbor observed that Judith Lavenhouse's enlisted son, George, "brought her food and his contributions were necessary as she did not have enough to support her adequately without his help."[145] York Biggs "contributed toward the support" of his mother, Maria, "by his labor" and sent her "eight dollars per month" before he succumbed to yellow fever in 1864.[146] Easter Brown lived on her own labor and the money her son, Jerry, sent home regularly in his letters.[147] Another woman's son sent her part of the money he earned every month by working for the quartermaster.[148] After enlisting in the Union Army, Julia Neel's son continued his contributions to her support, sending his earnings home regularly with his letters from the field.[149]

NEW BERN AT WAR'S END

As the war drew to a close, the black population of Union-occupied zones of eastern North Carolina burgeoned. During the last weeks of the war, a thousand more freedpeople arrived in New Bern. In the wake of this final influx, the population of the Trent River settlement swelled to about three thousand.[150] Living conditions were cramped, but residents were determined to make the best of the situation. In January 1865, Rev. Horace James, who was the first appointed superintendent of Negro affairs in North Carolina and, after March 1865, became the assistant commissioner of the North Carolina Freedmen's Bureau, reported on developments in the camp. He said that freedpeople had replaced tents with shanty-like houses; the Freedmen's Bureau had set up its office; and a school had been established, along with a blacksmith shop, a hospital, and several churches. Residents planted gardens and sold vegetables in neighboring communities.[151]

The return of black soldiers and the constant flow of maritime workers in and out of New Bern added to the social, economic, and political changes already taking shape in post–Civil War years. Whites who returned to the city had to adjust to a new social and political reality: resident blacks and returning veterans assumed posts in the local police and fire departments, and at the municipal level, they served as magistrates. The former supporters of the Confederacy also had to contend with a new group of Northern-born whites who had arrived during the war and decided to make New Bern their permanent home. White Southerners referred to them as carpetbaggers, but they preferred to think of themselves as entrepreneurs. The black fugitives who entered New Bern during the Civil War and its prewar black inhabitants left an indelible impression on the city. Once inhabited by prominent slaveholders and the state's largest concentration of free blacks, New Bern remained a beacon of freedom as black newcomers sought to reclaim their lives and assert their identities as free men and women.

Military officials found that the majority of freedpeople in North Carolina lived in three areas: New Bern (10,782), Beaufort and vicinity (3,245), and Roanoke Island (3,091).[152] These numbers pale in comparison to the unofficial estimates given by contemporary observers. In late June 1865, Harvey M. Watterson, a former congressman and longtime friend of President Andrew Johnson, estimated that "forty to fifty thousand" blacks, "and even higher" were living in and around New Bern.[153] Colonel F. D. Sewall, the acting inspector general for the Freedmen's Bureau, offered a more conservative but nonetheless stunning figure for the black refugee population: "There are other collections of freedmen in and around New Bern, but not regularly organized camps. Most of the men are at work. It is estimated that within a radius of six miles at this point, there is a colored population of 12,000."[154] These numbers place New Bern's refugee population on par with more populous urban centers where blacks settled at the war's close.

2

The Black Community in New Bern, 1865–1920

Freedpeople wasted little time celebrating the abolishment of slavery and the new possibilities on the horizon. In eastern North Carolina, black people who had been living in and around Union Army–occupied areas, such as New Bern, including those who had been free before the war, enslaved people who had labored for whites, and migrants who had entered the city in wartime, forged new communities with a panoply of social, religious, and political institutions. Wartime upheavals fundamentally altered the racial demography of New Bern, where blacks remained the majority population until the twentieth century.[1] Aspects of the city's history—particularly the influx of black newcomers during the wartime years—made New Bern a particularly fertile staging ground for black political struggles, especially for black Union veterans and their families. In the days and weeks following the war, the population of the city and surrounding area neared 15,000, but by 1870, it had settled at around 5,849, and by 1900, it had grown to 9,086.[2]

Demonstrating freedpeople's readiness to engage fully in electoral politics, representatives from New Bern attended the statewide colored conventions in 1865 and 1866. When 120 black delegates assembled in Raleigh's African Methodist church on September 29, 1865, James Walker Hood, pastor of the African Methodist Episcopal Zion (AMEZ) church of New Bern, was elected president, and the outspoken Abraham Galloway delivered a fiery speech. Delegates spelled out the rights they believed blacks must have in the wake of emancipation, which included the right to serve on juries, education for their children, legal recognition of their families, protection from violence, and the right to vote.[3] The convention's final resolutions, however, made no mention of equal rights before the law.[4] Blacks in New Bern further led the way in claiming their rights. In March 1867, an article in the *Newbern Weekly Journal of Commerce* announced: "The colored people of Newbern will be the first of their race in the State to vote under the Sherman Act."[5] In Wilmington, a "very large number of colored women attended the Radical Mass Meeting," where Abraham Galloway addressed the crowd.[6] Black men gained voting rights under the Fourteenth and Fifteenth Amendments, which were ratified in 1868 and 1870.[7] Craven County's black voters helped to elect thirty-two black state legislators who served in the General Assembly from 1868 to 1872. Minister Brevett Morris, Clinton D. Pierson, and three others hailed from New Bern.[8]

Military employment and enlistment in the Union Army laid the basis for the postwar expansion of black businesses and black women's relationship with the federal government in two crucial ways: by creating a population in need of government relief and by simulating migration to urban areas to take advantage of government resources. Black Union veterans and their families in New Bern, like those in Norfolk, Virginia, and Memphis, Tennessee, were well positioned to build and sustain a relationship with the federal government. In 1865, offices of the Freedmen's Bureau were established in New Bern, as well as in Raleigh and Wilmington, including branches of the Freedmen's Savings and Trust Company Bank, which Congress had just chartered. The black masses who lived in or near the city had at least some access to the federal government and its agencies.

Meanwhile, calls for the removal of black children and vagrants from the city streets grew louder in local papers. One editor charged that a group of black children gathered in front of the notable Gaston House on South Front Street had disrupted city dwellers with "inconvenience and insults."[9] Fearing the growing numbers of blacks occupying public space, New Bern's mayor and town commissioners introduced Ordinance 20, which authorized the arrest of "all idle or vagrant persons . . . who have no visible means of support" within the city's limits.[10] Vagrancy, a misdemeanor crime in which the court had full discretion in deciding the penalty, had detrimental consequences for the unemployed and landless.

This chapter reconstructs and analyzes black women's efforts to establish independent households, families, neighborhoods, and community institutions. Their efforts are essential to understanding black women's view of themselves as worthy women because, as Tera Hunter and Nancy Bercaw contend, it allowed them to define themselves beyond the confines of their work. In these spaces black people devised alternative notions of power and authority based on "a complex interweaving of relationships mediated by the community."[11]

THE IMMEDIATE AFTERMATH OF WAR

Emancipation advocates and northern agents of free labor assumed that the implementation of a system of contract labor would naturally improve working conditions throughout the South.[12] Immediately following the war, the Freedmen's Bureau and its agents aimed to assist people in transitioning from slavery to freedom and oversee abandoned lands. Agents managed disputes, distributed aid to the disabled and needy, protected freedpeople from white violence, settled civil disputes, and assisted the ill through dispensaries; eventually, they helped to establish schools for black adults and children.[13] Its state headquarters were in Raleigh, and the superintendent of the Eastern District set up offices in New Bern. Although freedpeople received uneven treatment from Freedmen's Bureau agents, blacks rallied behind the agency when President Johnson sought to discredit it in May 1866. Eight hundred blacks crowded into a Wilmington church to dispute the recommendation of two inspectors to remove the bureau from the South.[14] Two months later, at a mass meeting held at St. Andrew Chapel, blacks expressed their support for a Freedmen's Bureau agent who was "relieved from duty" at New Bern.[15]

The government's wartime analysis of dependency—embodied in the army and Freedmen's Bureau—set the tone for its postwar approach to managing black refugee populations. Just two months after the close of the war, charges of dependency and urgent calls to shut down settlement camps grew louder.[16] Home to two of the largest freedmen's camps in the South, new initiatives to reduce rations at black settlements had devastating consequences for vulnerable populations at the Roanoke Colony and the Trent River settlement camp.

Fanny Whitney and her young children resided at Roanoke as conditions worsened. Two black soldiers serving out their enlistment terms in Virginia apprised General O. O. Howard of the conditions at Roanoke. They called for the removal of an army administrator who withheld food and supplies from their families and refused to compensate men for their labor.[17] One soldier protested: "when I inlisted in the united states Service the Government made Promis for to hav them Taken Care off."[18] In a separate letter, a black army chaplain and a group of white missionaries in service at Roanoke Island appealed for additional resources and described the scene. "There are many who are sick and disabled whose ration has been cut off, and these instances are not isolated, but oft recurring and children crying for bread, whose husbands, Sons, and fathers are in the army today."[19]

In July 1865, roughly two months after official combat ended in North Carolina, Colonel Eliphalet Whittlesey became assistant commissioner of the Freedmen's Bureau for North Carolina. He announced to his agents and the white people of the state that freedpeople were "entitled to all the rights of man."[20] Agents of the bureau worked in conjunction with black community leaders, local authorities, and northern freedmen's aid societies in establishing schools and distributing relief. Focusing mainly on establishing an economy based on wage labor, Whittlesey worked diligently to promote and oversee employment contracts and to close settlement camps, which the families of black soldiers and the disabled populated—many depending on government assistance.

The problems of deprivation and poverty became increasingly acute in black settlement camps, where many families of black soldiers continued to live. In Commissioner Whittlesey's testimony before Congress's Joint Committee on Reconstruction, he outlined the circumstances in eastern North Carolina:

> We have at certain places large communities of blacks who have been gathering during the entire war on the coast—places of refuge from the interior—where they came within our lines. At those points the men have enlisted in the army, and left a large number of women and children dependent upon the government for support. These principal points are Roanoke Island and Newbern and vicinity. In all the rest of the State we have not more than five or six hundred who are receiving rations and support from the government.[21]

Distribution of rations to the most vulnerable refugees conjured up images of able-bodied black women living off the federal government's largess. Freedmen's Bureau agents, influenced by their own ideas about how to implement the wage-labor system called on black men, women, and children to sign labor contracts. Anything less could be construed as a form of "dependency." Despite these efforts, the agency remained the target of intense criticism from whites for distributing aid to freedpeople, which enabled blacks to avoid working for whites on the harsh terms that employers dictated.[22]

A little more than two weeks after bureau commissioner Howard issued Circular Order 13, directing assistant commissioners throughout the South to set aside abandoned lands and confiscated property for the use of refugees and freedmen, Whittlesey announced, "The Government owns no lands" in the state of North Carolina.[23] During this phase of dispossession across the South, in which the federal government effectively stripped away black claims to land and other forms of property, bureau agents compelled blacks to transition to the free labor system they envisioned.

The dissolution of freedpeople's camps throughout eastern North Carolina between 1865 and 1867, including the Roanoke Colony in 1867, prompted protest and resistance from inhabitants who had grown attached to the land.[24] The government's withdrawal of aid and protection from the most vulnerable at the freedpeople's colony at Roanoke amounted to little more than a forced relocation scheme. Fanny Whitney and her children lived through these days of dispossession and eviction on the Roanoke Colony, which historian Patricia Click has vividly depicted. When white owners returned to the island to reclaim their abandoned land, they promptly evicted freedpeople.[25] Some of the most destitute inhabitants pilfered food to keep from starving, while land restoration continued apace. The colony officially closed in 1867.

Hunger, illness, and coping with the loss of beloved community members were but some of the trials and tribulations Fanny Whitney and her kin endured while facing eviction from the Roanoke Colony. Relocating to New Bern ultimately meant returning to the place where Fanny had been born and potentially reconnecting with kin and community in the vicinity. Reconstructing Fanny's family and community relationships over long stretches of time shows that blacks who had been enslaved on Judge Donnell's Hyde County land continued to move along lines of kinship and local connections. They re-created complex family ties and familiar communities in new places, forming an intricate and expansive network that provided crucial support for women like Fanny, who was widowed when she was living on Roanoke Island in 1865.[26]

If freedom was to Fanny Whitney what historian Abigail Cooper defines as "the ability to move to one's kinship group," then she and her peers were successful.[27] This was also true for Charlotte Banks, whose travel to New Bern may have been more intentional than she let on in her early attempts to secure survivors' benefits. As it turns out, a group of formerly enslaved people who resided near Charlotte's Elizabeth City "neighborhood" settled in New Bern around the same time, including her cousin, whom she located shortly after her arrival.

In New Bern, Fanny and her boys—Adam, Harry, and Milton—settled on Jones Street, in the heart of the Fifth Ward, alongside a collection of common laborers, domestics, educators, and skilled artisans. Given what she and other black soldiers' families had recently endured on the Roanoke Colony, the strong presence of the Freedmen's Bureau in James City may have been disenchanting. Blacks living in James City, now a 180-acre parcel of land with 525 buildings, also struggled to maintain their right to stay there after the war. In February 1867, heirs to the property on which the Union Army had set up the Trent River camp filed a petition to take over the land. President Johnson's policy of allowing southern states to manage their own affairs alongside his pardon policy left bureau officials unsure of the legal standing of the Trent River settlement. The assistant commissioner of the North Carolina Freedmen's Bureau intended "to restore the whole or part of this property" and instructed agents "not to lease any of the land in question."[28] Black residents led by minister Benjamin B. Spicer protested their removal from their homes. Three months after Spicer directed a letter to Commissioner Howard, the land remained in government possession.[29] After the ordeal, nearly seventeen hundred blacks occupied the community, many of them veterans and their families and the survivors of dead black Union soldiers.[30] The Freedmen's Bureau terminated all provision to the residents of James City by the end of 1868, eventually shutting down its operation in the state.

Black women migrants sought the assistance and protection of military authorities, agents of the Freedmen's Bureau, and black Union soldiers, as well as for the mutual support and solidarity to be found in gathering together. Steven Hahn has shown how family and kin networks laid the foundation for black political communities in the late nineteenth century.[31] This was certainly true for black Union widows, who forged multifaceted relationships with the federal government in their search for the compensation they believed they deserved for their husbands' and their own services to the nation. Women also created social lives and neighborhood institutions that revolved around their encampments, which they turned into neighborhoods. They breathed new life into independent religious institutions, such as the AMEZ and various Baptist churches. New Bern, which a white military officer from the North deemed "a mecca of a thousand noble aspirations," continued to attract women because of the social and economic opportunities it offered.[32]

A small but rapidly growing black middle class lived sprinkled throughout the city, though especially concentrated in the Fifth Ward. Black veterans who had acquired literacy skills and learned a trade could accumulate wealth and status among their peers. Freedmen Allen G. Oden and Spencer Alexander were two such men.[33] Active in New Bern's civic arena, Oden taught school, worked as a shingle maker, and eventually learned the shoemaking trade.[34] His wife, Dicy, managed to open an independent business. Spencer Alexander, who was also a shoemaker, and his wife, Sophia, achieved a modicum of economic stability in the postwar years. As skilled craftsmen with resourceful wives, Oden and Alexander managed to stave off the acute economic problems that the majority of blacks in the area endured.

As in other southern cities, blacks and whites continued to pass one another on the streets and conduct business together, although residential neighborhoods remained segregated by race and class. Residents of James City, too, formed black-led religious and fraternal organizations where they could worship, socialize, and share stories. Only a few mixed race enclaves existed within the city's boundaries. Clark's Brick Yard, located about eight miles from New Bern in a wooded area, was exceptional in that it was home to a group of working-class blacks and whites who intermarried. A white observer described it in 1919: "That particular neighborhood is pretty well filled up with descendent[s] of negroes and low down whites who had lived together regardless of race up until now there are all shades of color to be found there."[35]

White northerners who arrived in New Bern during the war remained there after combat ended. They mostly took up residence in the Second and Third Wards of the city, areas historically inhabited by white elites. Veteran Ethelbert Hubbs was one of the few northern-born city officials to live in the Fifth Ward among a cadre of whites and professional blacks. War correspondent and Treasury Department employee Edward Carpenter settled in a hotel with a host of other whites in the Second Ward. The few blacks who lived in the hotel were hired to serve the white military officers, businessmen, and other occupants. After Captain William L. Palmer recovered from his bout with yellow fever, he served two terms as New Bern's mayor and settled in the First Ward among a cluster of northern-born military administrators.[36] Henry G. Bates served in the U.S. Army "during the entire period of the war" but did not arrive in New Bern until 1869, when he became assistant surgeon in the Marine Hospital. Bates resided on East Front Street and later served as city and county physician and coroner before his death in 1890.[37] After George Tinker's military duties with the Tenth Connecticut Infantry ended, he remained in New Bern, working as a court clerk and living in the Second Ward.[38] Augustus Seymour, who was elected to serve in North Carolina's House of Representatives in 1868, resided in the Third Ward.[39] These men would be some of the first to assist black women's initiate petitions for survivors' benefits.

Charles Alexander Nelson, a white northerner who arrived in New Bern in 1864, served as a civil engineer in the Quartermaster's Department; he later served as a Reconstruction administrator and lived in a black neighborhood in the Sixth Ward.[40] With Horace James, Hubbs, Carpenter, and Seymour, Nelson petitioned the municipal leadership to "erect a home of worship to be occupied by the Congregational Church and Society" in New Bern. According to their petition the men hoped to secure a "religious home for the free and progressive element" of their community.[41] White female school teachers and missionaries representing the Woman's American Baptist Home Mission Society of Chicago settled in James City and conducted classes at the Cedar Grove Baptist Church. Harriet Duggins, a black missionary who worked alongside Waugh and Williams, testified to the saintliness of some of her black female neighbors.[42]

Freedwoman Sarah Oxly rebuilt her eating house in the city's business district on Broad Street after losing the building to a fire in 1864, but another fire in 1867 destroyed the "handsome property."[43] After her sister, Frances, contracted yellow fever and died, Sarah took full custody of her sister's daughters.[44] In need of "a comfortable home for herself" and growing family, she took on additional work as Edward W. Carpenter's housekeeper.[45] While juggling her responsibilities as a household worker and raising her nieces, Sarah managed to establish an ice cream parlor at her residence. Advertisements appeared in the *New Berne Times* and *Newbernian* listing Sarah's Ice Cream Parlor at 59 Broad Street near the southwest corner of Middle Street.[46] Oxly was one of a small group of black female entrepreneurs, which included Lucy Jackson, who ran a boardinghouse on New South Front Street, and Lydia Pierson, a soldier's widow who sold spirits.[47]

The return of black Union troops undoubtedly inspired feelings of pride in black neighborhoods. As they rejoined their families, these veterans integrated themselves into newly constituted communities with a new sense of worth that their army service engendered. Turner Norman's military experience, combined with his skills as a lumberman, earned him a reputation as a "high priced man."[48] When Joseph Harvey returned to New Bern, "he was dressed in a new suit of uniform blue—had on a new Cap with a B on the front of it & had his haversack on his back and a stick in his hand—he had money—$75.00."[49]

Blacks in New Bern gave meaning to their freedom by formalizing their marriages and uniting their families. They fought to secure legal recognition for their families and to make unimpeded choices about their personal lives. With the discharge of black regiments recruited in North Carolina beginning in June 1866, a stream of returning soldiers transformed New Bern's social landscape. Men who returned from war marked their transition to freedom by securing marriage licenses with their partners, publicly declaring their status as married couples. Some took the opportunity to end their prewar marriages and sought new relationships on their own terms. These weddings were among the most elaborate and cherished events in the aftermath of the Civil War. Women orchestrated wedding ceremonies, prepared meals, set tables, and held candles. Men borrowed suits, and women hired seamstresses to make wedding dresses. One woman planned an elaborate ceremony with six bridesmaids. Some weddings attracted crowds. When Maria Wallace married veteran Hezekiah Richardson at Watson's Tabernacle "there were over a hundred present. . . . The church was full and there were nearly as many out the doors as there were in the church."[50] One guest recalled that she "could only get in the door."[51] These celebrations served as places for socializing and community formation.

Jubilant celebrations throughout the city and the triumphant return of black soldiers to their homes dismayed white southerners. Their objections to the presence of black troops in and around New Bern surfaced almost immediately. Any behavior that signaled blacks' free status made them anxious, and they interpreted black veterans' lack of deference as a threat. New Bern's Committee on Correspondence, which was made up of former slaveholders, notified President Johnson of daily offenses, "since Colored Troops are sustained in their acts of violence and Breaches of peace." According to the group, citizens—a status that, in their view, only whites enjoyed—had been "shot down" and "ladies elbowed and shoved off the sidewalks."[52] On October 17, 1865, members of the statewide convention, which admitted only white men, passed a resolution ordering the president of the gathering to "request [that] the President of the United States" remove all black troops from the state of North Carolina "at the earliest practicable period."[53] Five days later, the 135th regiment, a black infantry unit organized in Goldsboro, North Carolina, was mustered out of service.

Civil authorities also harassed black veterans who occupied urban spaces. In August 1865, "four or five U.S. colored soldiers were arrested" for walking about Wilmington without "passes."[54] In January 1866, a black veteran reported that white militia members threatened, beat, and searched the homes of black soldiers for weapons. As one returnee said, "We left our wives & children here & was bound to come back to them, to take care of them."[55] In Memphis, in contrast to New Bern, whites' racial hatred exploded: among the many acts of violence blacks endured during the Memphis riots of 1866, "which began as a clash between black Union soldiers and city police," historian Hannah Rosen lists the rape of black soldiers' wives and family members.[56] Additionally, white men lynched black men after accusing them of raping white women—when, in fact, as antilynching activists noted, the reverse was true.[57] Symbolically, these acts represented the determination of white men to reclaim and reassert their power over black people, especially black soldiers who had recently been decommissioned and disarmed.[58] As of October 28, 1866, all the black regiments organized in North Carolina had been disbanded.[59]

BLACK LIFE AND LABOR IN POSTWAR NEW BERN

Black men and women routinely appeared in the city's Mayor's Court for violating what historian Sarah Haley calls "quality of life crimes."[60] Wright Parker was fined one dollar for "fast driving." Godfrey Becton and John Bryant were charged with "selling liquor to soldiers," but the charges were not sustained.[61] Susan Moore and Allen Pettiford were charged with stealing money from a store. Wright Hammond, who had served in the navy, was fined two dollars for violating a watering ordinance.[62] Black women, too, were regularly arrested. On August 17, 1865, Delia Johnson and Betsey Hanehan were fined "for being drunk and disorderly"; their fines ranged from five to ten dollars.[63] Julia A. Poole, Violet Moles, and Caroline Woodworth were fined for "disorderly conduct."[64] Mayor William Palmer fined Sarah McCoy and Carolina Woodard three dollars for "keeping a disorderly house."[65] Offenders had to pay their fines or work off their fees. David Washington was fined twenty dollars for using "threatening language to [a] policeman" and "attempting to create a disturbance." After defaulting on his payment, Washington was assigned to "work on the streets 30 days, with ball and chain."[66] Lewis Mercer was "sentenced fourteen days labor on the streets" for stealing food from the city storehouse.[67]

The return of black veterans to cities like New Bern and Wilmington, combined with the influx of their families and of black women and children whose soldier-husbands and fathers had died, posed new challenges to North Carolina's labor system. Blacks continued to dominate the local fish trade in New Bern. The occupation was physically taxing. One resident reflected: "You see fishing is work that exposes a man very much and even in the coldest weather a fisherman will at times have to take the water up to his waist or arm pits and it will eventually impair the health."[68] Joseph Ives, a white Union veteran and "fishing man" by trade, reportedly "stayed in the river so much it was enough to kill a man." One of his neighbors believed that "his experience as a fisherman killed him" in 1887.[69] Black veterans also returned to work in North Carolina's labor-intensive naval stores industry, which had declined during the war. Turpentine hands earned about sixteen dollars a month plus board, which was considerably more than most other black men earned.[70] "They were offering big prices for men to go South [to Wilmington] to work in the Turpentine Woods."[71]

New Bern's labor force was not isolated or stationary. Black veterans found work operating schooners and water taxis and regularly made trips between North Carolina and New York, Massachusetts, and Rhode Island. These routes were important channels of information for black workers. Veterans like Walter Jones worked on a boat that ran between Elizabeth City and New Bern; then he "got on a boat that ran from N.Y. to the West Indies."[72] Eliza Larkins, a Wilmington resident, in the wake of her husband's death embarked on seasonal migrations to the North, where she found live-in summer jobs with white families in Hempstead, Long Island, and Orange, New Jersey, and at a boardinghouse in Bristol, Connecticut.[73] Responding to repressive labor conditions and a sagging economy, black families hoped to start new lives in Massachusetts, Connecticut, and other New England states, where they earned up to twenty dollars per month.[74] In several cases women and children outnumbered the men on these journeys. The labor market black women confronted in the aftermath of emancipation was harsh. They toiled for long hours at tasks that were as heavy as those men performed, but women were almost invariably paid less. Many worked some of the time as domestics, mostly for white families, and at other times as day laborers, piecing together a range of jobs to earn a living.[75] Many found employment in white households and on white-owned plantations, where domestic workers could earn four to five dollars a month.[76] Jane Richardson returned to the Biddle plantation just outside New Bern sometime after the war, eager to reconnect with her husband, whom she had been separated from before the war. When that hope was dashed, she began working for the new land owner as a cook. Eventually she met veteran Thomas Reynolds, who had been born free in Hertford County and had started working on the same plantation "ginning cotton" a few months after he was discharged from the army in December 1865. Jane and Thomas eventually married.[77]

The transition to the free labor system proved challenging for all black women, but especially for those who had lost their husbands in the war and were responsible for supporting their children. War widows pursued various wage-earning strategies to sustain their lives and relied heavily on their social ties.[78] Some women took in boarders and collected rent, while others cooked meals or worked as housekeepers for single men. One woman cooked for a group of black men the federal government employed after her husband was killed in the battle of Honey Hill, South Carolina, on November 30, 1864: "I cooked and washed for them all. [Then] they all left for other places and I was left alone with my only child."[79] Another mended clothes for a decommissioned soldier.[80] In the early days of their widowhood, women like Sophia Alexander and her three children relied heavily on their neighbors and community institutions. Minister Washington Spivey and his wife, Nancy, hired Sophia as a live-in domestic shortly after her husband, a veteran, died in 1871. Nancy Spivey said, "I took her in my house because she had no house. She works for me occasionally and tries to make a living. Her son Charley stays her[e] and works for my husband."[81] Brevett Morris, a respected reverend in a local AMEZ church, hired a black woman in search of work "to help . . . clean up the house" until she married a veteran in 1866.[82]

Whether widowed or caring for a disabled husband, black women valued the child-raising duties they performed. Bringing up children and being mothers were important aspects of black women's identity and were incorporated into their evolving sense of respectability. Despite their poverty, freedwomen sought a better life for their children by establishing bank accounts for them, enrolling them in school, and setting up their own households. Before Mary Lee's husband, Simeon, died in 1869, she gave birth to their child, but the baby died nine months later. In later years Mary had the opportunity to mother an abandoned child, which was an alternative way to gain honor and respect in her community.[83]

New Bern's black families contended with the apprenticeship system, which was an especially exploitative form of labor contracting. In the system's initial form, North Carolina's General Assembly stipulated that county courts could apprentice the children of parents who were unable to support the children by their own labor. Purportedly created to protect poor children from becoming orphans and paupers, but in fact designed to protect taxpayers from providing even minimal public relief to the dependent poor, the state's postwar apprenticeship system was a labor regime former slaveholders used to reestablish their mastery, argues historian Rebecca J. Scott.[84]

After Mariah F. Hassell learned that her eldest son had fatally contracted smallpox while serving in the USCT, Benjamin Hassell illegally apprenticed her thirteen-year-old son to "work in the shingle swamp."[85] When Mariah's son came home to visit her, Hassell came to her house, confiscated her child, and threatened to "kill" her if she pursued custody. Like scores of women in similar situations, Mariah enlisted the support of the Freedmen's Bureau to reclaim her son. In February 1867, she told the bureau that the father of her son was deceased and that she had had "no notice of the application" for apprenticeship.[86] Although the resolution in her son's case is unclear in the Freedmen's Bureau records, the 1870 census indicates that he survived the ordeal and returned to his mother. This outcome is important because, although the North Carolina Supreme Court's ruling invalidated apprenticeship agreements throughout the state in 1867, single women remained vulnerable to its exploitation.[87]

Educational resources earmarked for freedpeople inflamed resentment among whites in New Bern. In 1864, poor whites threatened to blow up a black church where classes were held, and three white men set fire to one of the freedpeople's schoolhouses. A white female teacher was threatened with violence if she continued to teach blacks to read. With assistance from northern whites in the American Missionary Society and the New York branch of the National Freedmen's Relief Society, freedmen and freedwomen established schools in New Bern, as in other places across the South.[88] Lists from the Freedmen's Bureau records in December 1866 indicate freedpeople's preference for schools led by black people. Historian Roberta Sue Alexander estimates that some 432 black teachers taught in schools across the state without any affiliation to New England donors or government programs. In New Bern, black teachers taught in the schools New England mission societies established and set up their own institutions. James O'Hara, who later served two terms in the U.S. Congress, established the Queen Street school in the city and enrolled at least ninety-two black students in January 1866.[89] At least two black teachers taught at St. Cyprion's School, which had four teachers underwritten by the Freedmen's Aid Society. Reverend Morris of the local AMEZ church established a school with 143 students. The first public school for black students opened in New Bern in 1868. The New Bern Normal School, one of four institutions in the state that trained black teachers, was founded in 1871 and headed by George Henry White, a black lawyer who also served in the state legislature and in Congress.[90]

A branch of the Freedmen's Savings and Trust Company Bank, established at the corner of Middle and South Front Streets in New Bern in January 1866, gave veterans and their families a place to deposit their money, which came from their current earnings, their military pay, and the bounties they had received. Widows and mothers of deceased soldiers set up accounts, as did several white families and government agents.[91] Approximately one-third of the freedpeople who opened accounts, historian Karen Zipf finds, were female. Their deposits consisted mostly of their wages and the military bounties and pensions of their deceased husbands and sons. Of the approximately four hundred black women who opened accounts between 1866 and 1873 in New Bern, Zipf further demonstrates, 19 percent labored as cooks, 17 percent worked as laundresses, and 15 percent claimed they were farming for themselves.[92] When the bank closed in 1874, deposits in New Bern totaled a little more than forty thousand dollars.[93] Though the bank's collapse led to some distrust of financial institutions among freedpeople in the region, many later opened bank accounts at the National Bank of New Bern.

The religious affiliations and associations of black veterans and their families shaped their social lives and connections within their neighborhoods in profound ways. The church was a source of spiritual guidance and redemption, secular leadership, education, charity, and fellowship. As soon as they could, black Christians separated from white-controlled congregations and established their own churches throughout the county. Black veterans served in key positions in their religious homes, which included the Cedar Grove Baptist Church, Rue Chapel African Methodist Episcopal (AME) Church, Clinton Chapel AMEZ Church, St. Paul Baptist Church, Mount Shiloh Church (James City), and the Star of Zion, among others mentioned in the case files. James Walker Hood, the charismatic religious leader in the AMEZ church, began his southern assignment in New Bern in 1863. He organized St. Andrew Chapel, initially a Methodist Episcopal church, into a flourishing AMEZ congregation and maintained close ties with members of other denominations.[94]

Following the Civil War, black veterans charted the direction of their communities, took up key leadership positions in community institutions, advanced the question of black male suffrage, and held elected office. Indeed, black New Bernians maintained congressional representation as white repression and disfranchisement gained momentum. The Reverend George Rue, minister of New Bern's AME Bethel Church and chaplain of the Thirty-Second USCT, served as a delegate to the Freedmen's Convention held in Raleigh, North Carolina, in October 1866.[95] Veterans Phillip J. Lee, Andrew J. Marshall, and Alfred Small all became religious leaders, and Marshall, Lee, and Philip Wiggins were active in local politics. In 1873, Marshall was elected coroner and served a two-year term in Craven County.[96] He described what happened in an inquiry into the death of a fellow black soldier: "While coroner I was notified that there were parties drowned up Neuse River near Pitch Kettle. I summoned a jury [a group of citizens to investigate] and proceeded to search *for* the bodies. I found this body of one Harris hanging from a tree near Pitch kettle."[97] While the inquest listed drowning as the cause of death, the evidence of a hanging suggested white terrorist groups may have committed vigilante violence on a black man. Hannah Rosen contends that white vigilante violence was a form of "political expression that drew on gender to resignify race and to undermine African American citizenship."[98]

At the municipal level, black people found little available direct relief. During Richard Tucker's tenure as the head of Craven County's poorhouse in the 1870s, the black political leader distributed limited relief services to the impoverished in desperate need of assistance. Mutual aid among relatives and friends was much more important in the black community. After veteran Turner Norman died in a boating accident in December 1870, Mary Norman and their two surviving children took shelter with her eldest son (from a previous relationship) in the Fifth Ward. Freedmen and freedwomen established a system of support to address the needs of black soldiers and their families. Veteran Philip Wiggins was president of a burial society in James City that served veterans "up to about 1895." In his appointed role, he administered medicine to ailing soldiers and attended to them in death, taking care to wash and lay out their bodies.[99] Neighbors sustained one another through periods of illness and death. A white seamstress depended on the goodwill of her black neighbors during her husband's final illness.[100] Notions of familial obligation and community reciprocity informed men's and women's actions. Veteran George Lavenhouse "helped his mother by working about around hiring himself out and he took home pensions to her."[101] The low wages paid to black men meant that even if an able-bodied veteran was present in the household, the women in the household might also have to seek gainful employment.

Ceremonies mourning dead soldiers bonded the black community, promoted sociability, and magnified the significance of honor and sacrifice. Draymen transporting corpses to Greenwood Cemetery, a public burying ground for black bodies, and to New Bern's National Cemetery was a familiar sight. Black ministers eulogized veterans in churches and at the graveside, and women prepared meals and set tables for grieving family members. Neighbors paid their last respects to deceased veterans and their families by viewing the bodies and attending church services.[102] When Israel Anders died, "his death . . . was known to all citizens in the neighborhood" and "was announced at Church."[103]

Moving about the streets of postwar New Bern, blacks and whites increasingly experienced racial difference in concrete ways. Clashes broke out over race and public space in the months and years following emancipation. A man was ejected from a local theater after it was discovered that "he had colored blood in him."[104] Mixed race couples living openly in the city were threatened with arrest. After William Gardner's discharge, he returned to New Bern with his new bride, Laura Stott, and settled in with his mother, Harriet Gardner. Laura was the daughter of a white woman and a free man of color from the North, and her racial ambiguity drew whispers among black residents and threats of an indictment by city authorities.[105] In New Bern, even with its history of interracial exchanges, black majority population, and interracial liaisons, white men punished blacks who were perceived to have violated the racial hierarchy.

BLACK UNION WIDOWS AND THE PENSION SYSTEM

During the war the federal government took bold steps to provide resources to injured and dead soldiers and their dependent family members. In February 1862, the Republican-dominated Congress passed the first of a series of bills addressing the issue. The Act of July 14, 1862, which set up the general law pension system, provided pensions for the widows, children, and other dependent relatives of soldiers who died in military service or afterward from causes that could be linked directly to injuries received or diseases contracted while in service. The legislation also established a basic legal structure for the evaluation of widows' applications, which remained in place until 1890. The general law pension system required proof of legal marriage, which prevented widows who had been slaves from being recognized as the "legal widow" of a deceased soldier.

The tragic April 1864 massacre of black soldiers at Fort Pillow, Tennessee, inspired lawmakers to reassess the accessibility of the pension system for black dependents. The Supplementary Pension Act, enacted on July 4, 1864, provided that all "free persons" were entitled to a pension upon proof that the applicant and a deceased soldier had "habitually" recognized each other as man and wife for at least two years prior to his enlistment. Once again, federal lawmakers' failure to acknowledge the fact that formerly enslaved soldiers' marriages had been extralegal by necessity prevented a substantial group of black soldiers' widows from initiating successful claims during the war years.[106]

Blacks with a history of enslavement could not meet the bureau's marriage standard, and the families of black soldiers had trouble gaining access to government resources set aside for dependents and survivors. Black women in the North and the South complained about the government's failure to support them during and after their husbands' service in the Union Army. Ira Berlin, Joseph Reidy, and Leslie Rowland's documentary history of black kinship in the Civil War era details the issues that black women raised in their letters of complaint to federal officials. Rosanna Henson, the wife of a New Jersey soldier, wrote to President Lincoln: "I have four children to support and I find this a great struggle. A hard life this! I being a col woman do not get any state pay. Yet my husband is fighting for this country."[107]

After the war, lawmakers did away with previous distinctions embedded in the law so that the law would recognize the free status of all African Americans, but they continued to acknowledge the legacy of enslavement by keeping certain provisions—section 4703. The Act of June 6, 1866, recognized "slave marriage" retroactively and accepted black people's testimony as legitimate evidence.[108] Under this law, Congress repealed the section of the 1864 act on the legal status of blacks and profoundly and permanently altered black women's relationship to the federal government. The new law treated evidence of slave marriages, or cohabitation as husband and wife, a de facto marriage for Pension Bureau purposes, and the wives of black soldiers who died in service became "colored widows" or "colored claimants." The recognition of slave marriages in federal pension policy gave the bureau a way to manage the petitions of newly freed black women and to distribute economic aid to freedmen and their families.

The centrality of marriage to women's ability to secure survivors' benefits in the pension system cannot be overstated. If a woman remarried or engaged in sexual activity while collecting government aid, bureau officials had the authority to terminate her benefits permanently. In the event that a deceased soldier left neither a widow nor a child, certain other dependent relatives were eligible in succession to receive the pension: first mothers, then fathers, and finally orphaned brothers or sisters under sixteen years of age (orphaned brothers and sisters were to be pensioned jointly if more than one of them met the age requirement).[109] Without a firm construct of marriage in place, federal lawmakers worried about the potential financial burden that the newly freed women and "illegitimate" black children could place on the government's coffers.[110]

Laura F. Edwards has shown that North Carolina state laws, especially pertaining to the legal standing of freedpeople and their families and formal marriages, focused on establishing men's responsibility for the financial support of women and children.[111] Parallel conversations took place among congressional lawmakers during the Reconstruction era, which may have prompted legislators to carefully define the boundaries of legal widowhood while simultaneously recognizing slaves' marriages.

Given the history and legacy of enslavement in the United States, federal lawmakers had to address the real possibility that more than one woman might petition the government for survivors' benefits on the basis of their relationship with a deceased veteran. A Democrat from Maryland thus claimed that black Union soldiers, "not being conscious of any impropriety or immorality," had a "good many wives." A Unionist Democrat from West Virginia agreed with this premise: "It would be . . . safe to admit the fact that there is more than one wife in these cases." A Republican Senator from Iowa felt the "cohabitation" standard should be permitted for "all." Lawmakers were concerned both with morality and with the potential financial burdens imposed by single women and "illegitimate" children.[112] Pension Bureau officials had to devise a more systematic approach to deal with the increasing number of cases of this type. One solution could have been to acknowledge the rights of all the women who could substantiate their relationship with a soldier, but instead officials created a new administrative category, "contesting widows," and took it on themselves to determine which women had a legitimate claim to a pension.

Another set of concerns made explicit under the act of 1866 had to do with how soldiers' wives were expected to behave publicly and privately. Lawmakers expected soldiers' wives to act dutifully toward their husbands, providing excellent medical care and upholding the moral dictates of womanhood. Under the 1866 act, they banned from the pension rolls widows who failed to care "properly" for their deceased husband's children or who were entirely unable to care for them because of "immoral conduct."[113] As the marriage question progressed in the 1866 debates, the term *colored widow* was increasingly used to distinguish formerly enslaved Union widows from white widows, although the cohabitation policy also covered free black and Indian widows. All Union widows, white or black, were expected to remain sexually chaste and respectable. Black women would later harness these ideas in their favor while explaining the sacrifices they made on behalf of their husbands and families.

Perhaps the most controversial and misunderstood prohibition in the 1866 act involved the bureau's remarriage rule. If a Union widow opted to remarry after gaining admittance to the pension roster, she was expected to notify the Pension Bureau and relinquish her benefits. The government's rationale was that a pension was a stand-in for the soldier-husband's earnings, and a new husband would eliminate that need. A woman who had married before the 1866 law was introduced, however, remained eligible to collect benefits for the period of her widowhood. As early as 1868, commissioner of pensions Christopher C. Cox requested "discretionary power" to address widows' "flagrant violations of morality."[114] A related proposal involved pension agents and postmasters creating marriage rosters to expose Union widows who concealed the fact that they had remarried.[115] Not until lawmakers authorized the act on March 3, 1901, could "certain" widows of Union soldiers who had remarried and found themselves single once again reclaim their standing on the federal pension roster.[116]

The widows of black Union soldiers first became eligible for survivors' pensions in 1864, yet they would not make significant inroads in the system until after June 1866. Claiming the benefits promised to their beloved family members required a well-developed local infrastructure. It also required professional support in the form of a claims agent prepared to respond to gendered forms of racism embedded in the system's structure. Women whom the U.S. Pension Bureau recognized as the widows of Union soldiers were entitled to a pension of eight dollars per month, paid in cash on a quarterly basis.

Aside from scrubbing overt and implied references to an applicant's enslaved status, lawmakers did not do much more to help the widows of deceased black soldiers' lay claim to the benefits promised to them as early as 1864. Black women who applied for a pension faced particularly intense personal scrutiny, and their pension rights were the subject of continued political fights.[117] All widows had to establish that their husbands had died in battle or as a result of a disease stemming from their wartime service. They also had to prove the legitimacy of their marriages to Union soldiers. This requirement bore with special force on black couples who had been unable to contract legal marriages while enslaved and gave new meaning to their marriage rituals before, during, and after the war.

In areas like New Bern, where many freedpeople settled during the war, growing numbers of black women petitioned for and collected pension benefits through the late nineteenth century. They did so largely with the assistance of white northerners as black institutions recovered from the war and adapted to their new circumstances. The evidentiary requirement that plagued all prospective widows—both black and white—was the difficulty of demonstrating that their husbands had died as a result of wartime disease, disability, or injury. Proving that a soldier's death stemmed from his Civil War service would have been a Herculean task for any woman, but it was especially difficult for formerly enslaved women. Medical treatment, much less evidence of such treatment, was extremely difficult to procure, and medical doctors willing to provide testimony on behalf of the soldiers' widows were essential. One soldier's widow lamented that her husband "was too poor to have a Doctor all the time and he could only get medicines when he could after we got married."[118]

Widespread episodes of fraud and swindling of disabled black soldiers and Union widows throughout the South prompted the creation of the Bounty and Claims Division within the Freedmen's Bureau in March 1866.[119] Agents in New Bern and Wilmington distributed bounty and pension money to soldiers and their dependent relatives. Although the commissioner of pensions hoped the involvement of Freedmen's Bureau agents in the application and disbursement process would ensure that dependent women would be able to collect the money they were due and would reduce fraudulent practices, the results were uneven. Edward Conega, a soldier in the Thirty-Seventh Regiment of the USCT, died of typhoid fever in Wilmington, North Carolina, in the fall of 1865. With the assistance of Freedmen's Bureau agent William T. Drew, Conega's widow, Tena, filed for survivors' benefits and was admitted to the pension rolls two months later.[120] Mary Ann Sleight had more difficulty. Her husband, Alfred, had died in service, but Mary Ann had trouble securing his bounty and back pay: "I went to Major Coates who was here with the Freedman's Bureau and he wrote me a line which I carried to Mr. Carpenter. He tried for the pension . . . and he said I could not get anything any way and so I never tried anything and quit applying for a pension."[121] In September 1867, the assistant superintendent for the subdistrict reported that, although bureau officials would collect soldiers' bounties free of charge, the "greater portion of discharged soldiers filed their applications with claims agents."[122] Black people's apparent preference for local claims agents may reflect their reluctance to engage with federal officials. Many freedpeople felt that officials had run roughshod over them in settlement camps and saw no reason to trust them now that additional benefits might be available.

Unlike the Freedmen's Bureau, which had effectively ended its social welfare activities in 1868, the U.S. Pension Bureau expanded its commitment to the disabled and their families through the late nineteenth century. [123] Lawmakers, however, began to narrow the ground for the definition of marriage within the pension system. Whereas formerly enslaved women were allowed to present witness testimony to establish their marriages under the acts of 1864 and 1866, legislation passed on June 15, 1873, required evidence of an "obligatory" ceremony.[124] The strengthening of a marriage as an organizing component for women's legitimacy within the bureau would have a disproportionate effect on working-class black women.

At the same time, the Pension Bureau expanded. Under the Arrears Act (1879), pensions granted under the general law system would start at the soldier's date of death instead of when a woman filed her claim.[125] The pension system further expanded in 1890, with the introduction of the service law pension system.[126] As the research of Theda Skocpol attests, this system essentially turned the federal survivors' pension system into an old-age benefit for those who had served. The service law enabled survivors to secure benefits simply by demonstrating that their relative had served at least ninety days in the military, provided they were "dependent on their own labor for support."[127] Under this program, widows of veterans who died of old age became eligible for survivors' benefits. For the widows of black soldiers who had difficulty qualifying for benefits under the general law system, however, not much changed under the service law. Constructs of marriage and ideas about sexual morality remained key components of women's eligibility for pensions and the preservation of their standing on the pension roster.

Black women used their access to the federal pension system to press a multitude of claims, many of which did not fall within the intentions of the system. The stories they aired—expressing violations of the bureau's stated cohabitation rule—were critical in the reconfiguration of bureau policies aimed at women on the roster. The eventual passage of an act on March 3, 1899, enabled women to file claims against the men in their lives and publicize issues of nonsupport within the bureau and their communities. This law allowed wives of pensioned veterans to sue their husbands for one-half of their pensions when they abandoned their families. While abandonment and nonsupport did not entail the misery of death and disease, these claims posed new challenges for those who pursued this course of action. Speaking out against black men, especially those who served in the military, could result in social ostracism.

BLACK WOMEN AND THE BUSINESS OF FILING A CLAIM

The opening up of the pension system during the late nineteenth century brought new groups of professionals into contact with black citizens. Claims agents worked directly with veterans and their families and the widows of soldiers to file applications for benefits. Freedmen's Bureau agents throughout the South helped claimants apply to the Pension Bureau and distributed bounty and pension money to soldiers and their dependent relatives.[128] The Claims Division continued its services after the Freedmen's Bureau halted social welfare activities. The Freedmen's Bureau Claims Division was ultimately dismantled because blacks preferred to hire professional agents in their own communities.

In its initial phase, information about the opening up of the pension system to the newly freed was largely geared toward white professionals and military administrators. Articles appeared in the *New Berne Times* outlining the guidelines for filing claims for "colored soldiers" and "colored widows."[129] Poor black women depended greatly on the expertise of white claims agents to tackle the evidentiary requirements during the application process. The government paid claims agents fees based on a petitioner's admittance to the roster. This system of payment made the pension business potentially profitable and enabled poor women to keep their cases active over long stretches of time. The first group of pension professionals in New Bern to take on black women seeking to petition the government for federal aid were northern whites who made their home in the South after the war. Two such men, Augustus Seymour and Edward W. Carpenter, established themselves in New Bern's postwar economy by handling the cases of black and white Union widows. As Seymour quickly climbed the professional ladder in New Bern's legal arena, he turned his caseload over to Carpenter. Edward Carpenter and his brother, Seth M. Carpenter, who had arrived in New Bern sometime during the war, began helping black veterans and their families file paperwork for bounties and pensions.

Special examiners appointed to the Pension Bureau enforced its rules, sought and evaluated evidence, and investigated suspicious pension cases throughout the country. In the 1870s, the commissioner of pensions authorized examiners to go into a community and conduct their work secretly to ensure that claimants abided by the bureau's rules. Examiners were not required to notify beneficiaries of their purpose; consequently, a woman might not learn that she was in danger of having her benefits revoked until after the bureau officials made their decision.[130] Bureau officials assigned examiner George H. Ragsdale and several others to scrutinize the pension roster across eastern North Carolina around 1873, which coincided with a financial panic and an economic downturn sometimes referred to as the "first great depression."[131] Early confrontations between examiner Ragsdale and black female applicants around New Bern involved issues related to eligibility, evidence, medical records, and especially marriage, cohabitation, and respectability. Black Union widows complained to the commissioner of pensions that at least one black veteran, David Proctor, worked in concert with special examiners to expose them as being in violation of the bureau's remarriage and cohabitation policy. Carpenter's lucrative business representing the claims of poor soldiers' widows came to an end when examiner Ragsdale launched a successful criminal investigation into his business practices in 1873. The investigation resulted in Carpenter's permanent suspension from the claims business a year later. As a result, several men and women with pending claims lost touch with the Pension Bureau.

Increasing concerns about fraud and maintaining the sanctity of the pension system went hand in hand with the extension of benefits to the aging population of soldiers and their families in the late nineteenth century. During the 1870s, the northern public grew increasingly impatient with stories of fraud and exploitation of the pension system by undeserving beneficiaries. Exposés of pension fraud and sexual immorality in southern black communities appeared frequently in papers such as the *New York Times*, *Washington Post*, and *Chicago Tribune*. Claims agents and widows were frequently the targets of stories, and freedwomen were positioned as lawbreakers, victims, or both. Rampant racism and widespread disapproval of the government's largesse led to the creation of the Special Examination Division of the Pension Bureau in 1881.

Facing intense scrutiny by federal lawmakers, national newspapers, and the northern public, Pension Bureau officials weighed various procedural tactics aimed at ensuring the social and economic soundness of the federal system. When bureau administrators reconfigured the examination division, they introduced a new plan of special examination built on efficiency and transparency. This new type of examination placed black Union widows, especially freedwomen, under close inspection. The lack of standard documentary evidence of a marital union meant that examinations and investigations became a regular feature of black women's application process.[132] After 1888, special examiners operated out of the local post office and regularly walked the streets of New Bern and James City.

With the reorganization of the bureau, a cadre of black professional men in New Bern began to represent black women as they made claims on the government. Unlike the white agents who preceded them in the pension business, this emerging group of black claims agents functioned as cultural brokers, mediating the relationship between widows and the Pension Bureau. The most successful of them was Mary Norman's son, Frederick C. Douglass, a former slave from Jones County who taught in New Bern's black schools and held a prominent position in Clinton Chapel AMEZ. Douglass had a close professional relationship with Edward Carpenter, who may have assisted Douglass with his application for licensure as a claims agent in the pension system in 1879.[133] As the influence and reputation of New Bern's black claims agents spread among black veterans and their families, the local pension network expanded along North Carolina's eastern seaboard. These networks facilitated important dialogues among black veterans and their families, even as the Supreme Court chipped away at black citizenship rights in the Slaughter-House Cases (1873), which declared that certain rights of citizens remained under the jurisdiction of state governments. The Court continued down this path in its decision in the Civil Rights Cases of 1883, which invalidated the Civil Rights Act of 1875.[134] Amid the increasing restrictions on other rights that black people had briefly enjoyed, or at least been entitled to, claims agents empowered black women with a crucial body of municipal services in their neighborhoods and an influential voice in their congressional districts.

Claims agents worked diligently to prepare black women for face-to-face encounters with bureau examiners in their communities. Black soldiers' widows would experience intrusive questioning during the special examination process. But the process had unexpected benefits: it opened up a whole new world of legal action to the wives and mothers of deceased veterans. The federal pension system became one of the few federal agencies to which black women could air their grievances, and it gave widows means to file complaints against claims agents and special examiners. Participating in the ritual of the special examination also taught prospective widows about the examiners' function and authority in the Pension Bureau. The women understood that special examiners applied constructs of proper marriage and sexual morality that had a central role in the outcome of their cases.

As the expenditures for the federal pension system exceeded its budget, and criticism from the North increased, bureau officials looked for new ways to close gaps in the system and demonstrate its value to the public. The bureau's reorganization coincided with the introduction of the act of 1882, which denied or terminated a widow's pension if she was involved in a sexual relationship with a man or was otherwise deemed sexually immoral and unchaste. Bureau officials publicized their efforts to detect sexual immorality and illegal practices. For black women in the South, these actions generated more intense scrutiny of their personal lives and of the meaning of slave marriage. Bureau officials hoped that their efforts would calm public fears about the pension system. Their policies and practices criminalized black female sexuality in the pension apparatus.

Definitions of marriage and sexual regulation counterbalanced the racially neutral rules initiated in 1866 and 1890. No matter which system a woman filed a claim under, her standing hinged on a particular formulation of marriage. Oft characterized as licentious and lewd (the opposite of a virtuous and worthy widows), black women, particularly poor ones, suffered devastating consequences from the law of 1882. Most black women fell under suspicion, and a great number lost their standing on the pension roster. By 1890, contesting the construct of slave marriage resulted in another level of scrutiny for black women, further eroding their claims to a pension.

THE MEANINGS OF BLACK WOMEN'S CLAIMS ON THE GOVERNMENT

As the pension system opened up to the formerly enslaved, the federal government withdrew from the South, and Democratic officeholders reemerged in North Carolina's General Assembly. By 1880, the wives of disabled veterans and the widows of soldiers were adjusting to their uprooting and losses and finding their feet in freedom. They had established households, reconnected with kin, formed new ties, and discovered how hard it was to earn a living that would support them and their dependents, whether these were disabled husbands, children, or elders.

Recognition as a Union widow carried a measure of respectability, legal personhood, and a modest addition to their income for the life of the claim. After 1881, when the bureau reorganized itself, creating the Special Examination Division, and moving in the direction of recognizing rights, black women consciously echoed the bureau's language during the examination process. They used an eclectic blend of arguments and strategies to navigate the process and the pension system more generally. They were quick to learn the bureau's language of nuclear family forms and the norms for domesticity, and they mobilized these tools to defend their positions on the pension rolls. They came to understand which aspects of their private lives to expose to local examiners and which to conceal, and they learned to persuade these men to side with them against potentially damaging witness testimony. Many women blended aspects of the bureau's language with their everyday language to help them stay on the rolls. They criticized the presence of local examiners in their communities strategically, when it suited their interests in the system. On other occasions, women made overtures to bureau officials and invited examiners into their neighborhoods to investigate their cases, sometimes even asking these men for help.[135]

Southern black women's ability to sustain intense negotiations with the government in the decades after Reconstruction drew on neighborhood social ties, community networks, and black political power. At the turn of the century, Elizabeth Prigden formed an organization in Wilmington, North Carolina, to support soldiers' widows through all stages of the pension application process. The daughter of a turpentine distiller, Elizabeth attended school in Reconstruction-era Wilmington. While the specifics of the school she attended are not clear, the origins and expansion of black schools in Wilmington were much like those found in New Bern at the time. One examiner reported that Prigden was "instrumental in getting witnesses to testify" in one woman's case and found that she was "doing the same in other claims. She informed me that she is at the head of some kind of a colored organization that has for its purpose the looking after the interests of widows of colored soldiers."[136] Witnessing on behalf of disabled soldiers, widows, and other family members constituted a critical dimension of community building because it encouraged women to engage the state in a collective, fostering networks of reciprocity that sustained one another through periods of transition.

Conspicuous references to Post No. 22, a mostly black branch of the Grand Army of the Republic (GAR), an organization founded in 1866 for Union veterans and affiliated with the Republican Party, appear in the pension files of black veterans and their widows.[137] Though dedicated primarily to political advocacy in the late nineteenth century, the GAR functioned at times as a "charitable organization" dedicated to "good works." [138] The GAR post and its black members in New Bern outlasted most others in the South. As Cecilia O'Leary has shown, "the Ku Klux Klan had harassed Union veterans who moved to the South, and by the early 1870s most Southern GAR posts had disbanded."[139]

Savvy political alliances that crossed racial lines gave black North Carolinians an impressive amount of political power at the county level well into the late nineteenth century. Craven County was a part of the Second Congressional District—a Republican and black stronghold until the state disfranchisement amendment of 1900—which included nine other counties: Warren, North Hampton, Halifax, Edgecombe, Wilson, Wayne, Lenoir, Greene, and Jones.[140] Like the other counties in the Second Congressional District, Craven had a black majority population, but it stood apart from these counties because of the high concentration of black Civil War veterans and their families. Republicans, both black and white, served as sheriffs, clerks of the superior court, postmasters, stewards of the poor, coroners, and other officials during this period. Four black Republicans represented the district in Congress: John A. Hyman, James E. O'Hara, Henry P. Cheatham, and George H. White. O'Hara settled on Pollock Street with his family after serving in Congress from 1882 to 1887. He resumed his law practice with his son and helped black soldiers' widows petition the government for aid. White, the former principal of New Bern's black schools, resided in the Fourth Ward at the corner of Queen and Pasteur Streets. White was the only black representative in Congress in 1899, and he never forgot the black Union veterans and their survivors who had put him in office.

For black women, navigating the pension apparatus, which was constantly changing, involved building strategic relationships with members of the professional class, corralling neighbors to "witness," maintaining relationships with other Union widows, sharing community knowledge, learning the Pension Bureau's highly restrictive laws, testifying before government officials, and urging Washington bureaucrats to intervene in their cases. They had to be patient, adaptable, and willing to replace a professional pension agent at any moment. This was especially true of the clients of black and white claims agents in New Bern, who experienced regular scrutiny and investigation, as did the agents themselves. Two criminal investigations, one in 1889 and the second in 1894, resulted in Douglass's permanent suspension from the bureau. The suspensions and removal of claims agents threatened to weaken, and even eliminate, black women's prospects for filing successful claims.

Special examiners' efforts to discredit the work of agent Frederick Douglass and the many others who assisted black Union widows in New Bern and beyond occurred at a critical juncture in North Carolina's history. In the wake of the Populist alliance between poor whites and blacks, elite white supremacists moved to establish total authority in the region. A new Democratic state legislature began crafting amendments to the state constitution to disfranchise black men in 1899, and by 1901, one of these amendments had passed.

As civil and political rights collapsed across the South, the commissioner of pensions often heralded the success of Pension Bureau reform efforts in the region, which included rooting out pension fraud and purging sexually immoral widows from the pension rolls. The commissioner's reform agenda included conducting countywide investigations in southern black communities to ensure that veterans and their survivors continued to abide by the pension rules and regulations. Examiners Thomas Goethe and Charles D. McSorley carried out many of the individual investigations of the mothers and widows of dead black soldiers, but at least four other men were stationed in the area to do investigations as well. Among those investigated were Mary Lee and Fanny Whitney. At a time when the Pension Bureau was liberalizing its policies, which included supporting ex-Confederate soldiers, it also took determined steps to sanitize the federal pension roster. Notably, government officials steadily purged black women from the pension rolls based on racialized, gendered principles. Southern black women, however, found creative ways to intervene in the pension process on their own behalf.[141]

These are the contentious and constantly shifting social and political conditions with which black women had to contend when they pursued survivors' benefits in the federal pension system. Though not always successful, black women managed to extend their Reconstruction era vision of citizenship by petitioning for and obtaining survivors' benefits and then maintaining their presence on the pension roster through the early twentieth century. Claims agents, both black and white, played a decisive role in black women's ability to keep the issues of poverty, injustice, and inequality alive after the defeat of civil rights. These women, with all their individual complexities, struggles, disappointments, and achievements, are the subjects of the remaining chapters.

ENCOUNTERING THE STATE

PART II

3

Her Claim Is Lawful and Just

Black Women's Petitions for Survivors' Benefits

Just as Congress resolved the matter of slave marriage, and the Pension Bureau adapted their guidelines, freedwomen began petitioning the government for survivors' benefits under the 1866 law. With the help of claims agents and an assortment of pension professionals in New Bern, Fanny Whitney, Charlotte Banks, and many others leveraged their status as Union widows, asserted their citizenship, and offered evidence of their prewar marital unions. Change unfolded rapidly while these women waited for government officials to respond to their petitions. In 1867, North Carolina's Supreme Court struck down the discriminatory provisions of the state's revised apprenticeship code, which had subjugated black people in ways that harkened back to slavery.[1] In 1868, black men registered and cast their vote for the first time since 1835.[2] Also in 1868, "twelve colored men" in James City (formerly the Trent River settlement) were sworn into office as deputy sheriffs, with the authority granted to all deputies. Record numbers of marriages took place in black churches across New Bern as couples either reaffirmed old commitments or started new official legal relationships.

Petitioning the federal government for survivors' benefits must have been painful for Fanny Whitney and Charlotte Banks. Before the war broke out, Charlotte and Caesar were separated by sale, and only three of Fanny and Harry's nine children survived. Then each woman learned of the death of her beloved soldier-husband. The opportunity to petition the government for benefits required Fanny, Charlotte, and thousands of other newly freed black women to reduce their recollections of marriage and family life under enslavement to short affidavits and personal statements. Applying for a pension was far more than a bureaucratic process, and for southern black women it typically began with securing a claims agent.

Black women across the South inundated claims agents and attorneys with their pension business. Although the titles pension agent and claims agent were often used interchangeably at the time, they were not the same thing. Pension attorneys had been admitted to the bar and had litigated cases as part of their professional legal practice; claims agents represented cases only within the Pension Bureau, not outside it. The Pension Bureau approved all attorneys who worked within the bureau. Men who were certified to represent veterans and their survivors within the bureau did not need to have legal training or pass the state bar, but they did have to demonstrate their capacity to originate and carry through claims.

Conflicts involving black women, claims agents, and Pension Bureau officials arose shortly after federal lawmakers recognized slave marriages retroactively as the pathway to recognition of freedwomen in the federal pension system. Fueled by reports of fraud, suspicion grew among bureau officials that black women were fabricating claims based on relationships that did not qualify as marriages. In the spring of 1873, Pension Bureau examiners began searching southern neighborhoods for evidence of pension fraud.[3] Bureau examiners such as George Ragsdale, who conducted his work in eastern North Carolina and Virginia, exercised a great deal of power in these investigations because no coherent set of guidelines for examiners to follow existed. Evidence of cohabitation or remarriage while receiving survivors' benefits was interpreted as fraud against the government and in some cases resulted in a stiff prison sentence.[4]

Black women—single, married, or widowed, and with or without children—made decisions about how to live their lives in the spaces in between slavery, wartime emancipation, and freedom. The decision to enter an intimate relationship after surviving war, the loss of a spouse, and displacement has animated the study of emancipation for many decades, and these were precisely the questions that Fanny Whitney and Charlotte Banks pondered as the war subsided. What may seem trivial had measurable consequences for black women seeking survivors' benefits in the decades following the Civil War. This chapter traces the development of black women's early struggle for survivors' benefits in the federal pension system and analyzes their petitions and their protests between 1866 and 1877. Facing intense scrutiny by federal lawmakers, national newspapers, and the northern public, pension officials weighed various procedural tactics aimed at monitoring federal resources and allaying fears of fraud within the federal pension system. Women's conflicts with examiners calls attention to their understanding of Union widowhood and the strategies they used to maneuver within the pension system.

WHITE CLAIMS AGENTS AND THEIR BLACK CLIENTS

Shortly after the federal government discontinued its support of black refugees and soldiers' families at Roanoke Island, Fanny Whitney resettled in New Bern and petitioned the government for survivors' benefits and support for her boys—Harry, Adam, and Milton (figure 3.1). Charlotte Banks, a washerwoman from Elizabeth City, filed a petition for a survivor's pension in 1869. Documents in the case files for both women are relatively thin; bureau officials required two witness statements to affirm the legitimacy of their marriages, which are largely pro forma.

By 1870, perhaps before, Fanny had settled into a home in the heart of New Bern's Fifth Ward, on the corner of Jones and New South Front Streets. The neighborhood was populated by a collection of her kin and community from Hyde County and growing black middle class made up of skilled artisans, teachers, ministers, and grocers. St. John Baptist Church (referred to as the Colored Baptist Church), led by the Reverend John S. Johnson, was situated to the west of Fanny Whitney, on the corner of New South Front and Bryan Streets. St. John's members included war widows such as Mary Lee (domestic), Amy Squires, and Charlotte Banks (domestic). Nearly a block away stood Clinton Chapel AMEZ, where war widow Mary Norman and her son, Frederick C. Douglass, and Emanuel Merrick held memberships. Though invisible in the pension records, Fanny and Charlotte surely drew on the resources from their neighbors and neighborhood institutions before they contacted Edward Carpenter, a wartime correspondent, to represent their claims.

Before his arrival in New Bern, Carpenter read law under the attorney general of the state of Wisconsin. He then supported the campaign of Charles Henry Foster, a pro-Union Democrat, to represent North Carolina in the U.S. House of Representatives in 1861. Carpenter assisted Foster's efforts by planting fictitious stories in the *New York Tribune* to give northern readers the impression that Foster was a viable candidate and that a federal election could be held in a Confederate state in wartime. Carpenter's affiliation with Foster and the underhanded tactics he employed in conjunction with Foster's campaign earned him the opposition of Benjamin S. Hendrick, a southern abolitionist who taught chemistry at the University of North Carolina at Chapel Hill before being dismissed in 1856.[5] Despite this controversy,

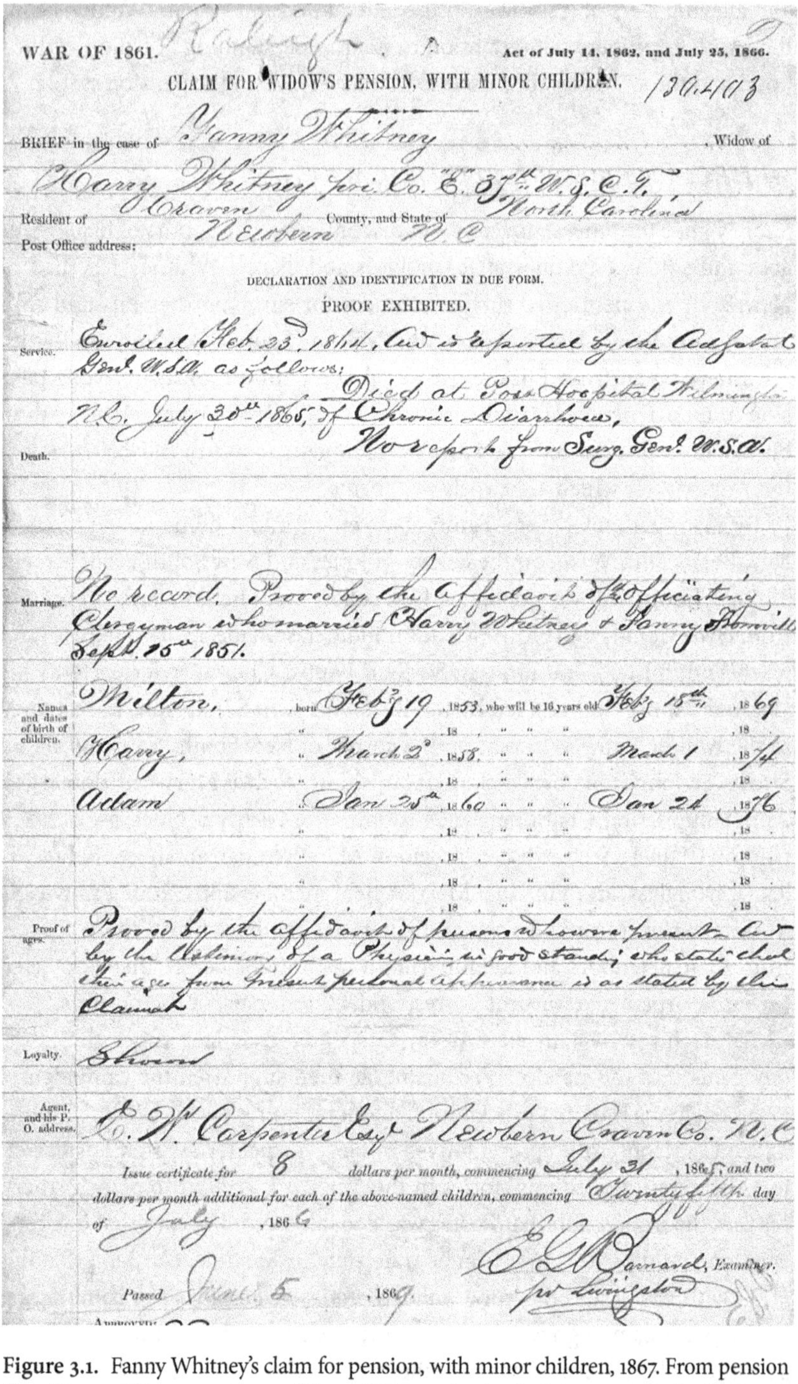

Raleigh

WAR OF 1861. Act of July 14, 1862, and July 25, 1866.

CLAIM FOR WIDOW'S PENSION, WITH MINOR CHILDREN. 130403

BRIEF in the case of Fanny Whitney, Widow of

Harry Whitney Pvt. Co. E. 37th U.S.C.T.

Resident of Craven County, and State of North Carolina

Post Office address: Newbern N.C.

DECLARATION AND IDENTIFICATION IN DUE FORM.

PROOF EXHIBITED.

Service. Enrolled Feb. 23d 1864, and is reported by the Adjutant Gen'l. U.S.A. as follows:

Died at Post Hospital Wilmington N.C. July 30th 1865, of Chronic Diarrhoea,

Death. No report from Surg. Gen'l. U.S.A.

Marriage. No record. Proved by the affidavit of the officiating Clergyman who married Harry Whitney & Fanny Bonwill Sept. 15th 1851.

Names and dates of birth of children.		born		who will be 16 years old	
	Milton,	Feb'y 19	1853	Feb'y 18th	1869
	Harry,	March 2d	1858	March 1	1874
	Adam	Jan 25th	1860	Jan 24	1876

Proof of ages. Proved by the affidavit of persons who were present and by the testimony of a Physician in good standing who states that their ages from present personal appearance is as stated by the Claimant

Loyalty. Shown

Agent, and his P. O. address. E. W. Carpenter Esq. Newbern Craven Co. N.C.

Issue certificate for 8 *dollars per month, commencing* July 31, 1865, *and two dollars per month additional for each of the above-named children, commencing* Twenty fifth *day of* July, 1866

E. L. Barnard, Examiner.
pr Livingston

Passed June 5, 1867.

Figure 3.1. Fanny Whitney's claim for pension, with minor children, 1867. From pension file of Fanny Whitney, widow of Harry Whitney (widow's claim 130403), Civil War Pension Index: General Index to Pension Files, Record Group 15: Records of the Department of Veteran Affairs, National Archives and Records Administration.

Carpenter's legal training won him an appointment in the U.S. Treasury Department. His wartime defense of Eugene Hannel, a hospital steward charged with raping a black girl, offers insight into Carpenter's perspective on the sexual respectability of black women.

> In Southern estimation, generally, as well as by the laws of North Carolina, a Negress is deemed incapable of an injury of this kind. . . . After a Negress has frequently enjoyed the amorous embrace of a white man, she among the Black Diamonds is considered a superior personage, and entitled to the honors of an aristocrat; they resort to stratagem to seduce and seek every opportunity possible to fulfill the measure of their so-called aristocratic ambition.[6]

Rooted in Carpenter's defense of Hannel was the pervasive notion that all black women were inherently unchaste and therefore sexually available to white men. But Rebecca Ann Cradle resisted, telling Hannel that "her body was hers and not his." He then struck and forcibly raped her, leaving her with severe injuries and in a state of "wild mania" that required treatment in the hospital in New Bern, where she had been employed. Finding Hannel's crime heinous and pronouncing Carpenter's defense of him "simply inhuman," the military courts sentenced Hannel to two years' imprisonment with hard labor at Fort Macon, North Carolina.[7]

Carpenter's government contacts and legal expertise enabled him to become one of the most influential white claims agents in the city. He represented white Union widows and black and white disabled veterans, although after 1866, black women made up the majority of his clientele. Celia Cuthrell, a white Union widow, hired Carpenter to file her pension application. Her husband had first "enlisted in the Confederate Militia" but soon "deserted" and joined the Union Army. In 1864, Confederates captured and hanged him in Kingston, North Carolina.[8] The commissioner denied Celia's initial attempts to secure benefits "on account of" her husband's service in "the Rebel army" but admitted her in 1872.[9] Fanny Whitney, who had been a client of Augustus Seymour, filed her initial claim in 1868. Years later she said, "Ed Carpenter was my Atty. He had the book of my husband and I went to him."[10]

Carpenter handled his expanding business by hiring white and black assistants. His brother, Seth, the editor of the Democratic newspaper *Newbernian*, helped disabled veterans and widows fill out paperwork and eventually became a licensed claims agent himself.[11] Like his brother, Seth harbored entrenched ideas about racial difference. In May 1874, Seth implored his white audience to "Read and Ponder" the recent appointment of a black trustee to lead "the Academy of New Berne,—a school of white children." Before closing his brief editorial, Seth urged his white readership to "go to the ballot box and thunder your protest."[12] War veteran David Proctor, a black barber, helped Carpenter to identify potential clients in black neighborhoods, before he began helping bureau agents to identify cases of fraud among black pension recipients.[13] Carpenter hired Phillip Coleman, whose mother, Eda, was one of Carpenter's clients, as an "errands boy" and to "wait on him."[14] Sarah (Richardson) Oxly, Carpenter's black housekeeper, occasionally delivered messages to his black female clientele.[15]

Born in bondage around 1836, Sarah Richardson was raised "7 m[iles] up Neuse River on Bill Mitchell's Plantation."[16] The fertile Neuse River valley had numerous small plantations and several hundred enslaved people.[17] Sarah's family included her enslaved parents, Moses and Elizabeth, and siblings Dorcas, Frances, Peter, and John. Sarah's father died when she was "small," and surviving records indicate that Sarah may have lived apart from her mother, who at some point resided on the "Woods estate."[18] Edward Downs, a free black artisan of some means, purchased Sarah's mother from the Woods family sometime before the war.[19] Just how Sarah acquired the surname Oxly remains a mystery.[20] Contemporary white male observers described Sarah as "very light—nearly white" and "of marked beauty and piety; refined and beloved." These physical attributes would have captured the imagination of male slaveholders, which makes it plausible that Sarah, like Dorcas, had been sold as a concubine. As scholars such as Darlene Clark Hine have pointed out, enslaved females tended to shroud such humiliating experiences in silence. Moreover, as Brenda Stevenson remarks, concubinage in small southern locales was concealed by "rural isolation."[21] Slaveholders with the surname Oxly in Craven, Bertie, and Jones Counties included John B. Oxley, a merchant who had a business on Broad Street in New Bern before he died of yellow fever in 1864. The 1860 federal slave census indicates that Oxley enslaved four women, one around twenty-three years old. An article in the *Newbern Journal of Commerce* on February 23, 1867, definitively linked Sarah to a "Mr. Oxley." According to a story that initially appeared in a "Northern Paper," Sarah lost her "fortunes" in the fires: "the first she acquired for herself, the other was left to her by Mr. Oxley." Sarah had apparently set aside money to establish a "theological school for colored youths."[22] Sometime around 1870, Sarah Oxly reestablished her eatery on Broad Street and began working for Carpenter.

Carpenter's connections to Proctor, Coleman, Oxly, and other black residents provided him insight into the lives of the clients he purportedly served. Though the Pension Bureau never licensed Proctor, he served as a community-based claims agent. Licensed agents regularly hired black men to roam neighborhoods believed to have high concentrations of disabled veterans and soldiers' widows.[23] Proctor's work as a barber, perhaps, authenticated him in the eyes of whites, while his status as a veteran afforded him a certain level of respectability among his black peers. With no licensed black claims agent operating in New Bern at the time, it is quite possible that Proctor worked in this capacity unofficially. At minimum Proctor offered Carpenter and other white professionals avenues into the trust of black soldiers and their families.

The connections that Carpenter and other white military administrators made from their association with prospective black clients afforded them a regular income and in some cases advanced their careers. Ethelbert Hubbs, a white Union veteran from New York, who was charged with administering the Abandoned Lands and Plantations Program in Craven County, North Carolina, penned personal endorsements for black women in the region. In 1871, Hubbs endorsed Julia Ann Foy's effort to secure benefits based on her son's service. "She is partially paralyzed in her right side and otherwise afflicted which disables her from earning her own support which leaves her in a destitute condition."[24] In Frances Holloway's case, Hubbs made a more impassioned plea: "I have for several years been personally acquainted with this claimant who is an invalid in very needy circumstances, well worthy of the kind consideration of the Government." Before closing the letter, he wrote, "her claim for a pension is lawful and just."[25]

William Palmer, after ending his terms as mayor, became a notary and began assisting women like Philis Harvey and Julia Neel to handle their affairs with the federal government. Harvey entrusted Palmer with her husband's "discharge paper" and secured her husband's back pay and bounty in the amount of $116.[26] Neel was a freeborn North Carolina woman who had survived on a small bit of land outside New Bern before the war broke out. It is unclear whether Neel owned the land, but she owned tools and animals, which she lost during the war. With the assistance of Palmer, Neel filed a petition for reimbursement through the Southern Claims Commission just a few months after it was established. Chartered by the U.S. Congress in 1871 to compensate pro-Union Southerners for property losses by the invading Union army, the agency was charged with investigating and reporting claims.[27] Julia hoped to recover compensation for the "hogs, beaver, wood, bee gum, pork, corn, bed, bedding and chairs" taken by the Third and Twelfth Regiments of the 121st Cavalry stationed at Rocky Run in Craven County. Unfortunately for Julia, the commission denied her claim on July 31, 1871.[28] Two months later, her son, veteran William Lewis, succumbed to death. Not until 1888 would Julia Neel assemble an application for a dependent mother's pension.

As the decade wore on, Palmer's involvement in pension matters increased. In December 1874, he placed detailed notices in the *New Berne Times* listing the individual names of black veterans, widows, minors, and their relatives, promising they would "hear of something to their advantage."[29] The relationships black women built with pension professionals, attorneys, judges, and clerks at the district courts in the surrounding counties enabled them to engage regularly with other federal institutions.

NORTH CAROLINA MARRIAGE LAW AND THE BUREAU'S MARRIAGE POLICY

The petitions white professionals filed on behalf of southern black women were subject to the policy interpretations and changes that took place during the Reconstruction era. Perhaps the most confounding was the Pension Bureau's construction of marriage and the consequences of cohabitation and remarriage. The recognition of slave marriage in the pension system gave government officials a framework in which to manage the petitions of newly freed black women and distribute economic benefits to freedpeople. If a woman met the government's marriage criteria, the government provided a monthly stipend that was meant to substitute for her deceased husband's earnings. When a beneficiary entered a new marital relation, however, she was no longer eligible to collect benefits. That Fanny Whitney, Martha Hammond, and Celia Cuthrell remained on the pension roster for the remainder of their lives means that these women probably forwent legal marriage.

In establishing "legal marriage," the bureau deferred to the marriage laws of the state in which the prospective beneficiary filed her claim. In Florida and Missouri, a slave marriage had no legal standing unless the couple lived together after emancipation. In Maryland, a "religious celebration" was essential in establishing a legal marriage. The South Carolina state legislature distinguished between "a moral marriage, entered into with the master's consent, and an illicit and unlicensed connection" between enslaved persons. In Tennessee and Virginia, after the Marriage Acts passed, the state legislatures recognized living together as evidence of marriage.[30]

North Carolina's Marriage Act of 1866 held that newly freed blacks who married within the state while slaves and who continued to live together as husband and wife after the abolition of slavery were legally married.[31]

As Pension Bureau officials interpreted North Carolina law, if a soldier was married before enlisting but the couple never lived together after he began his military service, the marriage was "null and void." Simply put, unless a soldier died in service, a marriage had to be satisfied by "subsequent cohabitation after the close of hostilities" to be considered legal in the bureau's eyes.[32] A woman's pensionable status, then, rested on whether she was married to or living with the soldier when the act became law in 1866.[33]

As in other southern states, North Carolina's Marriage Act was part of a broader set of laws by newly established governments that attempted to regulate the lives of the newly freed. Under the Black Codes, as they came to be known, North Carolina's General Assembly enacted race-neutral laws to contain the large population of blacks in cities like New Bern, where record numbers of blacks had settled during the conflict.[34] The apprenticeship codes—part of the Black Codes—became a system of controlling the labor of freedpeople.[35] Among the other discriminatory provisions of the code, black girls "could be bound out to the age of twenty-one while white girls could be only until their eighteenth birthday." Laura Edwards has shown that conservative white lawmakers promoted marriage to consolidate state power over newly freed blacks and absolved the state from financial responsibility for them, while blacks viewed the marriage covenant as an effective means to establish the integrity of their families within the legal system and governmental institutions.[36]

Poor women interpreted North Carolina's marriage mandate in ways that made sense to them. Though state lawmakers and Freedmen's Bureau agents regulated marriage, many black people maintained their own view of its meaning. Easter Brown, a freedwoman who lost her soldier son in battle, obtained a 25-cent marriage license and filed it with the Craven County register of deeds in accordance with North Carolina's marriage law. She clarified her intention: "Had no notion of marrying Baily Winn when I got the certificate from the Register of Deeds." Easter explained her reasoning: "When the 'narration' came that people living together had to get a certificate, I sold enough eggs to pay 25 cents for the certificate."[37] Easter married Winn in compliance and, like many poor women, remained self-supporting.[38]

Simply put, southern black women who lost their sons and husbands during the war were caught between state Black Codes and Reconstruction-era pension policies. In historian Noralee Frankel's study of Mississippi freedwomen, she found that several black soldiers' widows who applied for benefits based on their marital standing did not have a firm grasp of the Pension Bureau's policy on cohabitation. Many women may have unknowingly disqualified themselves from collecting survivors' benefits before the Pension Bureau announced its policy. When North Carolina's General Assembly enacted the Black Codes in 1866, it mandated that all black couples register their marriages by September or face a fine. Two months later, federal lawmakers opened up the pension system to black soldiers' widows. This was the policy dilemma Charlotte Banks and many other freedwomen in New Bern faced when they filed their petitions for survivors' benefits under the new law.

REMARRIAGE, COHABITATION INVESTIGATIONS, AND UNION WIDOWS

In the early 1870s, the commissioner of pensions dispatched bureau examiners across the South to investigate potential cases of fraud. Agents searched for evidence and interviewed people who knew the women they suspected. Examiner George H. Ragsdale immediately began conducting investigations and collecting evidence in eastern North Carolina, especially in New Bern. He scrutinized beneficiaries who had entered into new marital unions and continued to collect survivors' benefits from the federal government. Writing to the commissioner of pensions in April 1873, Ragsdale observed, "more than one half of the widows and mothers who are pensioners [in Craven County] were remarried under that law [North Carolina Marriage Act of 1866]." In Ragsdale's estimation, nearly "nineteen hundred couples took advantage of the act in this County."[39] He suspected that many women like Charlotte Banks were concealing remarriages to qualify for benefits.

Black residents' distrust of bureau examiners' conduct investigations in their neighborhoods made it difficult for Ragsdale and others to build a case against the women they suspected of marriage fraud. Any white stranger asking personal questions about women in black neighborhoods would have been regarded with suspicion, but examiners like Ragsdale, who worked regularly in New Bern between 1873 and 1875, stood out. One woman "forbid her [daughter] to have anything to do" with Ragsdale, "telling her not to sign any paperwork" when he was questioning witnesses in and around New Bern.[40] By 1879, a bureau examiner asserted that "most of the colored people of New Bern appear to understand the object of enquiries made concerning pensioners and it is but rarely one is willing to testify freely unless it is in the interest of the Claimant or pensioner."[41] Like E. W. Carpenter, Ragsdale relied on a network of community informants to build his investigation. With the assistance of David Proctor, the black disabled veteran who occasionally identified black clients for local agents, Ragsdale began searching neighborhoods for evidence.

Proctor was born into an enslaved family in Pasquotank County that included six children. His father died when "he was a small boy," and his mother sometime thereafter. At age twenty, standing five foot ten inches tall, Proctor first enlisted in the navy at Roanoke Island and labored on the USS *Ceres* until 1863. At enlistment, Proctor was assigned the rating of "boy," which was typically reserved for enlistees under eighteen. Later the same year he enlisted in the Second U.S. Colored Cavalry (USCC). Shortly after his discharge, Proctor married Caroline Shine and settled on West Street in New Bern. The couple had two children, George and Hannah, before they split. By February 1870, Proctor had established an account at the Freedmen's Bank, where he reported that he was the only surviving member of his family, which included two brothers and three sisters. The 1880 federal census recorded his occupation as a barber, though it is not clear who made up his clientele. Proctor's work as a barber may have provided him with a platform to interact with white patrons such as agent E. W. Carpenter. As historian Quincy Mills points out, white patrons "ceded little deference to their barbers, but rather they sponsored them."[42] Proctor married Marinda H. Dudley early in 1869, but that marriage ended too. Before he died in 1891, Proctor would marry two additional times.

Proctor's work among New Bern's white agents gave him special knowledge of women's financial status. Margaret Dudley, a freedwoman who gained admission to the pension roster in 1871, said that Proctor threatened her because she refused "to pay his house rent." Proctor reportedly asked Martha Hammond for money and warned "she would be sorry too."[43] Proctor threatened to report that Julia Ann Foy had remarried if she did not let him "have some money."[44] He eventually made good on his threats. When examiner Ragsdale began his investigations of New Bern's pensioners in the spring of 1873, he relied heavily on David Proctor's social connections. Proctor testified about Margaret Dudley's intimate relationship with veteran and boatman John Ireland: "One child is the fruit of their marriage," and "a colored minister" performed the ceremony. He told Ragsdale that Julia Ann Foy and Dilcy Jarmon were both living with men.[45]

A woman who violated the Pension Bureau's remarriage rule transgressed not only the bureau's policy but the boundaries of respectable Union widowhood. If a Union widow remarried or engaged in sexual activity while collecting government benefits, bureau officials had the authority to revoke her standing on the pension rolls. Women's testimonies during the 1873 cohabitation investigations suggest that many did not fully understand that when they remarried under the North Carolina Marriage Act, they forfeited their right to claim survivors' benefits from the Pension Bureau. Rebecca Spellman claimed a pension from 1869 to 1871 as the widow of Lewis Cherry, although she had remarried. When questioned on this point several years later, she explained, "Just as soon as I heard it was against the law for a married woman to draw a pension I at once discontinued to do so."[46]

The Pension Bureau's cohabitation rules and remarriage policies were not generally known to the public, though they were available to bureau examiners and claims agents.[47] Southern black women depended greatly on the expertise of professional claims agents when filing their petitions. Claims agents dispensed misinformation to their clients about the Pension Bureau's marriage policy, engendering deeper investigations into black women's private lives. Freedwoman Maria Biggs collected dependent mother's benefits though she knew that her son, York, had married a woman named Nancy before he died. When confronted by examiner Ragsdale in 1873, Maria Biggs placed the blame for the mishap in her case squarely in the lap of her claims agent, E. W. Carpenter. On his advice, Maria claimed that she believed that she was acting in good faith by dividing the money she collected with her daughter-in-law, rather than reporting the discrepancy to the bureau.[48] The amount in question totaled $198. Carpenter may have advised Maria to share the money with her daughter-in-law rather than face possible scrutiny and investigation. For one, it was a more immediate resolution than enduring bureau officials reprocessing the case. Moreover, Carpenter was probably also concerned about how such a revelation might affect his own standing in the bureau. Ultimately, Maria was "dropped from the rolls" because in the pension system, a widow's claim took precedence over the heirship claims of mothers and fathers; it appears that she escaped criminal prosecution.

Women attempted to adhere to their community's gender protocols as well as the Pension Bureau's rules. Churches regularly disciplined members for what were deemed moral faults, conducting investigations and interrogating those charged with an offense. If congregants promised to mend their ways, they were usually restored to good standing; if not, they were expelled. Ministers did not act alone in this regard; there was usually a committee of male or female elders, depending on the gender of the person accused of immorality.

Charlotte Banks and David Holloway secured a marriage license and went before a justice of the peace in compliance with North Carolina's marriage law in 1866. Their decision sparked substantial comment from the members of New Bern's St. John Baptist Church, who voiced their belief that it "would be better" if they had another ceremony performed in the church. Sometime thereafter, Charlotte and David went before their fellow congregants at

St. John's, where Rev. Hull Grimes and Rev. John S. Johnson officiated. Charlotte remembered "there were lots of people there."[49] Amelia Clark lived with veteran Anthony Walston until a minister from Pilgrim Chapel Baptist Church told them to go through a proper marriage ceremony or resign from the church. In her application for a widow's pension, Amelia explained, "The Church to which I belonged those days . . . forced all those who were living together to marry. It made no difference how long they had lived together if they had not been previously married by ceremony they turned them out unless they would agree to have the ceremony performed."[50] Amelia and Anthony formally married in 1880; not only did they maintain their standing in the church, but Amelia thereby became a veteran's wife.

Charlotte Banks's decision to marry in a religious ceremony invalidated her claim to Union widowhood within the bureau, yet she did not immediately feel the consequences of her decision. She filed an application for survivors' benefits as the widow of Caesar Banks three years after she remarried. She also took steps to secure Caesar's bounty money. Documentation of her initial petition is scant, but Charlotte appears to have presented a reasonable case for recompense because she was admitted to the roster in 1873. By that time, she had resettled on Norwood Street with her daughter, Pleasant, from a previous relationship, and her new husband, David Holloway (figure 3.2). She deposited the pension in her account at the Freedmen's Bank in New Bern.

Charlotte's admission to the pension roster in March 1873 coincided with Ragsdale's cohabitation investigation. Only weeks after she collected her first allotment, examiner Ragsdale notified Charlotte that she was living in violation of the bureau's cohabitation rule. He based his assessment on the evidence he had gathered from the county registrar's office, which recorded that Charlotte had married Holloway in August 1866. He then accompanied Charlotte to the Freedmen's Bank and demanded she hand over all the government money issued.

Publicly escorting women to the Freedmen's Bank and demanding that they withdraw money from their accounts became a public ritual of these early investigations. Hagar James recounted: "I made evidence and drew my pension after this remarriage being ignorant of the law which causes the payment of pension to be stopped after the widow['s] remarriage." Hagar then refunded $15.05 to examiner Ragsdale, "which," she explained, "is all I have."[51] Women's compliance with these visits to the bank may not have been as willing as these women let on in their affidavits.[52] Ragsdale threatened to report Margaret Dudley to the civil authorities and have her brought up on charges of "fornication and adultery" if she did not refund the money the

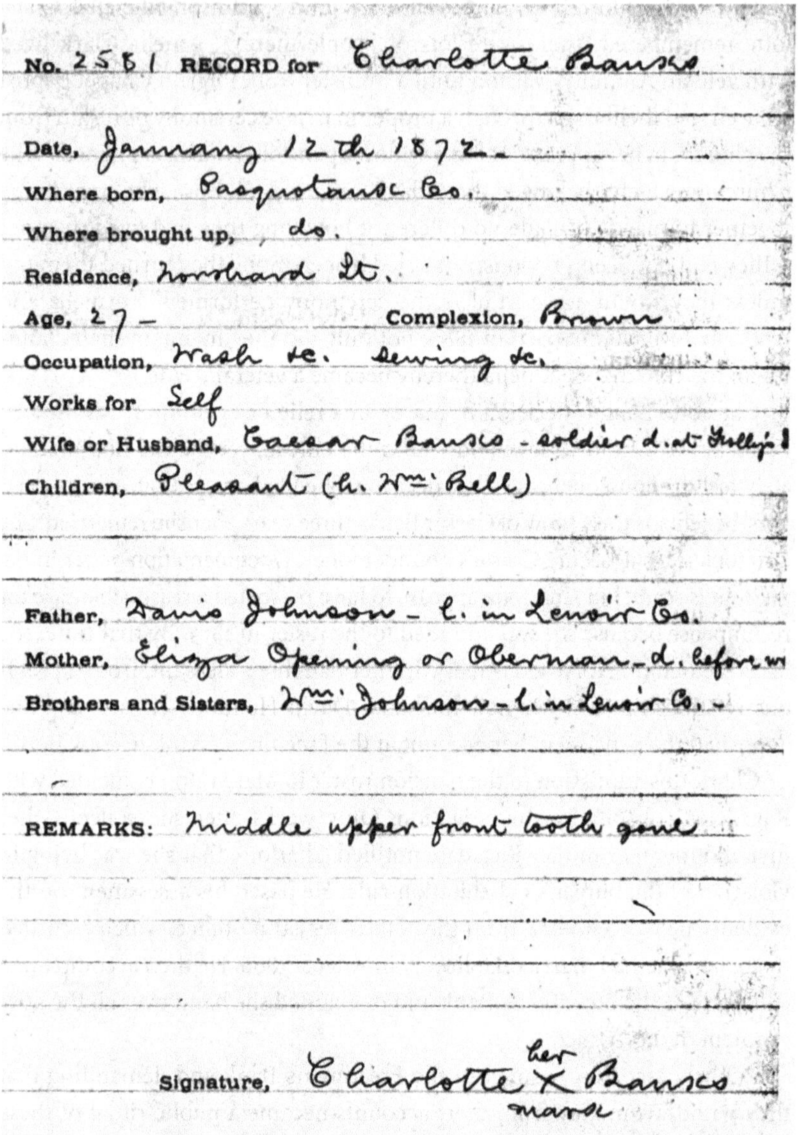

No. 2581 RECORD for Charlotte Banks

Date, January 12th 1872.

Where born, Pasquotank Co.

Where brought up, do.

Residence, Norrhard St.

Age, 27 — Complexion, Brown

Occupation, Wash &c. Sewing &c.

Works for Self

Wife or Husband, Caesar Banks — soldier d. at Folly's I

Children, Pleasant (h. Wm. Bell)

Father, Davis Johnson — l. in Lenoir Co.

Mother, Eliza Opening or Oberman — d. before w

Brothers and Sisters, Wm. Johnson — l. in Lenoir Co. —

REMARKS: Middle upper front tooth gone

Signature, Charlotte her X mark Banks

Figure 3.2. Charlotte Banks's bank record, January 12, 1872, Freedmen's Bureau Bank, New Bern. From Register of Signatures of Depositors in Branches of the Freedman's Savings and Trust Company, Record Group 101: Records of the Office of the Comptroller of the Currency, National Archives and Records Administration.

government had paid to her.[53] Margaret never regained her status on the pension roster, but her interactions with Ragsdale shed some light on the silences in Charlotte Banks's case history. With Ragsdale's propensity for retrieving funds by threatening arrest and criminal prosecution, it is conceivable that he did the same to Charlotte. Shortly after she turned over the money she had saved in her bank account, the commissioner of pensions terminated her pension on the grounds that it "had been improperly allowed because she had at the time another husband."[54]

CHALLENGING THE BUREAU'S COHABITATION RULE

Other women in and around Charlotte Banks's New Bern neighborhood faced similar charges and had to weigh their options under these circumstances. Though Pension Bureau officials suspended benefits for women who remarried, black women continued to file petitions and raise questions about the basis and application of the rule. The protest strategies of newly freed black women in these contested marriage cases appear unevenly and indirectly in the archival record. The testimonies of Harriet Morris, Ann Blackley, and Mary Hassell expose the economic vulnerability they endured in the aftermath of war.

Freedwoman Harriet Morris married Caesar Morris in mid-January 1850 on the Evans plantation in Beaufort, North Carolina. Caesar enlisted in the Thirty-Fifth Regiment of the USCT in 1863 and died two years later.[55] The couple separated during the war, and Harriet married a different man, David Clark, around 1864, under a license issued by the military authority. Sadly, Clark died "very shortly" after he married Harriet, who was left to raise three young children on her own. In 1869, believing that she, as the widow of Caesar Morris, and her children qualified for survivors' benefits, Harriet availed herself of the new law. In July the bureau issued Harriet a pension certificate for eight dollars per month, and an additional two dollars per month for each of her children. Three years later, a local examiner informed her that the bureau was terminating her benefits because she had not been Morris's widow at the time of her application. In a certified statement intended to contextualize her actions, Harriet explained her reasoning: "David Clark died very shortly after our marriage and when others who had been married to soldiers began to draw money from the Government I thought I was entitled to the same."[56]

Ann Blackley petitioned for a widow's pension in 1867, three years after her husband Abraham died of typhoid fever while serving in the Thirty-Fifth

Regiment of the USCT. Less than a year later, she remarried, thereby ending her pensionable status. Her new husband soon deserted her, but the bureau had no provisions for widows whose new marriages failed. Harriet Morris's and Ann Blackley's stories underscore the economic vulnerability women endured in the aftermath of war: marriages and women's financial health based on marriages were extremely precarious.[57]

Women countered the bureau's cohabitation rule by offering their own ideas about the meaning and function of marriage in their personal lives. When confronted by Ragsdale, black women underscored the significance of their relationships with men to their economic survival. Freedwoman Mary Hassell established her status as a Union widow around 1870. She collected a pension, although she had lived with Nelson Foy, her male companion, since around 1866. In her 1873 affidavit before examiner Ragsdale, Mary explained that she and Foy shared household responsibilities and that when her pension money came through, she bought a horse so that he could raise a crop.[58] Importantly, Mary did not construe herself as economically dependent on Foy, which was part of the Pension Bureau's model of marriage. In her view, living with Foy was not a way of scamming the government and did not involve questions of morality; rather, it was a matter of economic survival. Ragsdale decided that Hassell had relinquished her title to her pension because she was living with a man. More significant, her neighbors believed that Hassell's relationship with Foy constituted a marriage. Ragsdale "called on" Hassell "to refund the money." She responded by immediately heading to the Freedmen's Bank, withdrawing all her money, and hiding "in some of the colored settlements."[59] The examiner recovered only "21.00" dollars from the bank. Clearly, Mary Hassell disagreed with her neighbors' report and the examiner's interpretation of worthy widowhood.

Ragsdale had no compunction about when and where he confronted women about their private lives. He approached Dilcy Jarmon on Neuse Road (about two miles outside New Bern) and questioned her about the man Proctor had previously identified. "I was living with a man, doing washing and cooking & patching for him," she protested.[60] Ragsdale questioned another woman, Julia Ann Foy, at a local market after confiscating her bank book. Later the same day, while she chatted with a friend on the steps of her home, he attempted to question Julia Ann about the nature of her relationship with Henry Lofty. Julia Ann challenged Ragsdale's construct of domesticity by introducing issues of work and self-sufficiency into their dialogue: "He [Lofty] only boarded with me, I done his washing and cooking and he paid me for it."[61] Though "keeping house"—cooking and washing for single men—was not listed as an occupation on the census, beneficiaries identified it as a form of paid labor.[62] Some women lived with men as housekeepers without any intimate ties.[63] Others engaged in sex work to support themselves after their husbands died, but few would admit it in a public forum.

Women returned to their claims agents and urged them to file complaints and appeals as a result of their suspensions during Ragsdale's probe. Some women used the bureau's apparatus to protest what they deemed an unjust assessment of their intimate lives. Although formal appeal procedures would not be set in place until the creation of the Special Examination Division in 1881, bureau officials responded to women's complaints about local procedures and unethical suspensions. Lila Long, a forty-five-year-old freedwoman who lived in Beaufort, filed a complaint against Ragsdale after the commissioner of pensions revoked her pension. In a sworn statement, she explained that she had "never remarried since the death of my husband." She added "I have all the time lived with white people working in the field and about the house."[64] She was also surprised to learn of David Proctor's involvement in her case, as she "had no acquaintance" with him except in "Mr. Carpenter's office" when she had applied for benefits.[65]

Matilda Simmons, a washerwoman and cook, also countered the charge of remarriage by capitalizing on the bureau's preference for white testimony. A cohort of prominent white men in her community, including the assessor of the poor in Beaufort County, filed statements on her behalf. "She had no Husband nor has she had one since the Close of the Late war," they protested.[66] Five months later Matilda made her own case: "I have never been remarried or t[h]ough[t] of such an act. I have never had any man or men living with me except for my son Nelson." She closed by making a veiled reference to the powerful men who had petitioned the commissioner five months earlier.[67]

Both Lila Long's and Matilda Simmons's appeals prompted the commissioner of pensions to order new investigations into their cases. When examiner Michael E. Jenks descended on New Bern to investigate Lila's case, he noted that "the whole neighborhood say there is no foundation whatever to the charge Lila Long has ever remarried since the war."[68] Examiner Jenks recommended that Lila's pension be reinstated, and she remained on the rolls until she died in 1906. Jenks also conducted a swift investigation in Matilda's case. "I would recommend that the suspension in the case of Matilda Simmons be removed and that she be again restored [to] the Pension Roll."[69]

Pensioner Mary Counts appealed to the commissioner of pensions for a reconsideration of her case in 1874, about a year after a report by Ragsdale that she had secured a marriage license in 1866 and lived as the wife of

Mathew Simmons.[70] It was impossible for Mary to produce legal evidence of her marriage to Caesar, so she told her own story in an affidavit. Born around 1842, Mary was one of four enslaved women who resided on Lafayette Dillahunt's family farm in Jones County, North Carolina.[71] During her youth Mary saw her older sister, Maria Ann, suffer sexual violation by their owner's uncle. Maria Ann eventually gave birth to two "half white" children, Caroline and Census, before she was separated from her husband, Caesar, and sold to "speculators" in New Orleans; Mary never saw her sister again. Shortly after Maria Ann was sold, Lafayette Dillahunt gave consent for Caesar Counts to marry his wife's sister, Mary. The couple lived together and raised Caroline and Census as their own before Caesar enlisted in the army in 1863. Caesar died in a hospital in Beaufort County, North Carolina, seven months later.[72] Thus, from Mary's perspective, her sister had never embraced her identity as Caesar's wife. She argued that her own marriage to Caesar had more substance because her sister "was going with other men" and "did not own [acknowledge] him [Caesar] at first but afterwards did just as she pleased."[73] Mary outlined the contours of her relationship with Caesar: "When I took up with him I stayed with him all the time until he left me to go into the army." As further evidence of her marriage to Caesar, Mary offered details about their family. "I had one child by him. My sister never had any children by him. She had two children but they were of different color from him—they were half white. The Child I had by him was born before he left me."[74] Mary probably introduced the white paternity of Maria Ann's children into the official record to bolster her own case and gain power in the proceedings, rather than to castigate her sister. As further evidence of her marriage to Caesar Counts, Mary explained to the commissioner that when Caesar enlisted, he left "all of his clothes to me."[75] In telling her story, Mary confronted federal officials with the legacy of enslavement—particularly the sexual abuse black women had endured—while introducing a more complicated definition of marriage and family into the bureau's process.

What pension administrators construed as pension fraud and lax sexual mores in Charlotte Banks's early case history was far more complicated than their investigations actually reveal. "Remarriage suspensions" reveal a good deal about how poor and working-class black women navigated poverty during the Reconstruction era. Many African American women turned to Pension Bureau as a resource in their transition to a free labor society. As Tera Hunter makes clear, many poor black men and women used remarriage as a tool to offset the impact of a crushing labor market and turbulent life events such as death, abandonment, illness, financial crises, and displacement.[76] As the stories of Charlotte Banks, Harriet Morris, Mary Hassell, Ann Blackley remind us, marriage was a tool for economic survival not a reflection of their sexual virtue.

THE AFTERMATH OF THE COHABITATION INVESTIGATIONS

Fanny Whitney proved adept at gaining the attention of bureau officials while protecting the details of her private life during the 1873 cohabitation investigations. Shortly after settling with her children in New Bern, Fanny had a short-lived intimate relationship, which resulted in the birth of her daughter Malissa. The reputed father, William Henry Green, was a "fellow servant" who lived with Fanny on Donnell's holding in Hyde County.[77] It seems likely that Fanny apprised her extensive network of Donnell plantation family and kin of her situation. If this is true, then they might have known that any mention of Malissa's paternity—married or not—would have raised the level of suspicion, influenced examiner Ragsdale's perception of Fanny's worthiness, and jeopardized her ability to maintain her standing on the roster. This revelation could have left her vulnerable under the Pension Bureau's cohabitation rule.[78] It is also possible that Fanny wanted to avoid bringing undue attention to Green. Once identified to the civil authorities, Green might have been subject to a bastardy charge, with penalties of fines and imprisonment. Before Fanny died in 1911, however, the issue of her daughter's paternity would eventually surface.[79]

Glitches in a case file could take years to sort out, a desperate circumstance for women who had few wage-earning opportunities in a severely restricted labor market. Fanny Whitney caused a glitch of her own in 1873, when bureau officials noted that the ages of her children with Harry were incorrect on her application. The mistake cost Fanny her standing on the pension roster: the bureau suspended her benefits. Fanny then tapped into the network of freedpeople who had at one time lived on Judge Donnell's plantation. She contacted William Henry Green, the father of her young daughter, who "kept the record of the births on the plantation." Green had since returned to Hyde County, and Fanny hoped that his records would be enough to establish the dates of birth of her and Harry's surviving children, Harry, Milton and Adam.[80] "At a great expense to herself," Fanny sent Green money to travel to New Bern from Hyde County, "a distance of a hundred miles," and took him before the magistrate. To Fanny's dismay, Green said he had "little or no recollection" of her children, the magistrate misunderstood what was "required," and her "claim was left in a worse condition than it was before."[81]

The consequences of Green's forgetfulness must have hit Fanny especially hard since Green did not assist Fanny in supporting their daughter, Malissa. Frustrated with the entire process, Fanny directed her claims agent to express her desire "to have all of her children dropped from the Pension rolls" as she would be "content" to collect the pension "due her as the widow of Harry Whitney."[82] Fanny's pension was reissued four years later, but not before the postmaster had assessed her worthiness.

Around the time Fanny Whitney sought reinstatement to the pension roster, congressional lawmakers proposed various strategies to address the possibility that female claimants might collect pension benefits and enter into an informal marital union with a man. One such proposal involved pension agents and postmasters creating marriage rosters to expose Union widows who concealed their marriages.[83] Though this proposal never became a formal policy, bureau officials sought answers in Fanny Whitney's case a month before reissuing her benefits. On July 6, 1877, J. A. Bentley, the commissioner of pensions, asked the postmaster of New Bern if "Fanny Whitney, widow of Harry Whitney," had "ever remarried." The postmaster responded swiftly that Fanny "is a very exemplary and worthy woman" and described her witnesses as very "reliable."[84] By the time Fanny's name was reinstated, however, all her children had reached maturity.

Less sensational but equally important for what they reveal about black women's lives and labors in post–Civil War America are the case histories of the many women who remarried and reported the fact to the Pension Bureau. Black women weighed the decision to enter into a new marriage and forgo federal benefits with great care. Remarriage had ambiguous outcomes for soldiers' widows. Abandonment by their husbands, low-paying work, and the desire to live independently led some women to alter their personal lives. With few mechanisms to address their financial circumstances in their communities and no avenue by which they could petition the government for survivors' benefits, they sought jobs, asked for help from local sources, and migrated.

For women who had children, remarriage did not prevent them from trying to secure benefits for their children. Eliza and Jacob Banks married before the war and then recommitted themselves to each other in 1862, when they reached New Bern. Richard Tucker, a black minister and undertaker, performed the ceremony. Jacob enlisted in the USCT in New Bern in 1863. Less than a year later, he died in action. Eliza filed a petition for survivors' benefits in 1868 but rescinded her claim a year later when she married William Moore. Realizing that her three children still had standing as survivors of a

Union soldier, Eliza (now Moore) filed a petition on behalf of the children and identified herself as their guardian. Unfortunately, William Moore died sometime after 1870, and Eliza died five years later. Eliza's mother was appointed guardian of the grandchildren, but she too had died by the time the children came of age. The children's case stalled in the Pension Bureau until 1890.

CRIMINAL INVESTIGATION OF E. W. CARPENTER

Although black women's earliest dealings with the pension system were individual and seemingly uncoordinated, the women managed to respond to claims agents' unjust treatment with measurable success. Claims agents and trusted community figures exploited and thus angered black women, who desperately clung to the hope of government restitution and recognition.[85] Before Jane Richardson died in 1870, the protective grandmother penned an angry letter to the commissioner of pensions, saying, "Is it right that lawyer Carpenter should keep my grandson['s] money. Lawyer Carpenter drawed his pension and will not give it to me. I am the boy['s] grandmother and the Court of Craven has appointed me guardian for him."[86]

Multiple women who had hired Carpenter to assist with their cases failed to receive their monthly payments from the bureau several months or more after the bureau issued their checks. Their grievances revealed a trail of deception that led directly to Edward W. Carpenter's office. In one instance, the commissioner issued a check for more than $1,000 to a freedwoman whose husband had died of "colic" on Folly Island, South Carolina, in 1863. When she tried to follow up on her case, agent Carpenter informed her that "the claim was not paid."[87] Months later the woman's home "burned down together with all of her things." She returned to Carpenter's office to hear again that nothing had come through for her.[88] In yet another meeting, Carpenter explained that the delay was caused by a need to file more evidence. Nancy Cartwright told a bureau agent that she did not get her payment of $500, and Mary Counts reported that she never saw "a cent" of her first pension check. The Pension Bureau awarded Isabella Clark an arrears payment of $300, but she said she received only $175.[89]

Women's complaints about Carpenter during the cohabitation investigations of 1873 led to a formal investigation of him. Over the course of the investigations, examiner Ragsdale placed a good portion of the blame for the violation of the bureau's remarriage rule squarely in the lap of agent Carpenter. Ragsdale attributed a large number of the remarriage suspensions he uncovered in eastern North Carolina to claims agents' deliberate efforts to mislead the claimants about the Pension Bureau's marriage policies and regulations. In the case of Charity Moore, whose benefits were suspended in 1873 for living with a man, Ragsdale concluded that agent Carpenter was "no doubt to blame."[90]

Before Carpenter had completed the paperwork on Ann Blackley's behalf, she remarried, thereby ending her pensionable status. Ragsdale alleged that Carpenter filed Ann's application with the intent of collecting the monthly payout in her place. In an 1873 report penned to the commissioner, Ragsdale made clear his belief that Blackley "was induced to make her mark to the voucher for pension money through misrepresentation and did not mean to defraud the government."[91] He believed that Carpenter planned to cash the check for "$1,034.53." The mishandling of Blackley's money came to light shortly after her husband had "deserted her and she went to Carpenter's office in search of her check." Ragsdale recommended the bureau issue benefits to Ann from 1864, the date her husband died in service, to 1868, the date Ann remarried, "with as little delay as possible."[92] Before closing his June report to the commissioner of pensions, Ragsdale warned that "unless the power exercised over these ignorant pensioners by Carpenter and [Charles] Nelson is thoroughly broken down they will never get one half of their dues."[93]

Ragsdale labeled Carpenter "a pension crook" and instigated a relentless campaign for his suspension. Especially compelling were the reports from David Proctor, the black army veteran who worked as Carpenter's assistant. Ragsdale relied on Proctor's testimony and guidance as he built his case against Carpenter.[94] He was convinced that Carpenter planned to cash one woman's check himself when he learned that she planned to remarry. After Ragsdale filed his report with the commissioner of pensions, a judicial investigation ensued. Although a federal court in Raleigh ultimately dismissed the charges against Carpenter, the Pension Bureau prevented him from filing claims on behalf of veterans and war widows.[95]

Though it is difficult to know just what Carpenter intended, at no point during the cohabitation investigations did he work to help his clients appeal their suspensions. Carpenter lost his credibility among black veterans and their families, an important group in eastern North Carolina, which would become a factor when he later ran for office. Proctor was also deeply implicated in the bureau's criminal investigation, especially among black veterans and their families. Details surrounding David Proctor's troubles are scarce, though the evidence suggests that he went to jail in Raleigh sometime after 1873. One woman heard that Proctor "got into trouble and was imprisoned."[96] Indeed, Proctor did serve a prison sentence in Raleigh but returned to New Bern sometime around 1886 and married Margaret Ann Hines. The couple had two children, Minnie and James, before Proctor died in 1891.

The permanent suspension of Carpenter in 1873 left a large gulf in the local network.[97] Despite the criminal investigation, trial, and his subsequent suspension, Carpenter remained in New Bern and worked as a notary public and, without authorization, continued to assist freedwomen in securing their benefits from the government. An active member of the Republican Party, Carpenter combined his background in law and his relations with black voters in Craven County to gain public office. From 1877 to 1890, he served as clerk of the Craven County Superior Court. Carpenter achieved this ascendancy in large measure through his close relations with Craven County blacks, who voted until 1901. Had Carpenter aligned himself with the Democratic Party, as his brother did, perhaps he might have outlasted Republican rule, but he remained aligned with the Republican Party and the black community.[98] After his term as clerk of the court ended in 1890, Carpenter could still be found in his office on Broad Street certifying documents for black veterans and helping widows organize their paperwork. In one of his conversations with a distinguished minister of a local AMEZ church, Carpenter opined that it "is right [to] let the poor people get their money[;] they are entitled to it."[99]

CONCLUSION

Black women's interactions with examiners and their negotiations with claims agents during the 1870s educated them about the laws, regulations, and procedures governing their cases. During the cohabitation investigations of the early 1870s, they gained a deeper awareness of the system's construction of marriage, which was based on a monogamous union with continuous and exclusive co-residence. They also acquired familiarity with the local examination process and the role bureau agents played in their cases. Perhaps most importantly, in the years following the closure of the Freedmen's Bureau, freedwomen kept the issue of economic deprivation at the forefront of debate in the pension system by advancing their petitions for survivors' benefits. The various avenues they explored in their efforts to have their pensions reinstated reveal strategies that the women would later hone as they navigated the system over the course of their case.

Perhaps even more detrimental than Carpenter's suspension in the cases of black applicants was the narrowing of the construction of marriage, which was amended and now required evidence "that parties were joined in marriage by some ceremony deemed by them obligatory."[100] Meanwhile, bureau officials continued to authorize local agents to conduct covert investigations into Union widows' private lives. The matter of cohabitation was not resolved within bureau policy until August 1882, when Congress passed a new law that clarified how examiners and bureau officials alike would investigate cases of remarriage and evidence of sexual immorality.

4

Black Women, Claims Agents, and the Pension Network

While the criminal investigation of Edward W. Carpenter was underway, the wives of disabled veterans and widows of veterans established households, reconnected with kin, and formed new ties. While adjusting to uprooting, loss, and freedom, these women discovered how hard it was to earn a livelihood for themselves and those who depended on them, whether their disabled husbands or their children and elders. Fanny Whitney regained her place on the pension roster, and her daughter was about to start school. Louisa and Samuel Powers reordered their household to provide for their growing family. Charlotte Banks, who had lost her pension benefits in 1873, and her new husband, David Holloway, moved into a small home on Norwood Street, where they would raise four children, but Holloway died in 1874. The next year, Charlotte married Austin Caphart, with whom she lived until his death in 1887.[1] War widow Mary Lee, a domestic worker and farmhand, moved in to her stepfather's home on South Front Street. Black soldiers' wives and widows' marriage customs and flexible household organization reflected the collective ethos that congealed in black neighborhoods across the South in the wake of Reconstruction.

Amid the federal withdrawal from the South and the reemergence of Democratic officeholders in North Carolina's General Assembly, black North Carolinians "consolidated, expanded, and liberated" their own institutions from white intrusion.[2] In 1880, blacks continued to outnumber whites in the city of New Bern, and black women significantly outnumbered black men.[3] A new group of black professionals changed the landscape of New Bern's pension business when they began handling the cases of black veterans and their families. The shift from white to black claims agents signaled the maturation of black institutions, which laid the basis for a pension network in eastern North Carolina, especially in New Bern. Prospective beneficiaries built their own networks based on preexisting relationships and drew new participants into the pension application and examination process. Long-standing community-building activities that the black masses initiated, rising literacy rates, and the election of black men to municipal office all reinforced claims on the government by black soldiers' widows even as equality under the law was being eroded.

This chapter maps the lives and labors of black soldiers' wives, widows, mothers, and children in the wake of Reconstruction through the life histories of Louisa Powers and other veterans' wives; these active citizens and protective mothers fought with the U.S. Pension Bureau to assert their rights. The chapter then considers black claims agents' involvement in this process. Of particular importance for Louisa Powers's ability to navigate the pension system was the personal and professional positioning of Frederick C. Douglass, the son of Mary E. Norman—a black soldier's widow—when he began handling the caseload of claims agent Edward W. Carpenter. In hiring Frederick Douglass to represent her case in 1887, Powers tapped into New Bern's grassroots pension network. Soldiers' wives, widows, and mothers formed this network, developed local protocols, and exchanged information about the federal pension system in their homes and community institutions. Grassroots by nature, this pension network included communal practices and relationships separate from the formal bureaucratic structure. When combined with the skills of pension professionals, the resources Louisa Powers and hundreds of other women drew on to engage the bureau's application process proved remarkably adaptable and responsive to the government's shifting requirements.

LOUISA POWERS AND THE DILEMMAS OF WAGE-EARNING AND FAMILY

Louisa Powers's early history is especially hard to piece together because her reminiscences offer no clues about her prewar status and because of the absence of black lives from documentary records before the abolition of slavery. This gap testifies to the impact that slavery had on all black lives, whether enslaved or free. Louisa Jackson was born in Virginia around 1848. She was about sixteen years old when she met Samuel Powers (originally Rouse), a freeborn black soldier, in Richmond, Virginia.

Louisa traveled with Samuel for the duration of his service. When military administrators decommissioned the Thirty-Fifth Regiment of the USCT (formerly North Carolina Colored Troops) on June 8, 1866, Samuel collected his army pay in full; a year later, he received another hundred dollars. Believing in the sanctity of their relationship, they did not go before a justice of the peace or minister to renew their marital commitment, as the new North Carolina Marriage Act required. Sometime between his discharge and 1870, Samuel and Louisa settled in Harlowe, a farming community about twenty-six miles outside New Bern. They became part of a kinship and social network that they could depend on for their well-being. Their neighbors included freeborn and manumitted black farming families such as the Goddetts.[4] Until Powers's death, he and Israel Anders, a childhood acquaintance from Duplin County and fellow soldier, lived about "two miles apart."[5] Samuel and Louisa socialized at the Piney Grove AMEZ church and had six children (Rebecca, Rosanna, Siddy, Francis, Lizzie, and Samuel).[6]

Unlike many veterans and their spouses in New Bern, neither Samuel nor Louisa established an account at the Freedmen's Bank for themselves or any of their children. Instead they invested their resources in farming. With dreams of independence and financial stability, the Powers family rented "ten acres of land which cost about a dollar an acre" from a white sawmill owner.[7] Renting land was a distant aspiration for most freedpeople, who did not have the capital, tools, or animals required to work the land. Tenancy conferred a modicum of independence. Black veterans like Samuel Powers and Israel Anders secured land from white landholders willing to rent to blacks. They may have gotten worn-out horses and mules from the U.S. Army after it demobilized.

The injuries and illnesses Samuel Powers had suffered during the war impaired his ability to contribute to the family's income. He worked on and off as a field hand and did light work in the turpentine industry. A man who served alongside him in the army said, "He worked about there like the rest of us did, tried to farm, and picked cotton for other farmers and other work he could pick up."[8] Another neighbor said, "He was not able to do a full days work."[9] Samuel was in a slightly better position than another veteran, Peter Boyd, who spoke about the toll that his wartime disability took on his household: "I am wholly unable to perform any manual labor. . . . My wife [Annie Boyd] has tak[en] care of me since discharge."[10] Strikingly, Boyd and others outlined the bread and butter issues associated with disease and injury in a free market system. Gracy Archibald, describing her husband's ordeal, remembered, "He suffered all the time with his right arm or the stump of his right arm."[11] Gracy's testimony reminds us that as injured and disabled men returned to their families in refugee communities, freedpeople created new definitions of manhood that recognized men's wartime injuries.

Caring for an ailing husband was a heavy burden for poor women. Louisa Powers worked in the turpentine industry, a traditionally male occupation requiring considerable physical strength. Lana Burney's husband, Larry, served in the Thirty-Fifth USCT but developed severe pain in his left side. Once sought after for his productivity in the turpentine industry, Larry hoped that whatever was ailing him would "pass off." The final days of his life proved excruciating. "Just a short time before his death he was more helpless than a child," Lana lamented. "His bowels were so bad, I had to be continually changing the bed clothes."[12] Women like Lana Burney and Louisa Powers provided for their families while their husbands lay ill. Lana explained: "I had to work out to get something to subsist upon. I would leave him in the care of his mother."[13] Louisa Powers said, "I did the work to support the family."[14] For soldiers' wives, caregiving combined with earning wages was a form of respectable and worthy womanhood, even though it contradicted white norms of wifely dependency.

Women understood that both the household labor they performed—caretaking and mothering—and the wages they brought home were essential to their and their dependents' survival. Caregiving was a principal responsibility of the wives of injured veterans that added significantly to their household responsibilities. Many understood their caregiving work as well as their wage earning as a duty of womanhood. Like Peter and Annie Boyd's union, Louisa's marriage centered on caretaking. Diarrhea, coughing, chest pains, and sore legs confined Samuel to his bed for long periods.[15] Sometimes his legs, knees, and feet would swell, and Louisa would have to bathe them in "mullen." One neighbor saw him "bleed until he turned pale."[16] The uncompensated labor Louisa, Lana, and Annie performed as care providers was the basis for the petitions they filed in later years.

Delivering care to a veteran in need could be unpredictable, even life threatening. Veteran Jacob Moore served in the USCHA and was discharged in 1865.[17] Shortly after his marriage to Mary Jane (Sears), a freedwoman who labored as a domestic, Jacob became violent. Although caution must be taken in projecting twentieth-century medical knowledge onto the past, modern research on the psychological effects of war on the lives of veterans suggests that Jacob may have been struggling with post-traumatic stress disorder and alcoholism.[18] A relative found his behavior so appalling that she refused to visit: "He was so cruel to her [Mary Jane] that I did not care to go there. He would beat her so and I do not know the cause of his ill treatment."[19] A city official warned Jacob that "he had better leave Mary and go away or he would send him to jail if he was brought up before him again."[20] Heeding the official's advice,

Jacob separated from Mary Jane—though without securing a legal divorce or making financial provision for her. Shortly thereafter, Jacob "took-up" with another woman and moved to Raleigh, where he worked as a butcher.[21] As the pension system had no mechanism for providing financial support to soldiers' wives whose husbands had abandoned or abused them, Mary Jane Moore was left to support herself and their surviving child on her own.

Physical violence and failing to contribute to the support of one's family constituted major infractions among black New Bernians and Jacob Moore's peers.[22] Marriage and intimate relationships as black people understood them came with duties and obligations. Whether legally married or sweethearting, men expected the women in their lives to keep house—that is, prepare meals, do laundry, care for children, and nurse the ill—and to contribute wages to the family income. Women expected the men in their lives to work and turn their wages over to them in a timely fashion. Hettie Wendly's husband, George, labored in the shingle swamps along the Pee Dee River in South Carolina on the promise of higher wages while she worked intermittently as a farmhand and housekeeper. Hettie occasionally traveled to South Carolina to visit her husband, and together they traveled to Plantersville and Pine Bluff in a rowboat to trade goods. George continued to send money to support Hettie even after he started a new family in South Carolina. It is not clear whether Hettie knew of George's second family, but it is important to note that George continued to abide by societal expectations. The regular support that George sent Hettie, with the wages she earned as a domestic and as a farm laborer, enabled her to sustain an independent household in James City.[23]

Not all husbands acted thus, whether separated by geography or by emotional alienation. Leaders of the AME church stripped veteran William Frederick Harrison of his ministerial authority after he left his wife, failed to send support, and married another woman. A minister reported: "The A.M.E. Church doesn't keep any such preachers."[24] A laundress publicly condemned a man in her community because he "would not pay . . . nor help support his wife . . . so they quit living together."[25] The failure of husbands to provide financial support for their wives or intimate partners disrupted black women's ability to maintain their households. Several years after George's death, Hettie described him as "a good husband . . . worth more than a pension. . . . He did not drink and every Saturday night he brought his money home. There was not a lazy bone in his body. He certainly was a good steady hand and worked all the time and brought all his money home."[26]

Veterans' debilitating injuries and illnesses reordered marriage and family life in other significant ways. Wage earning separated some couples.

Sarah Latham had to live apart from her husband, Jesse, after he was discharged from the army because an injury limited his employment options. Sarah explained, "He left me . . . to get work and told me I better come to New Berne and get work as I was not strong enough to work in the country." She explained, "There was nothing whatever the matter between us—but we both had to work for our living." Unfortunately, because Jesse could not "do half a mans work . . . he went to work in the country."[27]

Samuel Powers's diminished earning capacity forced his family to reassign wage-earning responsibilities within the family. Louisa and Samuel's youngest children, Samuel and Francis, had mental impairments that limited their ability to earn wages.[28] The disastrous farming years of 1866 and 1867, coupled with Samuel's declining health, more than likely influenced the Powers family to relocate their children some distance from the land they rented "up the creek."[29] During this particularly bleak time, Samuel turned to suspended claims agent Edward W. Carpenter, who periodically loaned the family "money . . . as a matter of charity."[30]

Unable to fully support their family on the wages they earned raising crops, Samuel and Louisa negotiated work agreements for at least two of their daughters. The contracts Louisa negotiated mirror what Karin Zipf describes as an informal apprenticeship agreement, whereby mothers and fathers might hire their children out without involving state authorities.[31] Siddy lived with the family's black neighbors, Benjamin and Mary Ann Martin.[32] Mary Ann described the arrangement this way: "She is not bound to us she has lived with us constantly since she came to our house."[33] Benjamin elaborated: "She [Siddy] can leave me when she wants to. She came to live with me about a year after Saml Powers death and she has been living with me continuously since." William Gaskill, a white farmer and carpenter, took custody of Rosanna when she was about three years old. "She was not bound to me and I did not adopt her," Gaskill insisted. "My wife and myself are older and we want children around to help."[34]

Samuel Powers was the son of a poor white woman and a black man who attempted to live together openly in Duplin County, North Carolina, and apprenticeship had been a perpetual feature of the family's prewar existence. Samuel's parents, Rebecca (Becky) Rouse and Don Ketter, raised at least three children before Ketter disappeared from the historical record. It is not known whether Ketter was free or enslaved, and no one spoke on the record about the internal dynamics of their relationship. Rebecca bore ten children, at least three of whom were fathered by Ketter. State law placed severe restrictions on sexual relations between white women and black men, and the clandestine nature of Rebecca and Don's relationship probably made it difficult for Ketter to contribute to the economic support of his family. Ketter's name does not appear on the federal census before or after the Civil War, indicating that he may have been enslaved or fled the area.

Living in violation of North Carolina's prohibition of interracial marriage certainly qualified Samuel's mother to be viewed as "unruly" by her contemporaries.[35] Becky resided at the Duplin County poorhouse with at least three of her children: Prisy; May, who "was afflicted and suffered with fits"; and Barney, who was identified as white.[36] A law authorizing the arrest of unemployed blacks also empowered civil authorities to bind out as apprentices any free black child whose parents were not regularly employed. Samuel and all his mixed race siblings suffered this fate. As Zipf points out, these provisions applied "regardless of their mother's means of support and . . . regardless of their mother's race."[37] Rebecca apprenticed her daughters with Ketter to Jake Cole, the overseer of the poorhouse where she resided with her son Barney.

Samuel Powers's life of unfreedom differed greatly from that of New Bern's black male youth, who could acquire a skilled trade and a modicum of freedom through apprenticeship. Born in 1837, he was bound to a man named John Powers when he was a small boy until he turned eighteen.[38] There is no indication that he learned any sort of skill that would have prepared him to live independently while apprenticed to Powers.[39] At the end of his term of service, Samuel lived on his own for about four years and then reentered the state's apprenticeship system around the age of twenty-two or twenty-three. He bound himself to David West and "had for a wife Jene West a colored woman slave"; together they had three children. North Carolina's antebellum slave code made it illegal for free blacks to marry or live together as husband and wife with any enslaved person. Under provisions of this law, Samuel was "liable to indictment, and, upon conviction, fined and imprisoned, or whipped at the discretion of the court."[40]

Samuel paid dearly for his marriage to Jene. Sometime in the 1850s the local authorities indicted and fined him. To settle his fine, Samuel entered into a new apprenticeship with (Joseph) Kevin Boney, a white merchant who would later enlist in the Confederate army (March 1862). Around 1859, Boney traded Samuel's indenture to Max Myers, a German-born merchant who peddled goods throughout Duplin County. The terms of indenture bound Samuel to Myers "for 99 years."[41] Thus, for Samuel Powers, North Carolina's apprenticeship system was nothing more than "slavery by another name."[42] Much of what Samuel Powers experienced growing up in antebellum North Carolina had to do with the state's harsh and unjust legal system.

Despite Samuel's experiences, he and Louisa negotiated an informal apprenticeship arrangement for at least one of their daughters in the weeks leading up to his death in April 1877.[43]

ADJUSTING TO THE DEMANDS OF WIDOWHOOD

The death of a soldier or veteran represented a significant transition for their families. The most pressing issues were making funeral arrangements, paying burial costs, settling outstanding debts, and securing work and housing. Just as unmarried women and single mothers had to balance the demands of wage earning, motherhood, and community without male support, so too did war widows.

Complex family systems, including all-female households, enabled widows to survive. In 1880, the women of the Copes household—Sarah Copes (fifty-eight), Mary Whitby (Sarah Copes's daughter, a Union widow), and Rosannah Stevenson (Mary Whitby's daughter)—resided under the same roof on Crooked Street. Sarah and Mary "kept house" while Rosannah Stevenson contributed to the family support through her thriving dressmaking business in New Bern. In 1900, another widow of a Union soldier joined Mary Whitby's intergenerational household.[44]

Samuel Powers's death changed the conditions of Louisa's motherhood. Though widowed, Louisa was single in the eyes of the law, which made her vulnerable to the state's vagrancy and apprenticeship laws. As she had before, Louisa supported her family by a combination of fieldwork and housework at the homes of her neighbors. Her youngest child accompanied her on her rounds as a domestic worker, which included black and white household employers.[45] She continued working in North Carolina's declining turpentine industry by "raking boxes" (i.e., keeping turpentine trees from burning when the woods are fired to burn the underbrush), for which she earned about fifty cents per hundred boxes.[46]

When Louisa's youngest child, Samuel, reached age six, she enrolled him in school.[47] As scholars such as Linda Gordon have pointed out, mothers and guardians had to send their children to school clean, clothed, healthy, and on time. Two of Fanny Whitney's children, Harry and Adam, started school in 1870.[48] Both women's decision to enroll their boys in school represented an enormous sacrifice, especially because employers were eager to hire black boys. Louisa's decision may have been complicated by the fact that young Samuel was described as mentally impaired and unfit for manual labor.[49]

Mary Jane Moore attempted to rebuild her finances on her own terms after her husband left her. She explored the possibilities opened up by new intimate ties—even marriage—which resulted in four more children, and she embarked on a series of seasonal migrations.[50] After each of these relationships did not work out, Mary Jane was left to provide for herself and her five children (including her son with Jacob Moore) on the wages she earned from laboring as a domestic and a farmhand. Suffering from "heart trouble" and "paralysis" in her right leg, she migrated to Providence, Rhode Island, where her sister Charlotte White and a network of blacks from New Bern had established themselves. She probably hoped to earn a bit more money there, but as many southern black women who engaged in seasonal migration outside eastern North Carolina quickly learned, working conditions in the North did not always offer the boost they were seeking.[51] Mary Jane turned to sex work in Providence to make ends meet, and in 1886, she bore twins, who died some three months later.[52] Shortly thereafter she returned to New Bern.

Back home, Mary Jane rebuilt community ties by turning to the church for spiritual support and becoming an active member of Thomas Battle's congregation. A respected brick mason, Battle was affiliated with Andrew Chapel and St. Peter's AMEZ. The protracted struggle for survival in which black congregations had engaged since the close of the war suggests that Mary Jane could rely on the goodwill and charity of others in her church. She also managed to earn a little money by washing and cooking. Jacob Moore, her estranged veteran husband, sent Mary Jane a message by a fellow veteran informing her that he was sick. He died shortly thereafter, which opened up the possibility of her gaining regular monthly support as a soldier's widow. After another trip to the North, Mary Jane returned to New Bern permanently.[53]

With few municipal resources available to black women, right after a soldier's or veteran's death, bereft women depended on relatives, friends, and neighbors. Louisa Powers proved to be particularly resourceful. A few months after Samuel Powers died, she tested the waters with a new intimate companion, Jim Watson, a day laborer she had hired to help her cultivate the farm. Neighbors described Watson as a drifter and said he did not work hard. When Jim threatened Louisa with violence, her neighbors intervened. She told them how he had "knocked [me] around" and "forced [me] to stay with him." The neighbors "ran him away out of the neighborhood." A farmer who periodically employed Louisa said Watson came back to Louisa's home in the middle of the night and began "quarreling with her and called her a d—n bitch." To protect herself, Louisa "seized her gun" and, according to the farmer, "would have shot him if her daughter had not caught the gun."[54]

Louisa also fought back against a white farmer who physically assaulted her son. John A. Martin "struck" young Samuel on the head with a shovel as he was on his way to school. Witnesses reported that Martin hit the child with such force that he "knocked the blood out of the boy." Louisa confronted him as her neighbors watched, then filed a complaint with civil authorities. Several weeks later, Louisa "beat" Martin in court. In retaliation, John Martin compelled one of Louisa's daughters to go before the justice of the peace and file a complaint against her mother for fornicating with the Reverend James Bell.[55] Now the solicitor in Craven County, former pension claims agent George H. White indicted Louisa on charges of "fornication and adultery"; the case was adjudicated later that year and led to future problems with pension bureau administrators. This scandal further threatened to erode Louisa's standing in her community and isolate her from many of her neighbors, whom she relied on for support. As a single black woman raising five children in a mixed race farming community, Louisa Powers depended on the reciprocity and goodwill of her neighbors in times of trouble. Many of Louisa Powers's and Mary Jane Moore's decisions stemmed from the extreme challenges they faced as they coped with their widowhood in the postwar South.

For some years, Louisa Powers and Mary Jane Moore did not file petitions for survivors' benefits based on their standing as war widows. In the meantime, however, they and others cultivated ideas about themselves and the meaning of widowhood within their communities through their own experience. Long before they tried to adjust themselves to the Pension Bureau's definitions of moral behavior, they had formed judgments about what constituted worthy widowhood.

FREDERICK C. DOUGLASS

Pension Bureau officials suspended Edward W. Carpenter's license to represent veterans and their families to the bureau in 1873. They speculated that he had continued his business covertly through his dealings with Frederick C. Douglass. These officials interpreted the relationship between the two as one of convenience, in which Carpenter exercised all of the power. The chief of the Law Division said, "It is the common talk and belief in New Berne that Mr. Carpenter uses Mr. Douglass as a dummy, conducting the pension business under his name."[56] The commissioner held both Douglass and Carpenter responsible for the number of fraudulent cases originating from eastern North Carolina.

It is known to this Bureau that the white Mr. Carpenter and the colored Mr. Douglass have been inseparable in their business relations, so far as relates to the prosecutions of pension claims, since Douglass was admitted to practice; that they have made common use of the same offices; that Carpenter's former clients were turned over to Douglass, and that both men have worked in fleecing their dupes, but it has not been established that an actual, legal partnership has existed between them; on the contrary, the evidence so far obtained tends to show that there has been no actual division of legal fees, only a joint collection of illegal fees from the money derived from the first pension check in any given claim,—a far more profitable arrangement to both parties concerned.[57]

Bureau officials regarded Carpenter as the brains behind the entire operation: "The wide spread belief that he has and the fact that he has continued to practice before this Bureau by resorting to so transparent a subterfuge as the employment of Mr. Douglass tends to cast a grave suspicion upon him."[58] In fact, the relationship between Douglass and Carpenter was far more reciprocal than bureau officials understood. Douglass had an advantage over his white predecessors in the pension business: the respect of other members of the black community. That he was the son of Mary E. Norman, a union widow, gave Douglass special credibility among black veterans and their families.[59]

Born in Trenton, North Carolina, around 1830, Mary endured a series of family disruptions over the course of her enslavement in eastern North Carolina.[60] The first came at an early age, when she was separated from her parents, Marion and William Becton, most likely as a result of their owner's death and his heirs' business interests. Hardy Huggins, a slaveholder who lived about two miles from Trenton, purchased Mary around 1845. She later gave birth to her first child, a boy she called Fred, fathered by a man named Stalp Huggins. "I was not married to Stalp Huggins, the father of Fred Douglass, and have never seen him since Fred Douglass's Birth."[61] We can only speculate about Stalp's identity and Mary's relationship with him because she had little to say about him when she recounted her life history to a bureau examiner in a 1900 deposition. Nonetheless, the federal census records, coupled with the pension records, contain clues that shed light on Mary's and Frederick's lives.

In her 1900 deposition, Mary attested that she had been fifteen years old and a "slave to Hardy Huggins" at the time of her son Fred's birth. The Slave Schedule of the 1850 U.S. census lists Hardy Huggins as a resident of Jones County and owning three slaves: one black female aged twenty-three, and two black males, one aged five and the other aged two.[62] Mary's racial designation was listed as black or colored—which were interchangeable terms—on the federal censuses taken in 1870, 1880, 1900, and 1910.[63] She did not describe herself as mulatto—the conventional term used for any person with visibly mixed ancestry—in her application for a survivors' pension, nor did others use that term to describe her complexion or social identity in their testimony. Yet her son Frederick C. Douglass was identified as mulatto on the 1870 and 1920 manuscript censuses; the only time he was designated as black was on the 1910 census. Racial categorizations used in the federal census were applied inconsistently, and many individuals with biracial ancestry were listed as mulatto on one or more censuses but black on others. These were not self-descriptions but descriptions the census enumerator supplied, sometimes without seeing the individual.[64] This information suggests that Fred's father, Stalp Huggins, may have been of mixed race ancestry and may very well have been the enslaved son of his owner. While testifying in an investigation of her son's business practices eleven years earlier, Mary had referred to Stalp as her "former husband" but did not mention his name.[65] The record is incomplete, in part deliberately; as far as white slaveholders and the laws governing racial slavery were concerned, the paternity of slaves made no difference to their status.

Shortly after Mary gave birth to Fred, mother and child were sold to James C. Bryan, a farmer who lived in Pollocksville, an area of Jones County roughly two miles from where they had previously lived. Whether mother and son were sold together is not clear from the records. When Bryan died of consumption in 1850, Mary was "titled" to his son, Christopher.[66] He hired Mary out to David Scott, a mariner in Onslow County, roughly two miles from Swansboro, North Carolina.[67] While hired out to Scott, Mary gave birth to two girls, Laura and Martha. In 1900, she identified Scott as their father, a particularly eye-catching public revelation given that Scott's sister, Christian Willis, resided nearby on "So. Front Street" at the time of her deposition.[68] Other things Mary said about her intimate relationships in her deposition, coupled with what is known about white masters' sexual relations with enslaved black women, strongly suggest that this relationship was coerced. All enslaved women were unprotected against sexual abuse and rape. Under the law of slavery, indeed, the sexual violation of a slave woman was viewed solely as an offense against her owner, but only if he chose to complain. Nothing suggests that Christopher Bryan took issue with Scott for impregnating Mary. More importantly, we have no idea what either this relationship or her previous relationship with Huggins meant to Mary.

While hired out to Scott, Mary said, she had married a slave man, Dumar Hargett.[69] In her 1900 deposition, she described it as "slave marriage": "There was no ceremony but we got the consent of our masters."[70] Mary and Dumar, like most enslaved spouses, were subject to the control of their masters: they might live apart, be denied the opportunity to visit each other, be forcibly separated, or have their children taken from them. Mary and her husband had a daughter, Carrie, and another son, Godfre. When the war broke out, Dumar Hargett joined the Thirty-Seventh Regiment of the Union army but never returned to Mary. In 1884, he was "hung for killing a man name Fisher (colored) whose wife he was going with."[71]

Mary and her children fled to New Bern in 1862 and settled in the Trent River camp. The same year, she joined the Clinton Chapel AMEZ church in New Bern, where she married Turner Norman before he enlisted in the USCT. A shingler by trade, Norman found work in Plymouth, North Carolina, after he was discharged.[72] Mary's son Frederick may have enlisted in a black regiment, but his service remains a mystery. In affidavits and letters, he referred to his army service as "Capt of Lincoln Camp, No 1 Div. of Maryland."[73] In 1870, Turner Norman and "two other colored men" drowned in a boat on the Roanoke River, somewhere between Plymouth and Jamestown. The bodies were recovered months later.[74]

Ineligible for survivors' benefits under the government's general law system, which required widows to establish a link between the soldier's death and his wartime service, Mary and her daughter Carrie migrated to Warren, Rhode Island, in search of better wages. Warren is situated about fifty miles south of Worcester County, Massachusetts, where an activist black community aided the settlement of former slaves from New Bern during the wartime era.[75] She returned to New Bern for about a year and then went back to Warren, cleaning houses for about another year before moving to Providence. In the 1880s, Mary next moved to Brooklyn, New York, with Carrie, who worked as a live-in cook for a local storekeeper and his wife, while Mary worked as a housekeeper for a lawyer.[76] Sometime after 1885, Mary returned to New Bern without her daughter, who had since married, presumably to assist her son Frederick, whose wife Charlotte lay ill in the city "Asylum." Mary Norman's experience suggests that she regularly migrated to do seasonal work before she gained access to survivors' benefits. That same year, Frederick refiled a petition for survivors' benefits on his mother's behalf under the general law system.[77]

Frederick did well for himself in his mother's absence. Like his mother, Douglass joined the Clinton Chapel AMEZ church in New Bern's Fifth Ward. He learned to read and write, perhaps during the first years of freedom, and by 1870 he was teaching Bible classes at Clinton Chapel. He also taught in the "public schools of Craven County for more than ten years."[78]

Douglass may have belonged to one of New Bern's black lodges, presumably the King Solomon Masons. Over the years, in addition to teaching, he also worked as a barber, minister, and farmer.[79] He married a woman named Charlotte (Bryant), who is listed in his 1872 account records of the New Bern branch of the Freedmen's Bank. Described as "mulatto" on the 1880 census, Frederick had four children by Charlotte before she died.[80] Douglass remarried twice before he died in New Bern in 1928. His daughter Mamie attended Livingston College, an AMEZ institution in Salisbury, North Carolina, and his son Frederick Douglass Jr. migrated to New York and served in the military during World War I, returning to New Bern in 1958, the year he died.[81]

As Pension Bureau officials suspected, Frederick C. Douglass worked closely with Edward W. Carpenter throughout his time in the pension business. After all, despite Carpenter's disgrace in the Pension Bureau, he still held an important position among local white northerners. Carpenter may well have introduced Douglass to key professionals involved in the pension business, including William L. Palmer, Ethelbert Hubbs, and Henry G. Bates. Bates proved invaluable to New Bern's pension network because of his willingness to submit affidavits explaining the nature of the ailments from which diseased and disabled veterans suffered. A licensed medical examiner and one of the handful of white physicians who provided medical services to black soldiers and their families at the Marine Hospital in New Bern, he arrived in North Carolina in 1869. Bates, who was practicing medicine in New York when the war began, became a surgeon in the U.S. Army. After serving as medical director of the Emory Hospital in Washington, DC, for six months, he was sent to the front, where he ran a field hospital. After his second wife, Azariah, died in 1871, he remarried, this time to Ann Meadows, a resident of New Bern. Bates "gave medical advice gratis to the poor" for many years and had "hundreds of patients" in the city until he died in June 1890.[82]

By 1879, when Douglass filed his application with the U.S. Pension Bureau to become an approved claims agent, he was well connected to the social networks of freedpeople in New Bern, James City, and the rural areas of Craven County.[83] Six years later, Mary Lee, a thirty-five-year-old washerwoman, hired him. In addition to his mother, Mary Lee proved to be one of the most pivotal clients in his career as an agent.

Mary was born in Bertie County, North Carolina, and migrated to the Trent River settlement during the war. While there, she met young Simeon Lee, formerly enslaved by Edward Lee of Pasquotank County. In 1867, a year after Simeon was discharged, the couple married at Clinton Chapel AMEZ, with longtime acquaintances—including Frederick C. Douglass—attending the ceremony. Their son, born to the couple the following year, "died from diarrhea" when he was just one month old. Simeon, who suffered from chronic pain in his "legs and feet," died in early January 1870 without having applied for disability benefits. Mary began a new life on her own, working as a washerwoman, housekeeper, and farmhand. Sometime after 1870, she moved in with her stepfather on South Front Street, where black and white professionals and black veterans and their families were clustered.[84]

THE RISE OF BLACK AGENTS AND THE PENSION NETWORK IN EASTERN NORTH CAROLINA

Mary Lee's decision to hire agent Frederick C. Douglass was quite deliberate, for widows and veterans had many agents to choose from in eastern North Carolina. Between 1879 and 1920, eight black men worked as claims agents in New Bern, including the unflappable George H. White. Under the tutelage of William John Clarke, a former Confederate officer and retired judge, White studied law and gained his licensure through the state.[85] Douglass trained several of the men who worked in New Bern's pension network.[86] Most had been enslaved, though one was free before the Civil War. Two other black men who became claims agents were born after the war; at least one was the son of a black veteran. All these men resided in New Bern, which gave them firsthand knowledge of the local community, its culture, and black veterans and their families.[87]

A panoply of institutions rooted in black community life produced and authenticated the black male entrepreneurs who came of age in New Bern after the war. Some had been enslaved in North Carolina, served in the Union army, were literate, and had strong ties to religious, mutual aid, and fraternal organizations. They built relationships with white business leaders, municipal officials, and federal bureaucrats. These agents often lived on the same streets or in the same neighborhoods as the war widows they served.

Phillip Lee, for instance, enlisted in the USCT in New Bern, and when he returned from the war, he filed paperwork for a pension on his own behalf. Described as "a leader among his own people," Lee served as a political activist, a minister, and an educator in James City.[88] Benjamin Whitfield, an ambitious eighteen-year-old fish dealer, took the oath of allegiance at the Pension Bureau "to enable him to prosecute claims against the United States" government. Whitfield "prosecuted a limited number of claims" on the government before his health began to fail. He appears to have established his pension business with the assistance of Philip Wiggins, the former army recruiter with whom Whitfield lived before his death in 1886. Andrew J. Marshall, who had also served in the USCT, filed paperwork to gain licensure in the bureau in 1886.[89] While Marshall managed to represent several cases on his own, he also worked in concert with Douglass and Carpenter. Born in Hyde County and raised on Roanoke Island, Emanuel Merrick, one of New Bern's black grocers, occasionally worked on pension cases during this period of transition in the local pension network. Merrick's employer, Sheriff Ami Dennison, may have given him insight into the logistics of the pension system, as Dennison also appears to have dabbled in the business.[90]

Black veterans and war widows in North Carolina gained more influence as black men from North Carolina secured elected positions and became claims agents. James E. O'Hara, a New York–born black attorney who represented the Second Federal Congressional District of eastern North Carolina (which included Craven County) dabbled in the claims business before he died in the early twentieth century. O'Hara partnered with his son, Raphaela, but occasionally consulted agent Douglass. Douglass, Alfred Small, and Andrew J. Marshall identified themselves as ministers and claims agents in the pension records. Black women relied on these black and white pension professionals to sustain their communication with the federal government. These black grocers, undertakers, ministers, postmen, lawyers, policemen, schoolteachers, and municipal officials interacted daily with their clients and shared more important personal connections with them than did the earlier generation of white entrepreneurs who had handled their business in the immediate postwar years.

By the 1890s, Frederick C. Douglass dominated the pension business in eastern North Carolina, acting as claims agent and interacting with the Pension Bureau directly on behalf of a poor, black, and increasingly female clientele (figure 4.1). As his caseload expanded, Douglass groomed his son-in-law, Charles Cox, to enter the business. Although Cox worked on claims for at least fifteen years, the Pension Bureau never recognized him as an attorney. The pension business could be lucrative, as the government paid agents $10 for a straightforward case and $25 for a particularly difficult one. As of January 1, 1892, Douglass had collected $880 in fees from the federal government for his work on behalf of disabled veterans and war widows.[91]

Local businesses catered to New Bern's black Union widows at Douglass and Carpenter's behest. Merritt Whitely, a black undertaker, supplied caskets and conducted funeral services for many of their clients. Nearly three years after Whitely buried one war widow's husband, only three dollars of

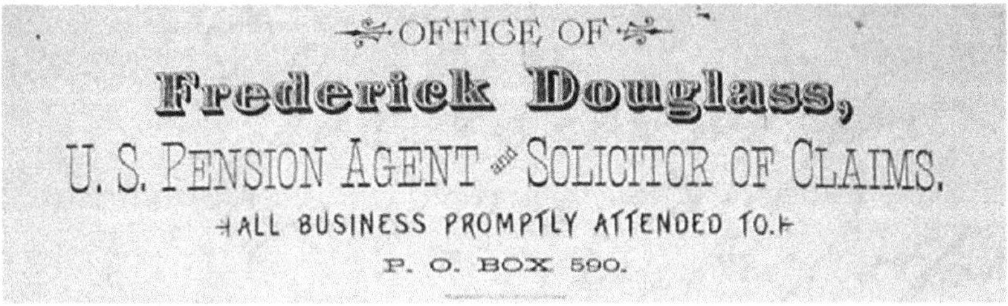
—OFFICE OF—
Frederick Douglass,
U. S. PENSION AGENT and SOLICITOR OF CLAIMS.
ALL BUSINESS PROMPTLY ATTENDED TO.
P. O. BOX 590.

Figure 4.1. Frederick C. Douglass's letterhead. From pension file of Caroline Sanders (widow's claim 340222), Civil War Pension Index: General Index to Pension Files, Record Group 15: Records of the Department of Veteran Affairs, National Archives and Records Administration.

the bill had been paid. "I have not pressed its collection," Whitely explained, "because I don't care to incur the enmity of Douglass or Carpenter, as it would injure my business by their sending their patronage to other parties."[92]

From Douglass's new home at 74 New South Front Street, he could see directly across the Trent River to James City, now a thriving center of black life. This enclave had its own post office, grocery store, and several churches. Among its 1,044 black residents, 60 percent (622) were women; the gender imbalance reflected deaths among soldiers and veterans. In New Bern, the wives of disabled veterans worked inside and outside their homes and, when necessary, acted as heads of households. Black soldiers' widows, who were generally unable to read and write, lived on their survivors' pension, about eight dollars a month, and took work when and where they could get it. Those who embraced the ethic of thrift, hard work, and piety were considered the "respectable poor."[93] Residents gossiped about some black women who spent their money on men, clothes, and good times.

THE STRENGTH OF COMMUNITY

Black neighborhoods in the Fifth Ward and James City constituted the core of the grassroots pension network black women mobilized to engage the government (map 4.1). Residents who labored as fishermen, turpentine workers, craftsmen, lumbermen, domestics, midwives, household workers, field hands, and cooks knew the intimate details of who married whom, when women gave birth, and their family histories. These neighbors measured how soldiers' wives cared for their husbands during periods of illness. They intervened and interpreted intimate partner violence and attended church with one another. As active participants in the grassroots network,

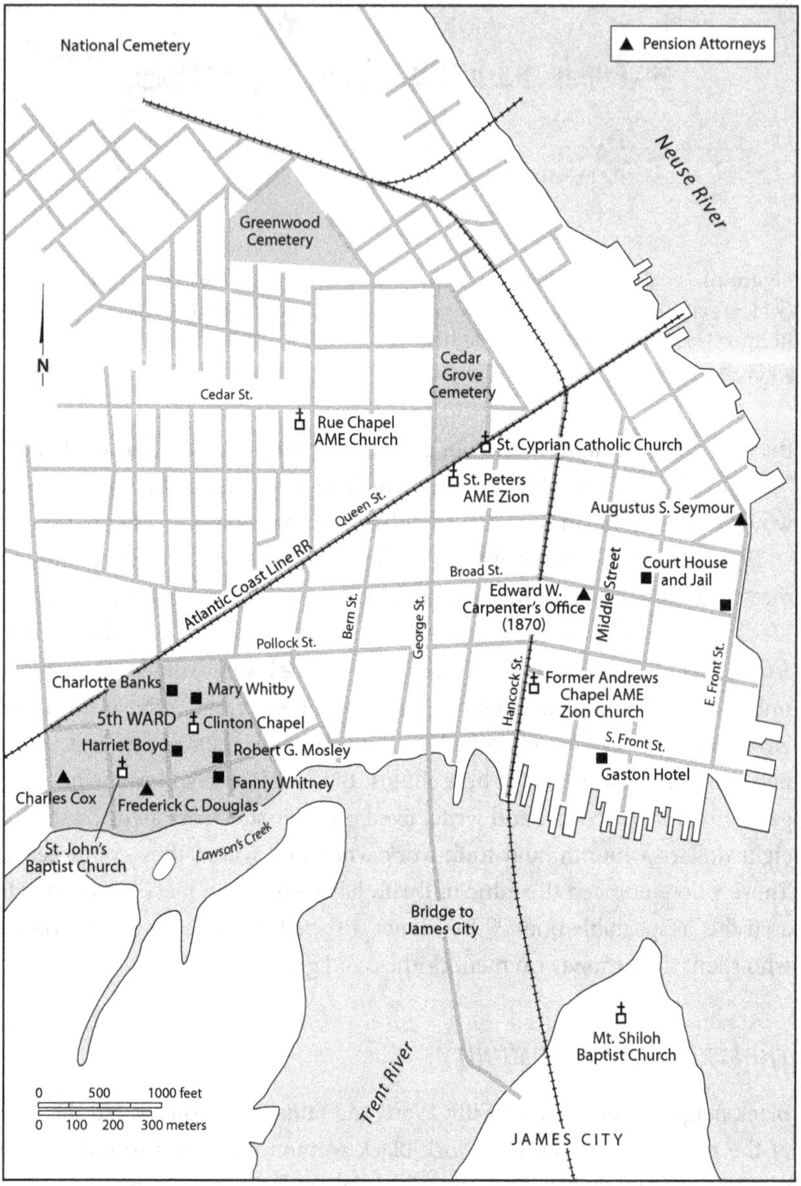

Map 4.1. Black Union widows and claims agents in New Bern, North Carolina, ca. 1870–1880. Map created by William L. Nelson.

war widows shared their individual histories with local claims agents. When special examiners arrived, members of the pension network guarded secrets; they came forward as witnesses. Neighbors also reported and surveilled black Union widows. Indeed, as Nancy Bercaw writes, "African Americans invested their communities with an active role in mediating relationships, displacing individual authority."[94]

Much of black people's communication about benefits for Union soldiers' families took place outside the bureau's purview, within black community institutions. They often exchanged information about the application process at black-owned businesses and local institutions. They attended meetings and public gatherings to learn about the federal pension system. Washington Spivey, a black farmer, merchant, and postmaster of James City Township (a political appointment made by the federal government), regularly helped black women fill out their paperwork. His office quickly became a meeting place for pensioners, who viewed him as a community leader.[95]

Churches functioned as a space not only for personal and spiritual development but also for sharing information about the application process and for advancing the full citizenship that black people envisioned. Scholars of African American history recognize religious institutions as sites for political meetings and circulating information within black communities. This was especially true in the South and in the case of the pension system. As one beneficiary recalled, "Papers came out saying that all widows of soldiers were entitled to money so I put in for it, several others tried at the same time. The notice was read from all the churches that there was money for all who applied for it."[96] The Reverend John S. Johnson, who led the historic St. John's Baptist Church, emerges as far more than a reassuring minister who testified on behalf of his congregants during the examination phase of the claims process. In 1881, along with other prominent black leaders in the Fifth Ward, Johnson urged cooks, washerwomen, nurses, farm laborers and all classes of colored people to organize a labor union for the "regulation and maintenance of wages."[97] This militancy spilled over into the grassroots pension network.

In black majority neighborhoods like James City, where black Union veterans and their families lived within "speaking distance" of one another, information about the pension application process traveled by word of mouth. Across the river in New Bern, where blacks lived in clusters throughout the city, news about pensions and special examiners circulated on the streets. Veterans came forward to support the wives of deceased soldiers and in many instances informed them of their eligibility for benefits.[98] Joseph Dunkin, who had served alongside Jacob Moore, persuaded Mary Jane Moore to file a petition for survivors' benefits on her return to the city.[99]

Although these communication networks provided remarkably accurate information, some women remained unaware of the application process for several years and expressed confusion about whether they were eligible for benefits. Mariah Hassell said that she did not know other women who were receiving pensions and did not apply for one until her friend "encouraged her to do so"; "I did not know that I could get my pension under law," she explained.[100] Sarah Latham stated, "The reason I never made application for pension as his [Jesse's] widow is that I never thought I was entitled to a pension as he was not drawing one. I thought a soldier had to draw a pension before his wife or widow did."[101] According to Sarah, although Jesse was a disabled veteran, "We knew nothing about pensions then during his lifetime."[102]

Securing community endorsement of women's applications for survivors' benefits was an important aspect of the pension network. Freedwomen could not present legal documentation of their marriages and birth dates, so they spent a good deal of their time corralling witnesses to come forward on their behalf. Black Union widows in eastern North Carolina used their own social networks to meet the bureau's evidentiary standards. Female witnesses were especially important since women's knowledge of marriage, family history, and extended kin could be helpful to those whose family ties had been disrupted by wartime migrations and who were still searching for loved ones. As black veterans died, women's knowledge of wartime events became increasingly crucial to widows' cases.

Reciprocity and goodwill, which were central to impoverished black women's daily existence, stood them in good stead as they sought pensions. Women such as Mary Norman and Mary Lee, who had settled in the Trent River camp outside New Bern at the onset of the war, emerged as key negotiators in the pension application process because they could provide information about individuals' intimate lives. Shortly after Mary Lee reached New Bern in 1862, she met Mary Norman. Nearly thirty years later, Lee helped Mary Norman establish her claim. In 1891, she testified for Mary Norman during a special examination: "I became acquainted with Turner Norman and his wife, Mary E. Norman . . . in 1862 at New Bern, NC."[103] The information that Mary Lee and Mary Norman traded about the application process, special examiners, and claims agents was evident in their testimony for each other.[104] Similarly, after Hettie Wendly hired Frederick Douglass, she enlisted the support of several women she had met in James City during the Civil War. Some then applied for pensions themselves: as one woman said, "Hettie got me and

Amanda Skinner to go to the office of Douglass."[105] These women gave testimony on behalf of Hettie Wendly over the course of her case. By witnessing for one another, black women gained recognition from the Pension Bureau not only as worthy widows but also as deserving citizens. For veterans' widows like Mary Lee, who did manage to secure witnesses and raise the funds necessary to petition for survivors' benefits, linking medical cause of death to wartime service sometimes proved impossible. Though Joseph Harvey's military records established his early discharge based on disease contracted during his army service, his widow encountered much difficulty establishing her claim under the general law pension system. She gained admittance to the pension roster in April 1888.[106] Medical treatment, much less evidence of such treatment, was extremely difficult for women to obtain. Lana Burney said sadly, "I did not have any physician to attend to him in his last sickness."[107]

Many other women could not apply for survivors' benefits because their husbands' death had no connection to the war. Tragedy struck Matilda Wells, an Elizabeth City freedwoman who had lived in the Trent River settlement, when her veteran husband, Toney, drowned while crossing the Neuse River. Matilda identified Toney's body nearly six weeks later because she recognized her husband's "jacket and the shirt."[108] The tragedy left Matilda and her four children in despair and ineligible to apply for survivors' benefits under the general law system. Widows of veterans who did not die of a service-related injury became eligible for pensions only in 1890, under the service law pension system.[109] Prior to this law, these widows had to cope with their precarious situation without survivors' benefits.

FREDERICK DOUGLASS AND THE CLAIMS-MAKING PROCESS

While Douglass was highly respected in New Bern as an influential religious leader and teacher, he still had to exhibit his professional acumen to his black clients. His early work on behalf of black veterans and their families focused almost entirely on vindicating the claims of black Union widows who had been suspended from the pension rolls during the 1870s cohabitation investigations. Women such as Julia Ann Foy, Rosanna Fosgate, Dilcy Jarmon, Matilda Simmons, and Maria Counts turned to Douglass for assistance.[110] He also helped women like Mary Ann Sleight, whose petition for survivors' benefits stalled when the Freedmen's Bureau left the state in 1870. Douglass's willingness to sort out particularly messy cases cemented his reputation as the leading black agent among black veterans and soldiers' widows in New Bern and throughout eastern North Carolina.

Rosanna Fosgate disputed agent Ragsdale's claim that she had remarried by explaining that she had begun working on a farm outside New Bern at the close of the war. She also provided witnesses' statements from respected black ministers Ellis Lavender and Amos York to show that she had married in 1873, not in 1866, as Ragsdale had reported. Rosanna managed to collect a small amount for a two-month period of her widowhood.[111] Some women lost their cases despite Douglass's efforts. Dilcy Jarmon insisted that the commissioner of pensions had mistakenly revoked her benefits on the grounds that she too had married under the North Carolina Marriage Act, but the commissioner refused to reverse his decision.[112]

Douglass routinely solicited the support of elected officials who represented the citizens of the Eighth Congressional District, which included Craven County. When Douglass suffered setbacks in his mother's case in 1880, he contacted James E. O'Hara. In the second session of the Forty-Eighth Congress, O'Hara introduced House Resolution 6192 to award benefits to Mary Norman, the widow of Turner Norman, but was unable to garner enough votes. Mary was eventually granted a pension in 1890 under the more liberal service law pension system, which did not require widows to link their late soldier-husband's death to his military service.[113]

Douglass used every tool at his disposal to move Lana Burney's case along. Fed up with what he perceived to be the commissioner of pensions' negligence, Douglass apprised Thomas Settle, a young Republican member of the North Carolina House of Representatives, of the widow's difficulties.[114] Settle filed an inquiry into the matter with the commissioner of pensions, but nothing came of it.[115] Douglass then prodded Republican U.S. senator Jeter C. Pritchard from North Carolina, who served between 1895 and 1903, to look into Lana's case. The commissioner denied Lana's claim because of her "inability to show . . . satisfactory evidence [of] the soldier's death."[116]

Professional black men's ability to gain a foothold in the pension system and the maturation of the pension network across the South largely resulted from black men's personal ambition combined with the endorsement of white community leaders, as well as black women's continual demands for recognition within the Pension Bureau. By the time their applications reached the bureau, black women had already built relationships with the claims agents, court clerks, public notaries, doctors, and local government officials, as well as witnesses in their neighborhoods. They had developed their own self-possessed public presence alongside the men who represented them to the federal government.

5

Encounters with the State

Black Women and Special Examiners

Black women's encounters with the Pension Bureau's special examiners exposed them to the agency's language and concepts. Through repeated meetings they learned bureaucratic jargon and harnessed it to reinforce their claims on the government. In the process some adopted the agency's understanding of Union widowhood and moved away from the concept of widowhood they had cultivated in their communities and among their peers. Their meetings with special examiners required mastery of the agency's formulations of marriage, dependency, virtue, and honor. Black Union widows understood their encounters with examiners as an opportunity to speak directly to government officials, refute erroneous evidence and inferences, and shape the outcome of their case. Some used special examinations to resist the power and intimidation of claims agents, who purportedly represented their interests.

The 1880s marked a time of change at the federal Pension Office. To keep up with the onslaught of claimants—black, white, and increasingly female—the office expanded and subdivided functions: Mail, Record, and Adjudicating; Review Board; Army and Navy Survivors; Law; Medical; Certificate; Stationery and Accounts; Special Examination; and Agents.[1] New laws extended the statute of limitations for filing claims, and the agency reorganized and introduced new guidelines for the special examination process, which altered the way new applicants and beneficiaries engaged the office. As a result of this restructuring and a new emphasis on rights, prospective widows began to make arguments on the basis of "rights" and equality.

The civil rights agenda that had prevailed throughout Reconstruction crumbled at the federal level. Waves of violence, fraud, and legal repression prevented black men from voting in the disputed elections of 1877. Federal courts severely limited the reach of the Fourteenth Amendment. In a final blow, the Court struck down the 1875 Civil Rights Act in an 1883 ruling. With the reestablishment of racial hierarchies and limitations on black citizenship, it was significant that black women were able to testify in the federal pension system, which was a rare arena in which black women could claim equal treatment under the law.

Black women, both freeborn and formerly enslaved, showed a determined resolve to secure survivors' benefits and to fulfill the gender expectations of their social world. In their communities, respectability meant attending church, raising children, and contributing to the family income. In front of the special examiners, however, they might present themselves as dependent wives. Their definition of worthy widowhood occupied an ambiguous territory between a necessary independence and what many examiners and community members perceived as tactless and insensitive treatment of their husbands.

DEPICTIONS OF PENSION FRAUD AND NORTHERN INTOLERANCE

Government officials condemned claims agents who aggressively pursued black Union widows' business. The national press characterized claims agents in the South as perpetrators of fraud and exploitation. Sensational cases of "pension swindling" appeared in the *New York Times* and *Washington Post*.[2] The media's portrait of black Union widows being taken advantage of by traveling pension swindlers positioned them as victims or even coconspirators.[3] This imagery suggested that public resources allocated to black women and their agents through the pension bureau represented fiscal waste. As of 1890, nearly 40 percent of the nation's budget went to support disabled veterans and their widows. That these discursive renderings gained traction in national and local newspapers coincided with the ratcheting up of suspensions under the act of 1882.

The end of Reconstruction preceded the reorganization of the pension system and the creation of the Special Examination Division by just a few years, yet some of the same impulses driving the changes in the Pension Office figured centrally in the rhetoric and power relations involved in the broader political shift. Eligibility criteria revolving around gendered and class-based notions of what constituted a worthy family limited the women's ability to petition the government successfully for survivors' aid and to maintain their position on the pension roster. The pension benefits of black Union widows were curtailed, along with other civil, economic, and citizenship rights, and these changes were justified by familiar charges of favoritism to black southerners, marriage fraud, corruption, and excessive public expenditure.

THE TRANSFORMATION OF THE PENSION EXAMINATION PROCESS

A general frustration with the government's largesse, accusations of fraud aimed at beneficiaries and pension professionals, and rampant racism led to the reorganization of the U.S. Pension Bureau and the creation of the Special Examination Division in 1881. The changes reflected Commissioner James A. Bentley's Reconstruction-era recommendations for a change in how bureau clerks vetted applications in the early stages of the process. This new type of examination placed all Union widows, but especially freedwomen, under close inspection. Their inability to provide standard documentary evidence of their marriages meant that black women applicants were regularly subjected to intrusive investigations of their intimate lives. Special examinations thus became a regular feature of their cases.

Commissioner W. W. Dudley, who followed Bentley, had convinced Congress that institutional reform was necessary to deal with the growing volume of claims in the years following the passage of the Arrears Act (1879). The agency's clerical staff was ill equipped to handle such demand, which resulted in lengthy delays.[4] Dudley recommended a larger clerical force. With the existing staff of 741 clerks, he argued, it would take nearly ten years for the agency to evaluate its current cases. Congress set aside nearly $2 million to hire more staff, and the clerical force ballooned to more than 1,500 in 1882 (figure 5.1).[5]

Examiners would now have the authority to evaluate the public and private conduct of pensioners at the community level. These investigations were conducted with much of the formality of a trial. Before showing up at a widow's home, examiners were obliged to issue a Notice of Special Examination, informing the claimant of her rights and privileges during the investigation. Widows had the right to be present during the examination, to be represented by their claims agent, and to rebut evidence. If the petitioner chose to be represented, her attorney had the right to cross-examine the Pension Bureau's witnesses. The special examiner was required to transcribe depositions and read them back to the witnesses to ensure accuracy before the

Figure 5.1. Pension Bureau Special Examiners, 1904. Brady-Handy Photograph Collection, Prints and Photographs Division, Library of Congress, https://hdl.loc.gov/loc.pnp/cwpbh.03423.

testimony was signed and entered into the record. Afterward, the examiner translated and interpreted the validity of black women's claims on the government in the application process.

At the same time, agency officials revised the *General Instructions to Special Examiners of the United States Pension Office* (1881). In the preface, Commissioner Dudley noted the "great hardships occasioned by the methods of inquiry" in previous years. The new set of guidelines was prepared with the goal of "eliminating from the practice" of the Pension Bureau "every objectionable feature of the secret investigation."[6] Another major change came in the form of an act designed to shore up the agency's policy on remarriage.

Lawmakers remained committed to some provision for widows but felt it necessary to close perceived gaps in a system that allowed for fraud. On August 2, 1882, Senator Thomas C. Platt (R-NY) presented a bill to amend section 4702 of the Revised Pension Statutes of the United States.[7] The first amendment dealt with Union widows who had been in violation of the law after the death of their husbands. If the widow in question lost her benefits because of immoral conduct but supported the children, the amendment would allow the children to draw the pension.[8] The second amendment clarified that "notorious and adulterous cohabitation by a widow" would terminate her pension. When Senator Henry G. Davis (D-WV) inquired whether the bill would require "additional expenditures," Platt answered concisely and confidently, "Nothing." Instead, Platt assured Davis that the Committee on Pensions would "diminish the expenditure." "There are cases now where the widow, when her husband dies, goes forward in violation of law, saying nothing about the death of her husband and draws pension." The present "remedy is to bring suit to recover that amount." This bill would "make the children's pension date from the time when the widow ceased to draw pension in violation of the law."[9]

This reform had a profound effect on how the federal government viewed Civil War widows.[10] The Pension Bureau policy had had no special category for women who had sex with men outside legal marriage. Examiners spoke of marriage, cohabitation, and remarriage, but without precision. Women who had intimate nonmarital relationships were regarded as engaging in a conspiracy to defraud the government.[11] The 1882 law aimed to close the gap between cohabitation and remarriage in pension law. The new emphasis on morality and sexual activity, especially as it was expressed in the press, made it appear that sexual immorality was a special problem among black women, politicizing what had been an administrative issue and creating a sense of moral panic about "colored widows." Making sexual morality a measure of women's deservedness and worthiness in law and practice denied widows who accepted survivors' benefits any semblance of a private life.[12]

Lawmakers viewed soldiers' widows who remarried, engaged in nonmarital intimate relationships, or had children while on the pension roster as a critical problem. The bureau's rules strictly forbade these types of relationships, but it had no set of uniform investigative procedures to adjudicate cases of perceived sexual immorality, so-called illegitimate children, and concealed marriages.[13] The 1882 law remedied this oversight, and women responded to the new policy. Some women elected to collect benefits from the government rather than marry the men in their lives. Others entered into nonlegal arrangements or opted to conceal their personal lives on entering the pension system. Regardless of woman's circumstance, the law of 1882 was far-reaching and retroactive.

SPECIAL EXAMINERS' GUIDELINES FROM 1876 TO 1881

Despite the Pension Bureau's high evidentiary standards for benefits, the increasing presence of black female beneficiaries led officials to clarify the protocols examiners should follow when handling the cases of "colored claimants." The recommendations revolved around these women's marital histories to ensure that only one woman could obtain benefits through her relationship with a given soldier.

On some questions, the examiners' guidelines offered a level of understanding and nuance concerning the experiences and situations of formerly enslaved petitioners. Recognizing the difficulty that freedwomen had in documenting their marriages and life histories, agency officials continued the Reconstruction-era practice of obtaining the testimony of the woman's former owner and "the fellow slaves of both the soldier and the claimant."[14] While officials seemed to appreciate communication from all parties, they ultimately treated the testimony of white deponents as more credible than that of black witnesses.

Freedwomen and their children were singled out in the "fifty-sixth" item of a large section of the *General Instructions* handbook, which was devoted exclusively to "colored claimants."

> Colored claimants (widows) adopt for the time being . . . children not their own, or substitute other children for those of their own who are dead, in order to obtain the increase allowed for minor children. . . . In some cases . . . it will be found upon careful examination, that the claimant was in no way related to the soldier, but has been picked up by interested parties to represent the widow or some other relative.[15]

Although crude in its delivery, this statement is partly true. Some freedwomen did adopt children, but their motives were not necessarily self-interested. When freedwoman Mary Counts applied for survivors' benefits, she named "a small boy" on her petition whom she and her deceased husband Caesar had adopted after Caesar's first wife was abruptly sold and sent away. In later years, Mary explained her reasoning to an examiner: "I understood the child was entitled to a pension as the child was raised by Caesar and myself."[16] Motherhood, in Mary Counts's view, was a matter of "claiming" and support and not necessarily of biology. In making this argument, Mary directly challenged the agency's construction of motherhood.

The *General Instructions* handbook delineated how to ascertain the paternity of black women's children: "Examiners should see all the children for whom pension is claimed. . . . Their color may sometimes indicate whether they are the children of the soldier and the claimant." Based on their observation, too, examiners were supposed to guess the children's "probable age," to identify whether they were too young to be the dead soldier's offspring. Examiner Dow McClain scrutinized paternity and the distribution of money paid to Eda Coleman, an ex-slave and veteran's widow. Prior to marrying Isaac Coleman, on whose service she claimed a pension, Eda was married to Thomas Wilson, a free black man, and bore several children.[17] Pension Bureau officials therefore sought to ensure the paternity of the three children Eda received a pension for in 1871. The questions are not recorded in her deposition, but Eda's answers suggest the examiner may have inquired about her sexual history: "I certain never had more than one man at a time. I am as certain that Isaac is the father of Mary as I am that I am her mother. No one ever told me that Mary was not the child of Isaac. All the plantation people knew that Isaac was named Coleman."[18] Eda maintained her standing on the pension roster until she died in 1904.

With these guidelines, the commissioner of pensions endowed examiners with the power to invoke difference based on race and status while simultaneously linking black female claimants to a powerful legacy of enslavement. Freedwomen did not shy away from their former status, but they recalled these legacies for different purposes.

SPECIAL EXAMINERS IN EASTERN NORTH CAROLINA

Informed about the law of 1882 and fortified with copies of the *General Instructions*, the examiners—all white males—brought their own ideas about marriage, morality, womanhood, and race to their interpretation of the law and application of the rules. Their understanding of Union widowhood and personal attitudes and beliefs necessarily played a critical role in their assessment of black women's claims on the government.[19]

Special examiners assigned to states other than their own were common in black communities across the South. In New Bern, they set up offices at the post office or rented office space from the likes of James E. O'Hara on Craven Street and Sarah Oxly's Ice Cream Parlor on Broad Street, which was next door to E. W. Carpenter's office.[20] They lodged at the Albert Hotel at the center of the city and interviewed witnesses on the streets. They traveled back and forth between New Bern and majority-black James City to investigate black women's cases. The examiners who appear most frequently in the pension files of women under examination in New Bern include S. M. Arnell (Tennessee), Rodney Chip (Colorado), Emmett D. Gallion (Pennsylvania), Charles Gilpin (Kentucky), Thomas Goethe (South Carolina), W. L. Harris (New York), Dow McClain (Kansas), H. P. Maxwell (Tennessee), William Porter (Massachusetts), J. O'C. Roberts (Alabama), I. C. Stockton (Illinois), H. F. Shontz (Ohio), C. D. McSorley (New York), and Grafton Tyler (West Virginia).[21] Over time, the black residents of New Bern came to know these men by name and called on them when it suited their own purposes.

Special examiners were often highly suspicious of black witnesses. They regularly commented on the inappropriateness of freedpeople's behavior, assumptions, and testimony. Over the course of a special examination, examiners rated witness testimony on a scale that ranged from "good" to "bad" and assigned a letter value.[22] An A was equivalent to a "good" rating, while an F meant that the witness was unreliable. Examiners often described black witnesses as "densely ignorant," biased, and incapable of offering reliable facts in an investigation.[23] One examiner complained that the racial politics of eastern North Carolina made it difficult to assess the honesty of the black or white witnesses: "I must say that it is especially difficult to fix a really correct rating here for colored claimants and witnesses, if you ask the vast majority of white people, they class them all alike as 'unreliable' and if you seek information amongst their own people they are all 'As.'"[24] Some examiners tried to strike a balance when assessing black witnesses. "In way of parentheses," one wrote, "I will state that, from a lifetime acquaintance with the negro, he has no idea as to dates, but his statements, if he tells the truth, may be depended on as a true and correct exposition of events happening."[25] Some took the time to build relations with the local population to gain the community's confidence. On arriving in New Bern, one examiner wrote, "I was fortunate in bringing . . . several introductions," so "I think reliable sources of information, or nearly so, will be open to me."[26]

Examiners described women's character using such labels as "conspirators," "defiant," and "untruthful" to describe women who they believed had committed perjury to get on the pension rolls.[27] Having a male companion or boarders, guests, furniture, and clothing that did not conform to the special examiner's expectations could convince him that a woman was "unfit" or "unworthy." Women who were believed to be sexually intimate with men who were not their husbands were characterized as "prostitutes," "women of the town," or just plain "immoral."[28] All these traits defied the characteristics of worthy widowhood, much less womanhood.

"The ordinary colored woman is devoid of virtue and her people will not testify against her."[29] This statement, buried in an examiner's report in one woman's case file, contributed to making black women's behavior appear pathological within the federal pension system, thereby severely limiting black women's chances to secure survivors' benefits. The ratings that examiners gave black women were affected by the women's increasing knowledge of Pension Bureau laws and their sophisticated ability to navigate the system. Women came well prepared when they met with the examiners. When examiner John Cole met with Maria Little in 1888, he immediately sized her up as "a yellow Colored woman of stout physical appearance and having about the average mental capacity of her class, neither educated, or well informed or able to express herself clearly."[30] Little, however, met examiner Cole with a firm understanding of the applicable laws and her own fully developed concept of honorable widowhood. She told Cole that she had not "remarried or cohabited with any man" and that she could "prove" all that she "had stated by good witnesses."[31] Examiner W. F. Aycock interviewed pensioner Hettie Wendly, a self-described housekeeper and farmer, and gave her high marks. Hettie more than likely used the time between the initial notification from the Pension Bureau and the meeting to prepare herself. "The claimant," Aycock wrote, "is neat and tidy in her appearance and bears all evidence of a hard worker."[32] Though impoverished, both Maria Little and Hettie Wendly were knowledgeable about how to stake their claim to survivors' benefits.

Examiners questioned the practices and protocols of the local pension network, particularly the practice of paying witnesses small sums of money (one to two dollars) to take time off work to file affidavits. A black laborer demanded that one woman "pay for his time."[33] Mary Franklin, who made her living "picking cotton," said that one of her witnesses "wouldn't testify" unless she paid him one dollar. She later revealed to a local examiner that she had paid all her witnesses: "Oh, yes sir, I promised to pay my witnesses before they testified and they were of course looking for something."[34] When asked if her attorney "advised" her to pay her witnesses, Mary responded that she had told them "I would pay them after I got my money."[35] Ann M. Cotton paid the eleven witnesses who appeared before the public notary "two dollars apiece" and another woman "one dollar."[36] Seven James City residents and invalid pensioners gave affidavits and depositions during two separate special examinations on Hettie Wendly's behalf.[37]

The reasons that a black working person and a professional person demanded fees were not the same. One physician resented having to testify before an examiner without receiving payment for his time. Charles Mason, a white physician who provided medical services for a black veteran in New Harlow, proved to be "a most unwilling witness." According to the examiner, Mason "kept up a sort of running quarrel" during his deposition "about receiving no pay for work he did in pension cases." Mason expected the examiner "to pay him for his affidavit" just as his black clients had.[38]

THE EXAMINATION PROCESS AND THE COMMUNITY

The examination phase of the pension application process required the cooperation and participation of the community writ large, as special examiners often summoned men, women, and children who knew the claimant to come forward and testify. Endorsement of black Union widows by family, neighbors, and employers was an especially important aspect of the application process. Community support reflected the ethos of mutuality that played out in other arenas of black community life. All this suggests the significance and seriousness with which most blacks understood the meaning of black men's and women's wartime sacrifice.

Protecting women's prospects for receiving a pension was a communal effort. The case of sixty-seven-year-old Mary Kent is instructive. Mary successfully misled examiner F. W. Galbraith when her case entered the special examination phase fifteen years after her husband, Henry Kent, died of "remittent fever." Galbraith collected detailed information about Mary's intimate life from her neighbors. Her neighbors, most of whom were freeborn and had resided in New Bern before 1861, eagerly attested to her moral conduct. A woman offered a detailed description of Henry and Mary's marriage ceremony: "I was present at the marriage. It took place here in this town: he was a white preacher who married them: she had never been married before."[39] A man said that "she had never been married nor lived with a man as his wife [and] has always been a woman of good reputation."[40] So impressed was examiner Galbraith that he remarked in his 1889 report, "I do not see the slightest reason for any further examination on any point nor really why it was ever sent out." The Pension Bureau eventually awarded Mary Kent a pension of eight dollars a month under the general law pension system. Mary and her neighbors, however, had concealed one very important detail from the examiner: Mary Kent had been recognized as the wife of George H. House, whom she had cared for until just before he died in the Craven County Poorhouse in September 1882.

Although many of the people who testified in Mary's case lived close to her, none hinted at her relationship with George during the investigation. It seems quite likely that Kent's neighbors were cognizant of her living situation but did not wish to reveal these details to the government when the stakes were so high. Since local black churches had their own procedures for prosecuting fornication and adultery, residents may have felt it unnecessary to bring the full gaze of white government officials into the homes of poor black women in their community. Perhaps Mary apprised her neighbors of the agency rules on cohabitation after the examiner notified her that the investigation was scheduled to take place. If this is true, then they might have known that any mention of her living situation—married or not—would have raised the level of suspicion, influenced examiner Galbraith's perception of Mary's worthiness, and jeopardized her ability to collect survivors' benefits. It is also possible that these men and women believed that Mary deserved to collect a pension regardless of her subsequent relationship. Rather than say anything that would risk Mary's ability to collect desperately needed benefits, these residents may have believed it more important to toe the community's line. In the end, Mary's neighbors upheld her claim to Union widowhood even though she was known as Bess House in her neighborhood.[41]

Neighbors had no problem exposing the behavior of women they deemed unworthy. When examiner J. Speed Smith opened an investigation to assess "the general merits" of Mary Ann Simmons's case, Simmons swore that she had remained single until she married veteran Alfred Bailey.[42] Over the course of Smith's investigation, he learned from Mary Ann's neighbors that she had actually married a man named Frank Williams in 1877. Williams died a year later. With ample testimony documenting her relationship with Williams, Mary Ann's assertion that she had not been involved with any other man until she married Bailey became shaky.[43] Under direct questioning, she explained, "Yes sir. I do know that I told you a falsehood but I never considered that I was married [to Frank Williams] he never done me any good."[44] Mary Ann managed to collect pension benefits from the time her widowhood began in 1877 to 1879, the year she married Frank Williams.[45]

Pension examiners' reliance on local testimony revealed mounting tensions between soldiers' widows and their neighbors. An adverse character report could jeopardize an otherwise positive case. Special examinations, then, could be a mechanism of social punishment, which made it difficult for examiners to discern just how accurate these characterizations were. Jealousy and envy were part of the claimants' and witnesses' very human relationships. Some believed, however, that benefits should be granted to women who labored and upheld community values regardless of their personal choices and intimate histories. Black women's autonomy, their standing as Civil War widows, and the meaning of Union widowhood in their neighborhoods increasingly became points of contention.[46] For a time, black New Bernians resisted the Pension Bureau's construct of honorable widowhood and its rigid definitions of marriage, family, and sexual morality as the primary indicators for women's worthiness to collect survivors' benefits.

LOUISA POWERS ENCOUNTERS THE STATE

Participating in the special examination ritual taught prospective widows about examiners' function and authority in the agency. "About a month after New Berne [was] quarantined against yellow fever," Louisa Powers began "looking after her pension claim." On December 31, 1887, she filed a claim under the general law, with the assistance of Frederick C. Douglass.[47] With questions looming about the cause of Samuel Powers's death, Louisa's case entered the special examination phase in late December 1888 and continued through March 1889.

Louisa Powers sat down with examiner Emmett D. Gallion, a local representative from the Pension Bureau, for the first time on December 17, 1888. The investigation took place in Harlowe, nearly twenty-six miles from New Bern. Claims agent Douglass accompanied Gallion to Harlowe for the entirety of the investigation. Gallion interviewed more than forty witnesses, both black and white, men and women, during his investigation. Louisa's neighbors and acquaintances offered observations, opinions, and character assessments of Louisa. Douglass appeared at every deposition taken in the case and assertively interviewed the witnesses too. Gallion transcribed every deposition in the case.

During her initial interview with Gallion, Powers described her life with her husband before and after the war and explained how she had supported herself and five children since his death in April 1877. Louisa spoke openly about her fleeting relationship with a "strange man," Jim Watson of neighboring Jones County. "He was the first and only man I had anything to do with since my husbands death and it was the only child I had since his death."[48] To acknowledge a sexual relationship with a man after a soldier's death, as Louisa had, left Gallion free to draw conclusions that might disqualify her claim under the law of 1882. But about an hour after Douglass certified Gallion's transcription of Louisa's deposition, he and Louisa appeared at the Craven County Courthouse to amend her statement. Louisa testified: "I want to tell you that the man who got the child I had nearly three years ago and of which I have told you came to my house in the middle of the night and come into my room where there was no one but this idiot girl and forced me to stay with him and I had to do it against my will."[49] Gallion repeated the amendment of her testimony in his report: "[She said] that it was the result of a Rape on her by James Watson a colored man, and that the child was dead[.] Douglass the Attorney contending such being the case that she was entitled to pension up to the date of birth of child."[50]

Gallion worked to contradict the portrait of Louisa Powers in the application her claims agent filed for her widow's pension. He first tried to determine the ages of Louisa's children. The birth of a child more than nine months after a veteran died belied a woman's assertion that she had not had intimate relations with any man since the veteran's death, thus undermining her claim to virtue. Examiner Gallion gathered Louisa's children "so that they might be identified," apparently planning to line them up to check their color and their age to determine if they were Samuel Powers's progeny. Gallion asked if Louisa had given birth to a boy and, if so, who was present when he was born. When she refused to answer, he probed the nature of her relationship with Watson. Ambrose Boyd, a witness, said that Louisa had been "about to marry Watson," though "he treated her roughly" and she "drew a gun on him but [not] because of having a bad connection with her."[51] At some point, Gallion learned that Louisa's child with Watson had not died but was alive and living with her. He pressed her on the point, asking her why she had told him in her original statement that the child she had had by Watson was dead. Louisa eventually recanted, saying, "The reason I did I thought you would take the child away from me." By systematically questioning Louisa about her children's living arrangements, Gallion painted a picture of a neglectful mother. He mocked Louisa's response in his retort: "Well if you had given the child away how could I get it and what reason would I have for taking the child?" Louisa's comeback was simple and direct: "By Law." Perhaps she was thinking about the North Carolina law of 1867, requiring single women and widows, both white and black, to apprentice their children to others.[52] She then refused to answer more questions: "I do not remember anything about it and I will not say I did or did not."[53] Examiner Gallion appeared confused by Louisa's reference to motherhood but did not seek clarification. Instead he used the moment to emphasize one of the major points he was seeking to establish through this line of questioning: that Louisa Powers was a neglectful mother and therefore a woman unworthy of the government's support. Gallion's piercing question to prove this, "Why should you be concerned about her welfare?" was negated when Louisa answered, "Because she is my child."[54]

In accordance with the Pension Bureau's definition of family, examiners zeroed in on the home life of widows who applied for monetary support for the children of dead black soldiers. In middle-class family systems, mothers were supposed to, above all, protect their children from immorality. Examiners were especially critical of mothers like Louisa Powers, who had pregnant unmarried daughters. Anticipating the commissioner of pensions' denial of Louisa Powers's benefits, examiner Gallion urged Louisa to secure a guardian to take control of her children's benefits. Gallion reported that Louisa was "excited . . . to tears" by this advice.[55]

Whether Pennsylvanian E. D. Gallion chose to recognize it or not, child-rearing standards in Louisa Powers's neighborhood were high, and mothers were expected to supervise, protect, and train young children.[56] Louisa attempted to mitigate Gallion's negative impressions of her by openly discussing her child-raising strategies. She expected all her children to contribute to the family economy, but she could depend on only one of her daughters for assistance: "Rebecca is the brightest child that I have and is the only one I can put any dependence."[57] She took Rebecca to live with Isaac Taylor's family as a "house girl" between 1884 and 1886.[58] For Louisa, childcare was an economic as well as a domestic responsibility. When Gallion questioned Louisa about her five children, she described the arrangement Samuel had authorized for at least one of his daughters before he died: "Siddy lives with Benj Martin where she has been since before my husband died and she went there with his consent and advise and it was not long before he died that she went."[59] "I do not take any control over her," she told Gallion in her 1889 deposition. "I promised Martin that as long as he treated her well she might stay with him." Benjamin Martin had a wife but no children of his own, and he was not related to Louisa. By emphasizing her daily labor at home, her own wage-earning activities, and the strategies she adopted to support all her children, Louisa Powers challenged and expanded the Pension Bureau's construct of motherhood beyond emotional nurturance and moral purity.

Gallion, in making his case for rejection, was especially critical of Louisa's moral influence on her daughters and held her accountable for what he regarded as their immorality: "Three of the daughters have been mothers without husbands and the youngest of the three Siddy was enc[ei]nte when I saw her for identification and she is not much over 16 years old."[60] In Gallion's view, not only was Louisa Powers a neglectful mother, but she led an openly immoral life. Both character traits threatened the sanctity of the pension system. He found the informal agreements Louisa negotiated strange and even negligent on her part. Freedmen's Bureau agents suspected black mothers of trying to exploit, rather than care for, their children.[61] Perhaps Gallion shared the sentiment.

Although examiner Gallion presented Louisa Powers's child-raising strategies as incomprehensible and her home life as suspect, black and white Harlowe residents evaluated Louisa's womanhood and worthiness very differently. Ten of her neighbors confirmed that she had been involved in an intimate relationship with Jim Watson. They described him as lazy and a drifter, but they reluctantly recognized Louisa and Jim as a couple who would likely marry. When Jim assaulted Louisa, the neighbors screamed at and kicked him as Louisa Powers waved her gun. The relationship resulted in the birth of at least one child, a girl named Rossie, but Louisa's decision not to marry Jim Watson meant that her chances to secure a survivor's pension remained viable.

A local farmer whom Louisa worked for periodically said that Louisa had "not remarried since" Samuel died but that she had "had one child since the soldiers death." When asked about Louisa's reputation, he said, "It is as good as any woman in the neighborhood."[62] Another man said, "She lives as straight a life as any of our people and I have heard scandal about her but not more than any other woman in our neighborhood." He continued, "If a woman goes out to church with any one she will be talked about."[63] Indeed, two contrasting conceptions of female virtue were operating at the center of Louisa Powers's case. As neighbors had done in Mary Kent's case, Louisa's neighbors resisted the federal agency's construct of honorable widowhood and its rigid definitions of marriage, family, and sexual morality as the primary indicators for women's worthiness to collect survivors' benefits. They believed that benefits should be granted to women like Louisa Powers who labored and upheld community values.

Louisa's neighbors' testimony played an especially important role during the examination, but it did not sway Gallion's opinion. As he did in Mary Lee's case, Gallion offered a multilayered argument for rejecting Louisa Powers's petition. Gallion told the commissioner of pensions that Louisa's dead husband, Samuel Powers (whom he described as "trifling and lazy"), had "beyond doubt" contracted "consumption" before his service in the Union Army, which made her ineligible for a war-based pension. In addition, he believed Louisa Powers had violated the Act of August 7, 1882, which terminated a claimant's eligibility to collect survivors' benefits if she later had an intimate relationship with a man. Drawing heavily on the testimony of her neighbors, Gallion established that Louisa had been sexually involved with at least one man since the death of her husband, which Louisa had admitted. He summarily dismissed Louisa's testimony as a lie that Jim Watson had raped her, relying instead on community testimony. Gallion emphasized that she had given birth to as many as two children since her husband's death.

The case, said Gallion's report, merited punishment for Louisa and "condemnation" for her claims agent, Frederick C. Douglass. She "has perjured herself beyond doubt"; she had not been "chaste since her husband's death," the proof being the "boy baby, she gave birth to about eighteen months after the soldiers death who died within a few months old." Gallion said, "Frederick Douglass should be disbarred for this and similar practice."[64]

Agency officials mentioned Gallion's report in an internal memorandum dated April 20, 1889: "The widow's claim is rejected because she gave birth to an illegitimate child about a year from soldier's death or a little over a year, leaving no pensionable status. . . . If a claim is filed for minors, action under 4706 is in order—to declare widow 'unsuitable' and provide for turning over pension [as] date of birth cannot possibly be determined."[65] On April 24, 1889, the commissioner denied Louisa Powers's claim "on account of claimant violation of Act of August 7, 1882, as to adulterous cohabitation."[66]

CHALLENGING THE PENSION BUREAU'S DECISIONS: MARY LEE AND LOUISA POWERS

As petitioners gained confidence and a better understanding of the Pension Bureau and its divisions, they took their claims to the next higher administration level, appealing to the Department of the Interior. The secretary of the interior held the power to review and change the outcome of decisions the commissioner of pensions endorsed.[67] Though prospective beneficiaries did not want federal officials peering into their private lives, they were not above inviting these men into their lives to investigate their cases.[68]

War widow Mary Lee's case overlapped with Louisa Powers's examination. The investigation, which began in December 1888 and lasted until February 1889, resulted in the commissioner of pensions denying her claim. Gallion suspected that her husband, Simeon, had died of syphilis, thus disqualifying Mary from collecting benefits under the general law system. In addition, Gallion voiced his suspicion that Mary Lee was not a virtuous woman: "It is probable that the clmt [claimant] did cohabit for brief intervals with other men since her husband's death but it is impossible to prove it among her associates."[69] Based on the medical evidence and Gallion's field investigation, agency officials ruled that Simeon Lee died of syphilis rather than a service-related injury and denied Mary's petition for benefits in 1889.

Mary Lee filed a succession of appeals highlighting the mishandling of her case and examiner misconduct. In her appeal to the secretary of the interior, she proclaimed, "The examiner ask me . . . unfair questions and told me that he had money for me in his pocket if I would do as he said. I told him I did not want his money."[70] In a follow-up affidavit, Mary declared, "I was told by Mr. E. D. Gallion the U.S. Pension Examiner that he intended to hold my claim until I got tired of it and give it up." She then addressed the syphilis diagnosis head on and faulted Gallion for rejecting her case: "I have every reason to believe that other Disease [syphilis] was instituted in the place of Hemorrhage and Reported in the Pension Department for the Purpose of Defeating me of my Just Rights."[71] Once again testimony from family, community, and fellow soldiers proved crucial. Those who came forward on her behalf gave detailed information about Simeon Lee's prewar marital history, dates of birth of any children, and his burial. The assistant secretary of the interior issued his ruling in Mary Lee's case in January 1892: "The Department [of Interior] agrees with the Bureau [of Pensions]. Syphilis was probably the cause of death. It would be unreasonable . . . to accept any other cause, or to believe that he brought any serious disability from service that was not so caused."[72]

As it happens, Louisa Powers's case had set the stage for Mary Lee's complaint. Seven months earlier, Louisa, with the assistance of Frederick C. Douglass, appealed the rejection of her case.[73] According to Louisa's sworn statement before a clerk in the Craven County Superior Court, she believed that her petition for aid had been rejected because of examiner Gallion's report "that I lived in adulterous cohabitation immediately after soldiers death and given birth to an illegitimate child about one year after the soldiers death. I declare that he reported . . . that he was going to [do] Everything he could against me." She said that she had reported being raped to her neighbors "the next morning and they ran him away out of the neighborhood."[74] After her husband's death, Louisa explained, "I went to cooking for Mr. Isaac Taylor and his wife [Eliza A.] Taylor (white) and I work with them six years every day and I had no child and I did not live or cohabit with any man as man and wife and I have not since and I can furnish credible witnesses and prove it by both white and colored."[75] During the weeks of searching for clues in Harlowe, Gallion had canvased her neighborhood several times and "told both white and colored that he was going to keep me off the money and was to[o] much for me to git. And when he would examine a witness he would lye and tell them that if they told him any lie . . . he would send them to prison. And he told me he was going to have me [im]prison[ed]."[76]

Nearly three months later, the assistant secretary of the U.S. Department of the Interior reversed the decision in Louisa Powers's case. Although evidence of adultery had been shown, the assistant secretary ruled: "The final clause of Section 2 of the Act proved August 7, 1882 is not applicable to claimants for pension, and, therefore, it does not bar any claimant from a pensionable status. The clause relates exclusively to widows who are pensioners."[77]

In other words, Louisa Powers was an applicant for survivors' benefits, not a pensioner, at the time of Gallion's investigation, so her name was duly entered on the pension rolls. She would receive nearly three thousand dollars in arrears and eight dollars a month for her own support thereafter, with an additional two dollars per month for each of her five children until each reached the age of sixteen, so long as she abided by agency rules. The ruling also implied that the Department of the Interior accepted the cause of Samuel's death. It is difficult to know with any certainty what this payout meant to Louisa Powers in the moment. Did she view it as recompense for the work that she had performed while traveling alongside her husband during the war?

The appeal Douglass filed in the Department of the Interior on behalf of Louisa Powers and the decision in her case served as a blueprint for appealing suspensions for "open and notorious cohabitation" in the years to come. With the assistance of agent Douglass, Ritty Titterton, a day laborer, gained admittance to the pension rolls two years after her claim was rejected. According to a decision issued by Cyrus Bussey, the assistant secretary of the Department of the Interior, on July 20, 1891, the law of 1882 applied to widows on the pension rolls, but not to claimants. As in Louisa's case, Ritty Titterton was granted a pension.[78] Indeed, not only did Douglass learn a new argument to contest successfully "open and notorious cohabitation" rejections for prospective widows, the ruling in Louisa Powers's case further strengthened his reputation among black veterans and Union widows in eastern North Carolina. As a consequence, his sense of his own influence must have grown.

THE CRIMINAL INVESTIGATION OF DOUGLASS AND CARPENTER

An 1889 criminal investigation of agents Frederick Douglass and E. W. Carpenter revealed deep-seated tensions and conflicts that were a part of the overall character and complexity of the pension business in New Bern. Examiners found the stories witnesses told consistent; especially striking were those agent Douglass presented. Other practices, including paying witnesses for appearing to testify, seemed irregular and suspicious.

One woman filed a complaint against agent Douglass with the commissioner of pensions in December 1893, saying, "Mr. Fred Douglass took charge of said certificate and I have never seen it since and can get no satisfaction from him[.] I have threaten to sue him now he says he has sent certificate back to the Department and there is no money for me."[79] Recognizing the extent to which disabled veterans had come to rely on Douglass, examiner William Porter recommended that the commissioner show him leniency. Douglass received a stern warning but was not formally tried or suspended on this occasion.[80]

Examiners discredited the work of black and white professionals who were part of the pension network. Examiner Gallion doubted Henry G. Bates's professional opinion because he accepted payment from claimants.[81] Examiner Palmer believed Bates to be "of good personal character" but thought his use of "narcotics" to treat his own illness took a toll on his mind and body. "I am sure his memory can not be depended on beyond what his books show."[82]

A few years later another examiner doing work in New Bern questioned Douglass's handling of his clients' mail. "The claimants say it gives them a great deal of trouble in getting official letters from the Department," Douglass responded, "because they claim they have to prove they are [the] parties letters belong to from time to time. In the country it is very hard for claimants to get letters"; one of his clients "had to go off and get witnesses to prove his identity [for] a letter I sent to him containing a matter in relation to his claim was returned to me."[83] The examiner remained unconvinced: "It occurs to me that it was high time that he was forbidden to carry on such high handed proceedings no matter what may be his motives."[84]

Carpenter was implicated during the investigation of Douglass's business practices. Examiner Isaac B. Dunn observed: "E. W. Carpenter (white) was formerly a claim agent[.] [S]pecial agent Ragsdale[,] who resigned in 1877, was instrumental in getting him indicted for pension frauds but the indictments were all killed as I am informed and he went free." In Carpenter's role as notary public, he "executes pension affidavits by the wholesale for colored claimants." Dunn further noted that Carpenter, like Bates, performed his services gratis when clients "have no money to pay fees" and remained "very popular among them." Dunn rented an office near Carpenter's living quarters, gaining insight into his personal life: "He is a bachelor. . . . I have been told [he] lives with a colored woman, which he denies." The woman the examiner mentioned in his correspondence to the commissioner was Sarah Oxly.[85] A few years later examiner E. D. Gallion linked the two in his report to the commissioner of pensions: "Mrs. Sarah Oxley a colored woman and reputed mistress of E. W. Carpenter."[86]

Sarah Oxly and E. W. Carpenter may very well have shared intimate ties, but the circumstances under which this relationship occurred must be placed in context.[87] She lived next door to Carpenter, whom she also identified as her employer in 1870. Both under slavery and after emancipation, "housekeeper" was a popular euphemism for women who performed both sexual and domestic labor for white men.[88] The fact that Sarah looked like a white woman and was affiliated with predominantly white religious groups, such as Christian Scientist, may have appealed to Carpenter.[89] The North Carolina General Assembly had outlawed interracial marriages, so it comes as no surprise that Carpenter and Oxly would have carried on their relationship in secret. Working as Carpenter's housekeeper may well have served as a cover because Sarah maintained her own residence and eatery on Broad Street until she died in 1906.

While the connection between Oxly and Carpenter was enough to spark rumor, they never lived in the same residence or acted as a married couple. Sarah never attempted to sneak through legal loopholes to protect her economic standing nor informally used his surname. Oxly surely would have detested Carpenter's wartime defense of Eugene Hannibal, though his work on behalf of injured veterans and the families of dead black soldiers may have softened her opinion. Wealthy white men often set aside inheritances for their children with black women, as J. B. Oxley may have done for Sarah.[90] Carpenter was by no means wealthy and made no similar provision for Sarah in his will (he died in 1904).[91]

CONCLUSION

In the face of intrusive questions and personal scrutiny, black women emerged as skillful negotiators in all aspects of the pension application process. They used an eclectic blend of arguments and strategies to navigate the special examination process and the pension system generally. Sometimes they appropriated the agency's own language to defend their position on the pension rolls, and they were quick to learn its concepts of acceptable marriage and family formations as well as its norms for domesticity. They learned how to present their cases to local examiners and to manipulate these men to side with them against potentially damaging witness testimony. They also relied on kin networks and the knowledge of community witnesses to help them retain control of their position on the rolls. They criticized the presence of examiners in their communities, but only when it suited them. In some instances, they even asked the same men for help.[92] As women continued to hone their critique of the pension system and its flaws, lawmakers introduced a new program into the pension system that allowed dependents to claim benefits without establishing the medical cause of their husbands' deaths.

6

Marriage and the Expansion of the Pension System in 1890

In a major policy change, the Dependent Pension Law of 1890 (referred to as the service law of 1890) allowed the widows of deceased soldiers to collect survivors' benefits based on their husbands' service.[1] Unlike the general law pension system, petitioners did not have to demonstrate that their husbands had died as a result of service-related injuries. Scholars have mainly focused on the law's expansion of the government's responsibility to veterans and their dependents. Political scientist Theda Skocpol, for example, estimated that "between 1880 and 1910, the U.S. federal government devoted over of a quarter of its expenditures to pensions."[2] Historians have paid less attention to how notions of marriage, proper family life, and respectable womanhood maintained class divisions and racial disparities in the administration of pensions.

Black women continued to challenge the construction of marriage embedded in the structure of Union widowhood. Marriage, from their perspective, could not and should not be divorced from its historical context and the experience of enslavement. Yet, the Pension Bureau's configuration of Union widowhood did exactly that. Pension Bureau officials and examiners stripped marriage down to a contractual relation and infused its meaning with notions of middle-class domesticity and individualism, thereby dictating just how such resources should be allocated within a claimant's household. Deviating from such conceptions could result in intrusive investigations.

After the passage of this law, black Union widows pursued federal benefits with new fervor. The service law made it possible for women to gain a pension solely on the basis of their husband's military service. Mary Norman, mother of agent Frederick C. Douglass, made a successful claim under this law. Mary Lee, although remaining convinced that her husband had died of a service-related injury, was finally successful in obtaining survivors' benefits under the new law. Before the secretary of the interior rendered a decision in Louisa Powers's appeal for reconsideration, she had filed two petitions under the service law.[3]

Black Union widows managed to make deep inroads into the pension system after 1890, but one issue affecting their eligibility remained constant: competing constructs of marriage. Indeed, no matter which system a woman claimed benefits under, she still had to meet the agency's marriage criteria. Black women whose intimate lives fell outside the dominant white construction of feminine domesticity continued to endure intrusive scrutiny. Moreover, in 1882 the perceived cohabitation loophole had been sewn up with a more stringent law, which suspended benefits from a claimant if it was determined that she was sexually involved with a man. The federal government's ongoing retreat from Reconstruction-era policies that allowed formerly enslaved women to gain recognition in the pension system was evident from the law of 1882 and congressional proposals calling for further limitations on the retroactive recognition of slaves' marriages.

This chapter discusses the success and failure of black women's pension claims under the service law of 1890. Taking seriously the concepts of worthy womanhood that black women put forth to justify their claims, I argue that black women's tendency to promote and publicize their identity as wage earners challenged the ideal of feminine dependency embodied in Union widowhood.[4] I follow the struggle of Charlotte Banks (now Caphart) to rehabilitate her claim for pension in the wake of her latest husband's death. The chapter also traces the efforts of women like Mary Lee to have their claims reclassified from the service law to the general law system as well as women suing their veteran husbands for nonsupport. All this occurred as the government began to retreat from its wartime construal of slave marriage, which was designed to open up the pension system to newly free black women. In the years leading up to the twentieth century, pension examiners used their investigations of slave marriage and nondivorce as a tool to purge women from the pension roster.

THE SERVICE LAW AND BLACK WOMEN'S CLAIMS

Before 1890, when the commissioner of pensions notified Mary Norman and Mary Lee that their claims had been denied, it was impossible for them to gain access to the pension system. Neither woman could link their husbands' death to a service-related disease or injury, which the general law system required. The general law pension system was then the only program under which Union widows could file claims. The new system allowed widows seeking pensions to claim benefits without establishing that their husbands had died of war-related causes, if they could demonstrate that they had married a veteran, remained celibate, and supported themselves by their own labor.

Matilda Wells submitted her petition shortly after lawmakers introduced the new system. Her veteran husband, Toney, had drowned in 1881 while crossing the Neuse River. Matilda easily met the bureau's criteria to file a claim under the service law; she had married Toney in a religious ceremony in 1868, she earned wages "washing and cooking," and she supported her children by her own labor. Still, a number of personal misfortunes stood in her way. Personal tragedy struck again when her young daughter, Hannah, died of pneumonia.[5] In the wake of her daughter's death, Matilda moved in and around New Bern to support her surviving children. She returned to Wicksville, a rural area near Elizabeth City in Pasquotank County, with her children around 1882. In Wicksville, Matilda leaned on the support of kin and community members while she earned wages cooking and working alongside men as a field hand. After the service law system opened up a new route to benefits, Matilda relocated to New Bern because several black veterans who had served alongside her husband lived there and could provide testimony to support her case. She also gained the support of black professionals and white merchants, who described her as "an ignorant negro woman but . . . honest and upright."[6] A widow's pension would have been life changing for Matilda, but her case stalled until 1896, when the bureau called for a special examination.

Widows who petitioned under the law of 1890 faced a means test: they qualified for benefits if they had no other means of support than their own labor and had a net income of no more than $250 per year.[7] At Allen G. Oden's death on September 30, 1894, he left his widow, Dicy, with a home and death benefits from memberships in organizations and mutual aid societies. "My husband and I owned one house on New South Front Street valued on Tax List 400 dollars" and "one shoe shop on Craven Street . . . valued at three hundred dollars." But, she continued, "I have no income . . . only from my own Daily Labor."[8] Dicy's petition eventually went through, and she remained on the pension roster until she died in 1928.

Lawmakers restricted eligibility to women who had married before the act became law. The commissioner of pensions suspended Caroline Butler's benefits under the service law because she and the deceased veteran John

Jackson married after the service law had been passed.[9] The policy captured looming fears about lady swindlers—women who married dying soldiers in anticipation of collecting federal benefits.

With expectations for soldiers' wives spelled out in numerous pension system rules, black women embraced new lines of argument under the service law system. They now offered detailed descriptions of their working lives to refute charges of unworthiness and sexual immorality. Casting themselves as hard workers and calling attention to their economic circumstances, these women challenged the agency's constructs of marriage and family. At the same time, they introduced a liberating concept of widowhood in the pension system. Issues of marriage, labor, work, and family emerged as key points in their petitions.

For many Americans, white and black, economic and social forces made the Victorian family ideal unattainable, while others never espoused it for themselves.[10] In this respect, black veterans' families had much in common with the families of farmers, immigrants, and members of the urban and rural working class. Some women found themselves in unusual living arrangements as a matter of necessity. As pension applicants, women who lived separately from their husbands for long periods had to find ways to frame their husband's absence from the marital home. Although Mary and Henry Bragg had lived apart for "5 years or more" when he died, she asserted that her marriage was intact: "He kept writing me and he sent me money every month whenever he . . . could make any. He sent me $5 at a time."[11] Hansey Jones's husband worked as a stevedore on a boat that "ran from NY to the West Indies"; sometimes she would see him twice a week, and sometimes she would not see him for two months.[12] Like Mary Bragg, multiple women had to substantiate the legitimacy of their marriages during the examination process because they lived apart from their spouses for the duration of the marriage. Clarissa and Spencer Sparrow lived apart for four years before his death. "No we were never divorced—he just liked living in Onzelo Co.," Clarissa protested, "and I liked to live in James City."[13] Under further scrutiny, she explained, "No, he was not mad with me but he just preferred to live" there "for the reason that he could get work there that suited him better."[14] These women's living arrangements challenged pension officials' interpretations of marriage and the household.

From the outset, pension officials expected the wives of soldiers to act dutifully toward their husbands, providing excellent care while simultaneously upholding the moral dictates of womanhood.[15] Care labor was a principal responsibility of the wives of diseased and disabled veterans.[16] Prospective beneficiaries harnessed these ideals while explaining the sacrifices they made on behalf of their husbands and families. Presilla Flowers admitted the difficulty of combining caring for her disabled husband with working for wages. "He was sick going on four years before he died," the widow remembered. "He was so helpless I had a hard time."[17] Maria Little "lived with and took care of" her disabled husband, Benjamin Little, "constantly." "He did not make wages enough to keep us in the necessaries of life." Maria said she always "hired out to work at anything" she could do and "used the earnings for his support."[18] Peggy Slade's husband, Miles, "was for many years unable to work . . . sat around with his arms folded and waved about at times. . . . He was out of his mind before he died."[19] A nearby neighbor remembered watching Miles deteriorate: "I saw him everyday he was able to be about. . . . He was not able to work at all when I first knew him—a beggar on the street and insane."[20] Though the accounts are compelling and illustrative of their circumstances, not all of these women gained admission to the pension roster.

Elsia Askew attempted to reimagine the terms of caregiving and wage earning in her marriage to Isaac Askew, a disabled veteran, whom she married in 1874. Sometime after Isaac secured invalid benefits from the Pension Bureau, Elsia moved to Orange, New Jersey, with her sister "and got a job to cook" to pay off "a little home" and Isaac's GAR dues.[21] Elsia's decision touched off a local debate about who would care for him in her absence. As Isaac's health rapidly declined, a neighbor informed Elsia that Isaac was near death, but "she wrote back that she could not come."[22] One veteran remembered that "her letter cause considerable comment. . . . A Minister read it aloud before his congregation and commented on it in a not very favorable way." Not until after Isaac died in 1903 did Elsia resettle in New Bern. A fellow veteran and member of Isaac's GAR post believed that Elsia "came to his burial so as to have grounds to apply for a pension."[23]

When Elsia applied for survivors' benefits in 1904, she faced a series of obstacles. Communal notions of worthiness often derived from the perceived dedication with which women performed care labor for a dying soldier. Elsia Askew's neighbors felt she had failed to live up to their expectations of a veteran's wife. Hulda Jane Smith, Isaac Askew's caregiver, vented her frustration with Elsia: "I consider I did the work very cheap for I did things for Mr. Askie that no one else would do along the entire street. . . . He was in such a dreadful condition that many thought he had a contagious or bad disease and would not touch him."[24] Hulda and a man who took care of Isaac during his last illness complained that Elsia failed to compensate them for work they performed. Moreover, Hulda believed that the government should compensate her for the work she did on behalf of the soldier. In the

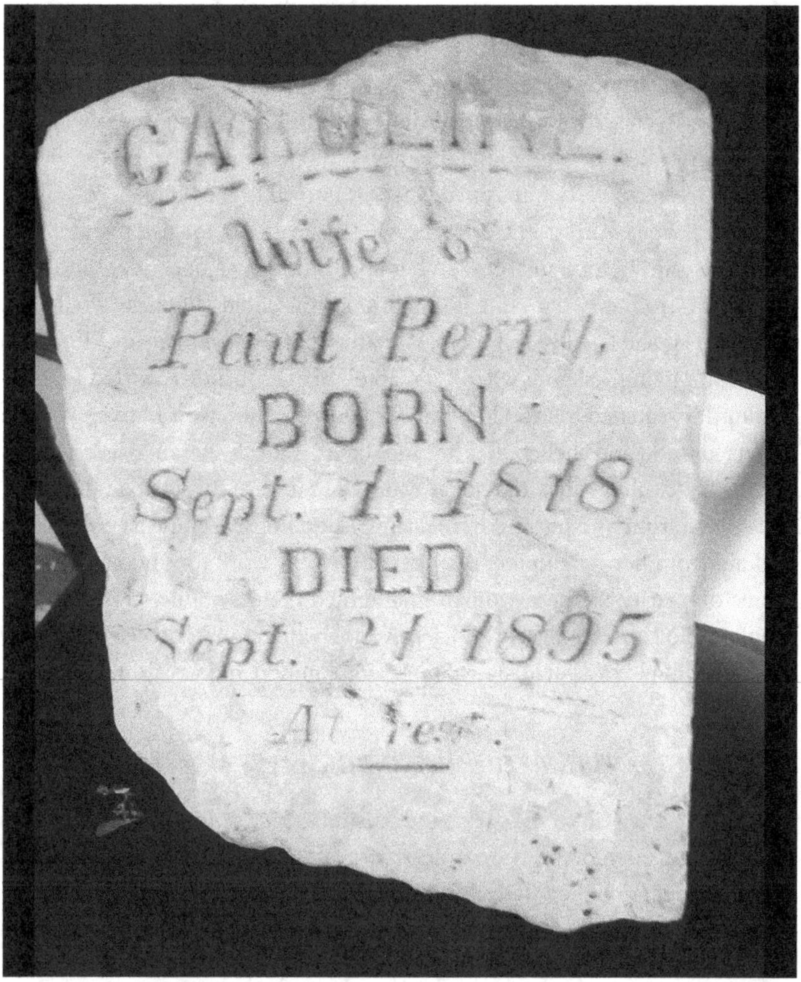

Figure 6.1. Headstone for Caroline Perry, mother of Luke Perry. Bryan Cemetery, James City, North Carolina. Photo by author.

community's opinion, Elsia was unworthy and ineligible for a pension. But by standing her ground and making her own claims, she garnered recognition by the bureau. Elsia Askew's analysis expanded the meanings of widowhood in the Pension Bureau and of womanhood in her community. Elsia collected the pension until she died in 1928.

A key requirement for widows seeking assistance under the service law system was their ability to demonstrate that they remained "dependent on their own labor for support."[25] Under the service law, wage work offered evidence of their worthiness and commitment to the family relationships. One widow said, "I did anything I could get to do before I was allowed a pension."[26] Harriet Boyd told an examiner, "Before I got my Pension I did all sorts of work for a living—cooked, washed, and did everything."[27] During the seven-year period between filing a petition for benefits and obtaining the pension, widow Jamsey Green's poverty intensified. She was known to earn money by collecting loose "paper from storekeepers . . . which she sells at the fish market."[28]

While waiting for a decision on her application for a dependent mother's pension, Caroline Perry estimated that her household supplies "would not bring $10" if she tried to sell them. Caroline told a pension agent, "I have to work for a living washing when I am able."[29] Lana Burney reported that her landlord threatened to evict her family.[30] Judy Lavenhouse had to beg on the streets for food and shelter after her son died.[31] A local veteran assisted her by "giving her clothes shoes and house room."[32] Mary Lee survived on the wages she earned from nursing children, farming, and housekeeping as well as gifts and aid from her neighbors: "All I gets is What I work for and get through hands of charity."[33] These women highlighted the economic strategies they employed to combat poverty and deprivation while simultaneously depicting their working lives as evidence of their womanhood and worthiness.

CHARLOTTE BANKS AND THE MEANING OF SLAVES' MARRIAGES

Three years after Charlotte's husband Austin Caphart died, Charlotte Banks Caphart considered the economic return and social implications of survivors' benefits on her daily life. Suspended from the pension roster for violating the bureau's cohabitation rule in 1873, Charlotte faced an uphill battle. Given her experience with examiner Ragsdale, she understood that the possibility of relief from the Pension Bureau had been foreclosed. Yet she pressed on, illuminating the varied meanings that she and formerly enslaved women like her attached to the claims-making process and Union widowhood.

The great difficulty black war widows like Charlotte Banks had configuring their marital relations in "the discourse" of the U.S. legal system underscored the need for claims agents. With agent Frederick C. Douglass now in charge, Charlotte hoped to recover her status as a Union widow. Rather than translating Charlotte's definition of marriage and vision of widowhood into a compelling challenge to the agency definition of marriage, Douglass pared down the details of Charlotte's case to conform to Pension Bureau rules. On April 8, 1890, Douglass filed an application on Charlotte's behalf to "recover the arrears of pension due her under a recent Act of Congress": the Arrears Act of January 29, 1879.[34] This law provided that pensions granted under the general law pension system begin from the date of death or discharge.[35]

The appeal Douglass filed for special action made no mention of the death of Caesar Banks, the timing of Charlotte's marriage to David Holloway in the 1860s, or the recent death of her last husband. Douglass made a far more linear and narrow case. He argued that Charlotte had been a pensioner until she remarried in 1866. Now, being a widow again, Charlotte deserved consideration for reinstatement to the pension rolls.[36] It is not entirely clear from Charlotte's case file why Douglass streamlined her marital history. The most obvious explanation is that he was seeking her best chance of regaining her pension. But it is also possible that his own class identity came into play. By the 1890s, Frederick C. Douglass had firmly established himself in New Bern's black middle class. As historian Glenda Gilmore writes, among middle-class blacks, "marriage itself was political" and a direct challenge to whites who viewed black families as degenerate.[37] Perhaps Douglass took this tactic not only to collect his claims agent fee but also to make a larger point about the legitimacy of black marriages to the Pension Bureau. Minimally Douglass believed that Charlotte could recover a small amount for the two-year period of her widowhood.

The "special action" Douglass sought for Charlotte's case did not materialize. She and Douglass probably hoped that the secretary of the interior would call for a new investigation into her case, including a special examination. Charlotte, like many other similarly situated women, did not necessarily oppose government intervention in her case, but she wanted to control when and on what terms the government might call for an investigation. Again, the commissioner of pensions notified Charlotte that her marriage to David Holloway in 1866 prevented her from collecting benefits as a Union widow. "Claimant is not the legal widow of the soldier," said the assistant secretary of the Department of the Interior, never "having been married to him except by slave custom and by cohabitation which terminated sometime prior to his death."[38] Perhaps what Charlotte was trying to establish was that their marriage had ended because their owner had separated them, rather than from their personal decision. The denial of Charlotte's marital life with Caesar was by no means new; in some ways, it was a symbolic replay of the events that had befallen her as an enslaved woman.

Charlotte Banks was not alone in her struggle. Marriages and family relationships among enslaved people reflected the brutal conditions of their bondage. Formerly enslaved petitioners had to spell out the difficulties of maintaining their marriages under slavery. Slaves' "marriages were recognized by the white folks," an ex-slave explained, "but if they got ready to sell you they would not let the marriage or anything else stand in the way."[39] Charlotte's marriage to Caesar meant a good deal to her even though she was involuntarily separated from her husband and began living with David Holloway sometime during the war. Though enslaved people were terribly vulnerable, perhaps their choice to marry without their owner's consent was, in their minds, an assault on the master's power to control them.[40] Ultimately, pension officials took the stance that separation by owner translated into a formal separation, thereby making the owners' decisions and practices paramount in black women's cases.[41]

Historian Megan McClintock has shown that the Pension Bureau gradually began to move away from its liberal marriage policy during the late nineteenth century.[42] This shift translated into deeper scrutiny of black women's intimate lives. One examiner discovered that Harriet Ellison had not secured a legal divorce from her first husband, Moses Webb, before she married veteran Mathew Ellison. Officials contacted Harriet in late July 1894 to inform her that the "allowance of your pension was . . . contrary to law."[43] Harriet was permanently removed from the pension roster. The very framework set up to create a legal pathway for the dependents of black soldiers to gain access to the pension system as a recognition of their sacrifice and their citizenship now served as a mechanism to purge the pension rolls.

The meaning of slave marriage was malleable and ever changing in black peoples' lives and in the Pension Bureau. For black women, the legacy of enslavement, wartime upheaval, poverty, and deprivation were all bound up in the meaning of marriage for blacks in ways that local examiners did not fully acknowledge and that agency rules did not fully recognize.

LEGAL WIDOWHOOD, VALID MARRIAGES, AND "UNDIVORCED WIVES"

When their marital relationships broke down, poor people did not necessarily turn to legal institutions to dissolve their marriages. Instead, separating couples might handle the logistics of financial support and childcare within their families or community institutions, such as the church or lodge. As pension officials clarified the definition of legal widowhood and the meaning of marriage in the pension system, there were direct consequences for those who continued to adhere to this common custom.

The case of Mary Ann Gatlin, a white Union widow, exhibits what historian Beverly Schwartzberg has identified as some of the "messier household and marriage patterns" behind the marriage contract in late nineteenth-century America.[44] Mary Ann petitioned for survivors' benefits shortly after her husband, veteran Riley Gatlin, died in 1889. She received a pension certificate on December 1, 1890, with an initial payment of $230.40 (less attorney's fee) and another $276.40 on her widow's claim. So long as Mary Ann remained a widow, she was eligible to receive twelve dollars per month. But Mary Ann's time on the pension roster was short. Two days after she collected her first stipend, a bureau examiner knocked on her door to inform her that another woman, named Mary Ann DeCree, had filed a petition "claiming to be the widow of Riley Gatlin." In a manner reminiscent of the cohabitation investigations conducted by examiner George H. Ragsdale in 1873, a bureau examiner instructed Gatlin "to return the money" to the government and said her case would have to be investigated. She complied with the examiner and returned "all of the money" but never regained her standing on the pension rolls.[45]

Women who could substantiate their marriages with certified documents also faced difficulties in meeting the agency's marriage standard and gaining the support of their communities. Nicy Smith's name was initially purged from the pension roster because pension officials believed she had been admitted based on fraudulent medical evidence. When she appealed the commissioner's decision in her case, the institutional dialogue shifted from illegal evidence to legal widowhood. Officials suspended her benefits because her deceased husband, James Smith, had not secured a legal divorce from his previous wife, Harriet Charles, before remarrying. Believing her marriage to be lawful, Nicy immediately applied to have her petition considered under the service law system. She confidently filed certified documents from Craven County's Register of Deeds with the Pension Bureau to prove the legitimacy of her marriage to Smith.

Nicy did not expect the testimony of black Union widows who had resided in the New Bern area since the war to carry the same weight as the legal evidence that she filed, but her neighbors called into question the legality of Nicy's marriage to James Smith. Mary Norman, a Union widow and the mother of agent Frederick Douglass, recalled that "James Smith was never divorced from Harriet." "They parted" without securing a legal divorce, customary in their neighborhood, and Harriet remarried before she died.[46] The testimony of women who knew Harriet Charles in the Trent River camp and veterans who served alongside James Smith ultimately outweighed the legal documentation Nicy filed with her case. This time, the commissioner denied survivors' benefits to Nicy Smith on the basis of marriage. Nicy filed a succession of petitions to protest the decision before she died in January 1917.[47] In one instance, the commissioner used particularly callous language: "You were never the lawful wife of the soldier and have no status as his widow." The letter arrived four months after Nicy died.[48]

INTIMATE RELATIONSHIPS AND THE PROBLEM OF REMARRIAGE

Historical and cultural forces led many blacks to enter into a broad range of domestic arrangements after the war, including maintaining separate households. Fluid and flexible marriage patterns existed side by side with legally sanctioned marriages. There were one-, two-, and three-generation households, extended and fictive kin, and co-residential two-parent households.[49] Indeed, as Tera Hunter finds, by the end of the nineteenth century, former slaves and their descendants had engaged in multiple, serial marital relationships.[50] Economic pragmatism also drove marriages: remarriage proved transformational in Charlotte Banks's quest to alleviate poverty in the post-Reconstruction South.

For soldiers' widows whose claims the Pension Bureau did recognize, the decision to marry again was fraught with uncertainty and risk. It meant surrendering their survivors' benefits, and it exposed them to poverty, abandonment, and other dangers.[51] The level of influence the Pension Bureau had on shaping marriage and family choices is difficult to assess. For some, the economic security of survivors' benefits was worth far more than the promise of marriage. Women's reasoning ran the gamut. Violet Wiggins contemplated remarrying, but when "I found I could get a pension I threw him over."[52] Still, many viewed the prospect of marriage with hope, and marriage and family were sources of personal fulfillment, companionship, and legitimacy for black women in their communities.

White women faced the same dilemmas. For Penelope Ives, a white seamstress who resided on Pollock Street in the Third Ward of New Bern, the decision to remarry ultimately shut her out of the pension system and made her vulnerable. Penelope successfully secured survivors' benefits as the widow of veteran John Ives in 1887. Three years later she married Joseph Barber but left him shortly thereafter because he treated her "cruel."[53] Joseph demanded that Penelope turn over the money she had collected from the government, but she refused to "let him have it."[54] Penelope attempted to resolve the matter on her own rather than turn to the local courts to dissolve her marriage or involve the Pension Bureau. She continued collecting survivors' benefits—as if she had never remarried. Faced with the possibility of criminal prosecution in 1893 for collecting benefits while married, Penelope explained her logic: "I did not feel as though I was married to him [John Barber] at all, and hence drew the pension allowed as widow after I had married him." She continued, "I hope I will not be further punished but I am now telling the truth."[55] Perhaps Penelope hoped to salvage her position on the pension roster by exposing Barber. The investigating examiner determined that Penelope's "confession and refundment" demonstrated her effort to make "reparation" to the government. He said, "She is an ignorant white woman and has show[n] a disposition to act honest in the matter now."[56] The commissioner of pensions suspended Penelope's benefits, but she avoided the criminal prosecution and public shaming that her black female neighbors endured.

The steady flow of petitions from beneficiaries who remarried underscores the centrality of marriage and citizenship for all women in the nineteenth century. The case files of Charlotte Banks, Penelope Ives, and many others provide clear evidence of poor women's push to advance "remarriage claims" before lawmakers took on the question. Beyond providing benefits, the Pension Bureau had become a resource for Union widows, both black and white, in their struggles against poverty and marital discord. Women's petitions exposed the economic vulnerabilities women experienced when they surrendered their pensions on the promises of marriage. Efforts to address the problems associated with remarriage in the pension system seem to have been influenced by the groundswell of complaints from poor women across the racial spectrum. Their claims outpaced the efforts both of federal lawmakers, who eventually passed a remarried widows pension act in 1903, and of middle-class feminists, who rallied for mothers' pensions in 1910.[57] A small victory came in 1901, when lawmakers introduced a program that allowed for women who had surrendered their benefits in compliance with the remarriage rule to rejoin the pension roster at a reduced rate.[58]

MARRIAGE, FAMILIAL RELATIONS, AND THE PENSION BUREAUCRACY

Blacks attached a wide array of meanings to their intimate relationships in the post-Reconstruction era. It was the job of claims agents to translate those relations into viable claims in the petitions sent to the Pension Bureau; agents such as Frederick Douglass may also have concealed aspects of the intimate lives of their clientele. In 1892, Julia Neel filed a petition for a dependent mother's pension based on her son's wartime service. Though Julia's original petition for survivors' benefits indicated that she had married after her son's death, when her case reached the examination phase in 1892, she made the conscious decision to disguise her marital history after the death of her son's father, Frederick H. Lewis. She may have been aware of the Pension Bureau's regulation on cohabitation and morality and anticipated the denial of benefits in light of the 1882 law authorizing bureau examiners to probe the private lives of widows and mothers and remove those who remarried from the pension roster. What Julia Neel did not know at the time was that her standing as a dependent mother would have allowed her to pursue an alternate path to benefits within the Pension Bureau.

Easter Brown succeeded in persuading officials to reinstate her benefits as the dependent mother of Jerry Brown, who drowned in St. John's River, Florida, while serving in the USCT. She had collected her son's army pay and drawn a dependent mother's pension under the general law pension system until May 1873, when examiner Ragsdale reported that she had remarried.[59] The pension system rules for compensating the parent of a deceased soldier were conceived around a notion of reciprocity, whereby adult male children were expected to provide for their parents when they became infirm and unable to support themselves.[60] The rules required a mother to establish the absence or incapacity of her spouse or other sons to qualify for a pension.[61] Thus, Easter had to demonstrate that she received support from neither the man she had married, Baily Winn, nor any of her other living sons. "Winn has not contributed to my support for years, if it was not for my neighbors I would suffer greatly."[62] Easter explained that her oldest son had been sold away, another had died, and she had lost communication with her youngest son, Oliver, when he went to war. Now, "totally blind," Easter lived with her daughter, Eliza Smith.[63] Easter's name was reinstated to the pension roster in 1896. The legal reviewer at the Law Division reasoned that despite her marriage to Baily Winn, Easter was "without other means of support."[64] Easter was awarded a mother's pension on May 28, 1892.

Familial relations exposed fault lines in bureau policy and amplified family discord. When William Gardner died in July 1887, his mother, Harriet Gardner (also known as Harriet Woodus), petitioned for a dependent mother's pension. She expected the government and William's wives to recognize her status as well. The case revolved around marriage because William's mother, Harriet, challenged Laura (Stott) Gardner's claim to widowhood. Harriet's petition pivoted on the subject of Laura's racial identity; Laura was a white woman, and interracial marriage was illegal under the North Carolina marriage statutes. Harriet's witnesses attempted to offer incontrovertible evidence about Laura's white racial identity: "I have heard

Laura A. say that she did not have a colored relation in the world before she lived with the soldier and she always claimed to be white."[65] Fannie Bryant, the mother of William's daughter Lillian, openly questioned Laura's racial identity: "I never heard her called 'colored' until after she filed her claim or rather recently."[66] Harriet even presented a handwritten letter from William's sister, Helen Jones, which categorically declared: "NO! Laura and William were not married[.] And they didn't sleep together either. For they could not get the minister to marry them because it was against the law because she was a white woman."[67] Harriet and her family cast Laura as a transgressive white woman. A black woman who met Laura shortly after she arrived in New Bern "always understood she was a white woman living with a black man. I never knew of any 'mulatto' about her."[68] According to Harriet's logic, Laura was ineligible for benefits because as a white woman she could have never legally married Harriet's son.

Perception equaled reality in the southern context. The mere appearance of sexual impropriety between a black man and a white woman was enough to ignite violence. Even in New Bern, with its history of interracial contact, black-majority population, and legacy of interracial liaisons, the racial hierarchy punished blacks in instances of a perceived violation. Harriet probably believed that the perception of Laura as white and female invited trouble for her son. The intense political climate of the Black Second could also have influenced Harriet's thinking. In the months leading up to William's death, Harriet had witnessed Israel B. Abbott's unsuccessful run against Congressman James E. O'Hara. Abbott argued that O'Hara's mixed race background made him unfit to represent the Eighth Congressional District, which included New Bern. The Republican vote split, thereby allowing Furnifold Simmons, the Democratic candidate, to win.[69]

Laura Gardner countered Harriet's maternal claim when she hired agent Frederick C. Douglass and petitioned on her own behalf.[70] It is difficult to reconstruct this case from Laura Gardner's perspective: her testimony no longer exists in her pension file. It is, however, clear that she testified; she marked the claimant's final statement acknowledging Frederick C. Douglass as her attorney and her satisfaction with the way the examination was carried out on November 11, 1892. It is, therefore, hard to know exactly how Laura positioned herself during the investigation; however, there is enough testimony from witnesses to reconstruct the basic outlines of her response to her mother-in-law's claim.

After William Gardner's discharge, he returned to New Bern with his new bride, Laura Stott, and settled with his mother, Harriet, in the city's Fifth

Ward. The daughter of a white woman and a northern-born free man of color, Laura's racial ambiguity provided fodder for New Bern's black community and civil authorities alike. Born in Summerville, South Carolina, Laura was relegated to a subservient position within her family. Eliza Mayo, a black woman who grew up with Laura, said she was "not considered clear white because her father was not a white man. . . . She always went with me and colored girls. I used to associate and do yet with her." To further establish Laura's racial identity, Mayo emphasized Laura's status within her family: she "was a servant for her own people and waited on others."[71] The testimony of black veterans who served with William Gardner and of a few Union widows who migrated from South Carolina to New Bern proved especially important in establishing the marriage between William Gardner and Laura A. Stott.

A crucial voice in the struggle between Laura and Harriet Gardner was that of Fannie Bryant, the black woman William "took-up" with. In such relationships, the woman might wash, cook, clean, and contribute to the family income while the man would contribute to her and the children's maintenance. These relationships were not always monogamous and could coexist with common-law or formal marriages; in some cases they were eventually legalized. It was the substance of the relationship and community recognition that constituted a marriage.[72] Informal relationships presented examiners with the challenge of determining whether evidence of cohabitation constituted a legal marriage. Because the Pension Bureau adhered to each state's definition of marriage, local examiners usually decided these issues on a case-by-case basis.

The possibility of Fannie Bryant petitioning as the legal widow would have transformed the investigation into a contesting widow's case. When veterans maintained more than one household, pension officials charged examiners with the responsibility of figuring out which wife was eligible for survivors' benefits. The possibility of two women seeking benefits as the widow of a deceased soldier was the type of scenario lawmakers predicted and examiners dreaded. It placed the question of marriage front and center and raised the potential of a contesting widows' case. In response to one of Douglass's unrecorded questions, Fannie replied, "I lived with Sgt. Wm. Gardner for years with me he live in my bed. I acted as his wife and he begot by me a child named Lilly Bryant. I do not claim to be married to him the child is half blood. I never considered him my husband while living in house and be with him."[73] With these words, Fannie effectively eliminated herself from consideration as Gardner's legal widow for purposes of the Pension Bureau, but not necessarily in the eyes of her community. It is not clear why

Fannie denied being Gardner's legal wife after emphasizing that she "acted as his wife." Fannie never petitioned for benefits, choosing instead to remarry.

Harriet Gardner lost her case because her matrifocal traditions conflicted with the pension system's patriarchal order. In siding with Laura Gardner, the Pension Bureau upheld the military's authority to declare what constituted a legal marriage and accepted Laura's racial identity as nonwhite, if not black. It also viewed Laura as a dependent, though she lived in a separate house with their three children and had established herself as a seamstress. Finally, as in many cases of this kind, Fannie Bryant and her daughter Lillian suffered an inordinate share of the consequences from the Pension Bureau. Recognizing Laura as William Gardner's widow made Fannie's relationship to William implicitly illicit or illegitimate, thus preventing her from filing a claim for her daughter as a legitimate heir.

Failure to ratify legally a marriage made behind Union lines had detrimental consequences for Thomas McCabe, the son of John McCabe. Thomas petitioned the Pension Bureau as the minor child of McCabe in 1890. Thomas's father had married his mother Cass Ann before the war, and the couple had three children together. Although they belonged to different owners, John occasionally visited Cass Ann's plantation at night. Thomas had to establish the legitimacy of his parents' marital union and his paternity. A former slave who knew them both said during her deposition in the case, "I know positively that they were regarded as being husband and wife. Cass Ann was just as near being the lawful wife of John McCabe as any slave woman could ever be the lawful wife of a slave man."[74] The examiner believed Thomas was John McCabe's offspring, but because John and Cass Ann had failed to ratify their marriage when they reached Union lines, the examiner said that Thomas was "illegitimate and had no title to pension."[75] Conceptualizing survivors' benefits through the lens of nuclear marriage had widespread implications for the families of deceased black veterans. This configuration was too rigid to accommodate the malleable and inclusive definitions of family that operated within black neighborhoods and communities.

PETITIONING FOR RECLASSIFICATION AND SUING FOR NONSUPPORT

Even after obtaining a pension under the service law, Mary Lee and many other women sought a reclassification of their case under the general law, which provided a higher level of benefits.[76] Pensions for widows of soldiers who died as a result of wounds or injuries received or disease contracted in the line of duty varied from twelve to thirty dollars a month. Under the service law, widows received a maximum of twelve dollars a month.[77] Women pursued this path as a matter of principle as well as monetary gain. Nancy Ann Bell, a cook and washerwoman who lived on New South Front Street, filed a series of petitions for survivors' benefits under the general law system because she "believed he [Lamb Bell] died of a disease which he contracted with in the army."[78] Pension officials refused to reclassify Mary's case and never approved Nancy Ann Bell's application.

The passage of the Act of March 3, 1899, permitted the wife of a pensioned veteran to sue her husband for one-half of his pension stipend.[79] In pursuing these claims, the wives of black soldiers joined a chorus of women who had revealed their economic vulnerability by filing claims for support that the Pension Bureau had not envisioned. The women called on pension officials to provide for the women and children of living veterans who neglected to contribute financially to their families. Indeed, pension officials had not contemplated how to support the women and children of veterans who had abandoned support of their families before 1899; until then, benefits were reserved for widows alone.

This law opened up space for women to publicize issues of nonsupport and desertion within the agency. Heretofore, these conversations had taken place in community forums, and though violators faced consequences in their communities, they suffered no consequences in the pension system. Women were acutely aware of the risks involved in publicizing issues of nonsupport both to the pension system and to their own communities. In addition to the agency's drawn-out process, speaking out against black veterans outside accepted community forums might result in social ostracization. Thus, prior to filing a claim against their husbands and exposing the interpersonal dynamics of their relationships with examiners, women made careful estimations about when and how to file petitions for nonsupport. They took stock of their financial circumstances, the time and money involved in pursuing such a case, and the potential that the community would repudiate their charges.[80]

Women who filed petitions for half their husbands' pensions tended to be in such desperate economic circumstances that the possibility of regular financial support outweighed the inconvenience of a protracted battle with their husbands. Jamsey Green's veteran husband, Robert, refused to contribute to her support for well over fifteen years. She sued him for half of his disability benefits. Robert responded in the proceedings by casting Jamsey as an immoral and unworthy woman. He told the investigator that she had "left home" while he was away working and removed all his belongings from the home. Robert said he owed Jamsey nothing because he "supported her and treated [her] all right before she left" him. He refused to live with Jamsey because he claimed she was running a "whorehouse." The entire disagreement with Jamsey had to do with money: "She did not want me, but all she wanted is my money," he protested.[81] Before pension officials resolved the dispute, Robert Green died. Jamsey Green was now required to file a new petition for widows' benefits. Marriage became an issue in the case. Nearly ten years after she began petitioning the government for half her husband's disability pension and then as a Union widow, Jamsey Green obtained a pension. A year later she died of a "stroke of apoplexy."[82]

Disabled veteran and pensioner Isaac Waters filed a series of letters to challenge his wife Sarah Waters's successful petition for half of his pension allowance. He attempted to undermine Sarah's claim by arguing that he had never married her in a legal or religious ceremony. He then questioned the government's decision to side with Sarah in the matter: "I am the soldier that is suffering not her. I am the one [who] lost my he[a]lth in the army."[83] Ultimately Waters blamed the government for failing to protect his rights and privileges. Veteran Benjamin Wallace similarly protested the commissioner's decision to award his wife, Hetty, half of his pension by painting her as sexually immoral. Wallace argued that he was a supportive husband before he brought up a deeply personal aspect of his medical history. He said that "he was afflicted with Syphilis" and that Hetty had passed that "loathsome disease to him."[84] Pension officials suspended Hetty's benefits and gave her an opportunity to respond to her husband's charges.[85] Following Benjamin's death, Hetty successfully established her standing with the bureau as Union widow.

CONCLUSION

Even with expansion of the federal pension system under the service law of 1890, definitions of marriage and notions of worthy womanhood remained a constant battleground among black women, examiners, and pension officials. When poor black women like Charlotte Banks stated their claims for widows' pensions, they offered alternative definitions of marriage, family, and widowhood, which translated into conceptualizations of their wants and needs that were sometimes new to the employees of the Pension Bureau. They also challenged the established boundaries between political, social, and economic issues in pension system policy. Finally, they carved out new spaces from which to publicize their social and economic struggles within government institutions in the post-Reconstruction South.

Some women pursued pensions as a matter of practicality and as a way to remedy the harsh conditions of the postwar labor market. With federal recognition as a Union widow, these women could buffer themselves from the social categories of "unmarried" and "single" and in some instances could maintain independent households. Black women—single, married, or widowed, and with or without children—made decisions about how to live their lives in the spaces in between freedom and modern society. Precisely how soldiers' wives and war widows decided to reconstruct their intimate lives after surviving war and displacement proved central to their engagement with the pension bureau in the postwar years. Scholars of gender and emancipation have provided important models of employing gender analysis to the Civil War and Reconstruction eras while integrating insights from policy history. Indeed, these were precisely the questions that Fanny Whitney and Charlotte Banks pondered as the war subsided. Answers to such questions had measurable consequences for black women seeking survivors' benefits in the years leading up to the twentieth century. In organizing their households on their own terms, these women might very well have been offering a broader critique of the fundamental inequalities at the center of the federal pension system while maintaining substantive relationships with the men in their lives.

7

Black Women and Suspensions for "Open and Notorious Cohabitation"

In early March 1894, examiner Emmett D. Gallion returned to New Bern. Shortly after his arrival, he learned, perhaps from community whispers or perhaps from examiner Charles Gilpin (also stationed in New Bern), that Louisa Powers, a soldier's widow and pension recipient, had appeared before justice of the peace E. G. Hill and had been indicted on a charge of "lewd and lascivious cohabitation" earlier that month.[1] Gallion took it on himself to inform the commissioner of pensions of the charges leveled against Louisa Powers. Gallion explained his involvement in the case in 1889 and his doubts regarding the medical cause of Samuel Powers's death. "It was shown the soldiers four daughters were prostitutes ranging in age from 14 years to 20 years old, had given birth to children or were at the time pregnant," he observed.[2] Gallion asked that Louisa's case file be sent to him so that he might start a new investigation. Nearly two months later Louisa received a notice from Commissioner Lochren that her name would be removed from the pension rolls on the grounds of "open and notorious cohabitation." The commissioner gave Louisa thirty days to file evidence to the contrary.[3]

About a month after reporting Louisa Powers to the commissioner, examiner Gallion took steps to have Charrity Brown removed from the pension rolls for violating the 1882 law. Charrity had been admitted to the pension rolls in 1888, when examiners Gallion and William Porter made their way through Craven County investigating claims from disabled soldiers and their survivors. A veteran and James City resident said Charrity had "given birth to a child within the last two years," and one of her children had since died.[4] With this testimony on record, Gallion conveyed the next steps of the investigation to the commissioner: "I do not care to disturb the Pensioner until I have the papers, as the colored people are in the habit under such circumstances of spiriting away the surplus children, causing no end of trouble in ascertaining the true condition of facts." Believing that many more women in the area had violated the bureau's policy, Gallion requested that "the names residences . . . of all widows in my Territory be furnished me. . . . I have no doubt that there are quite a percent who have gone wrong."[5]

Two days after investigating the Charrity Brown case, Gallion obtained evidence from a black undertaker's record books that Mary Lee, the woman he had investigated six years earlier, had also violated of the terms of the 1882 law.[6] He went directly to her home, where he found Mary talking with a disabled black veteran on the front steps, and began questioning her from the street: "I want to know how long your Husband been [d]ead, that you had Child and Buried him." Mary responded: "I had no Child of my own by Birth, but I had one given to me by the City Authorities." Gallion called her a "Liar" and told her he "would throw her off the roll." She told him, "I had no men," and admonished him to "go away . . . my House is no Quarling House." Mary then went inside and shut the door.[7] Six days later Mary Lee filed charges of "slander" against examiner Gallion at the Craven County Court and lodged a formal complaint with the U.S. Department of the Interior, which held supervisory power over the Pension Bureau's decisions.[8] Unlike Louisa Powers and Charrity Brown, Mary Lee managed to retain her pension.

The restructuring of the Pension Bureau, which preceded the 1882 law, included a change in how pension officials conducted special examinations. New guidelines gave examiners the latitude to assess the private conduct of pensioners in their communities. The examination system also gave widows a mechanism with which to make their voices heard by filing complaints against examiners and claims agents. The new examination process, together with the 1882 law, placed the private lives of all Union widows under close scrutiny. Yet black Union widows' inability to provide standard documentary evidence of their marital unions meant that special examinations addressing marriage, remarriage, and cohabitation remained commonplace during the application process. Consequently, narratives about sexual immorality abounded in their case files.

This chapter details how the claims of prospective beneficiaries changed through the experiences of Louisa Powers, Charrity Brown, Mary Lee, and several other women. New forms of sexual regulation countered the racially neutral rules initiated in 1866. At that time lawmakers opened up the system to the formerly enslaved and Indian people by accepting witness testimony to document marriage. Women argued their claims and navigated the pension system in light of this new law and its administration. Black women's experiences with the surveillance components of the pension system and criminal constructions of their sexuality were part of the larger process of consolidating the racialized gender state.

The social and political changes unfolding in and around New Bern in the last decade of the nineteenth century are central to understanding black women's relationship to governmental institutions and their citizenship claims. The large concentration of black Union widows who resided in and around New Bern amplified the investigations in the locality. At least six white Union widows lived in New Bern around 1894, but none were targeted under the 1882 law.[9] Race and class largely protected white women: they could legally document their marriages and shield their private lives.

Black women's responses to local examiners signaled women's increased awareness and understanding of the organizational shifts and the implementation of new laws in the examination procedures. The women made calculated decisions about how to respond to suspensions under the 1882 law. In addition, as a result of claims agent Frederick C. Douglass's support for women charged with violating the new law, some pension professionals endured intensified scrutiny of their own business practices.

BLACK WOMEN AND THE LAW OF 1882

The Act of August 7, 1882, sought to clarify the bureau's stance on remarriage by using sexual morality as a basis for determining whether Union widows would remain on the pension roster. When conducting investigations, pension examiners needed only to establish that a woman was living with a man or engaged in immoral conduct before terminating her pension. Before this law, pension administrators had to determine whether a woman had remarried according to state law, but there was no formal set of procedures for examiners to follow. With the passage of the new law, pension officials developed protocols for ascertaining women's moral conduct. Special examiners interpreted and applied the law's provisions.

Revisions to the examiners' instructions illustrate the increased power of special examiners to supervise the private lives of Union widows under the 1882 law. Four years after the law's passage, the commissioner of pensions clarified the protocol for administering the rule during special examinations by adding a paragraph to the examiner handbook. When an examiner learned that a pensioner had lived "with any man since the death of the soldier, in the absence of marriage ceremony," he was instructed to determine "what relations the parties maintained." If the widow "openly" presented herself as a married woman in her community or if she "lived in open and notorious adultery," examiners had to establish this fact and determine when the relationship began. In 1889 bureau officials issued new instructions to examiners to ensure the "uniform" administration of the law. Amended instructions directed them "to take a deposition from widow claimants" and ask, "Have you cohabited with any man as his wife since the death of the soldier?" The introduction of this new language marked an important turning point. Rather than viewing women as victims of duplicitous claims agents, local examiners increasingly discussed women using personal language, casting them as immoral, unchaste, and bad mothers.[10]

CLAIMING WORTHY WIDOWHOOD

Widows who sought survivors' pensions in eastern North Carolina had learned many lessons from the cohabitation investigations of the 1870s. They observed what happened in other women's cases and made the necessary adjustments in their own dealings with pension agents. Slowly and over time, they began to echo the agency's language on cohabitation and to model themselves on its image of honorable widowhood. One woman who had been falsely accused of remarrying and collecting survivors' benefits declared, "I have never had any desire or intention to get married."[11] While making her case for a dependent mother's pension, another woman told an examiner that she had "been true to his memory in every way."[12] Mary Lee rejected a suitor's overtures because "she was afraid of losing her pension."[13] Another widow explained her position on remarriage and sexual intimacy to a special examiner under direct questioning: "I was afraid I would get caught and what few pennies I get from the government would be stopped if I continued to [do] it."[14]

These women understood the provisions of the law of 1882, the examination process, and the bureau's concept of widowhood well enough not to disclose the details of their private lives. The repetition of words and phrases that conveyed shared constructs of chastity in the testimonies of black women suggests a collective strategy. The frequency and regularity of special examinations required black women to master the applicable rules, concepts, language, and examination process to the same degree the examiners themselves did. Thus, while each woman's relationship with the bureau and its examiners was highly individualized, as a group they developed an understanding of the law of 1882 and strategies to maintain their pensions.

Mary Vonveil, worried that the birth of her child would jeopardize her standing on the pension roster, tried to gain the cooperation of her neighbors and friends to conceal the birth. Less than an hour after giving birth, she summoned her neighbors, Henrietta and Charles Guion, to her home and asked if they could "take the child and keep it for a month." The Guions agreed to assist Mary and "carried the child home." "The pension agent was around," Charles said, "and she did not want the child to be in the way of her getting money."[15] Guion's revelation positioned Mary squarely within the purview of the law of 1882.

Examiner Charles Gilpin pressed Mary Vonveil for details about her intimate life: "Have you given birth to any children since the death of your husband? You state you have not cohabited with any man since the death of your husband. Are you sure that that is true?" Mary shot back, "I am sure." Gilpin then asked Mary if she was pregnant at that very moment. Mary responded, "Nothing the matter with me except a cold, and I have a large stomach any how."[16] Gilpin's report to the commissioner of pensions underscored his frustration. He requested Vonveil's complete file. Two weeks later, he informed the commissioner, "Since making my first report the pensioner has given birth to a child and I recommend that her name be dropped from the pension rolls."[17] Examiner Gilpin used the same aggressive style when he interrogated pensioner Mary Ellison Rodman in June 1895. Rodman had gained admission to the pension rolls a year earlier. At the time of her deposition, Rodman was pregnant. Gilpin pummeled her with a series of invasive questions: "Arn't you pregnant now?" "How long have you been swollen up?" "When did you have sexual intercourse with the man you spoke of?" In the face of these deeply personal questions, Mary obstructed the examiner's attempt to invade her private life and denied being pregnant. Eventually she said, "I will not state that I am not pregnant, although if I am I don't know it."[18]

Historians have shown that black women developed a code of silence around their intimate lives as a response to whites' attacks on their sexuality. According to Darlene Clark Hine, dissemblance in the face of intrusive questioning and oppressive situations was a survival tactic to protect their personhood.[19] Vonveil's and Rodman's refusal to answer examiner Gilpin's direct questioning about their pregnancies was a protective strategy, but it nonetheless had consequences. Mary Vonveil and Mary Rodman probably knew that he would report their names to the Pension Bureau for violating the 1882 law.

Rather than dissemble, as Mary Vonveil and Mary Rodman did, some women attempted to resist the reach of the law by articulating and promoting concepts of widowhood cultivated in their communities. Charrity Brown faced a similar situation when an examiner inquired about the father of her children during a special examination, but she refused to answer. "I do not tell anyone that," Charrity began, but then admitted, "Both of these children were born after I had commenced drawing pension."[20] With this statement, Charrity Brown systematically protected one aspect of her private life while exposing certain aspects of her intimate life that she believed were acceptable. In doing so, she rejected the pension system's construct of virtuous widowhood and positioned herself as an honorable Union widow. The examiner quickly moved to remove Charrity from the pension rolls, but not before describing what he viewed as a paradox: "This woman seems to have been more provident with her pension money than the average class of her race and owns a lot of ground with a very comfortable house on it. She seems to stand as well with her neighbors now as when she was considered virtuous."[21] The commissioner informed Charrity Brown in July 1894 that her pension benefits would be suspended.

While under investigation by E. D. Gallion, Mary Jane Moore attempted to force a redefinition of her character and explain her plight as an abandoned wife and mother. Mary Jane had obtained a pension in 1891. Gallion suspected that she had given birth while receiving a pension and began an investigation. Under direct questioning, Mary Jane admitted that she had given birth to seven children over the course of her marriage, but only one belonged to her deceased husband. Realizing that she faced suspension from the pension roster, she explained that Jacob had treated her "cruelly," had begun living with another woman, and had moved to another city. On her own and with their child to support, she turned to sex work and began "keeping house" for single men to earn wages. "I had to pursue this course of life after my husband left me."[22] By describing her sexual encounters as work, Mary Jane implied that these relationships did not constitute marriage because she collected pay and none of the men she had children with had contributed to her financial support. Mary Jane's argument did not persuade pension officials, who notified her of her impending suspension.

CHALLENGING SUSPENSIONS FOR "OPEN AND NOTORIOUS COHABITATION"

Given the growing sophistication and success of claims agents in eastern North Carolina, it is possible that Mary Vonveil, Mary Ellison Rodman, and Mary Jane Moore had been advised both to claim their children under oath to avoid criminal prosecution for perjury under federal law and to file an appeal. They may also have been relying on examiners' inconsistent interpretation and administration of the law as a basis on which to build an appeal.

Mary Jane Moore challenged her suspension in 1894. With the assistance of Curtis Palmer (presumably the son of William Palmer, the white veteran turned notary public), Mary Jane appealed to the chief of the special examination division of the Pension Bureau. In arguing for Mary Jane's case, Palmer reminded officials of how the secretary of the interior had interpreted Louisa Powers's case under the law of 1882 four years earlier.[23] Mary Jane's name was restored to the pension roster sometime thereafter, and she remained on the rolls until she died of heart disease in 1919.

Though Mary Lee maintained her standing on the pension roster during the 1894 "open and notorious cohabitation" investigations examiner Gallion spearheaded, she filed charges of "malicious slander" against the examiner at the Craven County Court and lodged a formal complaint with the Department of the Interior six days after he accused her of violating the law of 1882.[24] The precise words Mary Lee used in her complaint demonstrated her ability to frame her case for two distinct audiences. In her appeal to the Pension Bureau, she drew on the agency's concept of Union widowhood to undermine Gallion's. By presenting herself as an aggrieved Union widow whom Gallion had publicly shamed, she directly challenged the notion that she was a "Liar . . . having men" in the affidavit she filed with the Department of the Interior.[25] Publicizing her case in her community had an altogether different meaning. When she filed charges of malicious slander against examiner Gallion at the Craven County Court, Mary's chief objective was to vindicate her reputation and respectability within her community. She was successful in both settings.[26]

About six days after Mary Lee filed her complaint against Gallion in the Law Division of the Pension Bureau, the commissioner of pensions notified Louisa Powers once again that she would lose her pension for violating the law of 1882. Louisa painstakingly rebutted Gallion's rendition of the fornication and adultery charges she had faced at the county court. She denied violating the law of 1882 and attempted to rehabilitate her reputation as a worthy widow.

Powers urged the commissioner to authorize a new "hearing as soon as possible."[27] She explained that the pending fornication and adultery charges at the Craven County Court were the result of a community conflict. In exposing and publicizing the local "controversy" to the commissioner of pensions, Louisa hoped to instigate a new investigation. Her strategy was successful, because in August 1894, examiner Charles Gilpin arrived in Harlowe to gather new evidence in her case.

The witnesses who came forward in Louisa's investigation pointedly situated the charges of fornication and adultery in its local context. Gilpin began by gathering testimony from the principal witnesses who had testified in Craven County Court for the fornication and adultery case, including John Rowley, the laborer Louisa had "whipped" and kicked out of her home; Siddy Powers; and two local ministers. Few facts emerged from these witnesses beyond what Gallion reported in his March 1894 letter to the commissioner. On this occasion, however, the witnesses offered a scathing critique of Louisa's public and private behavior. Minister Isaac Waters said he "would consider her a lewd woman." Minister W. H. Fulford said, "It is believed by all the people in the neighborhood that she and James Bell are guilty of fornication and adultery." Fulford offered Gilpin another damaging piece of information about Louisa during his deposition: "She told me that when she was prosecuting her claim for pension she had to hide the child."[28] The most sensational and damaging testimony offered during Gilpin's 1894 investigation came from Louisa's daughter Siddy: "I have seen James M. Bell in bed with my mother. I have seen him in bed with her several times, he spend a great deal of time at my mothers house and I have seen them making love to each other and he would stay all night and sleep with her." Siddy told examiner Gilpin about her "one half sister" named Rossie. She believed Rossie's father was Jim Watson. Siddy also told examiner Gilpin that her mother had had "two children since the death" of her father. "She had a boy named Archie Gardner," who had lived only about a month.[29] Notably, John A. Morton, the white farmhand whom Louisa had filed charges against for assaulting her son, signed off on Siddy's testimony as a certifying witness.

Gilpin subjected Louisa Powers to a grueling round of questions with the same tone and style he displayed in the investigations of Mary Vonveil and Mary Ellison Rodman.

GILPIN: Were you not tried before him [E. G. Hill] during the month of March 1894?

LOUISA POWERS: Yes, sir.

GILPIN: What were you charged with?
POWERS: I was not charged with anything.
GILPIN: Isn't it true that you was charged with fornication and adultery?
POWERS: No sir, it is not. That is the first I ever heard of that.
GILPIN: Then you was charged with fornication and adultery, were you not.
POWERS: That's it. I remember it now and the case was carried to the Superior Court and I had to give a bond for my appearance at the next term of the Superior Court.[30]

Gilpin continued to press Louisa with deeply personal questions. He reminded her of the testimony she had given six years earlier:

GILPIN: On the 17 day of December 1888 you stated before special examiner E. D. Gallion that you had had one child a girl since the death of your husband.
POWERS: Yes sir, I remember now I did have a girl about thirteen or fourteen years ago, her name was Rossie, been dead for some time.
GILPIN: How many children did you have after the death of your husband.
POWERS: None but that one.

If Louisa seemed flippant and evasive regarding the charges, she was far more direct on the subject of how the charges came to be: "I am not guilty of the charge, the reason I was accused of it I found a man by the name of John [A.] Rowley in the bed with my daughter Siddie Ann." She told the court exactly how she disciplined the miscreants: "I took my buggy whip and whipped them both and they then accused me of staying with my neighbor James M. Bell." The next day Gilpin returned to Louisa's home to clarify the names and birthdates of Louisa's children: "In your statement before me on the 28th inst you state that your daughter Rossie has been dead for sometime, is that correct?" Louisa changed her answer again: "No, I was mistaken." After a few more questions Gilpin ended his questioning.[31] In Louisa's view, her case had to do with her assertive parenting style rather than her sexual activity.

Gilpin submitted a scathing field report to the commissioner of pensions. "Her character in the neighborhood in which she lives is about as bad as it could well be she is looked upon as being a lewd woman, and has been living in adulterous cohabitation for the last two years or more."[32] In Gilpin's opinion, Louisa Powers had "violated" the 1882 law, and he recommended that she be dropped from the pension roster. In September 1894, the commissioner permanently removed Louisa from the rolls.[33]

On suspension under the act of 1882, women were also notified that they would no longer be eligible to handle the benefits of their minor children. Both Charrity Brown and Louisa Powers took steps to protect their children's status as legal minors within the pension system. About a year after her own suspension, Louisa set out to secure disability benefits for her youngest child. She wrote to Commissioner William Lochren on behalf of her son Samuel Powers, who was an "invalid and not able to take care for his self." Samuel, she explained, "has been a invalid all his life and has not as yet been placed on the roll since she has been drop[p]ed." Louisa closed the letter by requesting his case be considered "and allowed in his favor. . . . He are upon my hands for his care and maintainance."[34]

After the Pension Bureau rejected Charrity's and Louisa's efforts to act as their children's guardians, which essentially meant handling their money, they appointed Robert G. Mosley to act on their children's behalf. Mosley, a respected black proprietor of free black ancestry, agreed to collect and distribute the children's benefits until they reached the age of majority. Pension officials awarded minor's benefits to Charrity's son, Henry Brown, in July 1896. Louisa Powers never secured benefits on behalf of her disabled son.

Black Union widows like Louisa Powers, who repeatedly ran up against agency rules and community scrutiny, add to our understanding of the surveillance working-class black women navigated.[35] Though neither Charrity Brown nor Louisa Powers had her name restored to the pension roll, it is significant that they attempted to challenge the system. Louisa's attempt to restore her pension by using everyday language and injecting social context back into her case posed a significant alternative to Mary Lee's casting herself in the image of the pension system's version of worthy widowhood. Charrity Brown, Louisa Powers, Mary Lee, and many others displayed the varying dimensions of black women's protest politics within federal institutions at the turn of the century.[36]

PENSION PROFESSIONALS UNDER ATTACK

During examiner Gallion's 1894 foray into New Bern, he seemed just as intent on purging the formidable black claims agent Frederick C. Douglass from representing veterans and widows as he was on removing widows for violating the terms of the 1882 law. He blamed Douglass for his own demotion in 1889 and sought to have Douglass's license from the Pension Bureau revoked. Gallion had been instrumental in an investigation of Douglass on suspicion of collecting illegal fees for his service to widows, and later that same year, before Gallion departed, the Pension Bureau had issued a stern warning to Douglass on the recommendation of another special examiner.[37] Now Gallion was busy collecting evidence for a new case against Douglass, tapping into dissent in the community of black veterans and their survivors.[38] After scrutinizing evidence from the files of at least six widows, Gallion found the case of Julia Neel promising for his purposes. He believed that he had enough evidence to file formal charges in the U.S. District Court in Raleigh against Douglass for collecting illegal fees.

Douglass mounted a successful defense of himself and his business. He showed that Julia Neel, the black mother of fallen soldier William H. Lewis, was much savvier than Gallion imagined. Recounting his version of events in his characteristically proud yet increasingly direct tone, Douglass described Julia as a challenging client in an affidavit taken under oath on April 21, 1894. She regularly borrowed money, asking for a dollar here, two dollars there, and an occasional horse and buggy for transportation, but she refused to pay him for his services. After he spent "three or four hours" helping her petition for dependent mother's benefits, she failed to compensate him for his labor, saying, "Much obliged to you Brother Douglass, the Lord Will Pay you."[39]

Douglass drew on gendered concepts of virtue to cast Julia Neel as an unworthy recipient of the nation's bounty.

> I have actually been inform that she has had two husbands since the death of William H. Lewis the soldiers Father to wit one [Carroll] Jones and one Neel who they say become blind and she drove him off and he was sent to the county poor house and there died. I am sure that she and part of her witnesses swore that she had not been Remarried or lived with any man since the Death of her Husband and that is the way she obtain Pension, that is William H. Lewis Father and Wm H. Lewis Father Died Just before the war so I was inform."[40]

The gist of Douglass's argument was that Julia had remarried twice and thereby violated the 1882 law. But the law did not apply to mothers; it applied only to widows.

Douglass seized the opportunity to criticize Gallion's conduct in the region: "Ever Since March 12th 1894, The Time Mr. E. D. Gallion, The Special Examiner of Bureau, Made his appearance in The City of New Bern, N.C. The City been in uproar. I never have heard or seen such illegal Prosceedings since March 1889, The time he was [here] before." According to Douglass, the special examiners who conducted investigations in New Bern before Gallion arrived had "acted as perfect gentlemen."[41] But Gallion began shadowing pension beneficiaries, digging up old cases, building cases against claims agents who represented widows, and accusing Douglass of "perpetuating fraud upon the [Pension] Office."[42]

Douglass's appeal did not win over the commissioner of pensions, who suspended Douglass's licensure to represent claims within the pension system on June 11, 1894. Nor did Douglass convince the judge, who moved the case against Douglass forward in federal court; pension officials paid close attention to the outcome. On October 26, 1894, Douglass faced a federal grand jury to answer claims that he had billed Julia Neel for fees beyond what the government allowed. Leonidas J. Moore, a white Democrat, represented Douglass; Charles B. Aycock, a white Democrat who later became governor of North Carolina, represented the U.S. government. The court minutes provide an account of the scene. Douglass, pensioner Julia Neel, and two black farmers, Elisha and Oliver White, sat in the court along with examiners Gallion and Gilpin. A jury of twelve men (eleven white and one black), whom agent Douglass described as some of "the Leading Citizens of New Berne," heard the case.[43] Two days later the jury acquitted Douglass of collecting illegal fees. Feeling vindicated, Douglass promptly sent certified copies of the district court trial records from Craven County to the commissioner of pensions, who refused to reinstate Douglass's privilege to represent pension claims; the commissioner said the evidence was "not sufficient upon which to recommend . . . restoration" of his license.[44]

The commissioner had sorely underestimated the depth of support for Douglass in eastern North Carolina. Few veterans or their widows had looked with favor on earlier efforts to prevent Douglass from serving as a claims agent. Local businessmen, politicians, and community leaders, both black and white, signed petitions in support of Douglass, and feisty black pensioners conducted their own fierce letter-writing campaign, inquiring about Douglass's case and recommending his reinstatement. White Democrats praised Douglass as an "honorable and truthful man." Even Furnifold M. Simmons, the collector of internal revenue at the time and a militant white supremacist who would play a leading role in the campaign to disfranchise North Carolina blacks, said that he was "very anxious to have Frederick Douglass restored to his position of U.S. Pension Agent."[45]

In an impassioned December 1894 letter to Nathan Bickford, a pension attorney and the department commander of the GAR, an organization of Union veterans, Frederick Douglass explained the details of his case.[46] He recounted his long ordeal with examiner Gallion, and Douglass turned Mary Lee's conflict with Gallion into the symbolic center of his battle to save his own professional standing within the Pension Bureau.[47] He replayed the pivotal incident between him and examiner Gallion during the investigation of Louisa Powers's case, quoting Gallion as saying, "'Fred Douglass I do not believe there is an Honest Colored Woman in North Carolina that they all was nothing but prostitutes and whores.' I made him take the words back he told me he would take the words back but he would fix me."[48]

In linking the narratives of examiner misconduct and the protection of black Union widows, Douglass drew on the black middle-class political discourse used to combat a calculated campaign white Democrats had deployed to recapture the majority in the state legislature.[49] Democrats propagated the white supremacist myth that black men's rapes of white women had increased as a result of black political power.[50] In Douglass's version of the story, black Union widows were actually the ones in need of protection from offensive special examiners.

Douglass asked Bickford to arrange his "restoral" to the Department of the Interior's list of approved agents.[51] Veteran Shadrick Tripp of James City gathered signatures from veterans and one widow, Clara Williams, on a petition supporting Douglass. Tripp then sent the petition to U.S. Senator Jeter C. Pritchard, a Republican and supporter of fusion arrangements with Populists in 1894, imploring him to give "serious attention" to the case and to present it to the commissioner of pensions.[52]

The campaign against New Bern claims agents Douglass and Carpenter went national in 1895. The *New York Times* carried this front-page headline on November 4, 1895: "PENSION FRAUDS IN NORTH CAROLINA. Jane Hill Sentenced to One Year's Imprisonment—Attorneys Indicted." The *Times* detailed "a formidable conspiracy in and around New-Berne to defraud the Government out of pensions. . . . The men at the bottom of the frauds are E. W. Carpenter, white, and Fred Douglass, colored, pension attorneys." Both had been indicted for "false claims."[53] "Numerous persons" were "charged with defrauding the Government by securing pensions to which they were not entitled."[54]

During his unsuccessful bid to restore his standing as a claims agent within the bureau, Douglass managed to reinvent himself. In 1897, he secured a position as a magistrate in New Bern.[55] In this capacity, he continued to assist widows by filling out and certifying documents. Douglass's advocacy on behalf of black Union widows, combined with his respected position, drew intense scrutiny from white supremacists. In the months before the Wilmington massacre, white Democrats ran a vicious publicity campaign equating black political empowerment with the sexual violation of white women. To invoke the specter of "Negro Domination," Democrats circulated inflammatory representations of black municipal leaders using their authority to invade white domestic space.[56] The *Charlotte News and Observer* reported that ten black magistrates in New Bern used their positions to harass white women. Frederick C. Douglass landed in the paper as a result of his involvement in the arrests of Edith Anderson and Mrs. Louis Habicht, both white women, based on a black woman's complaint.[57] W. H. Green, a black barber and justice of the peace, reportedly carried out the trial in his barbershop at Five Points, a black neighborhood in New Bern. Stories such as these inflamed whites' racial anxiety.

Douglass continued to use the federal apparatus and his local social networks against the charges of illegal conduct. Unlike the women he represented, whose testimonies were first shaped by claims agents, then by local examiners, and finally reprocessed into bureau memoranda, Douglass was able to present his own version of the 1894 "uproars," the illegal fees case, the trial, and his acquittal in Craven County Court to the commissioner of pensions.[58] His letters reveal the depth and reach of his personal contacts. Douglass explained the dilemma of his suspension to assistant secretary of the interior Webster Davis: "Under the Republican administration I had no trouble what ever but stood well before the Department I completed over fifteen hundred pension claim more or less. But under Cleveland's first administration General Black appointed the son of an ex-Rebel as an examiner."[59]

In an October 1897 letter, Douglass's daughter Mamie urged the secretary of the interior to reopen her father's case. A graduate of Livingston College, Mamie appealed on her father's behalf: "I know that you as Honorable man and Ex Judge do not believe this is Right."[60] Douglass also galvanized support from a cross-section of white and black municipal leaders, educators, and state-level political figures. Henry P. Cheatham, a black Republican who had represented the Second Congressional District in the U.S. Congress from 1889 to 1893, told the commissioner that "Mr. Douglass . . . is a very valuable man to us in New Bern."[61] William F. Fonville, assistant principal of the State Normal School for the Training of Colored Teachers in Raleigh, wrote, "He stands well in the immediate community as a Christian gentleman high up in the councils of his local church."[62] Mathias Manly, an ex-Confederate soldier who now served as postmaster in New Bern, told the secretary of the interior that Douglass was a "man of good character, honest in his obligation, and bears a good reputation for truth and fair dealings."[63] W. H. Jones, chairman of the Eighth Congressional District, sent a letter of support.[64] None of these testimonies made a difference.

The "Grand Army boys," in a July 9, 1897, petition, maintained that Douglass "has always stood ready and willing to assist a poor soldier and widow and orphan and defend father and mother." They joined the widows and orphans of black soldiers and several white and black leaders in defending Douglass as an "honest, truthful, high toned Christian gentlemen and therefore worthy of confidence."[65] The former principal of New Bern's black schools and now congressman George H. White, eager to address the concerns of his constituents in the Eighth District, met with "old soldiers Colored and White and other citizens of New Bern" to listen to their concerns regarding the handling of Frederick Douglass's case. He urged the commissioner of pensions to reconsider Douglass's application for licensure as a claims agent.[66] In November of the same year, Leonidas J. Moore, attorney and ex-state senator, asked the commissioner to "do this act of justice before a new administration comes in."[67]

White municipal leaders who helped black veterans and their survivors prepare evidence for their cases were not immune from scrutiny during the illegal fees investigation. A white northerner who actively campaigned for the Republican Party in New Bern, Edward Carpenter was no stranger to public ridicule. Not only had he been named in the 1895 *New York Times* story, but in 1898, a local Democratic paper launched a personal attack on him. At the time Carpenter was seeking to regain his former position as clerk of the Craven County Court on the Republican ticket. On September 15, the *New Berne Journal* published a letter signed "Democrat," accusing Carpenter of living "openly and defiantly" with a black woman and "a large family of Negro children."[68] The writer's reference pointed to Sarah Oxly. The letter revealed that he had formerly been a pension attorney but was "disbarred" for collecting illegal fees from his clients. On November 3, Carpenter fought back with a caustic letter to the editor denying any involvement with Sarah Oxly beyond "taking meals" at her boardinghouse.[69] He then addressed the case of Jane Hill, the fifty-three-year-old washerwoman who lived in the Trent City refugee camp with Douglass's mother during the war. Hill had been sentenced to twelve months in prison for collecting $2,400 as the widow of a soldier who was, in fact, still living at the time and had testified against her. "The government was made to believe that her pension claim was a fraudulent one," but the presiding judge "did not believe her guilty." Jane Hill "was given a light sentence" as she was "justly entitled to the pension."[70] Until his death in 1904, Carpenter continued to advise black claimants about their right to benefits from the government.

PROCEDURAL CHANGES AND BLACK WOMEN'S CLAIMS

In 1897, H. Clay Evans, the newly appointed commissioner of pensions, called for important changes to the implementation and administration of the law of 1882. In September of that year, Commissioner Evans, who had been in office since April, revised the guidelines for applying the law of 1882 in the handbook *General Instructions to Special Examiners*. In effect, the commissioner prohibited examiners from asking petitioners if they had "cohabited with any man as his wife since the death of the soldier" unless "the circumstances of the case or the evidence procured" suggested the petitioner had been living in adultery. If the examiner believed that a woman had violated the agency's evolving moral standards, then he had to show "the date when such relations commenced and ceased." Evans encouraged the examiners to carry out the investigation into the woman's private life "carefully and discreetly, so as not to cause unnecessary neighborhood gossip or scandal." Finally, he instructed examiners to make the woman aware of all the testimony gathered against her and give her an opportunity "to produce all evidence in rebuttal that she might desire."[71] Commissioner Evans announced these changes in his annual report a year later. The 1882 law, he began, "causes much friction and unkind feeling in the course of its administration," although "in the absence of such a law [women] would be encouraged and permitted to live in adultery and dishonor to the memory of their soldiers while enjoying the bounty of the government." Evans explained that "the widow who respects the law and honors society by legally entering into the marriage relation" would lose her pension.[72] These changes did little to alter how black women interfaced with the U.S. Pension Bureau, but they did make examiners even more aware of the linkages between survivors' benefits and the strictures of morality at the center of their investigations.

Prospective beneficiaries of the procedural changes Commissioner Evans introduced felt the difference in atmosphere at the Pension Bureau almost immediately. Louisa Little obtained a pension under the service law system a little more than twelve months after she had filed her petition. Examiner Gilpin, who had spearheaded the series of "open and notorious cohabitation" investigations less than two years earlier, conducted a brief investigation into Louisa's case. Although some fourteen years had passed since Louisa's husband, veteran James Little, had died in James City, examiner Gilpin did not question her motivation or her sexual morality. Perhaps Louisa's residence and employment as a domestic in a predominantly white neighborhood in the city's Eighth Ward convinced the examiner of her worthiness. The witness testimony

Gilpin procured portrayed Louisa as hardworking, pious, dutiful, and deserving. Winney Skinner, a household worker who had attended Louisa's wedding at the Pilgrim Chapel in New Bern, said Louisa was "a member of our church in good standing" and "a woman of good character."[73] Giles Blango, a fisherman and the son of a Union veteran, also testified to the marriage and to Louisa's "good character."[74] A black carpenter testified that Louisa had "not lived or cohabited with a man."[75] Gilpin's report rated the witnesses as "fair as to truth."[76] Louisa gained her pension less than a month later.

Before Commissioner Evans changed agency procedures, the principle that prospective widows had to prove their sexual virtue fell especially hard on laboring women such as Matilda Wells. Matilda Wells filed an application for a survivor's pension in 1890 but was not admitted until 1896. Her single state, combined with her wage labor, led pension officials to question Matilda's claim to worthy widowhood.[77] Officials scrutinized her application because of the gap between her husband's death and the date when she applied for benefits. Had Matilda engaged in any sexual activity after his death? Did she remarry or was she cohabiting? How had she supported herself? The commissioner of pensions ordered a series of investigation to answer these questions. Examiner D. H. Kincaid was initially assigned the case in March 1897. He traced Matilda's steps back to Elizabeth City, Pasquotank County, where she had worked as a field hand, cook, and domestic. Examiner H. P. Maxwell assisted with the investigation and questioned Matilda's sexual morality because she worked alongside men in the fields. She and her witnesses countered by emphasizing her hard work and reliability.

One witness said that Matilda had "worked for the white folks at anything she could get to do, whether as a domestic or as a common field laborer."[78] She also cooked for a sheriff and for workers at a fishery, whereupon the examiner questioned witnesses about Matilda's "reputation as to chastity." The testimony of her cousin, Fannie Spellman, a forty-three-year-old housekeeper, not the savvy rhetoric of a claims agent or high-profile pension firm, ushered Matilda's case through the examination process. Fannie provided insight into the gender conventions operating in the neighborhood where Matilda worked.

> So far as I know, she led a correct life but as I remember to have heard talk that she is too intimate with men, generally, but whether there was ground for such rumors I don't know. I never saw anything in her conduct to warrant it, the fact is any woman that has to work out with and among men will be talked about whether she is guil[ty] or not. And claimant had

to work in the field to support herself and her children. I did not regard her as a lewd or bad woman.[79]

While acceding to the requirements of the inquiry, Matilda Wells nonetheless challenged the government's prying into her private life. In October 1897, Matilda's case was handed off to examiner Gilpin, who questioned her closely about her relationships with men. Matilda expressed frustration and irritation at his sexually explicit line of inquiry. This time Matilda was better able to challenge the examiner. When he inquired as to whether Matilda had "lived or cohabited with any man" and clarified the question by adding "as his wife," she answered directly: "No sir I have not. God knows I haven't." Then his queries grew more specific and personal: "Have you had sexual intercourse with any man since the death of your husband?" She responded by explaining that she had "had womb trouble for several years." When he again asked Matilda about her relationship with James Williams, she asked him to explain the meaning of his question. "Now Mr. Gilpin," she began, "I will tell you I don't know if I understand what you mean by cohabiting, this man Williams use to wait on me, come to see me a few times and wanted me to marry him and I would not have him." The examiner retorted with another invasive question. "Did you have sexual intercourse with him?" Matilda continued to resist the meaning Gilpin attributed to her relationship with Williams, responding, "No sir not at all." She then referred to the conversation she had with examiner Kincaid back in May: "Mr. Kincaid told me he heard I had been living in adultery but would never tell me who told him." Gilpin was confused, asking, "Didn't you tell Mr. Kincaid that you had cohabited with James Williams?" Matilda explained that she had used those words in her deposition with Kincaid and that Williams "did court" her, "but I never told him that he had ever had connection with me and I asked Mr. Kincaid to put it down that he had not had intercourse with me." She said she "had nothing to do with him" thereafter.[80]

Matilda found the examiners' questions offensive. In one instance, she responded with categorical denials: "No sir I have not had intercourse with any other man other than James Williams since Toney Wells was drowned." The examiner demanded to know why Matilda had concealed her relationship with James Williams when her case had been under investigation a year earlier, and her reply suggests that she knew all too well the cost of revealing too much about her private life to local examiners: "It is not well for a woman to tell that she had anything to do with a man." "I have heard people here in town say that when a woman has anything to do with a man that she would not get a pension."[81]

Over the long period of questioning, Matilda Wells ended one of her depositions with these words: "I am ignorant and never paid much attention to dates of birth of my children—besides I have been a hard worker so I do not recall dates and circumstances like I would desire."[82] Instead of being construed as an immoral woman, Matilda presented herself as a hardworking mother and constructed her working life as evidence of patriotic sacrifice. The bureau granted her pension in 1898, and Matilda collected it until she died in 1905. The procedural changes Commissioner Evans championed opened a narrow space for Matilda Wells to make good on the promise the government had made to her husband after his military service ended.

PETITIONING GOVERNMENT OFFICIALS

As black Union widows and pension examiners were clashing over the law of 1882, important political shifts had begun in North Carolina's Second Congressional District, the Black Second. A coalition of black Republicans, white Republicans, and Populists forged an alliance to challenge Democratic rule in North Carolina. The issues they coalesced around included landlessness, poverty, and economic dependence. The victory of the fusion ticket of Populists and Republicans in 1894 and 1896 meant that blacks continued to play an active role in municipal and federal politics.[83]

Black Union widows, ever cognizant of changes in their communities and in the pension system, seized on a small opening created by the political advancement of state and federal leaders who were responsive to veterans and their families. If, as E. D. Gallion believed, black middle-class community leaders viewed the rise of Populist and Republican leaders at the municipal, state, and federal levels as a chance to work around local examiners, black Union widows interpreted fusion politics as an opportunity to plead their cases.

In 1897, roughly three years after losing her pension on charges of "open and notorious cohabitation," Louisa Powers petitioned the U.S. Congress to consider her version of events. Rather than drawing on the bureaucratized language of the state, Louisa used the common-sense reasoning of her community. She began by scrupulously tracing the details of her case from its inception in 1889. She then reminded the federal lawmakers of Gallion's history of misconduct in New Bern and subsequent suspension from the Pension Bureau: "I was informed that the Special Examiner E. D. Gallion was discharged on the grounds of bad conduct to the widows."[84] In rendering the events of her case in this order, Louisa implied her 1894 conflict with Gallion was another act of examiner misconduct, perhaps even retaliation against her.

Louisa Powers's single-spaced four-page affidavit revised the interpretive framework of her case by reminding government officials of the multiple episodes of examiner wrongdoing during the examination process and by repositioning herself as a worthy Union widow and mother of five minor children.[85] Although Louisa never regained her pension, her efforts set new standards for women's interaction with the pension system.

Mary Lee also once again sought reclassification of her claim under the general law pension system. On this occasion, she enlisted the support of Congressman George H. White, the only black representative in Congress in 1899. White turned Lee's case file over to the commissioner of pensions' office. In June 1899, the commissioner acknowledged receipt of White's inquiry but informed Mary Lee that the "rejected claim" would not be "reopened except upon new and material evidence." Despite her persistent attempt to bring attention to her husband's honorable service and to clear "syphilis" from his military record, bureau officials refused to reclassify Mary Lee's status. She remained on the pension roster under the service law system.[86]

Black women's petitions for survivors' benefits after the 1894 uproar and during the period of political realignment reflect the era's shifting political terrain. By marshaling their resources, which included legal evidence, witness testimony, and appeals in the bureau's own language, these women were often able to persuade examiners of their credibility and to regain their pensions. The strategies they developed, their political vision, the strength of their grassroots networks, and their unwavering struggle for economic justice illuminate black women's increasing understanding of ever-changing pension laws and ability to maneuver within government institutions.

CONCLUSION

During the 1890s, pension eligibility examinations became a dueling ground between black Union widows and claims agents on one side and the examiners of the U.S. Pension Bureau on the other, determined to protect the nation's assets and to expose fraud. Examiners measured questions of women's worthiness against the law of August 7, 1882. This law terminated a widow's pension if she were involved in a sexual relationship with a man or deemed immoral and unchaste. In New Bern, black widows were singled out, but across the North and West, white women faced suspension and public cases. For federal policymakers, removing women from the pension rolls under the 1882 law was a matter of maintaining the integrity of the pension system, and it affirmed their adherence to middle-class social norms for women's behavior. Black women facing charges of open and notorious cohabitation attempted to engage the law as a political issue by challenging the tendency to cast women's benefits as a matter of domesticity and personal behavior rather than in economic terms. The women continued to highlight childcare, labor, and issues of poverty. By showing up, telling their stories, and infusing the local application process with their notions of womanhood, these women took advantage of the new space the special examination process created in the system to disseminate their own definitions of worthy widowhood. To protect themselves, some echoed the Pension Bureau's definition of honorable womanhood. Others, like Louisa Powers, asserted their grievances in the language of her community.

Black Union widows learned many lessons from the 1894 pension controversies and the intensified scrutiny that followed. This series of investigations and subsequent suspensions weakened the effectiveness of women's petitions in the pension system. Attention to issues of sexual immorality truncated women's attempts to highlight the structural conditions of their poverty and the inequities embedded in the agency's established definition of marriage. This series of investigations overshadowed black women's creative attempts to combat the multitude of ways issues of race, class, and gender intersected in their lives. Still, by challenging the established definition of widowhood, these women created a new space from which to raise and contest issues within government institutions.

What occurred in eastern North Carolina between 1894 and 1897, especially in New Bern, exposed the multifaceted, overlapping dimensions of race, gender, and class inequality in the region at a time of political change. Community members' involvement in the removal of black Union widows from the pension rolls through their testimony about these women's intimate lives exposed what Elsa Barkley Brown has described as "the increasing class and gendered nature of internal community politics"; it also signaled a reorientation of communal definitions of worthy widowhood more in line with the pension system's construct and in tune with the 1882 law.[87] At the same time, the investigation and subsequent suspension of Frederick C. Douglass intensified cross-class solidarity among an increasingly economically stratified group of black veterans. As the century drew to a close, black Union widows recognized that their ability to rely on public officials, local courts, and claims agents to challenge the power of the examiners had narrowed significantly. Many began to construct their ability to access and maintain their benefits increasingly as rights, just as local agents and claims agents had.

8

The Personal Consequences of Union Widowhood

Transforming black Union widows into unworthy recipients of the "nation's bounty" required constant surveillance and evidence of "criminal sexuality."[1] In 1899, the commissioner of pensions called for a countywide investigation of all pensioners who had had any dealings with claims agents Carpenter and Douglass, so a small contingent of examiners arrived in eastern North Carolina to root out fraud and immorality.[2] They delved into black Union widows' home lives, just as they had in 1894, to establish their worthiness to receive federal pensions. These federally sanctioned examinations made Union widows' homes and intimate lives even more public and subject to the intrusion of pension administrators, denying prospective and recognized beneficiaries any privacy. Intimate partnerships and sexuality had become a battleground within the examination process, especially in light of the law of 1882 and the bureau's evolving standards on marriage and cohabitation. As these men made their way through the region, they infused the examination process with a vocabulary of sexual immorality and racist imagery and caused the suspension of at least ten women's pensions.[3]

Although blacks across the South had been systematically disfranchised since the 1870s, blacks in Craven County were not only voting but serving at the municipal, state, and federal levels of government.[4] The election of George H. White, former New Bern resident, to the U.S. House of Representatives from 1897 to 1901 meant that the survivors of black veterans had access to an elected official who responded to their concerns. The electoral status of blacks in North Carolina changed dramatically at the turn of the twentieth century. In 1899, a new Democratic state legislature began crafting amendments to the state constitution to disfranchise black men, and by 1901, one of these amendments had passed. White, in January 1901, issued a blistering critique of blatant efforts to suppress the black vote across the South: "It is an undisputed fact that the negro vote in the State of Alabama, as well as most other Southern States, have been effectively suppressed, either one way or the other—in some instances by constitutional amendment and State legislation, in others by cold-blooded fraud and intimidation, but whatever method pursued, it is not denied, but frankly admitted in the speeches in this House, that the Black vote has been eliminated to a large extent."[5]

Black disfranchisement, the continuous presence of special examiners in their neighborhoods, and heightened scrutiny of beneficiaries' personal lives by neighbors recontextualized what it meant to be a Union widow in New Bern, North Carolina. Black women's pension networks, images of Union widowhood, notions of good womanhood, and narratives of sexual morality took on new meanings at the Pension Bureau and in their neighborhoods. Once honored by the federal government for their husbands' sacrifice and respected by their communities, black Union widows now endured criticism and dishonor from government officials and community members alike. Within New Bern's black neighborhoods, many conceived of survivors' benefits as an economic resource mediated by the community, rather than by the federal government. This understanding of the pension system regularly placed black women at odds with government officials, the black middle class, black veterans, or other Union widows. Black women's response to these changes varied according to their individual circumstances.

Soldiers' widows who lost their pensions and black veterans deprived of the vote faced severe challenges to their ability to petition government agencies. The pension bureau's marriage criteria, sexual regulation, and concepts of family normalcy effectively demonstrate how intersecting patterns of racism shaped gender constructs within the pension system. Moreover, evidence gathered in black Union widows' case files during the countywide investigations reveals the overlapping social constructs and political systems through which black women had to navigate.

UNRAVELING THE GRASSROOTS PENSION NETWORK AND PURGING THE PENSION ROLLS

After 1895, widows' opportunity to use the services of Frederick C. Douglass and E. W. Carpenter to challenge the power of bureau examiners narrowed. Douglass continued to struggle for restoration of his license as a claims agent.

In July 1898, he summoned the support of Arthur Simmons, a black North Carolinian who had enlisted in one of the black regiments recruited in Craven County. After discharge, Simmons settled in Washington, DC, where he eventually assumed a post as a White House messenger. Douglass maintained close contact with Simmons, made easier because Simmons's family continued to reside in New Bern. In a letter to Simmons dated July 29, 1898, Douglass recounted the story of the 1894 uproars with his usual flair: "Using obsean Language with Threats," examiner Gallion had told the black Union widows of New Bern that they had assisted the claims agent "in Robbing the Government." Douglass told Simmons how the examiner tried to force the women to file complaints against him, vividly telling the story of Mary Lee and of how Gallion enticed Julia Neel to "testify against" him.[6]

It is unclear whether Simmons responded to Douglass, but he did forward Douglass's materials to Commissioner H. Clay Evans less than a week later, along with a brief endorsement of Douglass's case: "You being the proper one I most respectfully ask will you investigate the matter as it seems from the reading of the papers that he has been unjustly dealt with."[7] Less than two weeks later, the commissioner acknowledged receipt of Simmons's letter and replied that the enclosures had been duly considered "in connection with the other papers on file . . . but the facts shown do not warrant this Bureau recommending any change in action."[8] Once again Douglass had lost in his effort to vindicate his position as a recognized claims agent.

As of April 1901, black Union widows could no longer rely on Douglass in any official capacity. Governor Charles B. Aycock assured the U.S. Pension Bureau that Douglass would no longer have a career in the pension business in North Carolina.[9] Rejecting Douglass's application for reappointment as a notary public, Aycock contributed to the contemporary campaign to overthrow black political power across the state.[10] Douglass's story of the 1894 pension system uproars remained relatively consistent throughout its various iterations, but he elaborated on the account in an October 1901 letter. Douglass denied the charges of filing "fraudulent evidence" on behalf of a disabled veteran and criticized the bureau for "unjustly" dropping the man from the pension roster. Before closing, Douglass claimed, as he had done in 1894, that he had been in the army but that he would "never claim anything under Such heads."[11] Denouncing the government's "unjust" treatment of black veterans and rejecting the idea of government benevolence, he wrote, "I rather Preach and Pray my Life away [than] to be Deal with in that way." Douglass closed the letter by embracing his religious identity, signing it "Rev. Frederick Douglass."[12] Once again, the commissioner of pensions refused to reinstate his license.

PROTECTING THE "NATION'S BOUNTY"

Public critique of the pension bureau's rising expenditures after the introduction of the service law reached a fever pitch in the late nineteenth century as pension examiners sought to sanitize the pension roster using familiar constructs of marriage, sexual morality, and family. During the countywide sweep, examiners reevaluated the legitimacy of the marital unions on which women's status as Union widows rested. The recognition of slave marriages in 1866 proved a double-edged sword: as initially conceived, it provided a legal pathway for black women, especially freedwomen, to gain recognition as Union widows in the Pension Bureau during the immediate postwar years. But bureau officials now investigated slave marriages to question black women's very right to collect a pension.

Nearly forty years after Mary Whitby had established her place on the pension roster, a pension examiner probed the nature of her relationship with an enslaved man before the war. Under scrutiny from federal officials, Mary used casual language to describe her relationship with Peter Stevenson, the man in question: "I don't think I mentioned Stevenson's name in my pension claim as I never was really married to him."[13] Mary may have said this to ensure her continued status on the pension rolls, rather than to renounce her relationship with Stevenson, the father of her daughter. Mary knew the difference between a "slave marriage" and a "took-up" relationship. In the social world where Mary grew up, free blacks and enslaved populations regularly came together. This reality was apparent in her own family history, as her mother was born free, and her father was enslaved. Whitby's fears of losing benefits were not far-fetched: other women associated with New Bern's pension network had their benefits suspended on similar grounds.

Examiners' analysis of the bureau's marriage standard, however, remained inconsistent. In 1910, examiner Thomas Goethe applied the bureau's marriage standard in Lavinia Kelley's case with leniency. Kelley sought recognition as the legal widow of Thomas Kelley in 1909. Questions arose about the validity of Lavinia's claim because the deceased veteran had been married to another woman before he married her in 1869. Examiner Goethe carefully scrutinized the evidence and interviewed her neighbors and the soldiers who had served alongside Kelley. He determined that Thomas's first marriage was "null and void" because he did not live with his first wife after he returned from the army. Goethe assured bureau officials that Thomas's first wife would not file a competing claim for benefits because she had died before the war ended. In his words, "she is safely disposed of."[14] Lavinia told examiner Goethe that she had married Thomas Kelley in New Bern, but she was vague about the date. She also said, "After our marriage we were never divorced or legally separated."[15] Goethe returned to Lavinia's home the next day to question her further. On this occasion Lavinia more precisely clarified the stages of her relationship with Thomas Kelley: "I was not lawfully married to Thomas Kelley . . . but after we lived here [New Bern] about two years after my husband's discharge we went through a lawful marriage."[16] Goethe reported to the commissioner, "Even had this woman never married the soldier by ceremony I believe their relations would have constituted a common law marriage."[17] As Thomas's recognized widow, Lavinia collected survivors' benefits until she died in 1914.

Bureau officials postponed their decision in Margaret Proctor's case when they discovered that her late husband, veteran David Proctor, had married Dinah Foy years earlier. David and Dinah had not secured a legal divorce before the veteran married Margaret.[18] Although examiner I. B. Dunn recommended further investigation before bureau officials rendered a decision, he judged Margaret's claim of "doubtful merit."[19] After locating and interviewing Dinah (now Jones) in Clifton, New Jersey, examiner L. F. Harrison stated: "I am of the opinion that the claimant, Margaret A. Proctor's marriage to the soldier was illegal for the fact that his marriage to Jones was legal and from whom she had no divorce."[20] The question of legal widowhood animated Margaret's case as late as 1918.[21]

Investigators thought that Hettie Wendly was rightfully pensioned as veteran George Wendly's widow, but there were other problems with her case. Examiners believed that Frederick C. Douglass had filed fraudulent medical evidence to gain admittance for Hettie under the general law. Bureau officials transferred Hettie from the general law to the service system, which significantly reduced her monthly payment. Even worse, Hettie owed the government money because the government contended that she had been overpaid for several years under the general law system.

During the county investigation, pension bureau examiners scrutinized black Union widows' intimate lives, despite the changes to the administration of the law of 1882 that Commissioner Evans had enacted three years earlier. Examiners continually portrayed black Union widows as unworthy in their summary reports. Although examiners working in the area rarely mentioned white supremacy propaganda in their correspondence with bureau officials, they shared an understanding of virtue and morality with white Democrats that allowed them to intrude on black domestic space and represent worthiness as a matter of women's personal—especially sexual—morality.

Just as white supremacists made arguments about the immoral character of black homes, by 1900, the language of dishonorable homes that had long been a part of examiners' vocabulary became a major theme.

Black Union widows' homes and intimate lives became even more public and subject to the interest of the federal government, thereby denying prospective widows and recognized beneficiaries any distinction between public and private life. If a widow shared a household with a man, examiners presumed that she depended on him financially and portrayed their relationship as a common-law marriage. Clara Williams, widow of Silas Williams, a private in the Thirty-Fifth Colored Infantry, simply refused to acknowledge that her living arrangements should be grounds for questioning, much less cutting off her benefits. "Notorious in and around" her neighborhood, Clara "took up" with a disabled veteran who was collecting a pension of his own, and, after an eight-month courtship, the two decided to live together "happily," as some said, "living together as man and wife," in what examiner Goethe described as a "neat little home." Some thought the two were merely "cousins and never mean no harm," and Clara told Goethe she and the veteran were not married, just "closely related." Goethe issued a stern report to the commissioner of pensions on July 13, 1900: "As will be seen from the evidence this pensioner is now living in adultery. . . . Both pensioner and her paramour make full confessions. . . . [T]he case is submitted for . . . violation of the act of August 7, 1882."[22] Clara Williams lost her status as a Civil War widow, and her pension stopped.

Fanny Whitney skillfully shielded her intimate life from Pension Bureau examiners during the 1873 cohabitation investigation. During the community sweep, questions surrounding Malissa's paternity surfaced. Fanny initially refused to disclose the information and shut down the entire examination. More than likely Fanny understood the consequences of such a revelation: permanent suspension from the pension roster and a possible prison sentence. It is also safe to assume that Fanny took issue with the pension examiner rummaging around in her personal life. Furthermore, such examinations were "witnessed" by someone other than the examiner in the room, which means that intimate details of black women's private lives took on a heightened level of visibility.[23] Fanny Whitney eventually acceded with the bureau's demand while her extended kin group in New Bern vigorously upheld her reputation in the community, arguing for her dignity and worthiness. An official in the Law Division of the Pension Bureau concluded that Fanny's relationship with Malissa's father never violated the bureau's cohabitation rule or the subsequent law of August 7, 1882.[24]

In contrast to their accusatory investigations of black Union widows, examiners adopted more measured practices when dealing with white Union widows. In New Bern, at least, white war widows benefited from the presumption that their "whiteness" signified their sexual purity. Influenced by powerful Democratic propaganda regarding the gendered meanings of race, special examiners used caution when investigating white Union widows. During the countywide sweep, they scrutinized the cases of white widows who had relied on the services of Carpenter and Douglass, but these investigations seemed straightforward, and examiners tended to steer clear of questions about their personal lives. Celia Cuthrell initially had trouble securing a widow's pension because her husband had enlisted in the Confederate Army before joining the Union Army. After this dispute was resolved, she managed to secure her pension and remain on the pension rolls until 1923. Given Cuthrell's business relationship with Edward Carpenter, we would expect examiners to "test the merits" of her evidence in the same manner as they did the cases of black Union widows, yet Cuthrell's pension file does not indicate that a bureau examiner ever interviewed her or even contacted her.[25]

Another white widow, Laura Hilton, hired George E. Lemon's pension firm in Washington, DC, to represent her case in 1877, but she relied on Edward Carpenter to get "the affidavits" in New Bern. Examiner Thomas Goethe interviewed the fifty-one-year-old pensioner during the county sweep, but the tone of the deposition reflected deference and respect for her that was consistent with the treatment of white "southern ladies." At no point was she asked, "Have you ever cohabited with a man?"

The dignity and respect that special examiners extended to white Union widows compared to that offered to poor and working-class black Union widows reflects examiners' class as well as racial assumptions. Laura Hilton, for example, had been the wife of a government agent turned notary public. Census records show that she lived on a street inhabited by men in middle-class occupations: barbers, fruit dealers, bookkeepers, and physicians. Although not noted on the census, Laura worked as a seamstress and kept house for her brother, Francis Augustine. White supremacist logic, current in the press, appears to reflect examiners' understanding of proper domestic relations. White Union widows may have benefited from Democratic Party propaganda that urged the protection of white domestic space. Historians Crystal Feimster and Sarah Haley have shown how ideas about the category of womanhood are constructed by and through discourses of protection and the home.[26] Within the Pension Bureau such ideas reinforced beliefs about the inherent worthiness of white widows while linking black women to criminality and fraud. To be sure, white Union widows were not exempt from suspicion of open and notorious cohabitation; the pension records are replete with examples of white women being suspected of engaging in sexual relationships while collecting pensions outside North Carolina.[27]

As black women's capacity to earn wages diminished, the survivors' benefits they collected became increasingly important to their daily survival. Elsie Bishop, Dicy Oden, Lucy Spencer, and many other black women spoke openly about their reliance on their pension to maintain their households. Elsie Bishop collected half of her husband's disability pension before he died. In the wake of his death, she had to take on extra work to make up for the loss while she waited for her application to make its way through the system.[28] After the death of Dicy Oden's husband, she said that she relied on her pension and what work she "can get to make my living."[29] Lucy Spencer said that she combined housework for others and farming to provide for herself: "I have been supported principally by my pension."[30]

REPORTING MISCONDUCT

Black Union widows and the men who represented them challenged special examinations of the 1890s and early 1900s. As they had in the past, black war widows seized this moment and called attention to examiner misconduct during the investigations that the commissioner of pensions sanctioned. War widow Sophia Alexander, who lost her pension in 1901, complained about how the bureau examiner conducted his investigation of her: "I was not advised of my rights to be present with counsel at the examination . . . nor was I present at the examination of any witnesses against me. A gentleman representing the Pension dept. asked me some questions, hurriedly read over a paper and ordered me to sign it which I did."[31] Mary E. Kent testified that she "was taken in a room with no person present but the officer who closed the door," and he accused her of "living in adultery." After Kent denied living with a man, she said the examiner "became very angry" at her and then ushered her into another room, where a different examiner told her to "sign a paper" that had not been read to her. Kent said she signed the document "not knowing the contents or its purpose."[32]

Black Union widows also complained that claims agents embellished evidence, thus jeopardizing their claims. Hettie Wendly, a domestic worker, broke step with agent Frederick Douglass and the pension network to preserve her place on the rolls. Facing a possible suspension in 1901, she hired a new claims agent and offered a new narrative for her case. After being sworn in, Hettie answered the examiner's questions carefully and at length about how she had filed her claim. But then Hettie did something that most black Union widows affiliated with New Bern's pension network did not do: she launched a stinging critique of the professional men who had helped her assemble her petition. When questioned about the doctor who had treated her husband in his final illness, Hettie said, "I don't know what Dr. Bates swore to in my claim. So far as I know my husband's death might have been caused by the kick of a horse." "All them lies are on Fred Douglass and its Only the goodness of the government that I got my pension at all." In short, she blamed all the inconsistencies in her application on her pension attorney.[33] Before the deposition closed, Hettie added: "It makes me feel right bad that folks will swear to such lies."[34] In making such arguments, Hettie Wendly and others sought to capitalize on pension system ideology that positioned black women as victims of unscrupulous claims agents.

NEIGHBORHOOD POLITICS AND COMMUNITY INTERVENTION

By the early twentieth century, the Civil War was widely remembered and portrayed more as a battle for national unity than as a struggle over slavery.[35] In eastern North Carolina, some black Union veterans and their families responded to these shifts in sentiment in their own communities. In the years leading up to and following black disfranchisement in North Carolina, middle-class blacks devised a series of strategies for resisting white definitions of black domestic space. Middle-class community leaders, especially black veterans, assumed greater responsibility for black Union widows as white supremacy campaigns escalated and black men lost their voting rights. Certain aspects of these class-based initiatives made their way into the pension process.

Conflicts arose in black neighborhoods over what was considered acceptable behavior in public and at home. Black middle-class efforts to rebuff claims of "sexual danger" and "dishonorable homes" in North Carolina politics overlapped and intersected with the Pension Bureau's drive to eliminate fraud from the system. Glenda Gilmore's research on middle-class black reformers' efforts to undermine the gendered logics of white supremacy and the hardening of racial segregation in turn-of-the-century eastern North Carolina provides important insight into what might have caused the shift in perception of black Union widows. Black middle-class efforts to disprove "statistical discourses of black dysfunctionality" and rebuff white supremacists' depictions of black sexual degeneracy merged with their political and social reform efforts to "uplift the race."[36] Believing that domesticity offered a vehicle for expressing both ambition and moral integrity, black reformers such as Harriet Duggins, who lived and worked among the black poor of James City, extolled the virtues of respectable home life to their working-class sisters.[37]

Tensions between war widows and others in the community grew more pronounced in the months immediately after black disfranchisement. In the contested social and political conditions of that time and place, Union widowhood underscored key issues of gender, class, political expression, and community building. As black Union widows faced new levels of public scrutiny, some of their neighbors took out their frustrations on widows who were receiving federal pensions. In the past, community members had upheld widows' claims and interceded on their behalf, but now some black residents condemned women they believed did not deserve their pensions—in some cases with serious consequences.

The public behavior of some black Union widows upset certain black community leaders, and the women were subject to gossip and intimidation in their neighborhoods. The pension commissioner suspended Mary Ellison Rodman's name from the pension roster in 1895 on evidence that she had violated the act of 1882. She appealed the decision five years later. Liddia Moore, a James City resident, interceded on behalf of widow Rodman, saying that Mary had "had some Trouble" with a woman in the neighborhood, who then retaliated by spreading false rumors. Importantly, Moore made clear that Mary Rodman had redeemed herself in the eyes of her neighbors: "Her character have been good. . . . She join the Church and have been living a Christian Life."[38] Another resident argued, "There was no open and notorious cohabitation," adding that "she is now [in] poor circumstances she become so she could not pay rent and was put out of Doors two weeks ago."[39] The evidence was submitted on August 28, 1900. Officials issued a terse response a little over a month later, ruling that Mary Rodman's appeal was "Approved for rejection on the ground that the evidence filed in rebuttal" did not "warrant a change in former action."[40]

On November 9, 1898, an angry letter from a resident of New Bern landed on the desk of Commissioner Evans in Washington. "This woman Tammer Latham . . . ant Nothing livin on the U.S. of her dead husband an have every man she can get." In all likelihood one of her neighbors was fed up with Tammer's public behavior. Tammer had been awarded survivor's benefits in 1888. Whoever penned the letter had a clear understanding of the rules of the pension system and was familiar with other cases: "The State dont a low her to do that. . . . you stop Mary Ellerson [Rodman] from Drawing Money on the count of that mean act. Stop her [Tammer Latham] to."[41] Bureau officials suspended Tammer's benefits, but not for violating the law of 1882, as the anonymous letter writer suggested. Instead, the reason was that Tammer's husband had failed to secure a divorce before marrying her, thereby invalidating her marriage and her standing in the bureau.[42]

Violet Ann Wallace's name came to the attention of pension officials when an anonymous letter writer accused her of having children well after her soldier husband's death. After giving Wallace's street address, the critic claimed that "she has bin married since the death of her soldier husband . . . and has had children since the death of her last husband and have Rais a daughter that a Bastard on government money." Wallace had migrated to James City and filed a petition for survivor's benefits around 1888, but her neighbors openly questioned her standing: "These People came from Hyde County, N.C. and this was done ther."[43] An investigation in Hyde County showed that Violet Ann did have a daughter well after her husband died. The examiner "made an effort to see if" it could be shown that Violet had violated the 1882 law, but he eventually recommended no further action in the case; he believed that Violet had not violated the law because she never "lived openly" with the father of the child.[44] Violet Ann retained her pension until she died in 1925. Lydia Pierson, a Union widow and successful laundress, came under investigation by the Special Examination Division in August 1916, after a letter accused her of "keeping a disorderly house and secreting men and women for immoral purposes." The letter went on to expose Pierson's "dealing in wines and liquors."[45] When the case was sent out for investigation, "no evidence could be obtained pointing to a violation."[46]

Mary Lee, the Union widow who had successfully withstood examiner Gallion's charges of sexual immorality, became the target of new rumors of sexual impropriety. Veterans accused her of being intimate with five men in her neighborhood. Particularly damaging was the intimate relationship that she was suspected of carrying on with Lawrence Cotton, a disabled veteran and deacon at the Second Missionary Baptist Church. Attempting to remain above the fray, Lee emphasized her working life. She told examiner McSorley: "I have lived in New Bern, N.C. and worked out for a living. I have not lived with anybody but white people who I have worked for. There have been charges made against me that I had lived with Nathan Jackson but I proved that I never did. I have not lived with any man as his wife since his [Simeon's] death."[47] Emphasizing her employment implied that she was morally irreproachable, since white people would not allow a woman they believed immoral into their homes; it also suggested the superior reputation she had earned among white families who hired her. Then she expressed her own conclusion about the accusations of sexual immorality aimed at her over the course of the yearlong investigation: "These colored people have it against me that I am getting a pension." In making this statement, Mary Lee attempted to revise the interpretive framework of her case by casting neighbors' testimony as "unreliable" and repositioning herself as a worthy woman.[48]

Mary Lee successfully countered the charges of sexual immorality and retained her pension. Her community status, connections with black middle-class leaders, and earlier experience with examiner Gallion set Mary Lee apart from many working-class black women but did not protect her from open and notorious cohabitation charges. Nevertheless, her familiarity with the examination process and her knowledge of the bureau's well-defined rules, especially regarding the law of 1882, placed her in a better position than the majority of women who faced off against middle-class black leaders and local examiners.

Black women's presence on the pension roster and their choices about how they spent their allotment exacerbated tensions among blacks as well. Neighbors, veterans, and widows derided women's choice to pursue love interests, describing their behavior as sexually immoral.[49] Some faced class-based judgments while others faced gender-based criticisms of their personal lives. Historian Dylan Penningroth's analysis of the cultural significance of black property holding in the nineteenth-century South enriched scholars' understanding of black people's evolving notions concerning the distribution of economic resources and ownership throughout the post-emancipation South.[50] Contests that erupted between black Union widows and their neighbors over how they dispensed their resources and lived their lives reveal tensions and anxieties about a group of women who rebuffed behavior patterns dictated by the federal government.

Exposing Union widows to bureau examiners was a public matter for black veterans and Union widows alike, presenting opportunities for community building and applying the agency's definitions of female respectability through sexual morality in a new political context. What could be more worthy than helping examiners root out unworthy widows in a pernicious campaign to rid the pension rosters of excess? Pensioner Sophia Alexander became the target of public chatter because she had had a public relationship with a younger man "for a number of years." Hettie Wendly, who had recently had her status reclassified, reported that Sophia "used to go around the street" with her young beau.[51] Sophia expressed regret and disappointment about the relationship: "I have been sorry since I had anything to do with him but I thought so much of him. I couldn't really help it. I bought him . . .

clothes and lots of stuff and he took my pin from me and never relinquished it." Sophia's candid expression of hopefulness, love, and disappointment captures perfectly what historian Kali Gross views as an important challenge to "the larger rhetoric of normalcy" circulating in Sophia's neighborhood.[52]

Stories of neglect overlapped with and reinforced narratives of sexual immorality. Louisa Little had secured a survivor's pension with relative ease in 1897, but black veterans later condemned her for failing to care for or provide financial support for her disabled husband. A man who served in the same regiment as her husband described Louisa as "mighty mean to the old soldier," while another believed "she cared nothing for him." One said that Louisa lived in "adultery," while a different man charged her with "deserting" her husband and "leaving him destitute."[53] Another of her husband's fellow soldiers said, "I know she cared nothing for him, never attended to him when sick and left him to die alone for she was not present when he died."[54] In short, worthy widowhood was a social act, and Louisa Little failed to measure up to her neighbors' expectations because she moved away while her disabled husband died in squalor. A black drayman said that Louisa's home was "considered nothing more than a house of ill fame."[55] Veteran Philip Wiggins, who served as the president of a mutual aid society in James City in the 1890s, reported that a male visitor stayed the night at Louisa's house after Isaac died. Wiggins told an examiner that a man "would be inside" of her house "in the evenings at 10, 11, and 12 at night," but he "never saw them in bed together."[56] Louisa Little's status as a Union widow no longer garnered protection and respectability from her peers.

On October 3, 1900, the investigating examiner homed in on Louisa's marital history and pummeled her with intrusive questions: "Did you ever co-habit with a man named David Barfield? Did you or did you not have sexual relations with him? Were you ever married to David Barfield?"[57] Louisa refused to respond to any of the examiner's questions. Issues of race and immorality were the key points in the examiner's final report.[58] Significantly, his characterizations of Louisa as "defiant," "insincere," and unchaste rested on the testimony and corroboration of black residents (veterans), wives of veterans, and disgruntled neighbors. Their critiques often echoed the bureau's construction of Union widowhood. The examiner described Louisa's home as a "resort" for "various men," concluding that Louisa "had no equitable claim for pension as the soldier's widow as she deserted him and dropped his name and lived in adultery."[59] That the comrades of Louisa's husband offered such harsh criticism of the widow raises interesting questions. These men could have provided the same testimony when Louisa initially applied for survivor's aid in 1897, but they did not. Less than a week after the examiner submitted his report in February 1901, the commissioner of pensions notified Louisa of her violation of the law of 1882. Louisa had thirty days to refute the charges, or her name would be permanently removed from the pension roster.

Hostility toward black Union widows like Sophia Alexander, Violet Wallace, Mary Lee, Louisa Little, and Lydia Pierson during the early twentieth century might have sprung from frustration with the federal government in general and the pension system in particular. Indeed, quite a number of disabled veterans and Union widows were denied benefits. Moreover, the general sense of honor and respect bestowed on black Union widows was now reserved for those who followed the dictates of middle-class respectability. In some instances, black veterans and community members began to promote a view of Union widowhood that more closely mirrored the bureau's ideal of worthy widowhood and portrayed women's care labor as an essential measure of their worthiness. They described women who abandoned their ailing husbands as "mean and cruel" and raised suspicions about women they believed were out "to get pension."[60] Once the women were on the rolls, veterans monitored the women's homes and kept track of who visited them and if anyone stayed overnight. Finally, amid the shifting social and political conditions of the federal government, the influx of substantial cash payments to black women, most of whom were poor, raised important and contested issues of gender, class, political expression, and community building.[61] In this moment, communal aspects of Union widowhood once fortified by women and their neighbors unraveled in the face of white supremacist political campaigns and intrusive investigations that the women themselves sometimes initiated.

CALLING FOR SPECIAL ACTION AND PETITIONING FOR REINSTATEMENT

The suspension of claims agent Frederick C. Douglass and the erosion of the fusion coalition required claimants and prospective widows seeking vindication to employ new forms of protest politics at the Pension Bureau. As they had in the past, black women identified small windows of opportunity to maintain their communication with the government. The women called on elected officials—black or white, Republican or Democrat—to intervene and help them advance their cases through the pension bureaucracy. Ever cognizant of the changes in the pension network, new pension laws, and larger political changes taking shape at the municipal and federal levels, they seized on opportunities to plead their position to political leaders attuned to interests of veterans and their families at the municipal, state, and federal levels.

Louisa Little filed evidence to disprove the salacious charges leading to her impending suspension. She enlisted the support of a host of prominent white city officials, including her employer, Leonidas J. Moore, an attorney and influential Democrat. The mayor of New Bern, the chief of police, and the Craven County sheriff signed a petition that called on the commissioner of pensions to "reconsider" Louisa's case.[62] In addition to signing the petition, Moore wrote a personal letter to the commissioner on Louisa's behalf. Clues as to how Little managed to motivate these men to endorse her claim run throughout Moore's letter. "As a citizen" of the city, he began, "I wish to say that I have known Louisa Little for over (20) years, that she is a woman of excellent character."[63] Moore's description of Louisa Little's "excellent character" contrasted with black residents. He explained that she lived among "white people almost exclusively" and that if she did not "behave herself" she could not live among whites.[64] Louisa Little's case file offers evidence of the distance she had created between her personal life and her employers. As Moore rendered it, Little was an obedient servant with few ties to the black community. Little attempted to cash in on the interpersonal relationships she had built with these men and their families while cleaning their homes to drown out the accusations of unworthiness her black neighbors voiced. Despite Moore's intervention, the commissioner and the assistant secretary of the Department of the Interior found no ground on which to open another investigation or reverse the decision in her case.[65]

Louisa Little failed to have her name restored to the pension roster, though her maneuvering showcased her complex understanding of the value bureau officials and local examiners placed on white men's testimony. What is perhaps most intriguing about Little's self-defense is the way she attempted to disrupt lines of authority and regulation in her community. Women frequently called on their employers to advocate on their behalf, but the difference in Louisa Little's case is when and how she involved their testimony. She rejected the prescribed duties of Union widows in her own community, lived on her own terms, and chose her intimate partners based on her own preferences rather than the dictates of the bureau's policy and local custom.

White residents regularly came forward, occasionally stridently, on behalf of black Union widows during the examination phase of the pension application process. Three prominent white female missionaries who worked "among the colored people of James City, New Bern, and vicinity" under the auspices of the Woman's American Baptist Home Mission Society of Chicago interceded on Dianna Peldon's behalf.[66] R. Amelia Williams and Carrie Waugh described Dianna as a "virtuous woman and highly respected by all classes of people in James City." Harriet Duggins, the black missionary who collaborated with Williams and Waugh, confirmed that Dianna had been "a member of the Missionary Bible class meeting almost daily for . . . nine years."[67]

Nearly seventeen years after pension officials rendered Mary Ann Gatlin, a white seamstress, "the illegitimate wife of Riley Gatlin," she filed a new petition calling for "justice."[68] In 1908, with Frederick C. Douglass's help, Mary Ann pressed Senator Furnifold Simmons for action in her case. "I am a poor widow of a soldier and I want my just right," she protested. "I am entitled to a pension from Jan. 2, 1889 to the present time. . . . That is just what I am entitled to and I aske that the Congress of the United States to please give me justice."[69] Mary Ann told Simmons that she "had Every Reason" to believe if placed "in Special Examiner Hands . . . the true facts" would come to light. She then appealed to Simmons directly: "I believe that you can demand a thorough Examination and they will not allow it otherwise." Simmons found Gatlin's case compelling enough to forward the evidence to the commissioner of pensions with a request to reopen her case. After the case stalled for several months, Mary Ann urged Simmons to use his influence with the commissioner to allow her claim "or put the [case] in the Hand of a Special Examiner who will do Justice by me."[70] Officials refused to reopen Mary Ann's case on the basis of the new evidence, reasoning that "it could not overcome the evidence on file." Mary Ann Gatlin did not regain her pension before she died in New Bern in 1912.

In a final act of desperation and assertiveness, Hettie Wendly, now seventy-six, turned to an unlikely source to regain her pension. She realigned herself with agent Douglass and, with his assistance, appealed to Senator Simmons, a man who worked tirelessly to disfranchise blacks in North Carolina, endorsed the rule of white supremacy, and led the state's Democratic Party.[71] His political transformation was as calculated as Hettie's correspondence with him. At one time, Simmons represented the black citizens of James City in a heated land dispute against a member of a prominent white land-owning family in New Bern. Perhaps that is why Hettie reached out to Simmons. In a handwritten letter, Wendly said, "I was taken off the rolls for telling the truth when the examiner ask where did my husband die at I told him that he died in South Carolina. The same that I told when I was getting the money." Wendly's letter explained her desperate condition: "If you pleas I am suffering for food and something to wear. I can not do any work at all I am nearly blind."[72] As Simmons did with Mary Ann Gatlin's case, he followed through on Hettie's request by forwarding her letter to the commissioner and asking him to investigate this matter further.[73] The commissioner responded to Simmons three days later, but the decision in Hettie's case remained intact. She retained her status as a Union widow but did not receive any federal allowances before she died in 1910.

The definition of marriage remained a battleground between black women, examiners, and pension officials at the dawn of the twentieth century. Charlotte Caphart (formerly Banks, then Holloway), after her appeal was dismissed in 1890, waited fourteen years before contacting the bureau again.[74] Her new appeal consisted of six affidavits and a certified statement from Craven County's Register of Deeds indicating that she had gone before the county clerk on August 28, 1866. Pension officials had suspended Charlotte's benefits because they believed she had begun living with David Holloway before Caesar Banks died. In 1904, the commissioner ordered a new investigation to resolve the question of Charlotte's marriage. Examiner Thomas Goethe led the charge.

Among Charlotte's surviving peers, the legacy of enslavement remained the starting point for interpreting marriage and the meaning of Union widowhood in her case. It was customary for enslaved men and women to find spouses on adjoining farms in Charlotte's Elizabeth City neighborhood without their owners' consent. Of Charlotte and Caesar, one freedman recalled, "They . . . called themselves husband and wife and were so recognized by those who knew them."[75] Another said, "Plenty of slaves lived on one plantation while their wives would live on another."[76] Caesar's owner, Thadeous Banks, allowed him to visit Charlotte on Saturdays until he moved to a farm nearly twenty miles away. Separation by sale remained another central point of contention Charlotte's peers addressed. Freedman Jacob Pool recalled that slave "marriages were recognized by the white folks but if they got ready to sell you they would not let the marriage or anything else stand in the way."[77]

While testifying before examiner Goethe, Charlotte discussed marriage in a more specific way than she had in her earlier petitions. She identified a definitive beginning and ending to her relationship with Holloway: "I swear I never lived a day with David Holloway before we got the twenty five cent license." She said she was living as "the lawful widow of Caesar Banks" at that time. Not until a month after the marriage license was issued did Charlotte and David Holloway formalize their vows at "the church wedding."[78]

Pension officials refused to reinstate Charlotte's benefits after the 1904 special examination. A board of review within the Department of the Interior rejected her appeal, reasoning that her relationship with Holloway, which began during the war, invalidated her prewar marital union with Caesar.[79] From the perspective of pension officials, Charlotte had never had a pensionable period of widowhood. This ruling must have stung, for in the midst of her case, federal lawmakers opened up a new pathway for remarried widows to regain their pensions under the Act of 1901. This law allowed for soldiers' widows who had previously lost their benefits to regain their status on the pension roster.[80] By declaring that Charlotte had no pensionable period of widowhood, pension officials effectively eliminated any future attempt by Charlotte to petition for survivor's benefits under the newly construed act of March 3, 1901.[81]

But Charlotte was persistent. In 1905, at about seventy-one years old and partially disabled by a "bad sore leg," she prepared a new petition, this time to the secretary of the Department of the Interior, seeking "justice" in her case.

> I do not believe I was given justice by the Commissioner of Pension in rejecting my case I their fore petition you Hon Secretary of Interior to please have my claim investigated. I ask that you will please take my case under your consideration and if theire has any injustice been done me in the rejection of my claim I ask that you will have the claim allowed in my favor. . . . I only ask for justice at your hands.[82]

Two years later, Jesse Wilson, the assistant secretary of the Department of the Interior, rendered a lengthy opinion in her case. Consistent with the commissioner's earlier decision, Wilson ruled that "the evidence shows that she is not the soldier's legal widow [and that] the cohabitation which began in slavery" ended before the soldier died and thus that Charlotte did not "regard herself as the widow of Caesar Banks" when she filed her initial petition for survivor's benefits in 1869.[83] Charlotte's disappointment with this decision must have been especially bitter because the separation cited by the officials resulted from her owner's disruption of her family, not from her personal choice. According to the 1910 federal census, Charlotte's last known address was on Fleet Street in the Fifth Ward of New Bern, where she lived with her granddaughter's family.

By challenging their suspensions and pressing their senators for intervention in their cases, Louisa Little, Dianna Peldon, Mary Ann Gatlin, Hettie Wendly, Charlotte Banks, and countless other women attempted to carve out space within the pension system from which to disseminate their interpretation of what constituted a legitimate claim on the government.[84] As demonstrated in the case of Louisa Powers (see chapter 7), women filed petitions with the Department of the Interior when they felt they had exhausted all their options at the Pension Bureau. When read as texts, their petitions testify to how impoverished black people thought about federal institutions and how they expected the government to uphold its promises to black soldiers' families, even under the repression of Jim Crow.

NEW FREEDOMS AND FIRST PURCHASES

When women collected survivors' benefits from the government, they had to conform to the bureau's rules. Union widows could not remarry or carry on a public relationship with a man and maintain their position on the pension rolls. Black women who received federal support therefore had to decide whether to remain single or to remarry and give up their cash benefits. This was no easy decision. At the same time, pension awards opened new avenues toward economic power.

When Caroline Brown's application for survivor's benefits stalled in the early 1900s, she had no children or other family members to look after. Caroline embraced this new freedom and used it to explore opportunities in the North. She first settled in Massachusetts, with a family "named Reeves." The husband of the family "had a training school at Newton Center near Boston, Mass." Caroline worked for the Reeves, a white family, for "about five years," during which time the family moved to a streetcar suburb. Caroline was lonely: "I did not get acquainted with anyone up there. I was the only colored woman in Newton Highlands." About six months after settling in the Boston area, Caroline saved enough money to assist her friend Mattie C. Windsor with her train ticket, and the two "worked up there for nearly six years."[85] Mattie surely relished the chance to pursue employment opportunities outside the South, given that she had formally trained to teach music in New Bern but was unable to find a teaching position. After spending five years as domestic workers in Massachusetts, Caroline and Mattie returned to Caroline's home in New Bern but "did not remain there long."[86] In 1913, Caroline and Mattie decided to head north again, but this time they moved to Brooklyn, New York, where "a number of Newbern . . . residents of Craven County, were residing."[87] Both Caroline and Mattie "worked out in service there" but never thought of their stays in Boston or New York as permanent. Caroline Brown said: "I did not consider that I had left here when I went to Boston to work. I still considered this my home." After their return, Caroline and Mattie pooled their money and built a house in New Bern.[88] Caroline remained on the pension roster until she died in 1920.

Black Union widows' first purchases after a pension award reflect their needs, desires, and interests. Thavolia Glymph has argued that the desire for "a pretty dress or a home with kitchen utensils and blankets . . . was a central part of freedom's making, of demonstrated control over one's life."[89] After receiving her first pension check, especially if awarded a lump sum payment, a widow typically deposited a good portion of it in a bank and paid the fees of notaries, agents or attorneys, and witnesses. Then she made purchases and investments. Margaret Dudley bought "a good house and lot."[90] Julia Ann Foy "bought a lot and had a house built on it."[91] Jane Hill, a fifty-five-year-old washerwoman, purchased a prominent piece of property, which caused quite a stir.[92] In the city's official books, it was "known as the Academy Ground," on the north side of Broad Street adjoining the Craven County Court, but residents referred to it as "the old engine house."[93] After collecting her first check, Sophia Alexander moved from her employer's James City residence and eventually purchased a house across the river in New Bern.[94] Louisa Little bought a small home across the street from the Craven County Jail, where women who did laundry sold their services. Shortly after their pensions were issued, Mary Jane Moore built a house, and Charrity Brown purchased "a lot of ground with a very comfortable house on it."[95] Hettie Wendly spent fifty dollars for a lot in Graysville, three miles outside James City, and built a small house containing "a cook room, two bed rooms and a little sitting room."[96]

Though the pension was not necessarily permanent, the financial resources associated with respectable Union widowhood enabled black women to navigate the early twentieth-century landscape in ways that unmarried women with children and married women could not. Their personal choices offer compelling evidence that these women sought a degree of autonomy that went well beyond the roles the bureau and their own communities permitted.

CONCLUSION

Black Union widows forged new public identities and rejected Pension Bureau examiners' assumptions that regarded them as unworthy of the nation's financial support. They did not merely submit to the examination process, invasive as it had become; they shrewdly shaped it for their own purposes. They treated the pension system as a resource in their struggle to change the terms of their relations with working-class black men, the black middle class, their white employers, and the state itself. That bureau officials kept a close eye on the black Union widows in New Bern and special examiners entered the community to investigate individual cases had as much to do with the stubborn persistence of poor black women as it did with the desire of federal officials to purge the pension rolls. Walking a tightrope between retaining their federal benefits and protecting themselves from public criticism, black Union widows tried to bend special examinations to their will. They were uncomfortable with white examiners coming into their community and monitoring their behavior, but they attempted to influence the examination process and the government's levers of power to shape the outcome of their cases.

Black Union widows regularly initiated official intervention, even when the stakes were high and knowing the investigation would be deeply personal. Demands of this sort came from women such as Mary Lee, Louisa Powers, Charlotte Banks, Mary Kent, and Clara Williams, who imagined a different kind of relationship with the federal government and who believed that their rights had been denied. In doing so, working-class black women cultivated a flexible and coherent political vision around issues of poverty and inclusion in government institutions. At the same time, they forged their own public identities while rejecting the implications of the bureau's rules and black middle-class uplift ideology that branded them as unworthy women.

Conclusion

Newly freed and living in the post-emancipation South, black women whose husbands had died while serving in the Union Army were grief stricken and anxious about the future, though many hoped that the federal government would honor its promise to their families. The pension system had been designed primarily for soldiers. Pensions for the wives and children of deceased soldiers and veterans were later additions, and pensions for the families of the formerly enslaved were added even later. Marriage was the cornerstone of bureau policy; unless a woman could authenticate her marriage to a deceased soldier, she could not establish her legal widowhood, the legitimacy of their children, and the survivors' eligibility for a pension.

As potential beneficiaries, black women—many of them formerly enslaved—had access to one of the largest governmental bureaucracies and to official recognition as Union widows. Union widowhood was not a static status or condition. Southern black women toiled for wages, raised children, confronted poverty, and migrated in search of better conditions of life and labor. They supplemented their earnings by taking in lodgers and boarders, serving meals to single men, or collecting trash on the streets. Some contemplated forming new intimate relationships, and others embarked on new marriages. All these experiences and decisions typified the realities of Union widowhood for Fanny Whitney, Charlotte Banks, Louisa Powers, Mary Lee, and other black southern women who sought benefits.

In contrast to prevailing paradigms explaining late nineteenth-century black protest politics, which chart how middle-class blacks appealed to the federal government for enforcement of the Reconstruction amendments and civil rights laws, this study has demonstrated that poor and working-poor black women infused their distinctive experiences into their definition of Union widowhood and, by extension, their claims of citizenship. They insisted on a broader definition of marriage and family than the Pension Bureau's narrow, racially biased terms. Accepting the validity of relationships constrained by enslavement obligated the federal government to allow the black women survivors of deceased soldiers and, later, veterans to apply for benefits. The widows' construct of marriage acknowledged the oppressive conditions of enslavement, including family separation and sexual violence. Aware that black women were socially valued mainly for their labor and asserting the centrality of care work as well as paid employment, they frequently spoke about the work they performed inside and outside the home to indicate that they deserved the benefits promised.

Black women petitioned for benefits in a system dedicated to upholding patriarchal family systems, but their class and race excluded them from the system's very privileges of womanhood. They had to fight for whatever measure of recognition they gained. Consequently, their petitions for widows' benefits in the U.S. pension system had greater implications than the material outcome of their claims. As Union widows, they challenged the fundamental constructs of female dependency enmeshed in pension law and southern culture, which were used to justify the exclusion of black women from the pension roster. These women viewed their wartime sacrifice and their husbands' honorable service as sufficient evidence of their worthiness. Their alternative definitions of marriage, family, and widowhood reflected distinctive conceptions of their wants and needs. From their position as Union widows, black women described their experiences and confronted federal officials to contend with the legacy of enslavement and the reality of postwar inequality. They carved out new spaces from which to publicize their issues within the Pension Bureau by using special examinations, filing appeals, and lodging complaints. Astute strategists in their own right, these women learned to shape their answers to meet the bureau's criteria to maintain their benefits, even if it meant feigning ignorance, refusing to answer questions, or hiding to avoid imprisonment.

POOR BLACK WOMEN VERSUS THE U.S. PENSION SYSTEM

In response to black women's proactive use of the pension system to claim benefits the government had promised, bureau officials introduced new investigative strategies and launched inquiries into the women and the pension professionals who served them. The creation of the Special Examination Division, the presence of special examiners in black neighborhoods throughout the South, and the attention paid to black Union widows point to a larger paradox. The constant presence of federal agents in southern black communities was partly a result of institutional reform and partly a response to the pressure black Union widows brought on their own behalf. Black women initiated contact with government officials and reported perceived abuse by special examiners and pension attorneys. The pattern of interaction that unfolded in eastern North Carolina during the late nineteenth and early twentieth centuries is central to understanding how impoverished black women maintained a close, albeit combative, relationship with government officials long after the end of Reconstruction.

Black women who had worked directly for the Union Army found it nearly impossible to gain military recognition in the form of a pension. Harriet Tubman had helped hundreds of runaway slaves escape bondage through the Underground Railroad, but it was her work as a spy and scout for the army that formed the basis of her petition. Tubman's case is unique because she petitioned based on her wartime service, in addition to her standing as a Union widow. Tubman received compensation as a Union widow, not on the basis of her war work.[1] Even today the government's failure to compensate Tubman's work for the military continues to be a source of controversy, as her descendants still seek recognition of her military labor. Tubman's experience with the Civil War pension system highlights the injustice that has shaped the position of black women in relation to the federal government, even when they performed the same vital military tasks as men.

Antiracist and feminist scholarship point to many linkages between the experiences of black Union widows and the state and those of their counterparts in more recent historical periods. Black women's struggles with the pension system enhance our understanding of the development and limits of the welfare state in twentieth-century United States.[2] Racialized constructions of gender have continued to shape federal policies, practices, and decision making in both the legislative and executive branches. The conceptions of black women that were embedded in the Civil War pension system accompanied black women and families into public employment and relief programs well into the twentieth century.

Black women's treatment in the pension system as subjects, petitioners, and claimants was central to the racialized gender surveillance adapted in modern iterations of the state. Implementation of such policies and practices anticipated the protocols of welfare programs such as Aid to Dependent Children (ADC) and Aid to Families with Dependent Children (AFDC). Social and economic transformations in the early twentieth century led to the expansion of black women's claims on the nation-state. Poor black women pursued paths of opportunity and struggled for justice, whether or not the government compensated them for their husbands' military service. The intensification of segregation across the South, denials of opportunity, and systematic violent attacks propelled thousands of black women and their families to leave the South. Middle-class blacks sought to ward off such attacks by adopting a politics of respectability, which embraced middle-class gender norms to undermine notions of black inferiority and conferred on middle-class blacks the responsibility for lifting up the black poor. Wage-earning black women, refusing to accept the idea that their poverty resulted from their moral deficiency, sought better material conditions as industrial and service workers in urban centers. Among them were Union widows like Mary Norman, Caroline Brown, and Harriet Council.

By 1911, diverse groups of women had demanded and won subsidies for impoverished widowed mothers. Mothers' pensions took the form of state-sponsored subsidies for women in need who could not work outside the home due to their childrearing responsibilities or who were unable to earn a living wage. But black women were rarely deemed eligible for mothers' pensions because they were expected to work for wages when they had young children. Moreover, black mothers who headed their own households were seen as morally suspect; even those who could prove that they were widows rather than unwed mothers were given only small sums to supplement their earnings.[3] As had happened under the Civil War pension system, racialized conceptions of motherhood prevented most black women from securing benefits. In petitioning state governments for mothers' pensions, black women defined the impact of poverty in their own terms while seeking recognition as mothers and citizens.

When World War I opened up wage-earning opportunities in the industrial North and Midwest, a mass exodus from the rural South began.[4] The lure of higher wages and greater personal freedom was particularly strong for black women, who were largely confined to domestic service and farm work in the South. The prospect of escaping the demands of household labor that placed them in close contact with hostile white employers and the daily threat of sexual violence, as well as the opportunity to affirm the meaning of their citizenship, prompted black women to move en masse. But northern employers' preference for immigrant and white ethnic labor in the munitions, iron and steel, railroad, automobile, and food-processing industries combined with limited housing options confined black women and their families to dilapidated urban spaces with few municipal resources. Black migration slowed as the nation fell into a recession.

Black men's and women's participation in the Civil War helped to secure the destruction of slavery and to win both citizenship and military benefits for black soldiers and their families, but black men's military service during World War I did not bring similar gains. Although the Selective Service Act of 1917 required black as well as white men to register for the draft, the military remained segregated and, fearing the specter of armed black men, often relegated them to physical labor rather than combat units. African Americans responded with ambivalence when activist intellectual W. E. B. Du Bois called on African Americans to "close ranks" and get behind President Woodrow Wilson's effort to make the world safe for democracy.

Under the Selective Service Act, Congress extended draft deferments to men "who supplied their families' livelihoods." Draft officials in the South viewed marriage as a reasonable reason for deferment, despite official regulations stipulating that what mattered was men's financial support of their families. The idea that black women had historically contributed to their families' economic survival through wage earning meant that fewer black men qualified for marriage deferments. In their husbands' absence, black women were deemed capable of wage labor outside the home. In November 1917, the Bureau of War Risk Insurance in Washington, DC, began paying monthly allowances to the dependent wives and children of servicemen, ranging from thirty dollars for a wife with no children to up to sixty-five dollars for a mother with six children. Black women struggled to gain access to these benefits, which gave them the kind of autonomy and bargaining power that women like Fanny Whitney had attained in the Civil War pension system.[5]

In the 1930s, the Hoover administration recognized the civic contributions and sacrifices of black Gold Star mothers and wives, but it relegated these same women to second-class status by segregating them during their state-sponsored travel to France to mourn their men. The segregated tours drew protests from black leaders such as James Weldon Johnson, the executive secretary of the National Association for the Advancement of Colored

People (NAACP). In the end, 279 black women joined six all-black groups and traveled across Europe. Hoover's administration viewed these segregated pilgrimages as upholding the U.S. racial system and projecting an image to the world of the United States as a homogeneous white nation. Black civil rights leaders and journalists advanced arguments about the responsibilities of "race mothers," who owed their loyalty to their beloved dead and the black community, not the nation-state. As Rebecca Jo Plant and Frances M. Clarke cogently point out, these poor and working-poor black women took "pride in their treatment as guests of the U.S. government, segregated though they were, while still harboring dreams of a radically transformed society."[6]

The Great Depression led to the end of most state-sponsored pension programs for mothers. In states that retained these programs, the implementation of new racial and family guidelines further limited black women's ability to use them. Unable to tap municipal and state resources, black women faced increased pressure to support themselves and contribute to the well-being of their extended kin groups. To make up for black men's underemployment and unemployment, many sold their labor on what was called the "slave market": street corners where black women waited for white women to pick them up for day work in their homes. On the whole, national and state welfare initiatives did not provide a safety net for domestic service workers.[7]

Black women "derived little tangible support from landmark social welfare legislation of the 1930s," especially the Social Security Act of 1935, which offered the first federal grants to those who were not veterans or their dependents.[8] This program set up distinctly different provisions for workers and for the poor. The social insurance program required contributions from employees and their employers and was therefore tied to work. Yet it failed to cover three-fifths to two-thirds of all black workers and more than half of all employed women. The outright exclusion of domestic service and agricultural workers from the program severely limited black women's ability to claim benefits based on their work.

ADC (later AFDC) was set up principally to ensure the well-being of young children. Governed by principles of "adequacy," the program allocated general revenues to states for means-tested welfare for poor and older citizens. Assistance was administered at the local level. In the segregated South, black women and their children were often excluded from ADC: welfare boards saw "no reason why the employable Negro mother should not continue her usually sketchy seasonal labor or indefinite domestic service rather than receive a public assistance grant."[9] Recipients were subjected to home inspections, rules governing sexual morality, and means testing. This set of programs was funded by taxpayers and was stigmatized by its resemblance to poor relief, while Social Security was supported by the contributions of beneficiaries who were regarded as deserving and was seen as an entitlement.

As Joanne Goodwin points out, southern congressmen all but eliminated a provision that would have authorized equitable distribution of public aid regardless of race, as had been true of the Civil War pension system—at least in theory. Amended in 1939, the Social Security Act added provisions for the widows and children of male workers in covered industries, but black women fared no better in the amended version of the act. Widows of industrial workers would receive a Social Security payment based on their husbands' work without the humiliating intrusive inspections ADC recipients had to endure.[10]

In the early 1940s, the rapid expansion of wartime industries and the shortage of male labor prompted even more African Americans to move from the rural South to urban centers in the North, West, and South. Black women escaped their previous confinement to low-wage, demeaning work, and "the war propelled [them] to stake new claims to citizenship in the arena of jobs, housing, public accommodations, [transportation,] and voting."[11] The almost complete exclusion of blacks from defense industries, such as shipyards and airplane plants, led to threats of mass protests. The planned March on Washington in 1941 prompted President Roosevelt to issue Executive Order 8802, banning racial discrimination by employers receiving government contracts. By 1944, some three hundred thousand black women had secured employment in manufacturing industries.

During the war, more than one million black men served in the military—again in segregated units. Initially relegated to construction, transportation, and other noncombat tasks, black soldiers endured such indignities as being forced to give up their seats in railroad cars to German prisoners of war.[12] But black GIs served valiantly in combat missions in both the European and Pacific theaters, and the Tuskegee airmen have recently enjoyed the recognition they merited. After the war, returning black soldiers met with white hostility, fear, and even lynching. Moreover, black veterans failed to get the benefits extended to millions of returning veterans under the Selective Service Readjustment Act of 1944 (GI Bill). Aimed at rewarding veterans with economic opportunities such as homeownership, higher education, subsidies for starting small businesses, and steady employment, the GI Bill was purportedly race neutral.[13] Because state and local agencies managed the benefits, however, black veterans, especially those living in the South, failed to receive just recompense.

Emboldened by their wartime gains, black people made demands on the federal government well before the 1954 *Brown v. Board of Education* Supreme Court decision. The modern-day black freedom struggle inspired new modes of protest politics and political claims. Through sit-ins, work stoppages, and petitions, poor black women pushed the federal government to uphold the promises of equal treatment before the law that were rescinded after Reconstruction. In their claims, black women continued to petition the federal government, providing a sustained critique of the racialized gender and class bias embedded in ostensibly color-blind policies such as the Social Security Act of 1935 and the GI Bill.[14]

Black military widows and black women in search of welfare were disproportionately excluded from government-sponsored benefits, and applicants endured intrusive home visits and sexually explicit questioning. In 1943 Louisiana adopted an "employable mother" rule, which authorized the denial of benefits to mothers if casual jobs in the fields were available. Georgia followed suit in 1952. In 1960 the Louisiana legislature passed a "suitable homes" law, which prohibited women in "common-law marriages" or those who had children outside legal marriage from receiving welfare assistance. In the months following implementation of this program, some twenty-three thousand women and children in Louisiana became ineligible for aid; black women and children formed the majority of those removed from the rolls.[15]

During the 1970s, after a quarter century of postwar prosperity failed to improve the situation of poor and working-poor African Americans, black women seized the opportunity Lyndon B. Johnson's Great Society programs created to press the claims of impoverished women and children. Formed in 1967, the National Welfare Rights Organization taught eligible women who were not receiving aid how to apply for benefits and avoid racial discrimination. With affiliate organizations in fifty states by 1971, the group galvanized poor black women and provided a national platform for these women to advance citizenship claims on their own terms. The organization claimed public benefits "as a matter of equality" and "as a component of their rights as citizens, mothers, consumers, and human beings." Importantly, black women were the majority of the National Welfare Rights Organization members.[16]

Civil War widows and mid-twentieth-century welfare rights activists took profoundly different approaches to engage the government. Black Union widows pursued monetary benefits to which they were entitled through their late husbands' military service. They regularly spoke of their labor to deflect racially biased charges of sexual immorality. In their eyes, their care work and their paid labor made them upstanding members of the community. A century later, welfare rights activists spoke more of dignity and its meaning in a consumer-based society. They sought to participate fully in the post–World War II consumer economy and viewed a decent standard of living as an essential sign of respect. Though black women on welfare were often stigmatized as lazy, welfare rights activists did not emphasize work—even though most welfare mothers had to earn money to get by. By the time welfare recipients founded the National Welfare Rights Organization, activists—most of whom were women of color—explicitly linked motherhood and childcare to equality and citizenship. In short, they were laying claim to a racialized formulation of domesticity to which poor black women had never had access. The fundamental differences between war widows' and welfare activists' concepts of entitlement and citizenship clarify black women's changing relationship to the state.

The history of conflicts between black women and federal officials over military pension benefits and welfare aid indicates that the racialized gender inequities and class biases that stigmatized black women had a powerful influence on social policy much earlier than current scholarship has acknowledged. Without a racialized gender perspective, it is difficult to grasp the full import of notions of marriage and sexuality that have marginalized poor black women and limited their rights as citizens of the nation-state throughout U.S. history.[17] The dominant racialized gender and class concepts of marriage and morality justified to the government the denial and removal of black women from the pension roster. Similar constructs justified black women's exclusion from Social Security entitlements and relegated them to AFDC, the most penurious and stigmatized side of the U.S. social welfare system. Gender- and class-based ideas about marriage and family have continued to inform the structure and provisions of entitlement and public assistance programs.[18] Racial and sexual stereotypes imagining black female welfare recipients as sexually immoral pervaded the public debates that preceded "the end of welfare as we know it" in the late 1990s.[19] The historical roots of these ideas and black women's responses to the implementation of such policies require deeper investigation.[20]

THE LEGACIES OF BLACK WOMEN'S CLAIMS

While *Claiming Union Widowhood* shows how poor black women contended with various forms of gendered racism and inequality, other considerations can be teased out from their case files. It is difficult to know just how many black women exposed their experiences of rape and sexualized violence during the special examination process or why some used this forum to air these traumatic experiences. Although they did not receive justice in the pension system or the courts, these disclosures nonetheless formed what Lisa Levenstein and Danielle McGuire characterized as "a form of direct action."[21] As the struggle for black freedom and gender equality has continued, black women's claims for citizenship and protests against rape have become ever more public. Poor black women also leveled careful and cautious critiques of black male abusers without estranging themselves from their communities.[22] They raised issues of domestic instability, abandonment, and intraracial intimate partner violence.

The acknowledgment of black women's pension claims as a form of political activity opens up new analytical pathways in studies of redress and reparations. Historian Robin D. G. Kelley urged proponents of reparations to consider how to both make restitution for women's unpaid labor, reproduction, and sexual abuse and clarify what constitutes a family.[23] Black women's post–Civil War claims reflect the means by which freedpeople reconstructed their families and communities and made a place for themselves in a society based on wage labor. Applying for and receiving federal benefits on the basis of women's marital ties to black soldiers and veterans simultaneously extended the gains of Reconstruction and served as a form of resistance to Jim Crow, which was then being established across the South. Through this social and political process, working-class black women attempted to negotiate the terms of their citizenship with the federal government and in their own communities.

The women whose claims are analyzed in this book understood their recognition as Union widows as both a personal matter and a means by which black women might begin to reconstruct their relationships within their households and communities and their ties with local, state, and governmental institutions. Significantly, the Reverend Isaiah H. Dickerson and Callie D. House organized the Ex-Slave Mutual Relief, Bounty and Pension Association along the same lines as the federal pension system. Leaders and members of this movement for reparations pressed for federal legislation authorizing financial compensation for all formerly enslaved people. Dickerson and House endured federal surveillance and, ultimately, imprisonment for daring to speak about the possibility of a pension as an entitlement for former slaves. The public's unwillingness to pay a subsidy to former slaves and their descendants also failed because of popular contemporary conceptions of black people as naked labor rather than as clothed in citizenship rights. In the twentieth century, Queen Audley Moore developed a "feminist, nationalist, and class-based politics" to organize on behalf of poor black women and children and to reinvigorate the idea of financial redress for African Americans. Moore's activism developed around sexual violence, which informed her reparations activities.[24]

The protracted battles that women like Charlotte Banks and Louisa Powers waged within the pension system expand our understanding of how the American welfare state unfolded for black women and revise our interpretations of black women's continuing struggle for full citizenship. Keenly aware of the political system in which they operated, nineteenth-century working-class black women adapted their language and actions to meet the Pension Bureau's evolving views on marriage and virtuous widowhood to secure the economic resources they desperately needed to sustain their families. At the same time, questions of citizenship informed their claims and their vision of their place in American society.

Notes

Abbreviations

Case Files Case Files of Attorneys, Agents, Pensioners, and Others Relating to the Prosecution of Pension Claims and the Investigation of Fraudulent Practices, Legal Records, Records of the Bureau of Pensions and Its Predecessors, 1805–1915, Record Group 15: Records of the Department of Veteran Affairs, 1773–2007, National Archives and Records Administration

Civil War Pension Index General Index to Pension Files, 1861–1934, Record Group 15: Records of the Department of Veteran Affairs, 1773–2007, National Archives and Records Administration

CMSR31–35 Compiled Military Service Records of Volunteer Union Soldiers Belonging to the 31st through 35th Infantry Units, Organized for Service with the U.S. Colored Troops, Record Group 94: Records of the Adjutant General's Office, 1780s–1917, National Archives and Records Administration

CMSR36–40 Compiled Military Service Records of Volunteer Union Soldiers Belonging to the 36th through 40th Infantry Units, Organized for Service with the U.S. Colored Troops, Record Group 94: Records of the Adjutant General's Office, 1780s–1917, National Archives and Records Administration

FSTC Register of Signatures of Depositors in Branches of the Freedman's Savings and Trust Company, 1865–1874, Record Group 101: Records of the Office of the Comptroller of the Currency, National Archives and Records Administration

FSSP Freedmen and Southern Society Project, Department of History, University of Maryland, last updated February 14, 2020, http://www.freedmen.umd.edu

IC Invalid's Claim

MC Mother's Claim

MI Minor's Claim

NARA National Archives and Records Administration

RBC Record Group 29: Records of the Bureau of the Census, National Archives and Records Administration

USCC	U.S. Colored Cavalry
USCHA	U.S. Colored Heavy Artillery
USCT	U.S. Colored Troops
WC	Widow's Claim

Introduction

1. Foner, *Reconstruction*, 148.

2. Du Bois, *Black Reconstruction*; Holt, "Empire of the Mind," 283–313; Schwalm, *Hard Fight for We*, 7.

3. Schwalm, *Hard Fight for We*; Bercaw, *Gendered Freedoms*; Frankel, *Freedom's Women*; Hunter, *To 'Joy My Freedom*; Edwards, *Gendered Strife and Confusion*; Romeo, *Gender and Jubilee*; Glymph, *Out of the House of Bondage*; Rosen, *Terror in the Heart of Freedom*; Farmer-Kaiser, *Freedwomen and the Freedmen's Bureau*; E. B. Brown, "Negotiating and Transforming the Public Sphere," 107–46; Clinton, "Reconstructing Freedwomen," 307–19; J. Jones, *Labor of Love, Labor of Sorrow*.

4. Schwalm, *A Hard Fight for We*, 3; Frankel, preface to *Freedom's Women*, xxx; Hunter, *Bound in Wedlock*, 4.

5. Frankel, *Freedom's Women*; Romeo, *Gender and Jubilee*.

6. Gordon, "Family Violence, Feminism, and Social Control," 467.

7. Hunter, *Bound in Wedlock*.

8. E. Anderson, *Race and Politics*.

9. Foner, *Reconstruction*, 78.

10. Kaye, *Joining Places*, 1–19.

11. E. B. Brown, "Negotiating and Transforming the Public Sphere," 107–46.

12. Hunter, *To 'Joy My Freedom*.

13. Hahn, *Nation under Our Feet*.

14. L. Alexander, "Challenge of Race," 50–60.

15. I have identified sixteen black men who served as licensed and community claims agents in New Bern. At least seven of the men were born enslaved, and another was free-born. Two of the remaining eight were born during the war, three were born after the war, and information about the remaining three is lacking.

16. In these petitions, claims agents crafted official narratives that framed the basis of a woman's claim in terms that the agents thought the bureau would regard as legitimate.

17. Holt, "Empire over the Mind," 299.

18. McClintock, "Impact of the Civil War," esp. 397n6.

19. McClintock, "Impact of the Civil War."

20. U.S. Pension Bureau, *General Instructions to Special Examiners*, 9.

21. Berry, *My Face Is Black Is True*, 47.

22. Act of June 27, 1890, 26 Stat. 182–83, chap. 634 (1890); McClintock, "Civil War Pensions," 464–65; Skocpol, *Protecting Soldiers and Mothers*, 110–11; Berry, *My Face Is Black Is True*, 47–48.

23. Hunter, *Bound in Wedlock*, chap. 6.

24. Higginbotham, "African-American Women's History," 251–74; Boris, "Racialized Gender State," 160–80; Randolph, "Evelyn Brooks Higginbotham."

25. L. Williams, *Constraints of Race*; Shaffer, *After the Glory*; Shaffer, "I Do Not Suppose"; Regosin, *Freedom's Promise*.

26. U.S. Pension Bureau, *General Instructions to Special Examiners*, 24–26.

27. These studies show how race and gender structured inequality in social welfare policy, which in many cases denied black women access regardless of their class status. Gordon, *Pitied but Not Entitled*; Mink, *Wages of Motherhood*; Kessler-Harris, "Designing Women and Old Fools." The history of regulation of work performed at home similarly reveals how concepts of womanhood and manhood, visions of proper home life and childhood, and the persistent ideological separation of home from work have structured state policy. Sapiro, "Gender Basis of American Social Policy"; Boris, "Racialized Gender State."

28. Haley, *No Mercy Here*, 5–10, 17–57. My use of the term *worthiness* has been influenced by Gordon; however, I am not using the term synonymously. Freedwomen brought their own sense of worthiness to their interactions with the Pension Bureau.

29. Romeo, *Gender and Jubilee*.

30. Penningroth, *Claims of Kinfolk*.

31. Rosen, "Not that Sort of Woman."

32. Rosen, "Not that Sort of Woman," 268.

33. Haley, *No Mercy Here*, 13. This work has profited immensely from Haley's analysis of the "gendered logics of race" in the carceral setting. Hunter, *Bound in Wedlock*, 221.

34. Edwards, *Gendered Strife and Confusion*, 64.

35. Boris, "Racialized Gender State."

36. M. Jones, *Birthright Citizens*, 11; Romeo, *Gender and Jubilee*, 11–38; Rosen, *Terror in the Heart of Freedom*, 222–41.

37. M. Jones, *Birthright Citizens*, 10.

38. M. Jones, *Birthright Citizens*, 137.

39. Rosen, *Terror in the Heart of Freedom*, 221–41.

40. Skocpol, *Protecting Mothers and Soldiers*.

41. McClintock, "Civil War Pensions"; Kretz, "Pensions and Protest."

42. Gordon, "Family Violence, Feminism, and Social Control," 475; Levenstein, *Movement without Marches*.

43. Fraser, "Struggle over Needs," esp. 203–4.

44. Shaffer, "I Do Not Suppose," 133–34.

45. *Claiming Union Widowhood* sits in dialogue with historians who have documented the important role black soldiers and veterans played in the expansion of citizenship won by black men. Berlin, Reidy, and Rowland, *Black Military Experience*; R. Reid, "Raising the African Brigade"; Foner, *Reconstruction*; Foner, *Freedom's Lawmakers*; Hahn, *Nation under Our Feet*. Shaffer, *After the Glory*, analyzes black men's occupational advancement and the symbolic meaning of their presence in black communities across the South.

46. Hicks, *Talk with You Like a Woman*, 12.

47. Hicks, *Talk with You Like a Woman*, 10.

48. *Claiming Union Widowhood* contributes to scholarly conversations that engage the politics of respectability from the vantage point of poor and working-class black women. Hine, "Rape and the Inner Lives of Black Women"; Higginbotham, *Righteous Discontent*, 185–229; Hicks, *Talk with You Like a Woman*, 12.

49. Boris, "On the Importance of Naming"; Canaday, "Building a Straight State."

50. I surveyed the pension files of widows associated with the Thirty-Fifth, Thirty-Sixth, and Thirty-Seventh Regiments of the USCT, the Fourteenth USCHA, and the Second USCC to identify the compilation of files referenced in this book. These pension files are indexed by military unit in Organization Index to Pension Files of Veterans Who Served Between 1861 and 1900, Record Group 15: Records of the Department of Veteran Affairs, NARA. I also used the Special Schedules of the Eleventh Census (1890) Enumerating Union Veterans and Widows of Union Veterans of the Civil War, Record Group 15: Records of the Department of Veteran Affairs, NARA.

51. Fuentes, introduction to *Dispossessed Lives*.

52. E. Anderson, *Race and Politics*; Bishir, *Crafting Lives*, 218; Gilmore, *Gender and Jim Crow*; Browning, *Shifting Loyalties*; Cecelski, *Waterman's Song* and *Fire of Freedom*; Mobley, *James City*.

53. Baptist, "Stol' and Fetched Here."

1. Black Life and Labor in New Bern, North Carolina, 1850–1865

1. Soon after the Swiss Germans and Palatine Germans arrived, they captured and sold members of the indigenous Tuscarora band into slavery. They were pushed out in the war of 1711–13. The survivors took refuge with the Iroquois Confederacy to the north.

2. Date from Martin, "Craven County (1705)."

3. Johnson, *Ante-Bellum North Carolina*, 115.

4. Johnson, *Ante-Bellum North Carolina*, 117.

5. The characterization first appeared in Hannigan, *New Bern*.

6. Johnson, *Ante-Bellum North Carolina*, 115–19; Bishir, *Crafting Lives*, 21.

7. Outland, "Slavery, Work, and Geography," 31.

8. Outland, "Slavery, Work, and Geography," 31.

9. In 1755, New Hanover had 1,374 slaves; Craven, 934; Edgecombe, 924; North Hampton, 834; and Beaufort, 567. Franklin, *Free Negro in North Carolina*, 8.

10. Berlin, *Many Thousands Gone*.

11. Seventy-three percent of families in North Carolina had no slaves, and more than half of the slaveholders had fewer than ten slaves. Finkelman, *Encyclopedia of African American History*, 463–69.

12. On the eve of the Civil War, less than 2.3 percent of the state's enslaved population (331,059) lived on large plantations. See Walbert, "Distribution of Land and Slaves"; testimony of Hattie Rogers, in Works Projects Administration, *Slave Narratives*.

13. A. Watson, *History of New Bern and Craven County*, 308.

14. Though large numbers of free blacks lived in New Bern and Wilmington, the majority of free blacks in the state lived outside these cities. Franklin, *Free Negro in North Carolina*, 14–57.

15. Cecelski, *Waterman's Song*, 159; Scarborough, *Masters of the Big House*, 366–67.

16. Wolfram and Thomas estimated that 220 slaves resided on Judge Donnell's Hyde plantation in 1850; the next-largest plantation had only 45. Wolfram and Thomas, *Development of African American English*, 58; Carawan, "Hyde County's Largest Plantation Owner," 37–41.

17. Deposition of Fanny Whitney, October 10, 1892, in the pension file of Elizabeth Jane Longest (Tooley), Isaac Longest, and Moses Longest, minors of Moses Longest, Thirty-Seventh USCT (MI 137141), Civil War Pension Index.

18. Bisher, *Crafting Lives*, 56–60.

19. Schweninger, "John Carruthers Stanly," 161. Schweninger determined that the correct spelling is *Stanly*, not *Stanley*.

20. Schweninger, "John Carruthers Stanly," 161.

21. Schweninger, "John Carruthers Stanly." John Wright Stanly owned the vessel that transported John C. Stanly's mother to America before the revolution. As further evidence of his paternity, Schweninger points to John C. Stanly's linkages with the white Stanlys, including his willingness to guarantee a "security bond" for his white brother, who eventually became a U.S. congressman. Stanly's family history is also captured in Vass, *History of the Presbyterian Church in Newbern, N.C.*, 135–37.

22. In November 1798, John C. Stanly took additional steps to fortify his free standing when he petitioned the General Assembly of North Carolina to pass a special act certifying his status as a freeman. Petition Analysis Record Number 11279805, Digital Library of American Slavery, UNC-Greensboro, accessed May 5, 2020, https://library.uncg.edu/slavery/.

23. Bassett, *Slavery in the State of North Carolina*, 43–46; Schweninger, "John Carruthers Stanly," 171; Bishir, *Crafting Lives*, 70.

24. Cecelski, *Waterman's Song*. Bishir, *Crafting Lives*, traces the lives and labors of black artisans.

25. Deposition of Mary Norman, July 9, 1900, pension file of Mary Norman, widow of Turner Norman, Thirty-Fifth USCT (WC 289190), Civil War Pension Index.

26. Deposition of Julia Ann Foy, February 26, 1901, pension file of Charlotte Banks, widow of Caesar Banks, Thirty-Fifth USCT (WC 157383), Civil War Pension Index.

27. Kaiser, "Masters Determined to Be Masters," 13. Kaiser's analysis of slave patrol records from Craven County highlights white concern about insurrection in the county near the end of the growing seasons and during holidays between 1818 and 1824 (58).

28. Deposition of Mary Whitby, June 22, 1900, pension file of Mary Whitby (Williams) widow of John Whitby, Thirty-Seventh USCT (WC 276505), Civil War Pension Index.

29. Schweninger, "Property Owning Free African American Women," esp. 15.

30. Walker, *History of Black Business in America*, 177. Reference to Catherine Stanly's property value noted in Franklin, *Free Negro in North Carolina*, 228. Both authors spell Stanly's name with an *e*. The 1860 manuscript census lists her residence in the Second Ward of the city. She is listed as a dressmaker with one thousand dollars of real estate and three thousand dollars of personal property. Eighth Census of the United States, 1860, RBC.

31. William P. Biddle, Wills and Probate Records, Craven County Records, North Carolina State Archives. Whether these were Biddle's children or were purchased by Biddle Sr. at the slave auction is unclear from the evidence in Jane's case file. Biddle's grandson James, who at the time of his deposition served as the register of deeds in Craven County, believed that Jane was given to one of his aunts after William Biddle's death. Deposition of James W. Biddle, September 22, 1892, pension file of Jane Reynolds (Atkinson), widow of Thomas Reynolds, Fourteenth USCHA (WC 349453), Civil War Pension Index. Edward White, a farmer who attended the auction where Biddle's enslaved property was sold off, felt certain that Pope actually purchased Jane. Deposition of Edward White, September 27, 1892, pension file of Jane Reynolds.

32. Affidavit of Jane Reynolds (Atkinson), September 19, 1892, pension file of Jane Reynolds (WC 349453).

33. *Newbern Daily Progress*, December 29, 1859.

34. *Newbernian and North Carolina Advocate*, November 13, 1849.

35. Greenwood, *Bittersweet Legacy*, 245.

36. Bishir, *Crafting Lives*, 298n20.

37. Eighth Census of the United States, 1860, RBC; Greenwood, *Bittersweet Legacy*, 245. By comparison, in 1850, 51 percent of the residents of Wilmington were black. Of its total population of 7,264, 42 percent (3,031) were enslaved blacks, and 9 percent (652) were free blacks. In 1850, Petersburg, Virginia, also a port city, counted a total of 7,345 blacks (2,616 free people of color, 4,729 enslaved) and 6,665 whites. On the eve of the Civil War, Charleston had a majority black enslaved population. Bishir, *Crafting Lives*, 298.

38. *Newbernian and North Carolina Advocate*, Shade and Arch, December 1843, Edny Manor, March 1848.

39. "NC Runaway Slave Advertisements," Digital Library of American Slavery, UNC-Greensboro, accessed September 12, 2018, https://library.uncg.edu/slavery/.

40. Johnson, *Ante-Bellum North Carolina*, 128.

41. Paul Heinegg, "Free African Americans of Virginia, North Carolina, South Carolina, Maryland and Delaware," Free African Americans, last updated November 1, 2019, http://freeafricanamericans.com/.

42. Eighth Census of the United States, 1860, RBC; pension file of Mariah Richardson, widow of Hezekiah Richardson, Fourteenth USCHA (WC 769899), Civil War Pension Index.

43. Kaye, *Joining Places*, 51–82, esp. 52–54.

44. I deduced that Sarah Williams (Copes) lived in the city by analyzing the names of her nearby neighbors (Sarah Richardson) and comparing them to the 1860 census, which notes the different wards of the city. Eighth Census of the United States, 1860, RBC; pension file of Mary Whitby (Williams) (WC 276505).

45. Deposition of Mary Whitby, June 22, 1900.

46. Deposition of Mary Whitby, June 22, 1900.

47. Section 1 of the apprenticeship code, North Carolina, *Revised Code*, 77–78.

48. Deposition of Mary Whitby, June 22, 1900.

49. Browning, *Shifting Loyalties*, 3. An enslaved woman from Edenton, North Carolina, remembered, "My owners carried me up the country." Amanda Skinner to the Hon. Commissioner of Pensions, September 30, 1882, pension file of Caroline Skinner, widow of Mingo Skinner, Thirty-Fifth USCT (WC 924480), Civil War Pension Index.

50. Browning, "Removing the Mask of Nationality," 589–620.

51. Bishir, *Crafting Lives*, 101–2; Patterson Green, *Fact Stranger than Fiction*, 4.

52. Berlin et al., *Wartime Genesis of Free Labor*, 78n193. The scale and scope of black migration to Union-occupied areas of the state during the wartime era are captured in census figures. A survey conducted in January 1865 counted 17,307 black people (apparently excluding soldiers) in the counties under federal occupation in eastern North Carolina.

53. Manning, *Troubled Refuge*, 65–76.

54. Kate Masur poignantly describes General Butler's use of *contraband* as nothing more than a "legal veneer" for holding enslaved people [at] the early stage in the Civil War. It allowed the U.S. military to hold people without returning them to Confederate rebels and avoid the question of emancipation. Masur, "Rare Phenomenon of Philological Vegetation," 1050; see also Greenwood, *First Fruits*, 29.

55. Colyer's appointment date from Berlin et al., *Wartime Genesis of Free Labor*, 123–24, doc. 7. The Department of North Carolina refers to the military department assigned to the occupied area. Colyer said that he could never get enough men to meet the military's demand.

56. Berlin et al., *Wartime Genesis of Free Labor*, 122, doc. 6.

57. No mention was made of work that women might do.

58. Berlin et al., *Wartime Genesis of Free Labor*, 122, doc. 6.

59. Mobley, *James City*, 23–24.

60. On the renaming of the Trent River settlement, see Mobley, *James City*, 27.

61. Colyer, *Report of the Services Rendered*, 9; deposition of Charles Collins, October 12, 1896, pension file of Mary Williams (Jourdan), widow of Henry Jourdan, Fourteenth USCHA (WC 435758), Civil War Pension Index.

62. Proof of Dependence and Support, Julia Ann Foy, pension file of Julia Ann Foy, mother of William Foy, Thirty-Fifth USCT (MC 156180), Civil War Pension Index.

63. Colyer, *Report of the Services Rendered*, 9.

64. Deposition of Ann Stamp, August 4, 1904, pension file of Charlotte Banks (WC 157383); for black women's wartime work in Virginia, see Krowl, "African American Women," 182.

65. Cecelski, *Fire of Freedom*, 69.

66. "Nurses and Nursing," in J. C. Smith, *Encyclopedia of African American Popular Culture*, 1:1033.

67. Greenwood, *First Fruits*, 4; Patterson Green, *Fact Stranger Than Fiction*, 4.

68. Berlin et al., *Wartime Genesis of Free Labor*, 93n12.

69. Nicholas Bray, a white farmer, and his wife, Harriet, came to New Bern claiming that a Union soldier had taken a woman they owned against her will. According to Vincent Colyer's version of the incident, Bray had been offered fifteen hundred dollars for Harriet, who had then taken refuge in the Trent River camp. After Bray took the oath of allegiance to the United States, Stanly allowed Bray to retrieve the woman. Incensed by the incident and the policies that Stanly sanctioned, a group of Union soldiers traveled to Bray's farm and held a gun to his head before taking the woman back to New Bern. Browning, "Removing the Mask," 611; Colyer, *Report of the Services Rendered*, 47.

70. Sumner was savagely beaten on the Senate floor in 1856 after delivering his "Crime against Kansas" speech. "The Caning of Senator Charles Sumner," U.S. Senate, Art and History, accessed August 22, 2017, https://www.senate.gov/artandhistory/history/minute/The_Caning_of_Senator_Charles_Sumner.htm.

71. Greenwood, *First Fruits*, 56.

72. R. Reid, "Government Policy, Prejudice," 384.

73. Click, preface and introduction to *Time Full of Trial*, xvii. In the spring of 1863, it became the setting for a historic experiment much like Port Royal, when General John G. Foster instigated efforts to transform the refuge on Roanoke into a federally sanctioned settlement. He instructed Rev. Horace James to supervise the colonization of the island with former slaves. From that point forward, it was referred to as a "colony" or "village" by missionaries, military authorities, and the Northern press.

74. Deposition of Fanny Whitney, February 9, 1901, pension file of Fanny Whitney, widow of Harry Whitney, Thirty-Fifth USCT (WC 130403), Civil War Pension Index. The movement from Donnell's plantation to the Roanoke Colony appears to have taken place around December 1863.

75. Bercaw, *Gendered Freedoms*, chap. 1.

76. Henry Jones to Mr. Donnell, September 11, 1862, box 6, John Heritage Bryan Papers, David M. Rubenstein Rare Book and Manuscript Library, Duke University; Cecelski, *Waterman's Song*, 159; Glymph, "Du Bois's Black Reconstruction," 492.

77. Second Confiscation Act, July 17, 1862, 12 Stat. 589–92, chap. 195 (1863), FSSP; Cook-Bell, "Self-Emancipating Women," 5.

78. Militia Act of 1862, July 17, 1862, 12 Stat. 597–600, chap. 201 (1863). Glymph, "Invisible Disabilities." Glymph offers a deeply nuanced analysis of various aspects of black women's wartime experiences: overrepresentation in freedmen's camps, trauma, and family separation.

79. Browning, "Removing the Mask of Nationality," 613.

80. General Order 46, December 5, 1863, cited in Berlin et al., *Wartime Genesis of Free Labor*, 168–74.

81. Berlin et al., *Wartime Genesis of Free Labor*, 169.

82. Singleton, *Recollection of My Slavery Days*, 48.

83. On Mary Ann Starkey, see Glymph, *Out of the House of Bondage*, 212; Cecelski, *Fire of Freedom*, xiv–xvi.

84. On Abraham Galloway, see Cecelski, *Fire of Freedom*; Cecelski, *Waterman's Song*, chap. 7; McClintock, "Civil War Pensions"; R. Reid, "Raising the African Brigade." On black soldiers' understanding of the government's promise to support their families, see Frank James to General A. G. Draiper, June 4, 1865, and endorsements, Sergt. Richard Etheredge and Wm. Benson to Genl. Howard [May or June 1865], Unregistered Letters Received, ser. 2453, Record Group 105: Records of the Assistant Commissioner of the State of North Carolina, Bureau of Refugees, Freedmen, and Abandoned Lands, NARA.

85. R. Reid, "Raising the African Brigade."

86. In 1860, the number of black males aged eighteen to forty-five in North Carolina was 60,170: 5,510 free, 55,020 enslaved. See table 1, "Black Soldiers in the Union Army and Black Male Population of Military Age in 1860, by State," in Berlin, Reidy, and Rowland, *Black Military Experience*. The enlistment percentage is on par with South Carolina, which is credited with 5,446 black soldiers (8 percent); though Virginia recruited a slightly higher number of black soldiers, the proportion was 6 percent of the black men aged eighteen to forty-five. There are several reasons to question these numbers, since blacks from neighboring states crossed state lines to enlist in the military. Moreover, compelling testimony from contemporary observers suggests that in many cases, the black men recruited—in North Carolina, at least—were underaged.

87. Deposition of Philip Wiggins, October 18, 1905, pension file of Alice Askie, widow of Isaac Askie, Thirty-Seventh USCT (WC 600768), Civil War Pension Index. Various documents spell the soldier's surname *Askie* and give the widow's name as *Elsie* or *Alice*. After interviewing her family members in Orange, New Jersey, the pension examiner explained the proper spelling of the name: *Elsia Askew*. See Mark J. Maloney to Hon. Commissioner of Pensions, July 19, 1905. For this reason, I have adopted *Elsia Askew* except in quotations and when citing the pension index.

88. Though generally known as *Sam Rouse*, his maternal surname, Samuel enlisted under the name *Powers*. Samuel Powers's military service records, roll 79, CMSR31–35. Samuel Powers may have been one of the thirty black prisoners freed from Duplin County Courthouse by a black regiment organized by General Edward A. Wild. Joseph E. Williams, a free black antislavery activist who served in the unit, penned a July 1863 letter to the *Christian Recorder* describing the ordeal: "When we arrived at the town of Duplin, we were informed that there were upwards of thirty colored prisoners . . . that were to be tried for their lives for attempting to escape inside the lines." After liberating the men, "two of them came to Newbern

to join Wild's Bridgade." Joseph E. Williams (Wild's Brigade) to *Christian Recorder*, July 11, 1863 (Letter 34), in Redkey, *Grand Army of Black Men*, 91–92.

89. In addition to the Trent River settlement, James set up two other temporary camps located outside the Union fortifications for black refugees near New Bern. A Confederate attack on New Bern and capture of blacks housed outside the city in January 1864 led to the consolidation of all the camps into the Trent River settlement. Mobley, *James City*, 24.

90. Deposition of E. W. Carpenter, September 14, 1892, pension file of Mary Ann Sleight, widow of Alfred Sleight, Second USCC (WC 367716), Civil War Pension Index.

91. Judy Blackwell, Burial Registers of Military Posts and National Cemeteries, 1862–1960, Record Group 92: Records of the Office of the Quartermaster General, NARA. Petition of Elizabeth Dempsey in the William L. Horner Collection, p. 295, and Elizabeth Dempsey's petition for a nurse's pension (application 1133591). S. K. Taylor, *Reminiscences of My Life in Camp*. On the racialized treatment of black and white army nurses by the pension bureaucracy, see Schultz, "Race, Gender, and Bureaucracy," 53–58; on Dr. Henry O. Marcy, see "Biographical Sketch of Dr. Henry O. Marcy," in I. A. Watson, *Physicians and Surgeons of America*; R. Reid, *Freedom for Themselves*; Daniel J. Vivian, "Dr. Marcy's March," *New York Times*, February 13, 2015.

92. Berlin, Reidy, and Rowland, *Black Military Experience*, 21; Shaffer, *After the Glory*, 13.

93. References to the men appear in the deposition of Martha Fulford, February 13, 1901, pension file of Fanny Whitney (WC 130403). They include Green Cradell, Ira Holwell (Holliway), Nathan Whitney, George Spencer, Moses Longest, Washington Whitfield, Frank Brimmage, and Harry Whitney. Date and place of enlistment and, in some instances, dates of death determined by military service records for Harry Whitney, roll 51; Nathan Whitney, roll 51; Washington Whitfield, roll 51; Green Cradell, roll 31; Moses Longest, roll 40; and Ira Howell, roll 36, CMSR36–40. I was not able to locate the enlistment dates and locations for Frank Brimmage and George Spencer in the military service records.

94. Deposition of Nathan Whitney, February 14, 1901, pension file of Fanny Whitney (WC 130403). See also the pension file of Mardecia Whitney, widow of Nathan Whitney, Thirty-Seventh USCT (WC 745221), Civil War Pension Index. Moses Longest may have enlisted at Roanoke before his pregnant wife and children arrived. Deposition of Margaret Blunt, September 10, 1891, pension file of Eliza Jane Longest (Tooley), Isaac Longest, and William Longest, minors of Moses Longest (MI 137141).

95. Deposition of Fanny Whitney, February 1, 1901, and Martha Fulford, February 13, 1901, pension file of Fanny Whitney (WC 130403); A. Cooper, "Away I Goin'," 451–52.

96. Deposition of Charles Oats, February 27, 1913, pension file of Presilla Flowers, widow of James Flowers, Thirty-Seventh USCT (WC 755483), Civil War Pension Index.

97. Deposition of Mathew Walden, September 26, 1892, pension file of Jane Reynolds (WC 349453).

98. Deposition of Frank Mardix, July 30, 1900, pension file of Sarah Mardix, widow of Frank Mardix, Thirty-Fifth USCT (WC 834642), Civil War Pension Index.

99. Glymph, "Du Bois's Black Reconstruction," 490.

100. Deposition of Mary Lee (Williams), December 19, 1888, pension file of Mary Lee, widow of Simeon Lee, Thirty-Fifth USCT (WC 329285); Cook-Bell, "Self-Emancipating Women," 5.

101. Williams to *Christian Recorder*, June 23, 1863 (Letter 33), in Redkey, *Grand Army of Black Men*, 90–91. Horace James reflected on the ceremony in his annual report published in the *New Berne Times*, September 12, 1865; *New York Times*, August 5, 1863.

102. Glymph, *Women's Fight*, 91. Williams's coverage of black activism and the Colored Ladies Union Relief work appeared in news outlets throughout the North. "Mass Meeting of the Colored People of Newbern, N.C.," *Liberator* (Boston), June 26, 1863. Glymph, *Out of the House of Bondage*, 212. It is possible that the name *Hannah Snell*, which appears on one of the few existing group statements, actually referred to Hannah Small, the wife of Alfred Small, a black soldier and James City minister. See the pension file of Hannah Small, widow of Alfred Small, Second USCC (WC 251123), Civil War Pension Index.

103. "The Colored Quakeress," *Newbern Journal of Commerce*, February 24, 1867. A more detailed article with the same title, aimed at soliciting funds on behalf of Oxly, appeared in the *Wilmington Daily Dispatch*, February 21, 1867.

104. Cecelski, *Fire of Freedom*, 134.

105. Click, *Time Full of Trial*, 4.

106. J. Jones, *Labor of Love, Labor of Sorrow*, 50. On the case of Rebecca Ann Cradle, see Silkenat, *Driven from Home*, 87; Barber and Ritter, "Physical Abuse," 54; Lowry, *Sexual Misbehavior in the Civil War*, 132.

107. Gutman, *Black Family in Slavery and Freedom*, 386–91.

108. Deposition of Esther (Easter) Brown, May 28, 1896, pension file of Esther Browne, mother of Jerry Brown, Thirty-Fifth USCT (MC 130542), Civil War Pension Index; Gutman, *Black Family in Slavery and Freedom*, 386–91. Documents in this file refer to the claimant as *Esther Browne* and *Easter Brown*, while her son is identified as *Jerry Brown*. I refer to the claimant as *Easter* and use the surname *Brown* when referencing the soldier or his mother but have retained variant spellings in quotations and when citing the pension index.

109. Reports of Union soldiers raping and sexually violating black women have been well documented. Crystal Feimster's work examines wartime rape: "General Benjamin Butler"; "Rape and Justice in the Civil War," *New York Times*, April 25, 2013. Sexual violence and the threat of rape must have taken an emotional toll on the women who resided in these camps. LeFlouria, *Chained in Silence*, writes of the toll sexual violence took on incarcerated black women's daily lives.

110. Romeo, *Gender and Jubilee*, 2–7, and chap. 1.

111. Gutman, *Black Family in Slavery and Freedom*, 372.

112. Gutman, *Black Family in Slavery and Freedom*, 373–74.

113. On the development of intergenerational communities of women, see Gray-White, *Arn't I a Woman?*; Berkeley, "Colored Ladies Also Contributed"; Hahn, *Nation under Our Feet*, 166.

114. According to Steven Hahn, "African Americans built their new political communities—as they had done under slavery—from many basic materials of everyday life: from the ties and obligation of kinship, from the experiences and struggles of labor, from the traditions and skills of leadership, and from the spiritual energies and resources of religion." Hahn, *Nation under Our Feet*, 166.

115. Deposition of Matilda Wells, July 2, 1904, pension file of Charlotte Banks (WC 157383).

116. Deposition of Martha Fulford, February 13, 1901.

117. Names of Harry Whitney's fellow black enlistees culled from deposition of Martha Fulford, February 13, 1901. Of those mentioned, Green Cradell, Ira Howell, and Washington Whitfield, along with Harry Whitney, died in the fall of 1865. Rolls 31 and 51, CMSR36–40. When a group of armed slaves went to Louisville to enlist in the army, a "great weeping and mourning" and "demonstration of sorrow" accompanied their departure. Gutman, *Black Family in Slavery and Freedom*, 369.

118. Deposition of Louisa Powers, December 17, 1888, pension file of Louisa Powers, widow of Samuel Powers, Thirty-Fifth USCT (WC 300875), Civil War Pension Index.

119. Affidavit of Louisa Powers, January 23, 1891, pension file of Louisa Powers (WC 300875).

120. The ceremonies could be quite elaborate.

121. Deposition of Lucy Crocker, May 27, 1916, pension file of Lucy Crocker, widow of William (Henry) Crocker, Thirty-Sixth USCT (WC 815127), Civil War Pension Index.

122. Gutman, *Black Family in Slavery and Freedom*, 372.

123. Clinton, introduction to S. K. Taylor, *Reminisces of My Life in Camp*, xxii.

124. Samuel Powers's wartime illness and injuries traced in his service records, roll 79, CMSR31–35. A reference to Louisa Powers's work as a contract nurse is mentioned in a letter of rejection from the director of the Widows and Dependents Claims Service. H. L. Bailey to Samuel Powers, April 12, 1935, pension file of Louisa Powers (WC 300875).

125. The inspection occurred in 1864. Farnham and King, "March of the Destroyer," 437.

126. Farnham and King, "March of the Destroyer," 451.

127. Farnham and King, "March of the Destroyer," 471.

128. Reports on the 1864 yellow fever outbreak and Captain William Palmer's illness appear in "Newborn [*sic*], N.C.; The Yellow Fever," *New York Times*, December 6, 1864. See the pension file of William Palmer, Captain and

Commissioner of Subsistence, New Bern (IC 362015), and related documents in his widow's pension file, Mariette Palmer (WC 501166), Civil War Pension Index. See Bay's discussion of yellow fever in the Mississippi Valley in *To Tell the Truth Freely*, 28–29. Palmer's term as mayor of the city (1867–1869) from the *New Bern Republican* and *New Berne Times*.

129. Farnham and King, "March of the Destroyer"; Bay, *To Tell the Truth Freely*, 28.

130. Nathaniel Harris's death on January 7, 1865, roll 269, Compiled Military Service Records of Volunteer Union Soldiers Belonging to the Artillery Units Organized for Service with the U.S. Colored Troops, Record Group 94: Records of the Adjutant General's Office, NARA; pension file of William Harris, minor of Nathaniel Harris, Fourteenth USCHA (MI 133916), Civil War Pension Index.

131. Berlin et al., *Wartime Genesis of Free Labor*, 182–85, Doc. 29.

132. Cecelski, *Fire of Freedom*, 136, puts the number at 1,000, while Farnham and King, "March of the Destroyer," 471, estimate that 650–700 people died, including black refugees and native inhabitants of the city along with military and military administrators. Mary Williams noted that her first husband died of yellow fever in her deposition taken on June 22, 1900; she subsequently married Henry Williams (Jourdan), pension file of Mary Williams (WC 435758).

133. Deposition of Flora Lucas, November 23, 1900, pension file of Biner Becton, widow of Moses Becton, Fourteenth USCHA (WC 712132), Civil War Pension Index.

134. Deposition of Flora Lucas, November 23, 1900; Delancy, "Vaccinating Freedom," esp. 300–301; Faust, *This Republic of Suffering*, 61–101.

135. Deposition of Flora Lucas, November 23, 1900. None of the available treatments for smallpox could do more than make the sufferers more comfortable.

136. Louisa Powers pension file suggest that her experience during the war in some ways resembled that of black women employed as army nurses. In 1940, Louisa's son, Samuel, applied for survivor's benefits, noting his mother's work as an army nurse in his application. E. L. Bailey to Samuel Powers, April 12, 1935, pension file of Louisa Powers (WC 300875); S. K. Taylor, *Reminiscences of My Life in Camp*; Schultz, "Race, Gender, and Bureaucracy."

137. Schultz, "Race, Gender, and Bureaucracy," 47–48. Much of black women's care labor would be conducted without compensation.

138. Deposition of Caroline Butler, February 20, 1879, pension file of Caroline Butler, widow of Godfrey Butler, Thirty-Seventh USCT (WC 134795), Civil War Pension Index.

139. Chaplain William A. Green was one of eighty-seven black officers who commanded blacks in the USCT. An esteemed minister before his enlistment, Green received his appointment as chaplain and was mustered into service at Fort Monroe, Virginia, on November 15, 1863. He became ill with intermittent typhoid fever while stationed at Camp Hilton near Wilmington, North Carolina. Complications from his wartime illness would later form the basis of his 1881 claim for disability benefits. After Chaplain Green mustered out of the army, he married

Brunette Prince and taught school in New Hanover and Pender Counties, North Carolina, until 1878. Unable to stand for long periods, Green had to "decline several offers for teaching" because he was unable to walk or stand all day. Affidavit of William A. Green, September 2, 1881, pension file of Brunette Green, widow of William A. Green, Thirty-Seventh USCT (WC 355330), Civil War Pension Index; deposition of Harriet Barlow, February 6, 1894, pension file of Harriet Barlow, widow of Philip Barlow, Thirty-Seventh USCT (WC 393620); deposition of Jane Williams, March 22, 1893, pension file of Jane Williams, widow of Aleck Williams, Thirty-Seventh USCT (WC 370646), Civil War Pension Index.

140. Deposition of Fanny Jackson, June 30, 1900, pension file of Caroline Butler (WC 134795). Many opted for black clergy to solemnize their marriages. Minister Richard Tucker married Eliza and Jacob Banks shortly after they arrived in New Bern in 1862. See F. W. Galbraith to Commissioner of Pensions, November 13, 1889, pension file of Eliza Banks, widow of Jacob Banks, Thirty-Fifth USCT (WC 265622).

141. Berlin, Reidy, and Rowland, *Black Military Experience*, 658; U.S. War Department, *War of the Rebellion*, ser. 3, vol. 4, 1219, 1228.

142. Gutman, *Black Family in Slavery and Freedom*, 377.

143. Cecelski, *Waterman's Song*, 179–201.

144. Deposition of Charlotte Banks, June 16, 1904, pension file of Charlotte Banks (WC 157383). See also the pension file of Mary Gatlin, widow of Riley Gatlin, First North Carolina Infantry (WC 278382), Civil War Pension Index.

145. Deposition of Angeline Williams, April 6, 1892, pension file of Judy Lavenhouse, mother of George Lavenhouse, Second USCC (MC 332918).

146. Claim for mother's pension, pension file of Maria Biggs, mother of York Biggs, Fourteenth USCHA (MC 130543), Civil War Pension Index.

147. Deposition of Esther (Easter) Brown, May 7, 1896, pension file of Esther Brown (MC 130542).

148. Julia Foy's mother's claim, pension file of Julia Ann Foy (MC 156180).

149. Deposition of Julia Neel, April 22, 1892, pension file of Julia Neel (MC 334373), 5, Civil War Pension Index.

150. Mobley, *James City*, 25.

151. Mobley, *James City*, 25.

152. "Annual Report of the Superintendent of Freedmen," *New Berne Times*, September 12, 1865. James counted an additional 94 freedmen in Plymouth and 95 in Hatteras Banks. The total number under his jurisdiction was 17,307. Click, *Time Full of Trial*, 11n24; number from Horace James's annual report, *Freedman's Affairs*.

153. H. M. Watterson to His Excellency Andrew Johnson, June 20, 1865, in Simpson, Graf, and Muldowny, *Advice after Appomattox*, 48–50.

154. Excerpts from F. D. Sewall's North Carolina tour of inspection report, May 14, 1866, cited in Hayden et al., *Land and Labor*, 758.

2. The Black Community in New Bern, 1865–1920

1. The first census taken after slavery recorded New Bern's population at around six thousand, with blacks making up the majority population. A. Watson, *History of New Bern and Craven County*, 548.

2. A. Watson, *History of New Bern and Craven County*, 548.

3. R. S. Alexander, *North Carolina Faces the Freedmen*, 17–31. Reports on the convention appeared in local newspapers. "The Freedmen's Convention," *New Berne Times*, October 6, 1865. Delegates from New Bern and other eastern counties dominated the meeting. Bishir, *Crafting Lives*, 178.

4. Scholars seem agreed that black delegates determined that an appeal for equal rights before the law and black male suffrage would have to be made to the delegates of the state's Constitutional Convention, which also met in Raleigh.

5. "Reconstruction—First Voting by the Colored People of This State," *Newbern Weekly Journal of Commerce*, March 22, 1867. The Sherman Act refers to the constellation of acts passed by Congress, overriding President Andrew Johnson's veto, that divided the Southern states into military districts and placed former Confederate states under martial law until they adopted constitutions guaranteeing civil and political rights to freedpeople.

6. "Look at This, Colored Men!" *Wilmington Morning Star*, March 25, 1868.

7. Free black men, including John C. Stanly, had voting rights in North Carolina until 1835. See 1835 amendment to the North Carolina State Constitution, section 3, North Carolina General Assembly website, accessed February 12, 2020, https://www.ncleg.gov/EnactedLegislation/Constitution/NCConstitution.html. Whites in Pasquotank County opposed the amendment to the state constitution. Barton, *Executing Daniel Bright*, 17.

8. E. Anderson, *Race and Politics*; Bishir, *Crafting Lives*, 217–17. Brevett (Bravet) Morris, minister of the AMEZ church, served in the North Carolina House of Representatives in 1868. Richard Tucker, George B. Willis, and Edward R. Dudley made up Craven County's all-black delegation in the House of Representatives. North Carolina, *Journal of the House*, 84; Foner, *Black Lawmakers*, 65–66 (Dudley), 214 (Tucker); 233 (Willis).

9. "A Nuisance Which Ought to Be Abated," *New Berne Times*, May 29, 1865.

10. "Ordinance 20," *New Berne Times*, September 20, 1865; R. S. Alexander, *North Carolina Faces the Freedmen*, 46; LeFlouria, *Chained in Silence*, 58–59.

11. Bercaw, *Gendered Freedoms*, 5, 49; Hunter, *To 'Joy My Freedom*, chaps. 2, 8.

12. Holt, "Empire over the Mind"; Click, *Time Full of Trial*, 168–69.

13. Du Bois, "Reconstruction and Its Benefits." In North Carolina, agents oversaw civil matters until July 13, 1866, when Freedmen's Bureau officials believed that the state of North Carolina removed all discriminatory laws. General Orders 3, A-10814, FSSP.

14. Hayden et al., *Land and Labor*, 127–38.

15. Endorsement of Col. Wiegel, *New Berne Times*, August 17, 1866.

16. “The North Carolina-Freedmen,” *Raleigh Daily Standard*, May 1, 1866; Hayden et al., *Land and Labor*, 709.

17. John M. Schofield, commander of the Department of North Carolina, issued an order for the reduction of rations in settlement camps; Click, *Time Full of Trial*, chap. 6. On the devastation at the Trent settlement, see Horace James to Lt. Beecher, September 20, 1865, in Hahn et al., *Land and Labor*, 714

18. Richard Etheredge and Wm. Benson to Genl. [Howard], [May or June 1865], in Berlin, Reidy, and Rowland, *Black Military Experience*, 729. See also Berlin et al., *Wartime Genesis of Free Labor*, 231–36.

19. Chaplain Green et al., June 5, 1865, in Berlin, Reidy, and Rowland, *Black Military Experience*, 727–30, quotation on 728.

20. Circular Order 1, July 1, 1865, by Col. Eliphalet Whittlesey, A-10802, FSSP.

21. Testimony of Colonel Eliphalet Whittlesey before the Joint Committee on Reconstruction, February 3, 1866, in U.S. Congress, *Report of the Joint Committee on Reconstruction*, 182.

22. Foner, *Reconstruction*, 148.

23. Jeffrey R. Kerr-Ritchie, “Forty Acres,” in Martin and Yaquinto, *Redress for Historical Injustices*, 224; Freedmen’s Bureau, “Circular No. 3,” *New Berne Times*, August 15, 1865.

24. Hayden et al., *Land and Labor*, 335–36.

25. Click, *Time Full of Trial*, 185–86.

26. Kaye, *Joining Places*, 4–7.

27. A. Cooper, “Away I Goin’,” 447.

28. Endorsement, February 28, 1867, in Hayden et al., *Land and Labor*, 358–59.

29. Endorsement, February 28, 1867, in Hayden et al., *Land and Labor*, 358–59. Spicer led the First Baptist Church, Cedar Grove Chapel, in New Bern. A later recommendation called for the owners to allow the occupants to pay a small rent for the area occupied until they could transition to new homes.

30. Mobley, *James City*, 101.

31. Hahn, *Nation under Our Feet*.

32. Haines, *Letters from the Forty-Fourth*, 109.

33. Biography of Allen G. Oden compiled from his pension application; pension file of Allen G. Oden, Thirty-Sixth USCT (IC 511342), Civil War Pension Index; Hood, *One Hundred Years*, 621; Bishir, *Crafting Lives*, 281–82.

34. Bishir, *Crafting Lives*, 281.

35. H. N. Fleming to Commissioner of Pensions, August 28, 1919, pension file of Mattie Jones, widow of Solomon Jones, Thirty-Fifth USCT (WC 882069), Civil War Pension Index.

36. Palmer served at least two terms as mayor of New Bern (1867–1870). His activities are documented in the *New Bern Republican* and *New Berne Times* (1867–1869). In 1890 Palmer began collecting a pension of his own on the basis of “the effects of the Yellow Fever and disabilities.” See the pension file of William Palmer (IC 362015) and related documents in his widow’s pension file, Mariette Palmer (WC 501166), Civil War Pension Index.

37. "Sketch of H. G. Bates," *New Bern Daily Journal*, June 13, 1890. For a discussion of Bates in relations to black women's claims and the pension network, see chapter 4.

38. Tinker enlisted on September 13, 1861, and discharged in New Bern on October 18, 1864. In 1905, he received a disability pension of six dollars per month for "partial inability to earn support by manual labor." He resided in the city of New Bern in 1880. Tenth Census of the United States, 1880, roll 960, RBC. Pension file of George E. Tinker, Tenth Connecticut Infantry (IC 1104251), Civil War Pension Index; "U.S. Clerk of Court," *Branson North Carolina Business Directory*, 936. George remained in New Bern until 1883, when he took up residence in Durham, North Carolina, for two years and then returned to Concord, New Hampshire.

39. Seventh Census of the United States, 1850, RBC; Eighth Census of the United States, 1860, RBC; Ninth Census of the United States, 1870, RBC; Freedmen's Bureau Bank Records, New Bern Branch, FSTC, records 1909, 2090, 2470; McCrady and Ashe, *Cyclopedia of Eminent and Representative Men*, 128–27.

40. Nelson is identified as a notary public in FSTC, record 1578. "Charles Alexander Nelson," in Wilson and Fiske, *Appleton's Cyclopaedia of American Biography*, 489–90.

41. Petition to New Bern City Council [1866?], in Charles Alexander Nelson Papers, Rare Books and Manuscript Division, New York Public Library.

42. The missionary work of Carrie E. Waugh and R. Amelia Williams is referenced in Whitted, *History of Negro Baptist*, 83–84; American Baptist Convention, *American Baptist Year Book*. The 1870 federal census lists Carrie Waugh, Matilda Barker, and Maggie Hutchins as schoolteachers living in James City. Ninth Census of the United States, 1870, RBC. Harriet Duggins conducted classes for poor black women on her own and with Waugh and Williams in James City. Williams, Waugh, and Duggins offered testimony in Dianna Peldon's case. Affidavit of R. Amelia Williams, May 24, 1904, affidavit of Carrie E. Waugh, May 24, 1904, Affidavit of Harriet Duggins, September 10, 1900, pension file of Dianna Peldon, widow of Isaac Peldon, Thirty-Fifth USCT (WC 387150).

43. "A Colored Quakeress," *Newbern Journal of Commerce*, February 23, 1867.

44. Frances appears to have died during the war, perhaps during one of the many epidemics that occurred in the city.

45. "Colored Quakeress."

46. "Ice Cream!" *New Berne Times*, June 24, 1873; "Extra Corn Meal," *Newbernian*, December 30, 1876; *Business Directory of the City of New Berne*, pt. 5, 53.

47. Lucy Jackson, Twelfth Census of the United States, 1900, RBC; advertisement in the *New Bern People's Advocate*, July 31, 1886; Advertisement for Dicy Oden's Eating Saloon, *New Bern Daily Journal*, September 25, 1884; pension file of Lydia Pierson, widow of Essex Pierson, Fourteenth USCHA (WC 623883), Civil War Pension Index. On black female property owners in slavery and freedom, see Schweninger, "Property Owning Free African American Women"; Hunter, *To 'Joy My Freedom*, 134–35. On black women boardinghouse operators before the Civil War, see Walker, *History of Black Business*, 177.

48. Deposition of Philip Wiggins, January 14, 1901, pension file of Mary Norman (WC 289190), Civil War Pension Index.

49. Deposition of Philis Harvey, April 25, 1887, pension file of Philis Harvey, widow of Joseph Harvey, Fourteenth USCHA (WC 243771), Civil War Pension Index.

50. Deposition of Maria Richardson, December 9, 1913, pension file of Maria Richardson, widow of Hezekiah Richardson, Fourteenth USCHA (WC 769899).

51. Deposition of Prescilla Bryant, December 9, 1913, pension file of Maria Richardson (WC 769899).

52. James Osgood et al. to President Johnson, in Simpson, Graf, and Muldowny, *Advice after Appomattox*, 86–87.

53. North Carolina, Constitutional Convention, *Executive Documents*, 69.

54. "City Provost Court, August 23," *Wilmington Herald*, August 26, 1865; "An Excitement," *New Bern Daily Times*, March 23, 1866. Excerpt documented the arrest of soldiers from the Thirty-Seventh USCT for disorderly conduct, reprinted from the *Wilmington Dispatch* in the *New Berne Times*.

55. Berlin, Reidy, and Rowland, *Black Military Experience*, 801–2. One of the men who signed the petition was Richard Weaver, the future spouse of Bettie Weaver. Pension file of Bettie Weaver, widow of Richard Weaver, Fourteenth USCHA (WC 868644), Civil War Pension Index.

56. Rosen, "Not That Sort of Woman."

57. Rosen, "Not That Sort of Woman," 273; Rosen, *Terror in the Heart of Freedom*, 61–83; Hodes, *White Women, Black Men*, 148–52.

58. Rosen, *Terror in the Heart of Freedom*, 61–83.

59. Sefton, *United States Army and Reconstruction*, appendix B, 261–62.

60. Haley, *No Mercy Here*, 113.

61. "Mayor's Court, Monday," *New Bern Daily North Carolina Times*, September 4, 1865.

62. "Mayor's Court, Tuesday (May 22)," *Newbern Daily Times*, May 23, 1866; Wright Hammond is identified as a navy veteran on the 1890 veterans' schedule.

63. "Mayor's Court—Wednesday, August 16," *New Bern Daily North Carolina Times*, August 17, 1865.

64. "Mayor's Court, Saturday, Oct. 28," *New Berne Daily Times*, October 30, 1865.

65. "Mayor's Court," *New Bern Republican*, June 15, 1867.

66. "Mayor's Court, Wednesday, August 16," *New Bern Daily North Carolina Times*, August 17, 1865.

67. "Mayor's Court, Saturday, September 2," *New Bern Daily North Carolina Times*, September 4, 1865.

68. Deposition of J. H. Clark, November 10, 1900, pension file of Daniel Smith, Twenty-Ninth Connecticut Infantry (IC 898550), Civil War Pension Index.

69. Deposition of Rhoda Willis, December 31, 1892, pension file of Penelophy Ives, widow of James Ives, First North Carolina Infantry (WC 332445), Civil War Pension Index. Various documents spell this name *Penelophy* and *Penelope*. I refer to her as *Penelope* throughout but have maintained variant spellings in quotations and when citing the pension index.

70. R. S. Alexander, *North Carolina Faces the Freedmen*, 107.

71. Deposition of Mary E. Bragg, January 22, 1900, pension file of Mary E. Bragg widow of Henry Bragg, Second USCC (WC 489846), Civil War Pension Index.

72. Deposition of Hansey Jones, November 27, 1900, pension file of Hansey Jones, widow of Walter Jones, Thirty-Seventh USCT (WC 289857), Civil War Pension Index.

73. Deposition of Eliza Larkins, December 8, 1890, and I. D. Luke to Hon. Commissioner of Pensions, December 15, 1890, pension file of Eliza Larkins, widow of Frank Larkins, Thirty-Seventh USCT (WC 280633), Civil War Pension Index.

74. On New England migration and wage rates, see R. S. Alexander, *North Carolina Faces the Freedmen*, 107n42. According to Alexander, the *Wilmington Journal* reported that 3,200 black North Carolinians left the state in 1866. See, for example, "The Flight from North Carolina," *New York Times*, December 7, 1879, 2; "Threatening Negro Emigrants," *New York Times*, December 19, 1879, 1; "Negroes Leaving a State," *New York Times*, August 10, 1889, 5; "A Persecuted Freedman," *New York Times*, October 30, 1880, 5. On black North Carolinians' migration to Massachusetts, see Greenwood, *First Fruits*.

75. J. Jones, *Labor of Love, Labor of Sorrow*, 112; Reiff, Dahlin, and Smith, "Rural Push and Urban Pull," 39–45; O'Donovan, *Becoming Free in the Cotton South*, 162–207, esp. 163.

76. Hunter, *To 'Joy My Freedom*, 44–73; Hayden et al., *Land and Labor*, 559.

77. A brief mention of Jane's first husband in deposition of Martha A. Hill, September 27, 1892, pension file of Jane Reynolds. Whitehead White purchased "the Cobb Place" around 1890; deposition of Whitehead White, September 21, 1892, pension file of Jane Reynolds (WC 349453). Various documents spell the name *Whitehead*, *Whichcut*, and *Whitecoat* White.

78. Pension file of Brunette Green (WC 355330).

79. Affidavit of Charity Moore, March 14, 1878, pension file of Charity Moore, widow of Charles Moore, Thirty-Fifth USCT (WC 127676), Civil War Pension Index.

80. Affidavit of John Jack, April 18, 1879, pension file of Caroline Butler (WC 134795).

81. Deposition of Nancy Spivey, June 16, 1884, pension file of Sophia Alexander, widow of Spencer Alexander, Thirty-Fifth USCT (WC 209079), Civil War Pension Index.

82. Deposition of Sarah E. Morris, April 23, 1894, pension file of Sophia Alexander(WC 209079). Minister Brevett Morris went on to serve in North Carolina's House of Representatives in 1868. Bishir, *Crafting Lives*, 218.

83. Deposition of Mary Lee, December 19, 1888, and affidavit of David Weeks et al., November 27, 1886, pension file of Mary Lee (WC 329285).

84. The provisions of North Carolina's apprenticeship policy, passed by the General Assembly in March 1866, appear in section 4 of An Act Concerning Negroes and Persons of Color of Mixed Blood, in North Carolina, *Public Laws*, 93–99. R. S. Alexander, *North Carolina Faces the Freedmen*, 45; Scott, "Battle over the Child," 101–2.

85. Deposition of Mariah Hassell, August 13, 1887, pension file of Mariah F. Hassell, widow of Aaron Hassell, Thirty-Fifth USCT (WC 158811), Civil War Pension Index.

86. The North Carolina General Assembly amended the discriminatory provisions of the state's apprenticeship law on January 26, 1867. Two weeks later the acting assistant commissioner of the Freedmen's Bureau instructed agents to cancel indentures made without proper permission by the parents. Zipf, *Labor of Innocents*, 101; Mariah Hassell to C. W. Dodge, February 16, 1867, Letters and Reports Received, Plymouth NC Sub. Asst., A-941, Records of the Assistant Commissioner of the State of North Carolina.

87. Farmer-Kaiser, *Freedwomen and the Freedmen's Bureau*, 97–118. Farmer-Kaiser shows how white southerners, the courts, and even Freedmen's Bureau officers interpreted "orphan" to mean fatherless (rather than parentless).

88. Hamilton, "Freedmen's Bureau in North Carolina," 54.

89. R. S. Alexander, *North Carolina Faces the Freedmen*, 164–65; James O'Hara, who later served in the 48th (1883–1885) and 49th (1885–1887) Congress, established the Queen Street School. Horace James to Friend, April 23, 1864, in New England Freedmen's Aid Society, *Second Annual Report of the New England Freedmen's Aid Society (Educational Commission)*, presented to the society, Boston, April 21, 1864. Statistics of Teachers and Schools in the District of North Carolina, from December 1, 1863, to March 31, 1864, 72, in Debates over Slavery and Abolition, Slavery and Anti-Slavery: A Transnational Archive, Gale, accessed May 16, 2018, https://www.gale.com/c/slavery-and-anti-slavery-part-i.

90. Justesen, *George Henry White*, 63–93. For the black middle class, literacy and education signified class standing. Gilmore, *Gender and Jim Crow*; H. Williams, *Self-Taught*.

91. Location of the Freedmen's Bank in 1871 from "National Freedmen's Savings and Trust Company," *New-Berne Daily Times*, March 21, 1871; Zipf, "Promises of Opportunity."

92. Zipf, *Labor of Innocents*, 72.

93. Zipf, "Promises of Opportunity."

94. J. W. Hood, *One Hundred Years*.

95. "Minutes of the Freedmen's Convention, Held in the City of Raleigh on the 2nd, 3rd, 4th, and 5th of October, 1866," Documenting the American South, University of North Carolina at Chapel Hill, https://docsouth.unc.edu/nc/freedmen/freedmen.html.

96. Deposition of Andrew J. Marshall, September 30, 1896, pension file of Mary Jourdan (WC 435758).

97. Deposition of Andrew J. Marshall, September 30, 1896.

98. Rosen, *Terror in the Heart of Freedom*, 221.

99. Deposition of Philip Wiggins, July 17, 1900, pension file of Dianna Peldon (WC 387150).

100. Pension file of Penelophy Ives, widow of James M. Ives, First North Carolina Infantry (WC 332445), Civil War Pension Index. Testimony in Ives's file shows that James died of rheumatism, exhaustion, and injuries acquired while in service.

101. Depositions of Martha A. Boyd, April 6, 1892, and Angeline Williams, April 6, 1892, pension file of Judy Lavenhouse (MC 332918).

102. S. Smith, *To Serve the Living.*

103. Affidavit of David Ambers, July 9, 1897, pension file of Mary Anders, widow of Israel Anders, Thirty-Fifth USCT (WC 461604), Civil War Pension Index.

104. Capt. Horace James to Col., July 25, 1865, A-536, FSSP.

105. Dailey, "Deference and Violence," 55–56; Gilmore, *Gender and Jim Crow*, 103.

106. McClintock, "Civil War Pensions," 473.

107. Free black and enslaved wives, mothers, and children of Union soldiers generated a good deal of correspondence in response to the loss of male support at the height of the Civil War. See especially in Berlin, Reidy, and Rowland, *Black Military Experience*, Jane Welcome, the mother of a Pennsylvania black soldier, to President Abraham Lincoln, November 21, 1864, 664; Soloman (Solomon) Sanders, North Carolina black soldier, to his wife, Merina Sanders, November 28, 1865, and Merina's affidavit, May 22, 1865, 670; and Rosanna Henson, the wife of a New Jersey black soldier, to President Abraham Lincoln, July 11, 1864, 680.

108. Act of June 6, 1866, 14 Stat. 56–58, chap. 106 (1866).

109. Glasson, *Federal Military Pensions*, 139.

110. Edwards, "Marriage Covenant," 91–92. Edwards maintains that conservative white lawmakers promoted marriage to consolidate state power over newly freed blacks and to absolve the state from financial responsibility for the newly freed, while blacks viewed the marriage covenant as an effective means to establish the integrity of their families within the legal system and governmental institutions.

111. Edwards, "Marriage Covenant," 85.

112. Edwards, "Marriage Covenant," 91–92.

113. McClintock, "Civil War Pensions" 477, n49; U.S. Congress, *Annual Report of the Commissioner of Pensions*, H. R. Doc. 40-1 (1868).

114. McClintock, "Civil War Pensions," 477

115. McClintock, "Binding Up the Nation's Wounds," 268n549. See also Cong. Globe, 41st Cong., 2nd sess., 343 and 4451 (1870); *Annual Report of the Commissioner of Pensions*, H. R. Doc. 42-2, at 1505 (1871); H. R. Doc. 46-2 (1911); 13 Cong. Rec. 6084, 6086 (1882). Evidence of a bureau official calling on a postmaster to evaluate the worthiness of widow appears in Fanny Whitney's case. J. A. Bentley to Postmaster, July 6, 1877, and Postmaster to Commissioner of Pensions, July 7, 1877, in the pension file of Fanny Whitney (WC 130403).

116. Act of March 3, 1901, amending sec. 4708, Revised Statutes, 31 Stat. (1901), U.S. Department of Interior, *Laws of the United States*, 51; Glasson, "National Pension System," 210.

117. The experiences of black Union widows throughout the pension application process have been well documented by historians. Regosin, *Freedom's Promise*; L. Williams, *Constraint of Race*; Shaffer, *After the Glory*; Shaffer, "I Do Not Suppose"; McClintock, "Binding Up the Nation's Wounds," 456–80; Schultz, "Race, Gender, and Bureaucracy."

118. Deposition of Lenna Carnell, January 16, 1893, pension file of Lenna Carnell, widow of Peter Carnell, Thirty-Fifth USCT (WC 367681), Civil War Pension Index.

119. Carpenter, *Sword and Olive Branch*, 220–23. In 1869, an internal investigation of black applicants and pensioners in southern states ordered by the commissioner of pensions reported "an amount of systematic extortion and fraud unparalleled in the experience [o]f this office." H. Van Aernam, Commissioner of Pensions, to J. D. Cox, Secretary of the Interior, October 31, 1870, in *Annual Report of the Commissioner of Pensions*, H. R. Doc. 41-1 (1870), pt. 10, 431–34, quotation on 434.

120. Undated widow's pension claim, pension file of Tena Conega, widow of Edward Conega, Thirty-Seventh USCT (WC 143470), Civil War Pension Index.

121. Deposition of Mary Ann Sleight, August 25, 1892, pension file of Mary Ann Sleight (WC 367716).

122. John M. Foote to Col. Jacob F. Chur, September 25, 1867, A-680, FSSP.

123. Oliver, *History of the Civil War Military Pensions*, 51. Pension laws passed between 1862 and 1879 all included a stipulation outlining the date that the right to pensions would begin. During the Civil War years, a period of twelve months was set within which a woman had to file a petition for a widow's pension. In 1864, the period was extended to three years. The act of July 27, 1868, stretched the limitation to five years from the date when the pension should have accrued.

124. Frankel, *Freedom's Women*, 88.

125. The Arrears Act significantly increased the government's responsibility to veterans and their dependent relatives without indicating a source of funds. Oliver, *History of Civil War Military Pensions*, 53.

126. Act of 27 June 1890, 26 Stat. 182–83 (1890).

127. Act of 27 June 1890; McClintock, "Binding Up the Nation's Wounds"; Skocpol, *Protecting Soldiers and Mothers*, 110–11; Berry, *My Face Is Black Is True*, 47–48.

128. Examples of Freedmen's Bureau agents' involvement in the application process appear in the pension files: Tena Conega (WC 143470); Mary Ann Sleight (WC 367716); Margaret Dudley, widow of Elias Dudley, Fourteenth USCHA (WC 152362), Civil War Pension Index; deposition of Caroline Butler, February 20, 1879, pension file of Caroline Butler (WC 134795). Eliza Banks collected her husband's pay, which included bounty money. See Eliza Moore (Banks), FSTC, record 1581; C. F. Herring, Acting Auditor, to Commissioner of Pensions, August 18, 1877, pension file of Elizabeth, Rachel, and William Banks, minors of Jacob Banks, Thirty-Fifth USCT (MI 265622), Civil War Pension Index.

129. "Pension Agency," *Newbern Daily Times*, March 22, 1866.

130. Oliver, *History of the Civil War Military Pensions*, 83.

131. Hahn, *Nation under Our Feet*, 412.

132. Brimmer, "Black Women's Politics," 6.

133. Documentation of Douglass's licensure and business dealings with Carpenter can be found in Wm. Lochren to Hoke Smith, September 11, 1894, pension file of Mary Ann Sleight (WC 367716).

134. *Slaughter-House Cases*, 83 U.S. 36 (1873); *Civil Rights Cases*, 109 U.S. 3 (1883).

135. Gordon, "Family Violence, Feminism, and Social Control," 467.

136. L. V. Stafford to Commissioner of Pensions, February 20, 1918, pension file of Harriet Council, widow of Elias Council, Thirty-Seventh U.S. Colored Infantry (IC 823021), Civil War Pension Index.

137. References to Post No. 22 of the Grand Army of the Republic are found in the pension files of Alice Askie (WC 600768) and Laura Gardner (WC 375176). On church membership and the pension process, see especially the pension files of Alice Askie (WC 600768) and Louisa Little (WC 465452). Reference to the Clinton Chapel Mutual Aid Society appears in the pension file of Jamsey Green (Cooper), widow of Robert Green, Thirty-Sixth USCT (WC 699829), Civil War Pension Index.

138. O'Leary, *To Die For*, 4.

139. O'Leary, *To Die For*, 65.

140. E. Anderson, *Race and Politics*, 4.

141. Vogel, "Redefining Reconciliation"; Cox-Richardson, *Death of Reconstruction*; Broadus, "South and the Pension Bureau."

3. Her Claim Is Lawful and Just

1. While the state's apprenticeship system was ostensibly created to protect poor freed children from becoming orphans and paupers, historian Rebecca Scott has characterized it as a labor regime that former slaveholders used to reestablish their mastery. The provisions of North Carolina's apprenticeship policy, passed by the General Assembly in March 1866, appear in section 4 of An Act Concerning Negroes and Persons of Color of Mixed Blood, North Carolina, *Public Laws*, 93–99; R. S. Alexander, *North Carolina Faces the Freedmen*, 45; Scott, "Battle over the Child," 101–2.

2. Franklin, *Free Negro in North Carolina*, 116.

3. Several women had their pensions stopped as a result of cohabitation investigations during the 1870s: Ann Blackley, widow of Abram Blackley, Thirty-Fifth USCT (WC 136493), Charlotte Banks, Gatsey Donald, widow of Moses Donald, Thirty-Seventh USCT (WC 159349), Rosanna Fosgate, widow of Jerry Fosgate, Thirty-Fifth USCT (WC 290837), Mary Hassell (WC 158811), Dilcy Jarmon, widow of Richard Jarmon, Thirty-Fifth USCT (WC 154826), Charity Moore (WC 127676), Rebecca Spellman (Cherry), widow of Lewis Cherry, Thirty-Fifth USCT (WC 132857), Lila Long, widow of Jerry Long, Thirty-Fifth USCT (WC 136802), Civil War Pension Index.

4. E. B. French to Commissioner of Pensions, December 16, 1876, pension file of Nancy Cartwright, widow of Aaron Cartwright, Thirty-Fifth USCT (WC 130992), Civil War Pension Index.

5. D. E. Collins, "Charles Henry Foster"; T. C. Parramore, "Foster, Charles Henry," *NCPedia*, January 1, 1986, https://www.ncpedia.org/biography/foster-charles-henry.

6. Carpenter's argument in defense of Eugene Hannel is quoted in Barber and Ritter, "Dangerous Liaisons," 6; Parramore, "Charles Henry Foster." Hannel's trial took place in March 1863. Lowry, *Sexual Misbehavior in the Civil War*, 132.

7. On Rebecca Ann Cradle, see Silkenat, *Driven from Home*, 87; Barber and Ritter, "Physical Abuse." Brigadier General Innis N. Palmer had doubts that the sentence would stand and reduced Hannel's sentence to three months in the city jail and a dishonorable discharge from the army. Barber and Ritter, "Dangerous Liaisons."

8. Deposition of Celia Cuthrell, June 28, 1900, pension file of Celia Cuthrell, widow of Charles Cuthrell, Second North Carolina Infantry (WC 155267), Civil War Pension Index.

9. Widow's Brief No. 1, pension file of Celia Cuthrell (WC 155267). Cuthrell did not face investigation into her domestic space but was questioned about her loyalty.

10. Deposition of Fanny Whitney, June 21, 1900, pension file of Fanny Whitney (WC 130403). Augustus Seymour was the original attorney for Maria Bartlett, Mary Counts, and Fanny Whitney before transferring power of attorney to E. W. Carpenter. See the pension files of Maria Bartlett, widow of Simon Bartlett, Thirty-Fifth USCT (WC 167635), Mary Counts (Simmons), widow of Caesar Counts, Thirty-Fifth USCT (WC 130402), Margaret Dudley (WC 152362), Fanny Whitney (WC 130403), Civil War Pension Index. Allan B. Rutherford, an attorney in Washington, DC, assisted women filing claims for pensions in Wilmington, North Carolina. See also pension files of Celia Walker, widow of Richard Walker (Futch), Thirty-Fifth USCT (WC 578743), Mary Ellen Banks, widow of John Banks, Thirty-Seventh USCT (WC 414337), Marinda J. Everett, widow of James E. Everett, Thirty-Seventh USCT (WC 234726), Nancy McCabe, widow of John McCabe, Thirty-Sixth USCT (WC 282600), Margaret Garris, widow of Kindred Garris, Thirty-Seventh USCI (WC 408889), Elizabeth Ives, widow of John Ives, Thirty-Sixth USCT (WC 153599), Civil War Pension Index.

11. Seth Carpenter's record of work on behalf of freedwomen is documented most directly in the case files of those women. Impressions of government officials are documented in his legal case file. Seth Carpenter, Case Files.

12. "Read and Ponder," *Daily Newbernian*, May 16, 1874.

13. A few black Union widows later referred to Proctor as a traitor in their bid to have their benefits reinstated.

14. Deposition of Eda Coleman, February 25, 1901, pension file of Eda Coleman, widow of Isaac Coleman, Thirty-Fifth USCT (WC 154770), Civil War Pension Index.

15. Sarah E. Oxley, FSTC, record 1538. In most archival sources, Sarah Oxly's name is spelled *Oxley*. I refer to Sarah as *Oxly* because that is how she signed her name.

16. Sarah E. Oxley, FSTC, record 1538.

17. Singleton, *Recollection of My Slavery Days*, 3. When Bill Mitchell died in 1827, his heirs sold much of his property to settle his debts. Enslaved families were divided among Mitchell's children, with no mention of Sarah's parents. Sarah Richardson Oxly's reference to the Mitchell plantation, then, may have been a reference to the land rather than her owner.

18. Deposition of John Richardson, April 3, 1894, in the pension file of Maggie Harrison, widow of William F. Harrison, Thirty-Seventh USCT (WC 874040), Civil War Pension Index.

19. Elizabeth Richardson's biography reconstructed from deposition of John Richardson, April 3, 1894. Edward Downs's family history is drawn from FSTC, record 1335. See Stevenson, "What's Love Got to Do with It?," 108, for analysis of concubinage outside of New Orleans.

20. Sarah is referred to as *Oxly* during the war, and it is possible that she self-identified as such before.

21. Stevenson, "What's Love Got to Do with It?," 108; Hine "Rape and the Inner Lives of Black Women." For Oxly's physical description, see Sarah Oxley, FSTC, record 1538; "Colored Quakeress."

22. "Colored Quakeress."

23. Brimmer, "Her Claim for Pension Is Lawful and Just," 208.

24. E. Hubbs, Special Dept. Collector, to Commissioner of Pensions, March 6, 1871, pension file of Julia Ann Foy (MC 156180).

25. E. Hubbs to Commissioner of Pensions, October 14, 1870, pension file of Frances Holloway, widow of Edwin Holloway, Thirty-Fifth USCT (WC 147997), Civil War Pension Index. Hubbs made a similar argument to the commissioner on behalf of Eda Coleman: "I am satisfied . . . that this is a just claim." E. Hubbs, Spl. Dep. Collector, February 28, 1871, pension file of Eda Coleman (WC 154770). See also the pension files of Julia Neel (MC 334373) and Ethelbert Hubbs, Ninth New Jersey Infantry (IC 87541), who served as the deputy collector of customs in New Bern, Civil War Pension Index.

26. Depositions of Philis Harvey, April 4, 25, 1887, pension file of Philis Harvey (WC 243771).

27. Krowl, "African American Women," esp. 195.

28. Julia Neale, July 31, 1871, record 4884, Barred and Disallowed Case Files of the Southern Claims Commission, Record Group 233: Records of the U.S. House of Representatives, NARA. Variant spellings of Julia Neel's name appear throughout the documents. I spell the claimant's name *Julia Neel* unless quoting or citing government records.

29. "Notice," *New Berne Daily Times*, December 29, 1874.

30. U.S. Department of the Interior, *Decisions of the Department of the Interior*, Florida, 14:383; Maryland, 13:71–74; Missouri, 10:362–63; South Carolina, 14:537–38; Tennessee, 8:249–51, 11:294; Virginia, 8:213, 11:167.

31. See *State v. Melton* (120 NC Reps 591), cited in pension file of Charlotte Banks (WC 157383).

32. Thomas Goethe to Commissioner of Pensions, July 14, 1910, pension file of Lavinia Kelley, widow of Thomas Kelley, Thirty-Seventh USCT (WC 705972), Civil War Pension Index.

33. For examples of African American marriages under the 1866 North Carolina Marriage Act, also referred to as a "25 cent license," see the pension files of Sophia Alexander (WC 209079), Clarissa Johnson (WC 517635), Mary Lee (WC 329285), Edia Lee (WC 669012), Hetty Wallace (WC 699108), Caroline Batts (WC 338072), and Harriet Gaylord (WC 250847), Civil War Pension Index.

34. R. S. Alexander, *North Carolina Faces the Freedmen*, 46.

35. Scott, "Battle over the Child"; R. S. Alexander, *North Carolina Faces the Freedmen*, 45.

36. Edwards, "Marriage Covenant," 85.

37. Deposition of Easter Brown, May 28, 1896, pension file of Esther (Easter) Brown (MC 130542).

38. Deposition of Easter Brown, May 28, 1896.

39. George Ragsdale to Commissioner of Pensions, April 29, 1873, Edward Carpenter, Case Files.

40. Ragsdale to John H. Baker, Commissioner of Pensions, undated, pension file of Margaret Dudley (WC 152362).

41. James H. Clement to J. H. Baker, March 2, 1879, pension file of Caroline Butler (WC 134795).

42. Mills, *Cutting across the Color Line*, 5–6. Mills defines relations between customers and their barbers, pointing out that in contrast to patrons, customers gave some "deference to their barbers while maintaining their own consumer power."

43. Affidavit of Margaret Dudley, May 27, 1874, pension file of Margaret Dudley (WC 152362).

44. Affidavit of Julia Ann Foy, April 17, 1889, pension file of Julia Ann Foy (MC 156180).

45. G. H. Ragsdale to Hon. J. H. Baker [1873], pension file of Margaret Dudley (WC 152362).

46. Deposition of Rebecca Spellman, February 22, 1904, pension file of Rebecca Spellman (Cherry) (WC 132857). Also pension file of Charity Moore (WC 127676).

47. E. W. Carpenter and Augustus Seymour to Sir, March 17, 1874, pension file of Margaret Dudley (WC 152362).

48. Affidavit of Maria Biggs, June 3, 1873, pension file of Maria Biggs (MC 130543).

49. Deposition of Charlotte Caphart (Banks), August 31, 1904, Assistant Secretary of the Interior to the Commissioner of Pensions, February 19, 1907, pension file of Charlotte Banks (WC 157383). Charlotte Banks married twice after the death of Caesar Banks. For the sake of clarity, I refer to her as *Charlotte Banks* throughout but reference her changing surname when citing documents in her case file.

50. Deposition of Amelia Walston, June 27, 1904, pension file of Amelia Walston, widow of Anthony Walston, Thirty-Seventh USCI (WC 577795), Civil War Pension Index.

51. Deposition of Hagar James, April 23, 1870, pension file of Hagar James, widow of Samuel James, Thirty-Fifth USCI (WC 130401), Civil War Pension Index.

52. Nancy Cartwright's refund of $169: C. H. Belven, June 11, 1873, pension file of Nancy Cartwright (WC 130992).

53. Carpenter and Seymour to Sir, March 17, 1874. The stamp on the document indicates that it was received in the Department of the Interior. William L. Palmer, former U.S. agent, submitted a letter to the commissioner of pensions on behalf of Margaret Dudley and Mary Sanders; Wm. L. Palmer to Hon. J. H. Baker, May 27, 1874. A petition for an arrears of pension under the Arrears Act was denied on October 10, 1879; pension file of Margaret Dudley (WC 152362).

54. Jesse W. Wilson to Commissioner of Pensions, February 19, 1907, pension file of Charlotte Banks (WC 157383).

55. Widow's claim, pension file of Harriet Morris (Clark), widow of Caesar Morris, Thirty-Fifth USCT (WC 131719), Civil War Pension Index.

56. Affidavit of Harriet Morris (Clark), May 16, 1873, pension file of Harriet Morris (WC 131719).

57. Ann Harper (Blackley), FSTC, record 3717; G. H. Ragsdale to Commissioner of Pensions, August 20, 1873, pension file of Ann Blackley (WC 136493); G. H. Ragsdale to J. H. Baker, Commissioner of Pensions, May 7, 1893, pension file of Charity Moore (WC 127676).

58. Affidavit of Mary Hassell, May 20, 1873, pension file of Mary F. Hassell (WC 158811).

59. Ragsdale to Commissioner of Pensions, June 5, 1873, pension file of Mary F. Hassell (WC 158811).

60. Affidavit of Dilcy Jarmon, March 14, 1887, pension file of Dilcy Jarmon (WC 154826). Various documents spell this name *Dilcy*, *Dilcey*, and *Delacy*. I refer to the claimant as *Dilcy* but have retained various spellings in quotations.

61. Affidavit of Julia Ann Foy, July 1, 1874, pension file of Julia Ann Foy (MC 156180).

62. Affidavit of Dilcy Jarmon, March 14, 1887.

63. Deposition of Fanny Wiggins, January 14, 1909, pension file of Gordon Wiggins, Fourteenth USCHA (IC 460093), Civil War Pension Index.

64. Affidavit of Lila Long, July 5, 1874, pension file of Lila Long (WC 136802).

65. M. E. Jenks to Hon. J. H. Baker, December 21, 1874, pension file of Lila Long (WC 136802).

66. February 11, 1874, petition, Pantego, Beaufort County, North Carolina, pension file of Matilda Simmons, widow of Willis Simmons, Thirty-Fifth USCT (WC 135034), Civil War Pension Index; Matilda Simmons's occupation and family history drawn from FSTC, record 1544.

67. In Matilda Simmons's words, "All the people in my neighborhood know that to be true." Affidavit of Matilda Simmons, July 2, 1874, pension file of Matilda Simmons (WC 135034).

68. Pension file of Michael E. Jenks, 104th Pennsylvania Infantry (IC 956175), Civil War Pension Index.

69. Petition to Commissioner of Pensions, February 11, 1874, Affidavit of Matilda Simmons, July 2, 1874, and M. E. Jenks to the Hon. Commissioner of Pensions, December 21, 1874, pension file of Matilda Simmons (WC 135034).

70. The surname *Counts* appears as *Koonce* and *Koontz* in documents. The precise year Mary (Counts) Simmons's affidavit was filed is not clear within the case file. With the assistance of Frederick Douglass, Simmons tried to collect the benefits she was owed from the time of her husband's death and her remarriage in 1891. The Treasury Department provided a certified copy of all the documents in Mary's case file on June 3, 1892. This document was included in the collection of documents provided. Affidavit of Mary Simmons, April 1, 1874, pension file of Mary Counts (Simmons) (WC 130402).

71. Eighth Census of the United States, 1860, RBC; Confederate service record of Lafayette Dillahunt, American Civil War Soldiers database, Ancestry.com.

72. F. W. Tayyard to Commissioner of Pensions, October 5, 1867, pension file of Mary Counts (Simmons) (WC 130402).

73. Affidavit of Mary Simmons, March 4, 1874, pension file of Mary Counts (Simmons) (WC 130402).

74. Affidavit of Mary Simmons, March 4, 1874.

75. Affidavit of Mary Simmons, March 4, 1874.

76. Hunter, *Bound in Wedlock*, 196–232.

77. Deposition of Fanny Whitney, June 21, 1900, pension file of Fanny Whitney (WC 130403); William Henry Green's life history has been culled from another daughter's pension file: Clarissa Silver (daughter of William, who remained in Swans Quarter, Hyde County, North Carolina, and Susan Green), widow of Thomas Silver, Thirty-Seventh USCT (WC 300188), Civil War Pension Index.

78. Zipf, *Labor of Innocents*, 88.

79. Fanny's later testimony suggests that her relationship with Green may not have been destined for marriage. She stressed that Green never provided any support for her or her daughter and that he had married and returned to Hyde County.

80. Affidavit of William Green, April 14, 1877, pension file of Fanny Whitney (WC 130403).

81. Affidavit of Fanny Whitney, June 26, 1877, pension file of Fanny Whitney (WC 130403).

82. Affidavit of Fanny Whitney, July 26 1877. William H. Green appears in Ninth Census of the United States, 1870; Tenth Census of the United States, 1880. Clarissa Silver to Hon. Commissioner of Pensions, December 6, 1916, pension file of Clarissa Silver (WC 300188).

83. See McClintock, "Binding Up the Nation's Wounds," 268; Cong. Globe, 41st Cong., 2nd sess., 343 and 4451 (1870); *Annual Report of the Commissioner of Pensions*, H. R. Doc. 42-2, at 1505 (1871); *Annual Report of the Commissioner of Pensions*, H. R. Doc. 46-2 (1871); 13 Cong. Rec. 6084, 6086 (1882).

84. J. A. Bentley to the postmaster, July 6, 1877, Ethelbert Hubbs to Commissioner of Pensions, July 7, 1877, pension file of Fanny Whitney (WC 130403).

85. Gordon, *Pitied but Not Entitled*, 44.

86. Jane Richardson to Dr. Van Aernam, August 9, 1870, pension file of William Harris (MI 133916).

87. G. H. Ragsdale to Sir, April 25, 1873, Edward Carpenter, Case Files.

88. Undated correspondence from G. H. Ragsdale, Edward Carpenter, Case Files; pension file of Ann Blackley (WC 136493).

89. G. H. Ragsdale to Jas. Lockey, Acting Commissioner of the Pension Bureau, April 14, 1873, Edward Carpenter, Case Files.

90. G. H. Ragsdale to J. H. Baker, Commissioner of Pensions, May 7, 1893, pension file of Charity Moore (WC 127676); also G. H. Ragsdale to Commissioner of Pensions, August 20, 1873, pension file of Ann Blackley (WC 136493); Ragsdale to Jas. Lockey, April 14, 1873, Edward Carpenter, Case Files.

91. Ragsdale to Commissioner of Pensions, August 20, 1873,

92. Ragsdale to Commissioner of Pensions, August 20, 1873.

93. Ragsdale to J. H. Baker, June 23, 1873, Edward Carpenter, Case Files.

94. On Proctor's reports against black Union widows, see affidavit of Dilcy Jarmon, March 14, 1887, pension file of Dilcy Jarmon (WC 154826).

95. T. A. Henry to Hon. J. Turner, May 21, 1889, Edward Carpenter, Case Files.

96. Deposition of Letitia Foy, June 6, 1892, pension file of Margaret Proctor, widow of David Proctor, Second USCC (IC 549011), Civil War Pension Index.

97. Carpenter's suspension from Jas. Lockey to the Chiefs of Divisions, July 15, 1873, Edward Carpenter, Case Files.

98. Hahn views the political relations between whites and blacks as a form of political biracialism, whereby "direct and indirect cooperation" between the two groups occurred. Hahn, *Nation under Our Feet*, 382. Dailey, "Deference and Violence," 553–90.

99. Deposition of B. W. Moore, April 30, 1894, pension file of Mary Jane Moore, widow of Jacob Moore, Fourteenth USCHA (WC 307664), Civil War Pension Index.

100. McClintock, "Binding Up the Nation's Wounds," 243n498; quoted from 17 Stat. 570 (1873).

4. Black Women, Claims Agents, and the Pension Network

1. Craven County, Marriage Records, 1741–2011; joint affidavit of John and Margaret Butler [March 15, 1904], pension file of Charlotte Banks (WC 157383).

2. Foner, *Reconstruction*, 78.

3. Of New Bern's 6,435 inhabitants, 36 percent (2,325) were black females, and 25 percent (1,604) were black males; 20 percent (1,264) were white females, and 18 percent (1,149) were white males. An estimated 1,500–2,000 people lived in the area surrounding the city. *New Bern, N.C. Directory*, 38.

4. Bishir, *Crafting Lives*, 24; Heinegg, *Free African Americans in North Carolina*. According to Heinegg, the Goddett family is believed to have descended from immigrants from Virginia during the early eighteenth century.

5. Deposition of Israel Anders, December 18, 1888, pension file of Louisa Powers (WC 300875).

6. Deposition of W. H. Fulford, August 30, 1894, pension file of Louisa Powers (WC 300875).

7. E. B. French to Samuel Powers, February 1, 1877. Isaac Taylor rented land to Samuel Powers: see deposition of Isaac Taylor, January 16, 1889 deposition of Louisa Powers, December 17, 1888 (children), pension file of Louisa Powers (WC 300875). Louisa's daughter Lizzie died one month after her father in 1877.

8. Deposition of Israel Anders, December 18, 1888, pension file of Louisa Powers (WC 300875).

9. Deposition of Benjamin Wright, December 18, 1888, pension file of Louisa Powers (WC 300875).

10. Deposition of Peter Boyd, April 19, 1894, pension file of Annie Boyd, widow of Peter Boyd, Thirty-Seventh USCT (WC 456677), Civil War Pension Index.

11. Deposition of Gracy Archibald, January 24, 1893, pension file of Gracy Archibald, widow of Henry Archibald, Thirty-Fifth USCT (WC 380041), Civil War Pension Index.

12. Deposition of Lana Wright (formerly Burney), April 3, 1894, pension file of Lana Burney (Wright), widow of Larry Burney, Thirty-Fifth USCT (WC 940147), Civil War Pension Index.

13. Deposition of Lana Wright (Burney), December 16, 1893, pension file of Lana Burney (Wright) (WC 940147).

14. Pension file of Louisa Powers (WC 300875).

15. Deposition of Louisa Powers, December 17, 1888, pension file of Louisa Powers (WC 300875).

16. Deposition of Benjamin Wright, December 18, 1888, pension file of Louisa Powers (WC 300875).

17. Moore's date of discharge from his military records; see pension file of Mary Jane Moore (WC 307664).

18. LeFlouria, *Chained in Silence*, 43.

19. Deposition of Mary Pender, Mary 7, 1894, pension file of Mary Jane Moore (WC 307664).

20. Deposition of Nicy Ann Moore (Hill), April 28, 1894, pension file of Mary Jane Moore (WC 307664).

21. Deposition of Nicy Ann Moore (Hill), April 28, 1894. Nicy Ann Moore (Hill) was Jacob's new companion.

22. For an example of a community's response to domestic partner violence, see the pension file of Louisa Powers (WC 300875); Louisa's neighbors involved themselves in Louisa's household when she leveled charges of abuse at her intimate companion.

23. Pension file of Hettie Wendly, widow of George Wendly, Thirty-Seventh USCT (WC 297220). Various documents spell this name *Hettie Windley*, *Hettie*

Windly, *Hettie Wendly*, *Hettie Wendley*, and *Hattie Wendly*. I refer to her as *Hettie Wendly* throughout but have retained the variant spellings in quotations.

24. Deposition of William J. McCall, January 16, 1904, pension file of Maggie Harrison (WC 874040).

25. Deposition of Nancy Grainger, April 3, 1900, pension file of Samuel Windly (Keatch), Fourteenth USCHA (IC 749574).

26. Deposition of Hettie Wendly, January 7, 190[1], pension file of Hettie Wendly (WC 297220).

27. Deposition of Sarah Latham, February 22, 1893, pension file of Sarah Latham, widow of Jesse Latham, Thirty-Fifth USCT (WC 368120).

28. Samuel, their youngest child, had significant health challenges that required care and constant attention from Louisa. Affidavits of Frank Fisher, August 26, 1935, and Alex Fisher, August 24, 1935, pension file of Louisa Powers (WC 300875). In her autobiographical accounts, Louisa described her daughter Francis as "not bright." Deposition of Louisa Powers, December 17, 1888. In the pension files, this name appears as *Francis* and *Franceany*.

29. Hayden et al., *Land and Labor*, 876; deposition of Isaac Taylor, January 16, 1889.

30. Deposition of E. W. Carpenter, January 2, 1889, pension file of Louisa Powers (WC 300875).

31. According to Zipf, apprenticeship relationships ranged widely, but typically children were indentured by "fathers who sought skilled training for their children yet wished to retain control" of them; Zipf, *Labor of Innocents*, 4.

32. Deposition of Mary Ann Martin, July 16, 1889, pension file of Louisa Powers (WC 300875).

33. Deposition of Mary Ann Martin, January 16, 1889, Louisa Powers (WC 300875).

34. Deposition of William Gaskill, January 7, 1889, pension file of Louisa Powers (WC 300875).

35. Bynum, *Unruly Women*, 6–8.

36. Bynum, *Unruly Women*, 6–8; Edwards, *Gendered Strife and Confusion*, 145–83; Sommerville, "Rape Myth in the Old South."

37. Zipf, *Labor of Innocents*, 27.

38. Deposition of Prisilla Pickett, March 29, 1889, pension file of Louisa Powers (WC 300875).

39. Bishir, *Crafting Lives*, 38–96.

40. North Carolina's General Assembly initiated multiple policies to restrict the dealings between free blacks and enslaved populations. North Carolina, *Revised Code*, 564–80, quotation on 576.

41. Deposition of [Max Myers], March 22, 1889, pension file of Louisa Powers (WC 300875).

42. Blackmon, *Slavery by Another Name*.

43. Samuel's personal history may have had a direct influence on the arrangements they established for their own children. Deposition of Louisa Powers, December 17, 1888; occupation of Benjamin Martin from Ninth Census of the United States, 1870, RBC.

44. Deposition of Elsia Askew, April 13, 1905, pension file of Elsia Askew (WC 600768). Mattie Jones, the widow of veteran Sanders Jones, moved in with Mary Lee; see deposition of Mattie Jones, August 14, 1919, pension file of Mattie Jones (WC 882069).

45. Deposition of Ambrose Boyd, January 2, 1888, pension file of Louisa Powers (WC 300875).

46. Deposition of Louisa Powers, December 17, 1888.

47. Affidavit of Frank Fisher, August 26, 1935.

48. Adam and Harry Whitney's schooling in Ninth Census of the United States, 1870, RBC; Harry Whitney's instructor from FSTC, record 2076.

49. Affidavits of Alex and Frank Fisher, who attended school with Samuel Powers Jr., August 26, 1935.

50. Three monogamous relationships resulted in four additional children. Mary Jane had two children with a man she hoped to marry before he died unexpectedly. A casual intimate relationship resulted in another pregnancy. A few years later, she married and had another child. Mary Jane's new husband abandoned her and the children when she became ill. None of the men who fathered children with Mary Jane provided financial assistance for the children. To alleviate some of the pressure, Mary Jane turned over the care and custody of one of her children, William Henry, to her estranged husband in Raleigh. Deposition of Nicy Ann Moore (Hill), April 28, 1894.

51. Hunter, *To 'Joy My Freedom*, 220–38.

52. Deposition of Charlotte White, October 5, 1894, pension file of Mary Jane Moore (WC 307664). In this deposition, Charlotte identified the father of the twins, Floria and Flossie Mae, as William Beasley.

53. Clark-Lewis, *Living In, Living Out.*

54. Depositions of Louisa Powers, December 17, 1888, and Ambrose Boyd, January 2, 1889.

55. Affidavit of James Bell, June 8, 1894, pension file of Louisa Powers (WC 300875).

56. Wm. Lochren to Chief of the Special Examination Division, January 20, 1894, pension file of Mary Ann Sleight (WC 367716).

57. Mary Sleight and William Lochren, Commissioner of Pensions, to the Secretary of the Interior, Hoke Smith, September 11, 1894, pension file of Mary Ann Sleight (WC 367716).

58. Assistant Chief of the Law Division to the Chief of the Special Examination Division, January 20, 1894, pension file of Mary Ann Sleight (WC 367716).

59. Mary E. Norman identified Frederick C. Douglass as her son in depositions dated February 19, 1889 (Frederick C. Douglass, Case Files), and July 9, 1900 (pension file of Mary Norman [WC 289190]).

60. Douglass's name honored the abolitionist leader, but the two men were not related.

61. Deposition of Mary E. Norman, July 9, 1900; Turner Norman, military service records, roll 78, CMSR31–35.

62. Seventh Census of the United States, 1850, Slave Schedule, Beaver Creek, Jones County, 799, RBC.

63. Ninth Census of the United States, 1870, Craven County, North Carolina, Schedule 1, 388B, RBC; Tenth Census of the United States, 1880, 5th Ward, New Bern, Craven County, North Carolina, Schedule 1, 50B, Providence, Rhode Island, Schedule 1, 38, RBC; Twelfth Census of the United States, 1900, 5th Ward, New Bern, Craven County, North Carolina, Schedule 1, 194A, RBC; Thirteenth Census of the United States, 1910, Brooklyn Ward 24, Kings County, New York, 11B, RBC. In 1880, Mary is listed in both New Bern and Providence, Rhode Island. The New Bern census was taken by George B. Willis, a man of color and a colleague of Fredrick C. Douglass. She is listed as "Black," whereas Willis is listed as "mulatto" by a different enumerator.

64. Fields, "Ideology and Race in American History"; Hodes, *White Women, Black Men*, 96–122.

65. Deposition of Mary E. Norman, February 19, 1889, Frederick C. Douglass, Case Files.

66. James Christopher Bryan is listed on the Population of the United States in 1860, Schedule 1, Pollocksville District, Jones County, 985, RBC; he also appears on the 1860 U.S. Slave Schedule, Pollocksville District, Jones County, with forty-six women and fifty-seven men in his holding, while his mother, Julia C. Bryan, owned sixteen women and twenty-four men.

67. David W. Scott appears on the Population of the United States in 1860, Schedule 1, Swansboro District, Onslow County, 116, RBC.

68. Christian Scott Willis appears on the Twelfth Census of the United States, 1900, Schedule 1, 8th Township, New Bern, Craven County, 163A, RBC.

69. Dumar (Demmar) Hargett, Thirty-Seventh Regiment USCT, military service records, roll 35, CMSR36–40.

70. Deposition of Mary E. Norman, July 9, 1900, pension file of Mary Norman (WC 289190).

71. Deposition of Mary E. Norman, July 9, 1900. Dumar Hargett's service records list his birth date as 1844 and place of birth as Onslow County. He enlisted in the Thirty-Seventh USCT on September 12, 1864 at Morehead City, North Carolina, roll 35, CMSR36–40.

72. Marriage date and location from deposition of Mary Norman, July 9, 1900. Deposition of Solomon Reddick, January 29, 1901, pension file of Mary Norman (WC 289190). Biography of Turner Norman, military service records, roll 78, CMSR31–35; pension file of Mary Norman (WC 289190). The couple had one child together, George Hardy Norman. Turner Norman was discharged in June 1866.

73. Despite making an extensive survey of the regimental records of black soldiers raised in North Carolina, I have not found enlistment or service records for Frederick C. Douglass. I suspect that he changed his name after the war, hence making it more difficult to identify him in the sources. Douglass made similar claims in correspondence to the Commissioner of Pensions about his wartime service in 1901. See Frederick Douglass to Hon. Wm. Lochren, Decem-

ber 19, 1894, Frederick Douglass to Nathan Bickford, December 27, 1894 (which he signed "Capt of Lincoln Camp No 1 Div. of Maryland"), Frederick Douglass to Hon. Henry Clay Evans, October 9, 1901, Frederick C. Douglass, Case Files.

74. Turner Norman's death, roll 3, Nonpopulation Census Schedules for North Carolina, 1850–1880: Mortality and Manufacturing, RBC; depositions of Mary Norman, February 1, July 9, 1901, pension file of Mary Norman (WC 289190).

75. Greenwood, *First Fruits*, 2.

76. Deposition of Mary E. Norman, July 9, 1900.

77. Affidavit of Mary Norman, September 5, 1885. Douglass filed an earlier claim in 1880; see widow's claim, filed on February 4, 1880, and rejected on January 6, 1881, pension file of Mary Norman (WC 289190).

78. Douglass refers to the "Plesant" Hill School and his work at Clinton Chapel School in his personal ledgers in Collection 265, the William L. Horner Collection, Frederick C. Douglass Papers, East Carolina Manuscript Collection, J. Y. Joyner Library, East Carolina University. He is listed as a schoolteacher on the Ninth Census of the United States, 1870, Craven County, Schedule 1, 388B, roll 1,132, and petition, March 26, 1889, Frederick C. Douglass, Case Files.

79. When Douglass faced charges of collecting illegal fees in 1894, two of his employees filed affidavits on his behalf and discussed the work they did under his employment. See affidavits of William H. Wiggins and William Halloway, July 7, 1894, Frederick C. Douglass, Case Files.

80. Tenth Census of the United States, 1880, New Bern, Craven County, North Carolina, RBC.

81. Mary Norman identified Frederick Douglass as her son in her depositions taken on February 19, 1889, Frederick C. Douglass, Case Files, and on July 9, 1900, pension file of Mary Norman (WC 289190). Douglass appears as Fred D. Norman in the 1870 census along with his mother, sister, and brother (Ninth Census of the United States, 1870, Craven County, Schedule 1, 388B, roll 1,132). Details of Douglass's married life with Charlotte Bryant come from FSTC, record 2569; Tenth Census of the United States, 1880. The 1880 census also shows his two daughters, Martha A. and Mary C. (Mamie) Douglass, and two sons, William and Frederick Douglass. Charlotte, William, and son Frederick disappear from the census after 1880. Tenth Census of the United States, 1880, New Bern, Craven County, North Carolina, RBC. A letter from Mamie to the commissioner of pensions on behalf of her father indicates that her mother, Charlotte, lay ill in an asylum as late as 1894. Mamie C. Douglass to Hon. Wm. Lochren, October 27, 1894, in Frederick C. Douglass, Case Files. Charlotte may have still been alive and living in an asylum when Douglass married Delilah (Delila) Chance on December 23, 1886; Craven County, Marriage Records, 1741–2011, 27B. Delilah and Frederick had a son, Frederick Douglass Jr. Douglass's son with Charlotte of the same name was born in May 1880 and may have died. Douglass's elder son Frederick was born in September 1888. Douglass is identified as a widower in the 1900 census, and another notation indicates that Delilah died around 1898. About nine years later, Douglass married Polly Joyner. Twelfth Census of the United States, 1900, Craven County, North Carolina, Schedule 1, Enumeration District

052, 194A, roll 1,190; Thirteenth Census of the United States, 1910, Craven County, North Carolina, Schedule 1, Enumeration District 0026, 4A, roll 1,104. On Frederick Douglass Jr., see draft registration card for Frederick Harrison Douglass, World War I Selective Service System Draft Registration Cards, 1917–1918, Record Group 163: Records of the Selective Service System (World War I), NARA. Brimmer, "Black Women's Politics," 12n29.

82. William Porter to the Commissioner of Pensions, 1889, pension file of Lena Jones, widow of Wendall Jones, Thirty-Fifth USCT (WC 254588), Civil War Pension Index; "Sketch of H. G. Bates." For more on Henry G. Bates's personal history: affidavit of Henry G. Bates, October 7, 1889, pension file of Annie Bates, widow of Henry G. Bates, Act'g Asst. Surg. Med. Dept. USA (WC 276090), Civil War Pension Index. I also traced his professional history and dealings with black Union widows through the pension files of the soldiers he treated and the cases he testified in. Depositions given by Bates, December 31, 1888, pension file of Mary Lee (WC 329285), January 2, 1889, pension file of Mary Hatch (WC 324189), April 6, 1889, pension file of Hannah Carter (WC 255751), November 26, 1889, pension file of Mary Jane Moore (WC 307664), November 26, 1889, pension file of Christina Hill (WC 696351), December 30, 1889, pension file of Della Miller, widow of Washington Miller (WC 705978), Civil War Pension Index; depositions of Margaret Ann Rogers and Nancy Ann Morris, November 5, 1889, pension file of Penelophy Ives (WC 332445).

83. On New Bern's black middle class, see Gilmore, *Gender and Jim Crow*; on James City, see Mobley, *James City*.

84. Pension file of Mary Green, widow of Essex Green, Second USCC (WC 248457), Civil War Pension Index. FSTC, record 3929, lists Mary Green's residence as South Front Street. Pension file of Margaret Dudley (WC 152362); Mary Dudley, FSTC, record 2300; Christina Spruell, wife of Aaron Spruell, FSTC, record 4090.

85. Justesen, *George Henry White*, 39.

86. I have traced Douglass's work on behalf of black veterans and dependent families in eastern North Carolina by cross-referencing the names listed in his personal ledgers in Collection 265, the William L. Horner Collection, Frederick C. Douglass Papers, East Carolina Manuscript Collection, J. Y. Joyner Library, East Carolina University, with the pension application files indexed in the Organization Index to Pension Files, the Frederick C. Douglass, Case Files, and the *Business Directory of the City of New Berne*, pt. 4, 42. Records from Douglass's work as a teacher in the mid-1870s also appear in his personal papers.

87. Bloomfield, "From Deference to Confrontation."

88. Dow McClain to Hon. Commissioner of Pensions, January 4, 1900, pension file of Edia Lee, widow of Phillip Lee, Thirty-Fifth USCT (WC 669012).

89. Deposition of Andrew J. Marshall, May 26, 1894, Frederick C. Douglass, Case Files.

90. Emanuel Merrick's family history was gleaned from a combination of sources, including FSTC, record 3097, which documents his parents, life on Roanoke Island, and employer Ami Dennison. For references to Merrick's work as a claims agent, see S. W. Cuddy, Chief of Law Division, to Chief of the Special

Examination Division, September 26, 1900, pension file of Daniel Smith, Twenty-Ninth Connecticut Infantry (IC 898550); Harriet Gardner's petition, pension file of Laura Gardner (WC 375176); Allen G. Oden in 1887, pension file of Dicy Oden (WC 414263); minors of Moses Longest (MC 137141).

91. W. T. Pierson, Assistant Chief of the Law Division, to the Chief of S. E. Division, January 24, 1894, pension file of Jane Reynolds (WC 349453).

92. Deposition of Merritt Whitely, April 25, 1894, pension file of Caroline Batts, widow of Isaac Batts, Thirty-Seventh USCT (WC 338072), Civil War Pension Index.

93. Mobley, *James City*, 68; Pauli Murray, interview by Genna Rae McNeil, February 13, 1976, interview G-0044, Southern Oral History Program Collection (4007), Documenting the American South, University of North Carolina at Chapel Hill, https://docsouth.unc.edu/sohp/G-0044/menu.html; Gilmore, *Gender and Jim Crow*, 6.

94. Bercaw, *Gendered Freedoms*, 6.

95. Mobley, *James City*, 68; pension file of Sophia Alexander (WC 209079).

96. Deposition of Chaney Blount, January 9, 1899, pension file of Abram Blount, Thirty-Seventh USCT (IC 423988).

97. "The Colored People and Their Welfare," *New Bern Daily Commercial News*, September 18, 1881.

98. Deposition of James Flowers, February 20, 1879, pension file of Caroline Butler, widow of Godfrey Butler, Thirty-Seventh USCT (WC 134795). For additional examples of soldiers notifying women about their pension eligibility, see the pension files of Caroline Batts (WC 338072) and Matilda Wells (WC 455514).

99. Deposition of Mary Jane Moore, April 23, 1894, pension file of Mary Jane Moore (WC 307664).

100. Pension file of Mary Hassell (WC 158811).

101. Deposition of Mary Jane Latham, February 25, 1893, pension file of Sarah Latham, widow of Jesse Latham, Thirty-Fifth USCT (WC 368120).

102. Deposition of Sarah Latham, February 22, 1893, pension file of Sarah Latham (WC 368120).

103. Affidavit of Mary Lee, January 29, 1891, pension file of Mary Norman (WC 289190).

104. Similar linkages are apparent between Philis Harvey, Sally Ann Bond, Amanda Skinner, and Harriet Gaylord. See the pension files of Sally Ann Bond, widow of Hannibal Bond, Thirty-Seventh USCT (WC 256386), Philis Harvey (WC 243771), Harriet Gaylord, widow of Hardy Gaylord, Thirty-Fifth USCT (WC 250847), Caroline Skinner (WC 924480), Civil War Pension Index.

105. Deposition of Philis Harvey, January 10, 1901, pension file of Hettie Wendly (WC 297220).

106. Pension file of Philis Harvey (WC 243771).

107. Deposition of Lana Burney, December 16, 1893.

108. Deposition of Matilda Wells, March 1, 1897, pension file of Matilda Wells, widow of Toney Wells, Thirty-Seventh USCT (WC 455514), Civil War Pension Index.

109. Several women filed claims under both systems to better their chances of receiving remuneration. See Isaac B. Dunn to Commissioner of Pensions,

August 20, 1892, pension file of Lizzie B. Moore, widow of Bryant Moore, Thirty-Seventh USCT (WC 290837), Civil War Pension Index.

110. Maria Counts was the former wife of Caesar Counts and the sister of Mary Counts. See the pension files of Mary Counts (WC 130402), Charlotte Banks (WC 157383), Charity Moore (WC 127676), Rosanna Fosgate, widow of Jerry Fosgate, Thirty-Fifth USCT (WC 29837), Civil War Pension Index.

111. F. H. Allen to Chief Depend Sec., December 4, 1890, pension file of Rosanna Fosgate (WC 290837).

112. Pension file of Dilcy Jarmon (WC 154826).

113. Anderson, *Race and Politics in North Carolina*, 124.

114. "Congressional," September 21, 1893, and Commissioner to Hon. Thomas Settle, March 18, 1894, pension file of Lana Burney (Wright) (WC 940147).

115. T. Settle to Commissioner of Pensions, "Congressional," September 21, 1893, pension file of Lana Burney (Wright) (WC 940147).

116. Commissioner of Pensions to J. C. Pritchard, April 15, 1897, pension file of Lana Burney (Wright) (WC 940147).

5. Encounters with the State

1. *Report of the Commissioner of Pensions*, in U.S. Department of the Interior, *Reports for the Fiscal Year Ended June 30, 1910*. By 1910, there were 562,615 invalid Civil War pensioners on the rolls, receiving $106,433,465, and the national population of males sixty-five years and over was 1,985,976.

2. "Bogus Pension Claim Agents: How They Have Swindled Poor People in Mississippi," *New York Times*, August 7, 1884. Though aimed at highlighting pension scams, these articles capture the vast communication network that filtered information about the pension system through southern black communities. "Bogus Pension Claims: How the Department Is Imposed upon by Tricks, Frauds and Subterfuges," *Washington Post*, July 22, 1883.

3. McClintock, "Binding Up the Nation's Wounds," 257. Rosen illustrates how sexualized depictions of black women in Memphis, Tennessee, established the ideological context for the violence inflicted on freedwomen during the 1866 riots; Rosen, "Not That Sort of Woman"; Gross, *Colored Amazons*, chap. 4.

4. Oliver, *History of the Civil War Military Pensions*, 71.

5. Oliver, *History of the Civil War Military Pensions*, 82.

6. U.S. Pension Bureau, *General Instructions to Special Examiners*, 3.

7. 13 Cong. Rec. 6759 (1882).

8. 13 Cong. Rec. 6760 (1882).

9. 13 Cong. Rec. 6760 (1882).

10. Act of August 7, 1882, 22 Stat. 345 (1882).

11. "Extensive Pension Frauds," *Washington Post*, December 15, 1880, 1. See also the case of Amelia A. Haynes, "Pension Swindlers Arrested," *New York Times*, December 6, 1887, 1; pension file of Amelia Clopton, widow of Willis Clopton, Fifty-Ninth USCT (WC 214007), Civil War Pension Index. Laura Ann Huggins of Norfolk, Virginia, was convicted of fraud and sentenced to five years hard labor

in an Albany, New York, penitentiary in 1893. "Five Years Pension Frauds," *New York Times*, December 16, 1893, 9; pension file of Laura Ann Gregory, widow of Samuel Gregory, Thirty-Sixth USCT (WC 94592). In eastern North Carolina, see pension file of Elizabeth Ives (WC 153599).

12. On worthiness and entitlement in discussions of mothers' pensions, see Gordon, *Pitied but Not Entitled.*

13. Brimmer, "Black Women's Politics," esp. 830.

14. "Fifty-Fourth," in U.S. Pension Bureau, *General Instructions to Special Examiners*, 24.

15. "Fifty-Sixth," in U.S. Pension Bureau, *General Instructions to Special Examiners*, 24.

16. Affidavit of Mary Counts, February 14, 1868, and deposition of Mary Counts, January 20, 1893, pension file of Mary Counts (Simmons) (WC 130402).

17. Dow McClain to Hon. Com. of Pensions, March 13, 1901, pension file of Eda Coleman (WC 154770).

18. Deposition of Eda Coleman, February 25, 1901, pension file of Eda Coleman (WC 154770).

19. Gordon, *Pitied but Not Entitled*; Mink, *Wages of Motherhood*; Kessler-Harris, "Designing Women and Old Fools."

20. O'Hara and Oxly's office locations from *Business Directory of the City of New Berne*, 85 and 59. References to examiners renting space from O'Hara and Oxly appear in Isaac B. Dunn to Commissioner of Pensions, February 23 1892, pension file of Amy Squires, widow of Taffy Squires, Fourteenth USCHA (WC 330588), Civil War Pension Index.

21. List compiled by the author by first identifying the names of the examiners who conducted investigations in 120 pension files of the petitioners from Craven County. Home states were taken from an appointment book but do not always represent place of birth. For example, Gallion was working in a government agency in Pennsylvania before his appointment to the Pension Bureau. Gallion, 1:105, 2:55, 3:103; Gilpin, 2:55, 3:106; Goethe, 2:51, 3:107; Maxwell, 2:132; Porter, 1:228; Roberts, 2:207, 3:249; Stockton, 2:225 in Register of Appointments and Assignments, Record Group 15: Records of the Department of Veteran Affairs, NARA. Appointments and home states for Harris, McSorley, and Stockton from Special Examiners' Division, box 3, Record Group 15: Records of the Department of Veteran Affairs, NARA. Once I compiled my list, I looked through the various volumes to identify as many examiners as possible. See National Archives, Guide to Records of the Veterans Administration, section 15.2.2, accessed May 12, 2020, https://www.archives.gov/research/guide-fed-records/groups/015.html.

22. Edwards, "Sexual Violence, Gender, Reconstruction," 243–44. Edwards shows how allegations of bad character in Reconstruction-era courtrooms placed poor women, black and white, at a disadvantage. For black women negative character assessments also invoked the racialized gender stereotype of Jezebel.

23. William Porter to Commissioner of Pensions, February 9, 1889, pension file of Lena Jones (WC 254588).

24. Porter to Commissioner of Pensions, February 9, 1889.

25. W. F. Aycock to Commissioner of Pensions, September 11, 1890, pension file of Mary Whitby (WC 276505).

26. Porter to Commissioner of Pensions, February 9, 1889.

27. Pension files of Elizabeth Ives (WC 153599), Clarissa Johnson (WC 517635), Louisa Little (WC 465452), and Louisa Powers (WC 300875). Laura F. Edwards outlines the impact the allegation of "bad character" had on court cases involving black women in the local court system; Edwards, "Sexual Violence, Gender, Reconstruction," 243–45.

28. Pension files of Sophia Alexander (WC 209079), Mary Lee (WC 329285), Louisa Little (WC 465452), Louisa Powers (WC 300875), Clara Williams (WC 374117), and Matilda Wells (WC 455514).

29. Gallion to Commissioner of Pensions, December 31, 1888, pension file of Hannah Small (WC 251123).

30. John C. Cole to Commissioner of Pensions, April 19, 1888, pension file of Maria Little, widow of Benjamin Little, Thirty-Fifth USCT (WC 397932), Civil War Pension Index.

31. Deposition of Maria Little, April 10, 1888, pension file of Maria Little (WC 397932).

32. W. F. Aycock to Commissioner of Pensions, September 13, 1890, pension file of Hettie Wendly (WC 297220).

33. Shontz to Commissioner of Pensions, March 31, 1902, pension file of Jamsey Green (Cooper) (WC 699829).

34. Deposition of Mary Franklin, July 19, 1900, pension file of Mary Franklin, widow of John Franklin, Fourteenth USCHA (WC 488092), Civil War Pension Index.

35. Deposition of Mary Franklin, July 19, 1900.

36. Deposition of Ann Cotton, March 13, 1894, noted on a folder in Frederick C. Douglass, Case Files.

37. Pension file of Hettie Wendly (WC 297220). It is not clear whether Hettie paid all of the witnesses who came forward. She did pay Dr. H. G. Bates for his affidavit. Deposition of Hettie Wendly, January 8, 1900, pension file of Hettie Wendly.

38. Thomas Goethe to Commissioner of Pensions, February 3, 1904, pension file of Sarah Haskill, widow of Pompey Haskill, Thirty-Seventh USCT (WC 584942), Civil War Pension Index.

39. Deposition of Julia Dewry, October 25, 1889, pension file of Mary Kent (Mary Elizabeth Dove, Bess House), widow of Henry Kent, Fourteenth USCHA (WC 261737), Civil War Pension Index.

40. Deposition of William Edwards, October 25, 1889, pension file of Mary Kent (WC 261737).

41. Deposition of Mary Kent, August 28, 1900, pension file of Mary Kent (WC 261737). The possibility that the community admired Elizabeth as a Union widow and the care she performed on behalf of George House may have informed their opinion.

42. Smith to Commissioner of Pensions, December 17, 1890, pension file of Mary Ann Simmons, widow of George Simmons, Fourteenth USCHA (WC 280817), Civil War Pension Index.

43. Depositions of Stephen Scott, Hester Jackson, and Lucinda Banks, December 16, 1890, pension file of Mary Ann Simmons (WC 280817).

44. Deposition of Mary Ann (Simmons) Bailey, December 16, 1890, pension file of Mary Ann Simmons (WC 280817).

45. The bureau initially awarded Mary Ann Simmons benefits from 1877 to 1882; the period of widowhood was adjusted to 1877–79 on learning of her relationship with Frank Williams. Pension file of Mary Ann Simmons (WC 280817).

46. Pension files of Jeannie Chadwick, widow of Moses Chadwick, Thirty-Fifth USCT (WC 380900), Ada J. Stewart, widow of Simon Stewart, Thirty-Sixth USCT (WC 842442), Mary Lee (WC 329285), Louisa Powers (WC 300875), Civil War Pension Index.

47. Deposition of William Gaskill, January 16, 1889, pension file of Louisa Powers (WC 300875).

48. Deposition of Louisa Powers, December 17, 1888, pension file of Louisa Powers (WC 300875).

49. Deposition of Louisa Powers, December 17, 1888, pension file of Louisa Powers (WC 300875).

50. E. D. Gallion to Commissioner of Pensions, March 31, 1889, pension file of Louisa Powers (WC 300875).

51. Deposition of Ambrose Boyd, January 2, 1889, pension file of Louisa Powers (WC 300875).

52. Zipf, *Labor of Innocents.*

53. Deposition of Ambrose Boyd, January 2, 1889.

54. Deposition of Louisa Powers, January 13, 1889, pension file of Louisa Powers (WC300875).

55. Gallion to Commissioner of Pensions, March 31, 1889.

56. My ideas about motherhood have been shaped in part by Gordon, *Great Arizona Abduction*, 126.

57. Deposition of Louisa Powers, December 17, 1889.

58. Deposition of Isaac Taylor, January 16, 1889, pension file of Louisa Powers (WC 300875).

59. Deposition of Louisa Powers, December 17, 1888.

60. Gallion to Commissioner of Pensions, March 31, 1889.

61. Schwalm, *Hard Fight for We*, 251; Scott, "Battle over the Child."

62. Deposition of Ambrose Boyd, January 2, 1889.

63. Deposition of Theopholis George, December 18, 1888, pension file of Louisa Powers (WC 300875)

64. Gallion to Commissioner of Pensions, March 31, 1889.

65. Unsigned memorandum, April 20, 1889, pension file of Louisa Powers (WC 300875). Section 4706 of the Revised Statutes of the Pension Law states, "Widows' pension to children, until they reach the age of sixteen, if she has

abandoned or become unfit for the care of them." Curtis and Webster, *Digest of Laws*, 516.

66. Some of the letters of notification in Louisa Powers's pension are incomplete. The summary report attached to the August 10, 1891, appeal summarizes the dates on which the government took steps to notify Powers of her suspension. Pension file of Louisa Powers (WC 300875).

67. For a succinct outline of the U.S. Pension Bureau and its powers, see McClintock, "Impact of the Civil War," esp. 397n6.

68. Gordon, "Family Violence, Feminism, and Social Control," 467.

69. Gallion to Commissioner of Pensions, February 14, 1899, pension file of Mary Lee (WC 300875).

70. Claimant's appeal to the secretary of the interior, October 9, 1890, pension file of Mary Lee (WC 329285).

71. Affidavit of Mary Lee, December 6, 1889, pension file of Mary Lee (WC 329285). The issue of syphilis infection in a soldier's claim comes up in the pension files of James Flowers and Wendall Jones. See Porter to Commissioner of Pensions, February 9, 1889, pension file of Lena Jones (WC 254588); S. M. Arnell to Commissioner of Pensions, January 21, 1898, pension file of Presilla Flowers (WC 755483).

72. Department of the Interior, "Decision Affirmed," January 13, 1892, pension file of Mary Lee (WC 329285).

73. Claimant's appeal to the secretary of the interior, May 15, 1889, pension file of Louisa Powers (WC 300875).

74. Claimant's appeal to the secretary of the interior, May 15, 1889.

75. Claimant's appeal to the secretary of the interior, May 15, 1889.

76. Claimant's appeal to the secretary of the interior, May 15, 1889.

77. See August 10, 1891, Appeal, p. 4, pension file of Louisa Powers (WC 300875).

78. Examiner Tyler references Secretary Bussey's July 20, 1891, ruling, which outlines how the commissioner "construed" adulterous cohabitation. Grafton Tyler to Commissioner of Pensions, March 11, 1893, pension file of Ritty Titterton, widow of Benjamin Titterton, Thirty-Fifth USCT (WC 370801), Civil War Pension Index; see also Bussey's ruling, Baber, *Cases Relating to Pension Claims*, 243.

79. J. W. Lane on behalf of Jane Atkinson to Commissioner of Pensions, December 15, 1893, pension file of Jane Reynolds (WC 349453).

80. William Porter to the Commissioner of Pensions, February 25, 1889, in Frederick C. Douglass, Case Files. Douglass filed an affidavit refuting the charges on March 22, 1889, as well as a petition signed by black veteran Allen G. Oden and white officials such as postmaster Matthias Manly (a Confederate veteran) and state lawmaker William E. Clarke. "Mch 28 89 answer recd is satisfactory" is noted on a folder in Frederick C. Douglass, Case Files.

81. E. D. Gallion to Commissioner of Pensions, July 27, 1889, pension file of Mary Hatch (WC 324189).

82. Porter to Commissioner of Pensions, February 9, 1889, pension file of Tena Jones, widow of Windall Jones, Thirty-Fifth USCT (WC 254588).

83. Deposition of Frederick C. Douglass, February 20, 1892, pension file of Amy Squires (wc 330588).

84. Isaac B. Dunn to Commissioner of Pensions, February 23, 1892, pension file of Ammy Squires (wc 330588).

85. Dunn to Commissioner of Pensions, February 23, 1892.

86. Gallion to Commissioner of Pensions, June 30, 1894, pension file of Maggie Harrison (wc 874040).

87. Rothman, *Notorious in the Neighborhood,* chap. 6.

88. Stevenson, "What's Love Got to Do with It?," 108; Barber and Ritter, "Dangerous Liaisons," 6–7.

89. Sometime after 1894, Sarah began to follow the teachings of the First Church of Christ, Science at New Bern. The church was established around 1894, when Mary Hatch Harrison, a white painter and a teacher, began holding religious classes at 17 New Street. Her monetary contribution to the church may have assisted with the permanent structure erected in 1907. Oxly's donation to the First Church of Christ, Science is documented in her probate records, North Carolina Wills and Probate, Craven County Records, North Carolina State Archives. Advertisements for Harrison's classes appear in the *Christian Science Journal* 22 (1904–5): xcii.

90. Carpenter may have assisted Oxly in financing a boardinghouse in November 1893. See "Mortgage Deed," November 17, 1893, Deposition of James M. Harrison, May 24, 1894, pension file of Jane Hill, widow of Edmond Hill, Fourteenth USCHA (wc 373140). Holder, "What's Sex Got to Do with It," 163. Holder discusses how black activists such as John Mitchell Jr. drew on a repository of common knowledge about interracial sex to challenge new legal definitions of race and citizenship based on white racial purity.

91. "E W Carpenter Dead," *New Bern Weekly Journal*, July 12, 1904.

92. Gordon, "Family Violence, Feminism, and Social Control," 467.

6. Marriage and the Expansion of the Pension System in 1890

1. Dependent Pension Law of 1890, 26 Stat. 182 (1890). I have adopted the language of William Glasson, who refers to the new system to as a "service" system to emphasize the basis of the entitlement. *Federal Military Pensions*, 25–26.

2. Skocpol, "America's First Social Security System," 85; Skocpol, *Protecting Soldiers and Mothers*, 107–11.

3. Power of Attorney, July 22, 1890, Declaration for Widow's Pension, September 23, 1891, pension file of Louisa Powers (wc 300875). David Williams Parker of Beaufort County, North Carolina, filed another claim for Louisa Powers under the service law (wc 300285).

4. On black women's wage labor, see Hunter, *To 'Joy My Freedom*; J. Jones, *Labor of Love, Labor of Sorrow*, chaps. 2 and 3. Laura F. Edwards discusses gender constructions within nonelite African American households in *Gendered Strife and Confusion*, chap. 4. See also Schwalm, *Hard Fight for We*; Sims, introduction to *Power of Femininity*.

5. Deposition of Matilda Wells, March 1, 1897, pension file of Matilda Wells (WC 455514).

6. Deposition of Andrew Marshall, October 27, 1897, pension file of Matilda Wells (WC 455514).

7. Glasson, "National Pension System." The provision calling for widows to demonstrate that their net income did not exceed $250 was added in May 1900.

8. Sworn statement of Dicy Oden, June 17, 1895, pension file of Dicy Oden (WC 414263).

9. Pension file of Caroline Butler (WC 134795).

10. Frankel, *Freedom's Women*, chap. 4; Schwartzberg, "Lots of Them Did That"; Slap, "No Regular Marriage"; Adler, "Bessie Done Cut Her Old Man," 126; Edwards, "Marriage Covenant"; Franke, "Becoming a Citizen."

11. Deposition of Mary E. Bragg, January 22, 1900, pension file of Mary Bragg (WC 489846).

12. Deposition of Hansey Jones, November 27, 1900, pension file of Hansey Jones (WC 289357). For other examples, see pension files of Sarah Jane Latham (WC 368120), Hettie Wendly (WC 297220), and Alice Askie (WC 600768).

13. Deposition of Clarissa Sparrow, July 25, 1900, pension file of Clarissa Sparrow, widow of Spencer Sparrow, Fourteenth USCHA (WC 438928).

14. Deposition of Clarissa Sparrow, July 25, 1900; see also pension file of Hettie Wendly (WC 297220).

15. Under the act of June 6, 1866, lawmakers banned from the pension rolls widows who failed to care "properly" for their deceased husbands' children or who were entirely unable to care for them because of "immoral conduct." See McClintock, "Civil War Pensions"; *Annual Report of the Commissioner of Pensions*, H. R. Doc. 40-1 (1868).

16. Glenn, *Forced to Care*, 88–120.

17. Pension file of Presilla Flowers (WC 755483).

18. Deposition of Maria Little, April 10, 1888, pension file of Maria Little (WC 397932).

19. Deposition of Norman Lee, November 20, 1899, pension file of Peggy Slade, widow of Miles Slade, Thirty-Fifth USCT (WC 486995), Civil War Pension Index.

20. Deposition of Shadrick Tripp, November 22, 1899, pension file of Peggy Slade (WC 486995).

21. Deposition of Elsia Askew, April 13, 1905, pension file of Alice Askie (WC 600768).

22. Deposition of Isaac Powell, May 29, 1905, pension file of Alice Askie (WC 600768).

23. Deposition of Isaac Powell, May 29, 1905.

24. Deposition of Hulda Jane Smith, April 15, 1905, pension file of Alice Askie (WC 600768). Complaints by caregivers also appear in pension file of Caroline Batts (WC 338072).

25. Act of 27 June 1890, 2 Stat. 182–83 (1890).

26. Deposition of Hannah Small, July 2, 1900, pension file of Hannah Small (WC 251123).

27. Deposition of Harriet Boyd, June 26, 1900, pension file of Harriet Boyd (WC 444113).

28. H. F. Shontz to Hon. Commissioner of Pensions, March 31, 1902, pension file of Jamsey Green (WC 699829).

29. Deposition of Caroline Perry, July 8, 1893, pension file of Caroline Perry, mother of Luke Perry, Thirty-Fifth USCT (MC 380896), Civil War Pension Index.

30. Affidavit of Lana Burney, October 16, 1902, pension file of Lana Burney (Wright) (WC 940147).

31. Deposition of Marinda Mumford, April 6, 1892, pension file of Judy Lavenhouse (MC 332918).

32. Deposition of Michael Boyd, April 6, 1892, pension file of Judy Lavenhouse (MC 332918).

33. Affidavit of Mary Lee, October 20, 1891, pension file Mary Lee (WC 329285).

34. Claim of Widow for Arrears of Pensions, Under the Act of January 25, 1879, April 8, 1890, pension file of Charlotte Banks (WC 157383).

35. Weber, *Bureau of Pensions*, 15; 20 Stat. 265 (1879).

36. Claim of Widow for Arrears of Pension.

37. Gilmore, *Gender and Jim Crow*, 17–18; Curwood, *Stormy Weather*, 13–51. Curwood writes that middle-class blacks "at the turn of the century" viewed marriage as "a signifier for sexual morality in a time when all black people were stereotyped as immoral" (15).

38. This wording appears in E. T. Ware (commissioner) to Charlotte Caphart, November 18, 1904, pension file of Charlotte Banks (WC 157383). The formal response to Charlotte's 1890 appeal is documented in this 1904 letter, by which time she had filed a succession of appeals.

39. Deposition of Jacob Pool, August 25, 1904, pension file of Charlotte Banks (WC 157383).

40. H. Williams, *Help Me Find My People*; for analysis of Henry Bibbs's interpretation of slave marriage, 55–57.

41. Pension officials in the Legal Division of the bureau had implied their interpretation of owner separation in other cases. See the pension file of Harriet Barlow, widow of Philip Barlow (Barrow), Thirty-Seventh USCT (WC 393620).

42. McClintock, "Binding Up the Nation's Wounds," 241–42n496; Grossberg, *Governing the Hearth*, 133–36. Examples of the bureau's acceptance of informal marriages occurred in 1873, when a delegation of Native Americans petitioned to be exempted from rigid proofs of marriage. That same year lawmakers granted survivors' benefits to the daughters of a deceased black veteran and a white woman in Kentucky. See Cong. Globe, 42nd Cong., 3d sess., 1117 (1873).

43. Commissioner of Pensions to Harriet Ellison, July 25, 1894, pension file of Harriet Ellison, widow of Mathew Ellison, Thirty-Fifth USCT (WC 382583), Civil War Pension Index.

44. Schwartzberg, "Lots of Them Did That," 573.

45. Affidavit of Mary A. Gatlin, December 20, 1907, pension file of Mary Ann Gatlin (WC 278382).

46. Deposition of Mary Norman, March 3, 1902, pension file of Nicy Smith, widow of James Smith, Thirty-Fifth USCT (WC 220928), Civil War Pension Index.

47. The internal correspondence between the commissioner of pensions and secretary of the interior reduced Nicy's case to a "fraud" but continued to point to James Smith's "undivorced" wife in its official correspondence to her. Pension file of Nicy Smith (WC 220928).

48. Nicy Smith died on January 22, 1917. Death Certificates, January 22, 1917, Craven County Records, North Carolina State Archives; Commissioner of Pensions to Nicy Smith, April 7, 1917, pension file of Nicy Smith (WC 220928).

49. Hunter, *Bound in Wedlock*, chap. 6. Flexible definitions of marriage included polygamy, abroad spouses, took-ups, and sweethearting along with monogamous cohabitations. Marriage and family remained fluid and flexible despite laws and social customs.

50. Hunter, *Bound in Wedlock*, 272.

51. As was evident in the lives of Charlotte Banks, Mary Hassell, Harriet Morris, and Ann Blackley decades earlier, marriage and family relationships reflected the harsh conditions of poverty, racism, and gender inequality black women endured in freedom.

52. Deposition of Violet Wiggins, June 21, 1900, pension file of Violet Wiggins, widow of Washington Wiggins, Fourteenth USCHA (WC 132859), Civil War Pension Index.

53. Penelope Ives to Mr. Douglass, October 9, 1892, pension file of Penelophy Ives (WC 332445).

54. Deposition of Penelope Ives, December 31, 1892, pension file of Penelophy Ives (WC 332445).

55. Deposition of Penelope Ives, January 2, 1893, pension file of Penelophy Ives (WC 332445).

56. Examiner Dunn to Commissioner of Pensions, January 9, 1893, pension file of Penelophy Ives (WC 332445).

57. Pension files of Charlotte Banks (WC 157383), Penelophy Ives (WC 332445), Harriet Morris (WC 131719), and Ann Blackley (WC 136493).

58. Under the bureau's rules, veterans' widows who made the decision to surrender their benefits and marry again could recoup benefits for the period of their widowhood. The act of March 3, 1901, included a provision for women's daily labor and women's net income not to exceed $250 a year. Glasson, "National Pension System," 210.

59. Sam'l Blackwell to Hon. Commissioner of Pensions, April 19, 1894, pension file of Esther (Easter) Brown (MC 130542).

60. Regosin, *Freedom's Promise*, chap. 5, 151–52.

61. Regosin, *Freedom's Promise*, 160.

62. Baily Winn's testimony further established Esther's financial need and clarified the internal dynamics of their household. "She never did assume my name," Winn began, but then added, "I have never received or applied for a

divorce" from Easter. Depositions of Easter Brown, December 2, 1895, and Baily Winn, December 3, 1895, pension file of Esther (Easter) Brown (MC 130542).

63. Depositions of Easter Brown, December 3, 1895, Eliza Smith, May 28, 1896, and Abe Toler, May 8, 1896 (quotation, totally blind), pension file of Esther (Easter) Brown (MC 130542).

64. Quotation and date of admission from undated dependent mother's pension, George Albertson, April 6, 1896, Easter's date of admission from undated board of review slip, pension file of Esther (Easter) Brown (MC 130542).

65. "A colored man named Jordan Wilson was the father of Charles and that was what caused him to separate from her." Deposition of Edmund Woodus, December 1, 1892, pension file of Laura A. Gardner (WC 375176).

66. Deposition of Fannie Bryant, December 15, 1892, pension file of Laura A. Gardner (WC 375176).

67. Helen Jones to "Dear Mother," December 6, 1892, pension file of Laura A. Gardner (WC 375176).

68. Deposition of Joanna Hargrove, December 26, 1892, pension file of Laura A. Gardner (WC 375176). In making these claims, Harriet and her witnesses made whiteness as a racial identity visible rather than the norm. C. Harris, "Whiteness as Property."

69. On the Black Second and Israel B. Abbott, see E. Anderson, *Race and Politics*, 65, 73, 103, 134–35; Foner, *Freedom's Lawmakers*, 1. See also deposition of Israel Abbott, February 4, 1882, pension file of Caroline Butler (WC 134795); LeFlouria, *Chained in Silence*, 40–41.

70. Claim of heirs for arrears pension, August 25, 1887, pension file of Laura A. Gardner (WC 375176).

71. Deposition of Eliza Mayo, November 30, 1892, pension file of Laura A. Gardner (WC 375176).

72. Frankel, *Freedom's Women*, chap. 4.

73. Deposition of Fannie Bryant, December 15, 1892.

74. Deposition of Rose Kennedy, November 10, 1904, pension file of Nancy McCabe, widow of John McCabe, Thirty-Sixth USCT (WC 282600), Civil War Pension Index.

75. Thomas Goethe to Commissioner of Pensions, April 3, 1905, pension file of Nancy McCabe (WC 282600).

76. Mary Lee filed for reconsideration under the general law system the same day she filed for benefits under the service law system. See pension files of Mary Lee (WC 329285), Mary Jane Moore (WC 307664); Caroline Batts (WC 338072), Nancy Ann Bell (IC 618836), Mary Norman (WC 289190), Hettie Wendly (WC 297220), and Esther Brown (MC 130542). See also D. H. Kincaid to Honorable Commissioner of Pensions, May 31, 1896, affidavit of Winnie Pope, July 24, 1893, pension file of Winnie Pope (WC 434931); pension files of Minerva Hines (WC 366205), Louisa Little (WC 465452), Mary Jane Green (WC 248457), and Laura A. Gardner (WC 375176).

77. Weber, *Bureau of Pensions*, 8.

78. Deposition of Nancy Ann Bell, November 26, 1901, pension file of Lamb Bell, Thirty-Seventh USCT (IC 618836).

79. 39 Stat. 1379 (1899) "provides that a pensioner who has deserted his wife or children under sixteen years of age, for a period of over six months, or who is an inmate of a soldiers' home, must give up one-half of his pension to his wife, she being a woman of good moral character and in necessitous circumstances." Glasson, *History of Military Pension Legislation*, 338.

80. See the pension files of Elsay Bishop, widow of Peter Bishop, Thirty-Eighth USCT (IC 810577), Faithy Bowden (WC 907154), Maggie Harrison (WC 874040), Jamsey Green (WC 699829), Hetty Wallace (WC 699108), and Sarah Waters (WC 553420), Civil War Pension Index.

81. Deposition of Robert Green, June 24, 1901, pension file of Jamsey Green (WC 699829).

82. Deposition of A. P. Davis, January 19, 1912, pension file of Jamsey Green (WC 699829)

83. Isaac W. Waters to Commissioner of Pensions, March 9, 1900, pension file of Sarah Waters, widow of Isaac W. Waters, Fourteenth USCHA (WC 553420).

84. Affidavit of Benjamin Wallace, June 17, 1905, pension file of Hetty Wallace (WC 699108).

85. Commissioner of Pensions to Hetty Wallace, April 11, 1905, pension file of Hetty Wallace (WC 699108).

7. Black Women and Suspensions for "Open and Notorious Cohabitation"

1. It is not entirely clear from the surviving evidence how Gallion learned of the charges against Louisa Powers. E. D. Gallion to Commissioner of Pensions, March 31, 1894, pension file of Louisa Powers (WC 300875); Indictment, March 1, 1894, Craven County, Superior Court Criminal Action Papers, North Carolina State Archives. In November 1894, a grand jury found Louisa Powers and James Bell guilty of fornication and adultery. "Superior Court. Monday's Proceedings," *New Bern Daily Journal*, November 27, 1894. The judge sentenced Louisa to "30 days jail with leave to hire out." "Superior Court: Wednesday's Proceedings," *New Berne Weekly Journal*, December 6, 1894.

2. E. D. Gallion to Commissioner of Pensions, March 31, 1894, pension file of Louisa Powers (WC 300875).

3. William Lochren to Louisa Powers, May 22, 1894, pension file of Louisa Powers (WC 300875).

4. Deposition of Philip Wiggins, April 12, 1894, pension file of Charity Brown (WC 253903).

5. E. D. Gallion to Hon. Commissioner of Pensions, April 12, 1894, pension file of Charity Brown (WC 253903). Charrity's first name is spelled *Charity* throughout her case file, but she repeatedly signed her name *Charrity*. I refer to her as *Charrity* throughout except when quoting or referencing the pension index.

6. In the midst of investigating Charrity Brown's case, Gallion obtained evidence that Mary Lee, the forty-four-year-old black Union widow he had

investigated back in 1889, had buried a newborn child while collecting survivors' benefits. Since her husband, Simeon, had died in 1870, Gallion believed that the burial records provided irrefutable evidence that Mary Lee was in violation of the 1882 law.

7. Undated newspaper clipping attached to affidavit of Mary Lee, May 16, 1894, pension file of Mary Lee (WC 329285).

8. "Pension Investigation in Trouble," *Daily Journal*, May 13, 1894.

9. Annie Bates, Celia Cuthrell, Ada Dinkins, Emma Porter, Mary Bosewell, Julia Conner, Laura Hilton, Penelope Ives, and Mary Gatlin. I have also examined case files of white Union widows from Dare County.

10. Modifications over time to the guidelines are referenced in H. Clay Evans to the Secretary of the Interior, September 10, 1901, *Annual Report of the Commissioner of Pensions*, H. R. Doc. 57-5 (1901), in U.S. Department of the Interior, *Annual Reports* (1901), 9–78, esp. 34–36.

11. Affidavit of Lila Long, July 5, 1874, pension file of Lila Long (WC 136802).

12. Deposition of Nancy Rouse, June 15, 1891, pension file of Nancy Rouse (MC 306427).

13. Deposition of James Green, May 1, 1901, pension file of Mary Lee (WC 329285).

14. Deposition of Mary Ellison Rodman, June 15, 1895, pension file of Mary Ellison Rodman, widow of William Rodman, Second USCC (WC 389409), Civil War Pension Index.

15. Deposition of Charles Guion, September 22, 1894, pension file of Mary Vonveil (WC 365340).

16. Deposition of Mary Vonveil, September 4, 1894, pension file of Mary Vonveil (WC 365340).

17. Examiner Charles Gilpin to Commissioner of Pensions, September 22, 1894, pension file of Mary Vonveil (WC 365340).

18. Deposition of Mary Ellison Rodman, June 17, 1895, pension file of Mary Ellison Rodman (WC 389409).

19. Hine, "Rape and the Inner Lives of Black Women"; Gaines, *Uplifting the Race*, 5–9.

20. Deposition of Charity Brown, May 8, 1894, pension file of Charity Brown (WC 253903).

21. Gallion to Commissioner of Pensions, May 15, 1894, pension file of Charity Brown (WC 253903).

22. Deposition of Mary Jane Moore, April 23, 1894, pension file of Mary Jane Moore (WC 307664).

23. Affidavit of Mary Jane Moore, June 23, 1894, pension file of Mary Jane Moore (WC 307664). Bureau officials ultimately determined that Mary Jane Moore was not a recognized widow at the time she had given birth to her additional children.

24. Undated newspaper clipping attached to affidavit of Mary Lee, May 16, 1894, pension file of Mary Lee (WC 329285).

25. Undated newspaper clipping attached to affidavit of Mary Lee, May 16, 1894, pension file of Mary Lee (WC 329285).

26. Brimmer, "Black Women's Politics." Seven months later, the jury issued a swift not-guilty verdict in *State v. E. D. Gallion*. "Superior Court: Wednesday's Proceedings," *New Berne Weekly Journal*, December 6, 1894.

27. Affidavit of Louisa Powers, June 15, 1894, pension file of Louisa Powers (WC 300875).

28. Deposition of W. H. Fulford, August 30, 1894, pension file of Louisa Powers (WC 300875).

29. Deposition of Siddy Powers, August 28, 1894, pension file of Louisa Powers (WC 300875).

30. Deposition of Louisa Powers, August 28, 1894, pension file of Louisa Powers (WC 300875).

31. Deposition of Louisa Powers, August 28, 1894.

32. Charles Gilpin to Commissioner of Pensions, August 30, 1894, pension file of Louisa Powers (WC 300875).

33. Acting Secretary of the Interior to Commissioner of Pensions, September 19, 1894, pension file of Louisa Powers (WC 300875).

34. Louisa Powers to Commissioner of Pensions, June 15, 1895, pension file of Louisa Powers (WC 300875). Earlier that year she had asked the commissioner to reinvestigate her case for survivors' benefits. Louisa Powers to Hon. William Lochren, January 30, 1895.

35. Cohen, "Deviance as Resistance."

36. Rosen, *Terror in the Heart of Freedom.*

37. Examiner William Porter recommended that the government show leniency in Douglass's first illegal fees case. See chapter 5.

38. Examiner Gallion attempted to build a case against Douglass by collecting evidence in the cases of Caroline Batts (WC 338072), Lenna Carnell (WC 367681), Sarah Latham (WC 368120), Caroline Perry (MC 380896), Julia Neel, (MC 334373), and Peggy Slade (WC 486995).

39. Affidavit of Frederick C. Douglass, April 21, 1894, Frederick C. Douglass, Case Files.

40. Affidavit of Frederick C. Douglass, July 7, 1894, Frederick C. Douglass, Case Files.

41. Douglass affidavit, April 21, 1894.

42. Douglass affidavit, April 21, 1894.

43. Frederick C. Douglass to Nathan Bickford, December 19, 1894, Frederick C. Douglass, Case Files.

44. Commissioner of Pensions to Douglass, November 24, 1894, Frederick C. Douglass, Case Files.

45. F. M. Simmons to Commissioner of Pensions, December 28, 1894, Frederick C. Douglass, Case Files.

46. Douglass had met Washington, DC, attorney Nathan Bickford earlier that year when Douglass contacted his firm to handle Henry Brown's claims for survivor's benefits after his mother, Charrity Brown, was removed from the rolls. Pension file of Charity Brown (WC 253903) and Henry Brown's minor claim (MI 429230).

47. See especially Frederick C. Douglass to Nathan Bickford, commander of the GAR, December 27, 1894, Frederick C. Douglass, Case Files.

48. Douglass to Bickford, December 27, 1894.

49. Gilmore, *Gender and Jim Crow*, 82.

50. Gilmore, *Gender and Jim Crow*; E. B. Brown, "Negotiating and Transforming the Public Sphere," 107–46.

51. Douglass to Bickford, December 27, 1894.

52. Shadrick Tripp to Hon. J. C. Pritchard, February 26, 1895, Frederick C. Douglass, Case Files. Documents in this file also spell this name *Shadwick Trip*. I refer to him as *Shadrick*, as he signed his name.

53. "Pension Frauds in North Carolina: Jane Hill Sentenced to One Year Imprisonment," *New York Times*, November 4, 1895, 1.

54. Douglass served as Jane Hill's pension attorney in the case. Carpenter was implicated because he sold her land during the transaction. See pension file of Edward Hill, Fourteenth USCHA (IC 1149932).

55. "Full Vote of Craven County by Precincts," *New Berne Weekly Journal*, November 5, 1896; Magistrate's Oath, April 8, 1897, Frederick C. Douglass, Case Files.

56. Prather, *We Have Taken a City*, 22; Gilmore, "Murder, Memory, and the Flight of the Incubus," 83; Edwards, "Captives of Wilmington," 115; Gilmore, *Gender and Jim Crow*, chap. 4.

57. "Newbern's Awful Plight," *Webster's Weekly* (Reidsville), September 29, 1898. The image accompanying the article is titled "Trial of a White Woman by a Negro Justice of the Peace at New Bern."

58. Douglass affidavit, April 21, 1894, Frederick C. Douglass, Case Files.

59. F. Douglass to Assistant Secretary of the Interior Webster Davis, July 2, 1897, Frederick C. Douglass, Case Files.

60. Douglass to Secretary of the Interior C. N. Bliss, October 5, 1897, Mamie B. Douglass to Commissioner of Pensions William Lochren, October 27, 1897, Frederick C. Douglass, Case Files.

61. H. P. Cheatham to Commissioner of Pensions, July 18, 1897, Frederick C. Douglass, Case Files.

62. W. F. Fonville to Commissioner of Pensions, November 22, 1897, Frederick C. Douglass, Case Files.

63. M. Manly to Hon. Hoke Smith, November 17, 1894, Frederick C. Douglass, Case Files. Manly is mentioned in Douglass's correspondence to Hon. D. A. Murphy, September 14, 1896, Frederick C. Douglass, Case Files.

64. W. H. Jones to Commissioner of Pensions, November 17, 1897, Frederick C. Douglass, Case Files.

65. Petition to the Commissioner of Pensions, July 9, 1897, Frederick C. Douglass, Case Files.

66. George H. White to Commissioner of Pensions, December 11, 1897, Frederick C. Douglass, Case Files.

67. Leonidas J. Moore to C. M. Gilpin, November 14, 1896, Frederick C. Douglass, Case Files.

68. "Voice of the People," *New Bern Journal*, September 15, 1898, 4; "Talking to Negroes," *New Berne Daily Journal*, November 2, 1898, 4; "Voice of the People: Some Pertinent Questions," *New Bern Journal*, September 17, 1898, 4, which calls on E. W. Carpenter to explain his involvement in the Jane Hill case.

69. "E. W. Carpenter's Answer," *New Berne Daily Journal*, November 3, 1898, 1; "E. W. Carpenter's Answer," *New Berne Daily Journal*, December 27, 1898, 4.

70. "Carpenter's Answer," November 3, 1898; pension file of Jane Hill, widow of Edward Hill, Fourteenth USCHA (WC 373140), Civil War Pension Index. Jane Hill's case file is enclosed in the Edmund Hill's case file. Part of the confusion in this case stems from identity. Jane Hill and her witnesses testified to her marriage to an Edmond Hill and the soldier was referred to as *Edmond* and *Edward* in the case file; another Edward Hill served in the same regiment and eventually filed a claim. Jane's case interfered with Edward Hill's ability to secure disability benefits, and doubt surfaced regarding whether an Edmund Hill had ever served.

71. H. Clay Evans's changes to the 1897 *Special Examiner* handbook are noted in U.S. Department of the Interior, *Annual Report of the Commissioner of Pensions*, 28–30.

72. U.S. Department of the Interior, *Annual Report of the Commissioner of Pensions*, 29.

73. Deposition of Winney Skinner, May 18, 1898, pension file of Louisa Little, widow of James Little, Thirty-Sixth USCT (WC 465452), Civil War Pension Index.

74. Deposition of Giles Blango Jr., May 18, 1898, pension file of Louisa Little (WC 465452).

75. Deposition of James Linear, May 18, 1898, pension file of Louisa Little (WC 465452).

76. Gilpin to Commissioner of Pensions, May 19, 1898, pension file of Louisa Little (WC 465452).

77. On scrutiny of middle-class black women, see Schecter, "All the Intensity of My Nature," 59.

78. H. P. Maxwell to Commissioner of Pensions, October 15, 1897, pension file of Matilda Wells (WC 455514).

79. Deposition of Fannie Spellman, October 12, 1897, pension file of Matilda Wells (WC 455514).

80. Deposition of Matilda Wells, October 23, 1897, pension file of Matilda Wells (WC 455514).

81. Deposition of D. H. Kincaid, May 12, 1897, pension file of Matilda Wells (WC 455514).

82. Deposition of Matilda Wells, March 30, 1897, pension file of Matilda Wells (WC 455514).

83. Fusionists endorsed the restoration of local self-government, making county commissioners supreme in administrative authority but lessening the power of justices of the peace. Edmonds, *Negro and Fusion Politics*, 117–19.

84. Appeal to the Honorable, the Senate and the House of Representatives of the United States of America in Congress Assembled, July 9, 1897, Frederick C. Douglass, Case Files.

85. The level of involvement Douglass had in Louisa Powers's 1897 appeal to Congress is uncertain, but several months later he used her story in a petition to the assistant secretary of the interior (Frederick Douglass to the assistant secretary of the interior, July 2, 1897, Frederick C. Douglass, Case Files). At no point is Douglass's name mentioned in Powers's petition, despite his pivotal role in her case. Noticeably, however, bureau officials filed the appeal in Frederick Douglass's legal case file rather than in Louisa Powers's pension file. Louisa Powers, appeal to Congress, filed in 1896, stamped July 9, 1897, Frederick C. Douglass, Case Files.

86. Commissioner of Pensions to Mary Lee, June 28, 1899; affidavit of Mary Lee, September 11, 1899, pension file of Mary Lee (WC 329285).

87. E. B. Brown, "Negotiating and Transforming the Public Sphere," 141n62.

8. The Personal Consequences of Union Widowhood

1. "Robbing the Nation," *Chicago Tribune*, December 22, 1897, 10. On criminal sexuality, see Frankel, *Freedom's Women*, xii; Romeo, *Gender and Jubilee*, 106–7.

2. McSorley to Hon. Commissioner of Pensions, July 13, 1900, pension file of Sophia Alexander (WC 209079).

3. Women charged with violating the law of 1882 during the 1899–1901 investigations: Dianna Peldon (WC 387150), Maria Little (IC 397932), Sophia Alexander (WC 209079), Mary Kent (WC 261737), Clara Williams (WC 374117), and Louisa Little (WC 465452). At least eight other women were suspected of violating the act of 1882: Violett Pickett (WC 268227), Mary Franklin (WC 488092), Nicy Smith (WC 220928), Caroline Brown (WC 831470), Tammer Latham (WC 259469), Mary Lee (WC 329285), Lydia Pierson (WC 623883), Matilda Wells (WC 455514), and Fanny Whitney (WC 130403).

4. Justesen, *George Henry White*, 276–311.

5. "Defense of the Negro Race—Charges Answered, Speech of George H. White, of North Carolina, in the House of Representatives, January 29, 1901," Documenting the American South, University of North Carolina at Chapel Hill, https://docsouth.unc.edu/nc/whitegh/whitegh.html.

6. Douglass to Simmons, July 29, 1898, Frederick C. Douglass, Case Files.

7. Simmons to Hon. H. Clay Evans, August 8, 1898, Frederick C. Douglass, Case Files.

8. Commissioner to Arthur Simmons, Executive Mansion, August 23, 1898, Frederick C. Douglass, Case Files.

9. P. M. Pearsall to Hon. Thomas Ryan, April 2, 1901, Frederick C. Douglass, Case Files.

10. Douglass to H. Clay Evans, October 9, 1901, Frederick C. Douglass, Case Files.

11. See Douglass's affidavit on April 12, 1894, illegal fees case, Frederick C. Douglass, Case Files.

12. Douglass to Evans, October 9, 1901.

13. Deposition of Mary Whitby, June 22, 1900, pension file of Mary Whitby (WC 276505).

14. Thomas Goethe to Commissioner of Pensions, July 14, 1910, pension file of Lavinia Kelley, widow of Thomas Kelley, Thirty-Fifth USCT (WC 705972), Civil War Pension Index.

15. Deposition of Lavinia Kelley, July 5, 1910, pension file of Lavinia Kelley (WC 705972).

16. Deposition of Lavinia Kelley, July 6, 1910, pension file of Lavinia Kelley (WC 705972).

17. Goethe to Commissioner, July 14, 1910.

18. Pension file of David Proctor, Second USCC (IC 549011).

19. I. B. Dunn to Commissioner of Pensions, May 20, 1892, pension file of David Proctor (IC 549011).

20. L. F. Harrison to Commissioner of Pensions, June 7, 1892, pension file of David Proctor (IC 549011).

21. Margaret Proctor's case file indicated that she was not admitted to pension roster. Deposition of Margaret Proctor, June 15, 1918, pension file of David Proctor (IC 549011). Another example of how bureau examiners interpreted the marriage standard in black women's case files appears in the pension file of Annie Hardy (Puss Stevens), widow of Alfred Stephens (Albert Stevens), Thirtieth USCT (IC 1045853), Civil War Pension Index.

22. Thomas Goethe to Commissioner of Pensions, July 13, 1900, pension file of Clara Williams, widow of Silas Williams, Thirty-Fifth USCT (WC 374117), Civil War Pension Index.

23. See Brittany C. Cooper's analysis of the politics of respectability, the body, and public space in *Beyond Respectability*, 15. Treva Lindsey offers a nuanced analysis of dissemblance and the politics of hyperfemininity in *Colored No More*, 16–18.

24. The chief of the Law Division determined that Malissa's "birth out of wedlock" did not bring Fanny's case into violation of the Pension Bureau's cohabitation policy. Chief of Law Division to Chief of S. E. Division, July 14, 1900, pension file of Fanny Whitney (WC 130403).

25. Pension file of Celia Cuthrell (WC 155267).

26. Feimster, *Southern Horrors*, 62–86; Haley, *No Mercy Here*, 8–10.

27. See pension files of Sarah E. West, widow of Westley West, Seventy-Eighth Ohio Infantry (WC 258998), and Ann Manning, widow of Sumner Manning, Eleventh Michigan Infantry (IC 462834)

28. Deposition of Elsie Bishop, January 24, 1912, pension file of Elsie Bishop (IC 810577).

29. Deposition of Dicy Oden, June 19, 1900, pension file of Dicy Oden (WC 414263).

30. Deposition of Lucy Spencer, June 29, 1900, pension file of Lucy Spencer, widow of Hosea Spencer, Thirty-Fifth USCT (WC 332780), Civil War Pension Index.

31. Sophia Alexander to Commissioner of Pensions, August 10, 1900, pension file of Sophia Alexander (WC 209079).

32. Affidavit of Mary E. Kent, November 21, 1900, pension file of Mary E. Kent (wc 261737).

33. Deposition of Hettie Wendly, January 7, 1901, pension file of Hettie Wendly (wc 297220).

34. Deposition of Hettie Wendly, January 8, 1901, pension file of Hettie Wendly (wc 297220). For similar examples of black Union widows reporting misconduct of claims agents, see Dianna Peldon to Commissioner of Pensions, May 26, 1909, pension file of Dianna Peldon, widow of Isaac Peldon, Thirty-Fifth USCT (wc 387150), Civil War Pension Index.

35. Shaffer, *After the Glory*, 195; Blight, *Race and Reunion*; M. K. Harris, "Slavery, Emancipation," 264–90; Vogel, "Redefining Reconciliation," 67–93. This sentiment is also captured in newspaper articles of the day; see, for example, "Federal Colored Troops: Thousands Drawing Pension Who Never Drew a Gun," *New York Times*, May 20, 1894, 20.

36. Hunter, *Bound in Wedlock*, 293–97; Gaines, *Uplifting the Race*; Hicks, *Talk with You Like a Woman*, 53–56.

37. Harriet Duggins's report in *Annual Report of the Northern Baptist Convention, 1910*, 112; Stowell, *Rebuilding Zion*, 205. I have yet to establish a definitive link between the work of black and white missionaries in James City and reporting violations to the bureau, but the work that these women did inside of poor women's homes is suggestive.

38. Affidavit of Liddia Moore, September 10, 1900, pension file of Mary Ellison Rodman (wc 389409).

39. Affidavit of Patience Roberson, September 1, 1900, pension file of Mary Ellison Rodman (wc 389409).

40. Handwritten note on "Restoration" of widow's pension, October 2, 1900, pension file of Mary Ellison Rodman (wc 389409).

41. Anonymous letter, November 9, 1898, pension file of Tammer Latham (wc 259469). Latham married Duggins in 1901; Marriage Records, Craven County Records, North Carolina State Archives.

42. Chief of Law Division to the Assistant Chief of the Law Division, Legality of Marriage in North Carolina, August 7, 1900, pension file of Tammer Latham (wc 259469).

43. Anonymous letter to Commissioner of Pensions, February 18, 1901, pension file of Violett Ann Wallace, widow of Peter Wallace, Fourteenth USCHA (wc 268277), Civil War Pension Index. Violet Ann and Peter Wallace are also identified as Pickett in the pension records.

44. Thomas H. Goethe to Hon. Commissioner of Pensions, March 14, 1901, pension file of Violett Ann Wallace (wc 268277).

45. Anonymous letter to Commissioner of Pensions, August [22?] 1916, pension file of Lydia Pierson, widow of Essex Pierson, Fourteenth USCHA (wc 623883), Civil War Pension Index.

46. John G. Tricher to Hon. Commissioner of Pensions, February 6, 1917, pension file of Lydia Pierson (wc 623883).

47. Deposition of Mary Lee, July 23, 1900, pension file of Mary Lee (wc 329285).

48. Deposition of Mary Lee, July 23, 1900. Lee was rated an "unreliable" witness in Jamsey Green's case. See the index to C. M. Gilpin, *Special Examiners Report*, undated [1893], in pension file of Jamsey Green, widow of Robert Green, Thirty-Sixth USCT (wc 699829), also widow of James Cooper, Fourteenth USCHA.

49. Glymph, *Out of the House of Bondage*, 210–11.

50. Penningroth, *Claims of Kinfolk*; Rodrigue, "Black Agency after Slavery," 48–50.

51. Deposition of Hettie Wendly, July 6, 1900, pension file of Sophia Alexander (wc 209079); deposition of Nancy Bell, September 3, 1900, pension file of Mary Lee (wc 329285).

52. Gross, *Colored Amazons*, 84–87; deposition of Sophia Alexander, July 13, 1900, pension file of Sophia Alexander (wc 209079).

53. Depositions of William Hobbs, October 27, 1900, and Nelson Leary, October 11, 1900, pension file of Louisa Little (wc 465452).

54. Deposition of John Blango, October 26, 1900, pension file of Louisa Little (wc 465452).

55. Deposition of Giles Blango Jr., September 25, 1900, pension file of Louisa Little (wc 465452).

56. Deposition of Philip Wiggins, July 17, 1900, pension file of Louisa Little (wc 465452).

57. Deposition of Louisa Little, October 3, 1900, pension file of Louisa Little (wc 465452).

58. On the production of racialized gender in the post-emancipation South, see Rosen, *Terror in the Heart of Freedom*; Boris, "On the Importance of Naming."

59. C. D. McSorley to Hon. Commissioner of Pensions, February 11, 1901, pension file of Louisa Little (wc 465452).

60. Deposition of Nelson Leary, October 11, 1900, pension file of Louisa Little (wc 465452).

61. Survivors' benefits affected community ties, gender identities, and the economic position of poor black women. Penningroth, *Claims of Kinfolk*; Hickel, "War, Region, and Social Welfare."

62. C. R. Thomas et al., petition to the Commissioner of Pensions, September 27, 1901, pension file of Louisa Little (wc 465452). See also the case file of Matilda Simmons from 1874 in her pension file (wc 135034).

63. L. J. Moore to Commissioner of Pensions, April 3, 1901, pension file of Louisa Little (wc 465452).

64. Moore to Commissioner of Pensions, April 3, 1901. Similarly, several prominent white men intervened in the case of Anna Jones after her claim was denied. See Thomas Goethe to Commissioner of Pensions, October 31, 1911, F. M. Simmons to James L. Davenport, December 13, 1912, Davenport to Simmons, December 16, 1911, pension file of Anna Jones, widow of Sanders Jones, Thirty-Fifth USCT (wc 714042), Civil War Pension Index.

65. F. L. Campbell, Assistant Secretary, Department of the Interior, to Commissioner of Pensions, April 17, 1901. After the decision was rendered in her case, Louisa Little filed a succession of appeals in the Department of the Interior. M. W. Miller, Assistant Secretary, Department of the Interior, to Commissioner of Pensions, May 31, 1905, pension file of Louisa Little (WC 465452). Anna Jones, a black washerwoman, utilized her white employers to advance her rejected case; pension file of Anna Jones (WC 714042).

66. Affidavit of Harriet Duggins, September 29, 1900.

67. Affidavit of Harriet Duggins, September 29, 1900, affidavit of R. A. Williams, May 24, 1904, affidavit of Carrie E. Waugh, May 24, 1904, pension file of Dianna Peldon (WC 387150). See also "A History of the Negro Baptists of North Carolina," *Reformed Reader*, accessed February 14, 2020, http://www.reformedreader.org/history/whitted/negrobaptists06.htm; American Baptist Convention, *American Baptist Year Book*.

68. V. Warren to Hon. F. M. Simmons, December 21, 1907, pension file of Mary Ann Gatlin (WC 278382).

69. Affidavit of Mary Ann Gatlin, December 9, 1907, pension file of Mary Ann Gatlin (WC 278382).

70. Mary Ann Gatlin to F. M. Simmons, March 6, 1908, pension file of Mary Ann Gatlin (WC 278382).

71. E. Anderson, *Race and Politics*; Mobley, *James City*.

72. Hettie Wendly to Hon. Sen. F. M. Simmons, September 19, 1907, pension file of Hettie Wendly (WC 297220); pension files of Anna Jones (WC 714042) and Lana Burney (Wright) (WC 940147).

73. F. M. Simmons to V. Warner, Commissioner of Pensions, October 7, 1907, V. Warner to Senator F. M. Simmons, October 10, 1907, pension file of Hettie Wendly (WC 297220).

74. Charlotte Banks's appeal for reconsideration of her case under the Act of March 3, 1901, is in her pension file (WC 157383). Act of March 3, 1901, 56 Stat. 1445–46 (1901). Under this new law, which amended R. S. 4708, the widows of Union soldiers who had remarried (and found themselves single once again) could reestablish their standing on the federal pension roster. See also the pension file of Rebecca Cherry (Spellman) (WC 132857).

75. Deposition of Thomas Godfrey, August 21, 1904, pension file of Charlotte Banks (WC 157383).

76. Deposition of William Cartwright, August 6, 1904, pension file of Charlotte Banks (WC 157383).

77. Deposition of Jacob Pool, September 5, 1904, pension file of Charlotte Banks (WC 157383).

78. Deposition of Charlotte Capehart, August 31, 1904, pension file of Charlotte Banks (WC 157383).

79. T. W. Dalton, Chief Board of Review to Chief of Section and Mr. Andrews, Reviewer, November 3, 1904, pension file of Charlotte Banks (WC 157383).

80. Pension files of Charlotte Banks (WC 157383), Rebecca Cherry (Spellman) (WC 132857), Henrietta Rutherford (Lane), widow of William Rutherford, Fourth USCT (WC 259817), Lana Burney (Wright) (WC 940147), Fanny Oats, widow of Daniel Oats, Thirty-Seventh USCT (WC 255702), Civil War Pension Index.

81. This law allowed "certain" remarried women to renew their standing on the pension roster act of March 3, 1901, amending section 4708, R. S., 31 Stat. (1901) and U.S. Department of the Interior, *Laws of the United States*, 51; Glasson, "National Pension System," 210.

82. Charlotte Capehart to the Hon. Secretary of the Interior, October 2, 1905, pension file of Charlotte Banks (WC 157383).

83. Jesse E. Wilson, Assistant Secretary of the Department of the Interior, appeal, February 19, 1907, pension file of Charlotte Banks (WC 157383).

84. Freedwoman Julia Ann Foy appealed to the secretary of the interior on two separate occasions, and in 1905, she contacted Senator F. M. Simmons to intervene in her case. She sought reinstatement to the pension roster under the general law system. Julia Ann was not able to rouse another special examination, as Charlotte Banks had in 1904, but the lengthy correspondence between the acting commissioner and Simmons indicates that she elicited a response from bureau administrators. Julia Ann remained on the pension rolls until she died in 1914; pension file of Julia Ann Foy (MC 156180); see also pension file of Hettie Wendly (WC 297220).

85. Deposition of Mattie C. Windsor, September 7, 1917, pension file of Caroline Brown, widow of John Brown, Thirty-Sixth USCT (WC 831470).

86. Deposition of Caroline Brown, September 6, 1917, pension file of Caroline Brown (WC 831470).

87. Chief of Law Division to S. E. Division, April 9, 1901, pension file of Mary Lee (WC 329285).

88. Deposition of Caroline Brown, September 6, 1917, pension file of Caroline Brown (WC 831470). Caroline died on August 26, 1920; Born in 1883, Mattie married Charles Thigpen seven years after Caroline's death; at age eighty-seven, Mattie died of asphyxiation in a 1970 house fire. Mattie Windsor Thigpen, Death Certificate, May 15, 1970, North Carolina Death Certificates, 1909–1976.

89. Glymph, *Out of the House of Bondage*, 209–10.

90. George H. Ragsdale to Commissioner of Pensions, undated special examiner's report, pension file of Margaret Dudley (WC 152362).

91. Affidavit of Miles Sheppard, January 22, 1894, pension file of Julia Ann Foy (MC 156180).

92. Deposition of James M. Harrison, May 24, 1894, pension file of Jane Hill (WC 373140).

93. Affidavit of James M. Harrison, May 12, 1894, affidavit of Joe L. Hahn, May 26, 1894, pension file of Jane Hill (WC 373140).

94. Deposition of Hettie Wendly, July 6, 1900, pension file of Sophia Alexander (WC 209079).

95. Pension files of Mary Jane Moore (WC 307664) and Charity Brown (WC 831470).

96. Affidavit of Hettie Wendly, October 30, 1907, notarized by James M. Harrison, pension file of Hettie Wendly (WC 297220).

Conclusion

1. Michael Blackman, "In Search of Back Pay for Heroine of Civil War," *New York Times*, November 1, 2003, B1. Tubman never received the five-dollar-a-month increase granted in 1899.

2. Vagrancy codes enshrined in state codes across the South criminalized black men, women, and children perceived as idle. Rose, "Gender, Race, and the Welfare State."

3. Mothers' pension legislation was passed in the majority of states after Illinois passed a model law in 1911. Scholars of social welfare typically begin their discussion of public provision with the administration of public aid to mothers through the mothers' pension programs. Goodwin, "'Employable Mothers' and 'Suitable Work.'"

4. Hicks, *Talk with You Like a Woman*, 23–52; L. Brown, "African American Women and Migration"; Clark-Lewis, *Living In, Living Out*; Lemke-Santangelo, *Abiding Courage*.

5. Hickel, "Justice and the Highest Kind of Equality," 750, 761.

6. Plant and Clarke, "Crowning Insult," 432.

7. J. Jones, *Labor of Love, Labor of Sorrow*, 171–73.

8. Kessler-Harris, "Designing Women and Old Fools."

9. Goodwin, "'Employable Mothers' and 'Suitable Work,'" 261. Though these programs were not set up with black women in mind, they assigned black women to mandatory work programs in exchange for relief in the 1930s. As of 1961, twice as many black women receiving AFDC worked for wages as white women; the disparity in the South was even greater. Kerber, *No Constitutional Right to Be Ladies*, 76.

10. Goodwin, "'Employable Mothers' and 'Suitable Work,'" 258–62; Kessler-Harris, "Designing Women and Old Fools," 94.

11. J. Jones, *Labor of Love, Labor of Sorrow*, 196; K. T. Anderson, "Last Hired, First Fired."

12. Foner, *Give Me Liberty*, 701.

13. Katznelson, *When Affirmative Action Was White*, 114–43.

14. Kessler-Harris, "Designing Women and Old Fools."

15. Farmer, "Reframing African American Women's Grassroots Organizing," 84.

16. Kornbluh, "To Fulfill Their 'Rightly Needs.'"

17. Boris, "On the Importance of Naming"; Feimster, "Impact of Racial and Sexual Politics."

18. Katherine Boo, "The Marriage Cure: Is Wedlock Really a Way out of Poverty?" *New Yorker*, August 11, 2003. See K. Y. Taylor's forceful critique of "color blindness" in *From #BlackLivesMatter to Black Liberation*, 51–73.

19. Gordon, *Pitied but Not Entitled*; Quadagno, *Color of Welfare*; Goodwin, "'Employable Mothers' and 'Suitable Work'"; Mink, "Lady and the Tramp"; Kessler-Harris, "Designing Women and Old Fools." Scholarship oriented toward the rise of ADC and later AFDC and black women includes Amott, "Black Women and AFDC"; Orleck, *Storming Caesar's Palace*; Kornbluh, *Battle for Welfare Rights*.

20. Canaday, "Building a Straight State."

21. McGuire, *At the Dark End of the Street*, 47; Levenstein, *Movement without Marches*.

22. L. Alexander, "Challenge of Race"; Levenstein, *Movement without Marches*; Gross, "African American Women."

23. Kelley, *Freedom Dreams*, 136. Kelley minced no words when he wrote, "Even the radical architects for reparations completely collapsed black women within an undifferentiated mass called the black community."

24. Berry, *My Face Is Black Is True*, 50–80; Farmer, "Reframing African American Women's Grassroots Organizing," 83–89.

Bibliography

Archival Records

Duke University, Durham, North Carolina

DAVID M. RUBENSTEIN RARE BOOK AND MANUSCRIPT LIBRARY

John Heritage Bryan Papers, 1735–1956

East Carolina University, Greenville, North Carolina

J. Y. JOYNER LIBRARY, EAST CAROLINA MANUSCRIPT COLLECTION

William Horner Collection: Frederick C. Douglass Papers

Library of Congress, Washington, DC

Prints and Photographs Online Catalog

National Archives and Records Administration, Washington, DC

RECORD GROUP 15: RECORDS OF THE DEPARTMENT OF VETERANS AFFAIRS, 1773–2007

Case Files of Attorneys, Agents, Pensioners, and Others Relating to the Prosecution of Pension Claims and the Investigation of Fraudulent Practices. Legal Records. Records of the Bureau of Pensions and Its Predecessors, 1805–1915.

Civil War Pension Index: General Index to Pension Files, 1861–1934.

Organization Index to Pension Files of Veterans Who Served between 1861 and 1900. National Archives Microfilm Series T-289.

Register of Appointments and Assignments, 1882–1905, vols. 1-3.

Special Examiners' Division, July 1902–1904.

Special Schedules of the Eleventh Census (1890) Enumerating Union Veterans and Widows of Union Veterans of the Civil War. National Archives Microfilm Publication M123, 118 rolls.

RECORD GROUP 29: RECORDS OF THE BUREAU OF THE CENSUS

RECORD GROUP 92: RECORDS OF THE OFFICE OF THE QUARTERMASTER GENERAL, 1774–1985

RECORD GROUP 94: RECORDS OF THE ADJUTANT GENERAL'S OFFICE, 1780S–1917

Compiled Military Service Records of Volunteer Union Soldiers Belonging to the 31st through 35th Infantry Units, Organized for Service with the United States Colored Troops. National Archives Microfilm Publication M1992, 86 rolls.

Compiled Military Service Records of Volunteer Union Soldiers Belonging to the 36th through 40th Infantry Units, Organized for Service with the United States Colored Troops. National Archives Microfilm Publication M1993, 116 rolls.

Compiled Military Service Records of Volunteer Union Soldiers Belonging to the Artillery Units Organized for Service with the United States Colored Troops. National Archives Microfilm Publication M1818, 299 rolls.

RECORD GROUP 101: RECORDS OF THE OFFICE OF THE COMPTROLLER OF THE CURRENCY

Register of Signatures of Depositors in Branches of the Freedman's Savings and Trust Company, 1865–1874. National Archives Microfilm Publication M816.

RECORD GROUP 105: RECORDS OF THE BUREAU OF REFUGEES, FREEDMEN, AND ABANDONED LANDS, 1865–1870

Records of the Assistant Commissioner for the State of North Carolina, National Archives Microfilm Publication M843, 38 rolls.

RECORD GROUP 163: RECORDS OF THE SELECTIVE SERVICE SYSTEM (WORLD WAR I)

RECORD GROUP 233: RECORDS OF THE U.S. HOUSE OF REPRESENTATIVES

Barred and Disallowed Case Files of the Southern Claims Commission, 1871–1880. National Archives Microfilm Publication M1407, 4,829 fiche.

New York Public Library, New York

RARE BOOKS AND MANUSCRIPT DIVISION

Charles Alexander Nelson Papers

North Carolina State Archives, Division of Archives and History, Raleigh

CRAVEN COUNTY RECORDS

Death Certificates, 1909–1976
Marriage Records, 1741–2011
Superior Court, Criminal Action Papers, 1778-1906
Wills and Probate Records

University of Maryland, College Park, Department of History

Freedmen and Southern Society Project

Other Sources

Adler, Jeffrey. "'Bessie Done Cut Her Old Man': Race, Common-Law Marriage, and Homicide in New Orleans, 1925–1945." *Journal of Social History* 44 (2010): 123–43.

Alexander, Leslie. "The Challenge of Race: Rethinking the Position of Black Women in the Field of Women's History." *Journal of Women's History* 16 (Winter 2004): 50–60.

Alexander, Roberta Sue. *North Carolina Faces the Freedmen: Race Relations during Presidential Reconstruction, 1865–67*. Durham, NC: Duke University Press, 1985.

American Baptist Convention. *American Baptist Year Book*. Philadelphia: American Baptist Publication Society, 1884.

Amis, M. N., comp. *North Carolina Criminal Code and Digest*. Raleigh, NC: Edwards, Broughton, 1866.

Amott, Teresa. "Black Women and AFDC: Making Entitlement out of Necessity." In *Women, the State, and Welfare*, edited by Linda Gordon, 280–98. Madison: University of Wisconsin Press, 1990.

Anderson, Eric. *Race and Politics in North Carolina, 1872–1901: The Black Second*. Baton Rouge: Louisiana State University Press, 1981.

Anderson, Karen Tucker. "Last Hired, First Fired: Black Women Workers during World War II." *Journal of American History* 69 (1982): 82–97.

Annual Report of the Northern Baptist Convention, 1910. Philadelphia: American Baptist Publication Society, 1910.

Baber, George, ed. *Cases Relating the Pension Claims, and to the Laws of the United States Granting and Governing Pensions*. Vol. 5. Washington, DC: Government Printing Office, 1892.

Baber, George, ed. *Decisions of the Department of the Interior, in Cases Relating to Pension Claims, and to the Laws of the United States Granting and Governing Pensions*. Washington, DC: Government Printing Office, 1892.

Baker, Paula. "The Domestication of American Politics: Women and American Political Society, 1780–1920." *American Historical Review* 89 (1984): 620–47.

Baldwin, Thomas, and J. Thomas. *A New and Complete Gazetteer of the United States; Giving a Full and Comprehensive Review of the Present Condition, Industry, and Resources of the American Confederacy*. Philadelphia: Lippincott, Grambo, 1854.

Baptist, Edward E. "'Stol' and Fetched Here': Enslaved Migrations, Ex-Slave Narratives, and Vernacular History." In *New Studies in the History of American Slavery*, edited by Edward E. Baptist and Stephanie M. H. Camp, 243–74. Athens: University of Georgia Press, 2006.

Barber, Susan E., and Charles F. Ritter. "Dangerous Liaisons: Working Women and Sexual Justice in the American Civil War." *European Journal of American Studies* 10. no. 1 (2015). https://doi.org/10.4000/ejas.10695.

Barber, Susan E., and Charles F. Ritter. "'Physical Abuse . . . and Rough Handling, Race, Gender, and Sexual Justice." In *Occupied Women: Gender, Military*

Occupation, and the American Civil War, edited by LeeAnn Whites and Alecia P. Long, 49–64. Baton Rouge: Louisiana State University Press, 2009.

Bardaglio, Peter W. *Reconstructing the Household: Families, Sex, and the Law in the Nineteenth-Century South*. Chapel Hill: University of North Carolina Press, 1995.

Barrett, John G. *The Civil War in North Carolina*. Chapel Hill: University of North Carolina Press, 1963.

Barton, Myers. *Executing Daniel Bright: Race, Loyalty, and Guerrilla Violence in a Coastal Carolina County*. Baton Rouge: Louisiana State University Press, 2009.

Bassett, John Spencer. *Slavery in the State of North Carolina*. Baltimore, MD: Johns Hopkins University Press, 1899.

Bay, Mia. *To Tell the Truth Freely: The Life of Ida B. Wells*. New York: Hill and Wang, 2009.

Beckel, Deborah. *Radical Reform: Interracial Politics in Post-Emancipation North Carolina*. Charlottesville: University of Virginia Press, 2011.

Bederman, Gail. *Manliness and Civilization: A Cultural History of Gender and Race in the United States*. Chicago: University of Chicago Press, 1995.

Bentley, George R. *A History of the Freedmen's Bureau*. Philadelphia: University of Pennsylvania Press, 1955.

Bercaw, Nancy. *Gendered Freedoms: Race, Rights, and the Politics of the Household in the Delta, 1861–1875*. Gainesville: University of Florida Press, 2003.

Berkeley, Kathleen. "Colored Ladies Also Contributed: Black Women's Activities from Benevolence to Society Welfare, 1866–1896." In *The Web of Southern Social Relations: Women, Family and Education*, edited by Walter J. Fraser Jr., R. Frank Saunders Jr., and Jon Wakelyn, 181–203. Athens: University of Georgia Press, 1985.

Berlin, Ira. *Many Thousands Gone: The First Two Centuries of Slavery in North America*. Cambridge, MA: Belknap Press of Harvard University Press, 2000.

Berlin, Ira, Steven F. Miller, Joseph P. Reidy, and Leslie S. Rowland, eds. *The Wartime Genesis of Free Labor: The Upper South*. Ser. 1, vol. 2 of *Freedom: A Documentary History of Emancipation, 1861–1867*. New York: Cambridge University Press, 1993.

Berlin, Ira, Joseph Reidy, and Leslie Rowland, eds. *The Black Military Experience*. Ser. 2 of *Freedom: A Documentary History of Emancipation, 1861–1867*. New York: Cambridge University Press, 1982.

Berry, Mary Frances. *My Face Is Black Is True: Callie House and the Struggle for Ex-Slave Reparations*. New York: Knopf, 2005.

Bishir, Catherine. *Crafting Lives: African American Artisans in New Bern, North Carolina, 1770–1900*. Chapel Hill: University of North Carolina Press, 2013.

Blackmon, Douglas A. *Slavery by Another Name: The Re-Enslavement of Black Americans from the Civil War to World War II*. New York: Vintage, 2008.

Blight, David. *Race and Reunion: The Civil War in American Memory*. Cambridge, MA: Harvard University Press, 2000.

Bloomfield, Maxwell. "From Deference to Confrontation: The Early Black Lawyers of Galveston, Texas, 1895–1920." In *The New High Priests: Lawyers in Post Civil War America*, edited by Gerald Gawalt, 151–70. Westport, CT: Greenwood, 1984.

Boris, Eileen. "On the Importance of Naming: Gender, Race, and the Writing of Policy History." *Journal of Policy History* 17, no. 1 (2005): 72–92.

Boris, Eileen. "The Racialized Gender State: Conceptions of Citizenship in the United States." *Social Politics: International Studies in Gender, State, and Society* 2 (1995): 160–80.

Branson North Carolina Business Directory. Raleigh, NC: Branson, 1884.

Brimmer, Brandi. "Black Women's Politics, Narratives of Sexual Immorality, and Pension Bureaucracy in Mary Lee's North Carolina Neighborhood." *Journal of Southern History* 80 (2014): 827–58.

Brimmer, Brandi. "'Her Claim for Pension Is Lawful and Just': Representing Black Union Widows in Late-Nineteenth-Century North Carolina." *Journal of the Civil War Era* 1 (2011): 207–36.

Broadus, Thomas A. "The South and the Pension Bureau." *American Review of Reviews* 23 (1901): 203–7.

Brown, Elsa Barkley. "African-American Women's Quilting: A Framework for Conceptualizing and Teaching African American Women's History." *Signs* 14 (1989): 921–29.

Brown, Elsa Barkley. "Imaging Lynching: African American Women, Communities of Struggle, and Collective Memory." In *African American Women Speak Out on Anita Hill–Clarence Thomas*, edited by Geneva Smitherman, 100–124. Detroit, MI: Wayne State University Press, 1995.

Brown, Elsa Barkley. "Negotiating and Transforming the Public Sphere: African-American Political Life in the Transition from Slavery to Freedom." *Public Culture* 7 (1994): 107–46.

Brown, Elsa Barkley. "'What Has Happened Here': The Politics of Difference in Women's History and Feminist Politics." *Feminist Studies* 18 (1992): 295–312.

Brown, Kathleen. *Good Wives, Nasty Wenches, and Anxious Patriarchs: Gender, Race, and Power in Colonial Virginia*. Chapel Hill: University of North Carolina Press, 1996.

Brown, Leslie. "African American Women and Migration." In *The Practice of U.S. Women's History*, edited by Susan Jay Kleinberg, Eileen Boris, and Vicki L. Ruiz, 201–20. Piscataway, NJ: Rutgers University Press, 2007.

Brown, Leslie. *Upbuilding Black Durham: Gender, Class, and Black Community Development in the Jim Crow South*. Chapel Hill: University of North Carolina Press, 2008.

Browning, Judkin. "Removing the Mask of Nationality: Unionism, Racism, and Federal Military Occupation in North Carolina, 1862–1865." *Journal of Southern History* 71 (2005): 589–620.

Browning, Judkin. *Shifting Loyalties: The Union Occupation of Eastern North Carolina*. Chapel Hill: University of North Carolina Press, 2011.

Business Directory of the City of New Berne, N.C.: To which Is Added Historical and Statistical Matter of Interest. Raleigh, NC: Edwards and Broughton, 1893.

Bynum, Victoria. *Unruly Women: The Politics of Social and Sexual Control in the Old South*. Chapel Hill: University of North Carolina Press, 1992.

Canaday, Margot. "Building a Straight State: Sexuality and Social Citizenship under the 1944 GI Bill." *Journal of American History* 90 (2003): 935–57.

Carawan, Sandra S. "Hyde County's Largest Plantation Owner of 1850 and 1860: John R. Donnell." *High Tides: Hyde County Historical Society Journal*, Spring 2000, 36–41.

Carby, Hazel V. "Policing Black Women's Bodies in the Urban Context." *Critical Inquiry* 18 (1992): 738–55.

Carpenter, John A. *Sword and Olive Branch: Oliver Otis Howard*. New York: Fordham University Press, 1999.

Cecelski, David. *The Fire of Freedom: Abraham Galloway and the Slave's Civil War*. Chapel Hill: University of North Carolina Press, 2012.

Cecelski, David. *The Waterman's Song: Slavery and Freedom in Maritime North Carolina*. Chapel Hill: University of North Carolina Press, 2001.

Chesnutt, Charles W. *The Marrow of Tradition, 1901*. Ann Arbor: University of Michigan Press, 1969.

Clark-Lewis, Elizabeth. *Living In, Living Out: African American Domestics in Washington, D.C., 1910–1940*. Washington, DC: Smithsonian Institution Press, 1994.

Click, Patricia. *Time Full of Trial: The Roanoke Island Freedmen's Colony, 1862–1867*. Chapel Hill: University of North Carolina Press, 2001.

Clinton, Catherine. "Reconstructing Freedwomen." In *Divided Houses: Gender and the Civil War*, edited by Catherine Clinton and Nina Silber, 307–19. New York: Oxford University Press, 1992.

Clinton, Catherine, and Nina Silber, eds. *Divided Houses: Gender and the Civil War*. New York: Oxford University Press, 1992.

Cohen, Cathy. "Deviance as Resistance: A New Research Agenda for the Study of Black Politics." *Du Bois Review* 1 (2004): 27–45.

Collins, Donald E. "Charles Henry Foster: A Unionist in Confederate North Carolina." In *The Human Tradition in the Civil War and Reconstruction*, edited by Stephen Foster, 64–68. Wilmington, DE: Scholarly Resources, 2000.

Collins, Patricia Hill. *Black Feminist Thought: Knowledge, Consciousness, and the Politics of Empowerment*. New York: Routledge, 1991.

Colyer, Vincent. *Report of the Services Rendered by the Freed People to the United States*. New York: Vincent Colyer, 1864.

Cook-Bell, Karen. "Self-Emancipating Women, Civil War, and the Union Army in Southern Louisiana and Low Country Georgia." *Journal of African American History* 101 (2016): 1–21.

Cooper, Abigail. "'Away I Goin' to Find My Mama': Self-Emancipation, Migration, and Kinship in Refugee Camps in the Civil War Era." *Journal of African American History* 102 (2017): 444–67.

Cooper, Brittney C. *Beyond Respectability: The Intellectual Thought of Race Women*. Urbana: University of Illinois Press, 2017.
Cott, Nancy. "Marriage and Women's Citizenship in the United States, 1830–1934." *American Historical Review* 103 (1998): 1440–74.
Cott, Nancy. *Public Vows: A History of Marriage and the Nation*. Cambridge, MA: Harvard University Press, 2000.
Cox-Richardson, Heather. *The Death of Reconstruction: Race, Labor, and Politics in the Post–Civil War North*. Cambridge, MA: Harvard University Press, 2001.
Crocker, Ruth. "'I Only Ask You Kindly to Divide Some of Your Fortune with Me': Begging Letters and the Transformation of Charity in Late Nineteenth-Century America." *Social Politics* 6, no. 2 (1999): 131–60.
Curtis, Frank B., and William H. Webster, comps. *Digest of Laws of the United States Governing the Granting of Army and Navy Pensions and Bounty-Land Warrants; Decisions of the Secretary of the Department of the Interior, and Rulings and Orders of the Commissioner of Pensions Thereunder*. Washington, DC: Government Printing Office, 1885.
Curwood, Anastasia. *Stormy Weather: Middle-Class African American Marriages between the Two World Wars*. Chapel Hill: University of North Carolina Press, 2010.
Dabel, Jane, and Marissa Jenrich. "Co-Opting Respectability: African American Women and Economic Redress in New York City, 1860–1910." *Journal of Urban History* 43 (2015): 312–31.
Dailey, Jane. "Deference and Violence in the Postbellum Urban South: Manners and Massacres in Danville, Virginia." *Journal of Southern History* 63 (1997): 53–90.
Delancy, Dayle B. "Vaccinating Freedom: Smallpox Prevention and the Discourses of African American Citizenship in Antebellum Philadelphia." *Journal of African American History* 95, nos. 3–4 (2010): 296–321.
Dickerson, Dennis. "George A. Rue: Missionary Minister in New England and North Carolina." *AME Church Review* 117 (2001): 46–54.
Downs, Jim. *Sick from Freedom: African American Illness and Suffering during the Civil War and Reconstruction*. New York: Oxford University Press, 2012.
Du Bois, W. E. B. *Black Reconstruction in America: An Essay toward the Part which Black Folk Played in the Attempt to Reconstruct Democracy in America, 1860–1880*. New York: Russell and Russell, 1936.
Du Bois, W. E. B. "Reconstruction and Its Benefits." *American Historical Association* 15 (1910): 781–99.
Du Bois, W. E. B. *The Souls of Black Folk*. Chicago: McClurg, 1903.
Edmonds, Helen G. *The Negro and Fusion Politics in North Carolina, 1894–1901*. Chapel Hill: University of North Carolina Press, 1979.
Edwards, Laura F. "Captives of Wilmington: The Riot and Historical Memories of Political Conflict, 1865–1898." In *Democracy Betrayed: The Wilmington Race Riot of 1898 and its Legacy*, edited by David Cecelski and Timothy Tyson, 113–42. Chapel Hill: University of North Carolina Press, 1998.

Edwards, Laura F. *Gendered Strife and Confusion: The Political Culture of Reconstruction*. Urbana: University of Illinois Press, 1997.
Edwards, Laura F. "'The Marriage Covenant Is at the Foundation of All Our Rights': The Politics of Slave Marriages in North Carolina after Emancipation." *Law and History Review* 14, no. 1 (1996): 81–124.
Edwards, Laura F. "Sexual Violence, Gender, Reconstruction, and the Extension of Patriarchy in Granville County, North Carolina." *North Carolina Historical Review* 68 (1991): 237–60.
Engels, Friedrich. *The Origin of the Family, Private Property, and the State*. Edited by Eleanor Burke Leacock. New York: International Publishers, 1972.
Escott, Paul D. *Many Excellent People: Power and Privilege North Carolina, 1850–1900*. Chapel Hill: University of North Carolina Press, 1985.
Evans, W. McKee. *Ballots and Fence Rails: Reconstruction on the Lower Cape Fear*. Chapel Hill: University of North Carolina Press, 1966.
Farmer, Ashley. "Reframing African American Women's Grassroots Organizing: Audley Moore and the Universal Association of Ethiopian Women, 1957–1963." *Journal of African American History* 101 (2016): 69–96.
Farmer-Kaiser, Mary. *Freedwomen and the Freedmen's Bureau: Race, Gender, and Public Policy in the Age of Emancipation*. New York: Fordham University Press, 2010.
Farnham, Thomas J., and Francis P. King. "'The March of the Destroyer': The New Bern Yellow Fever Epidemic of 1864." *North Carolina Historical Review* 73, no. 4 (October 1996): 435–83.
Faust, Drew Gilpin. *This Republic of Suffering: Death and the American Civil War*. New York: Vintage, 2008.
Feimster, Crystal. "General Benjamin Butler and the Threat of Sexual Violence during the American Civil War." *Daedalus* 138, no. 2 (2009): 126–34.
Feimster, Crystal. "The Impact of Racial and Sexual Politics on Women's History." *Journal of American History* 99 (2012): 822–26.
Feimster, Crystal. *Southern Horrors: Women and the Politics of Rape and Lynching*. Cambridge, MA: Harvard University Press, 2009.
Fields, Barbara J. "Ideology and Race in American History." In *Region, Race, and Reconstruction: Essays in Honor of C. Vann Woodward*, edited by J. Morgan Kousser and James McPherson, 143–77. New York: Oxford University Press, 1982.
Finkelman, Paul, ed. *Encyclopedia of African American History, 1619–1895: From the Colonial Period to the Age of Frederick Douglass*. Vol. 2. New York: Oxford University Press, 2006.
Foner, Eric. *Freedom's Lawmakers: A Directory of Black Officeholders during Reconstruction*. New York: Oxford University Press, 1993.
Foner, Eric. *Give Me Liberty: An American History*. 5th ed. New York: Norton, 2017.
Foner, Eric. *Reconstruction: America's Unfinished Revolution, 1863–1877*. New York: Harper and Row, 1989.

Forbes, Ella. *African American Women during the Civil War*. New York: Garland, 1998.
Foucault, Michel. *The History of Sexuality*. Vol. 1, *An Introduction*. New York: Vintage, 1990.
Franke, Kathrine. "Becoming a Citizen: Reconstruction Era Regulation of African American Marriages." *Yale Journal of Law and Humanities* 11 (1999): 251–309.
Frankel, Noralee. *Freedom's Women: Black Women and Families in Civil War Era Mississippi*. Bloomington: Indiana University Press, 1999.
Franklin, John Hope. *The Free Negro in North Carolina*. Chapel Hill: University of North Carolina Press, 1943.
Fraser, Nancy. "Struggle over Needs: Outline of a Socialist-Feminist Critical Theory of Late Capitalist Political Culture." In *Women, the State, and Welfare*, edited by Linda Gordon, 199–225. Madison: University of Wisconsin Press, 1990.
Fraser, Nancy. *Unruly Practices: Power, Discourse, and Gender in Contemporary Social Theory*. Minneapolis: University of Minnesota Press, 1993.
Fraser, Nancy, and Linda Gordon. "A Genealogy of Dependency: Tracing a Keyword of the U.S. Welfare State." *Signs* 19 (1994): 309–36.
Fuentes, Marisa J. *Dispossessed Lives: Enslaved Women, Violence, and the Archive*. Philadelphia: University of Pennsylvania Press, 2016.
Gaines, Kevin K. *Uplifting the Race: Black Leadership, Politics, and Culture in the Twentieth Century*. Chapel Hill: University of North Carolina Press, 1996.
Gilmore, Glenda Elizabeth. *Gender and Jim Crow: Women and the Politics of White Supremacy in North Carolina, 1896–1920*. Chapel Hill: University of North Carolina Press, 1996.
Gilmore, Glenda E. "Murder, Memory, and the Flight of the Incubus." In *Democracy Betrayed: The Wilmington Race Riot of 1898 and Its Legacy*, edited by David Cecelski and Timothy Tyson, 73–94. Chapel Hill: University of North Carolina Press, 1998.
Glasson, William H. *Federal Military Pensions in the United States*. New York: Oxford University Press, 1918.
Glasson, William H. *History of Military Pension Legislation in the United States*. New York: Columbia University Press, 1900.
Glasson, William H. "The National Pension System as Applied to the Civil War and the War with Spain." *Annals of the American Academy of Political and Social Science* 19 (1902): 40–62.
Glenn, Evelyn Nakano. *Forced to Care: Coercion and Caregiving in America*. Cambridge, MA: Harvard University Press, 2010.
Glenn, Evelyn Nakano, Grace Chang, and Linda Rennie Forcey, eds. *Mothering: Ideology, Experience, and Agency*. New York: Routledge, 1993.
Glymph, Thavolia. "Du Bois's Black Reconstruction and Slave Women's War for Freedom." *South Atlantic Quarterly* 112 (2013): 489–505.
Glymph, Thavolia. "'Invisible Disabilities': Black Women in War and Freedom." *Proceedings of the American Philosophical Society* 160 (2016): 237–46.

Glymph, Thavolia. *Out of the House of Bondage: The Transformation of the Plantation Household*. Cambridge: Cambridge University Press, 2008.

Glymph, Thavolia. "Rose's War and the Gendered Politics of a Slave Insurgency in the Civil War." *Journal of the Civil War Era* 3 (2013): 501–32.

Glymph, Thavolia. *The Women's Fight: The Civil War's Battle for Home, Freedom, and Nation*. Chapel Hill: University of North Carolina Press, 2020.

Goodwin, Joanne L. "'Employable Mothers' and 'Suitable Work': A Re-Evaluation of Welfare and Wage-Earning for Women in the Twentieth-Century United States." *Journal of Social History* 29 (1995): 253–74.

Gordon, Linda. "Black and White Visions of Welfare Reform: Women's Welfare Activism, 1890–1945." *Journal of American History* 78 (1991): 539–50.

Gordon, Linda. "Family Violence, Feminism, and Social Control." *Feminist Studies* 12 (1986): 453–78.

Gordon, Linda. "Gender, State and Society: A Debate with Theda Skocpol." *Contention* 2 (1993): 139–56.

Gordon, Linda. *The Great Arizona Abduction*. Cambridge, MA: Harvard University Press, 1999.

Gordon, Linda. *Heroes of Their Own Lives: The Politics and History of Family Violence*. New York: Viking, 1998.

Gordon, Linda. *Pitied but Not Entitled: Single Mothers and the History of Welfare*. New York: Free Press, 1994.

Gordon, Linda. "Response to Theda Skocpol." *Contention* 2 (1993): 185–89.

Gordon, Linda, ed. *Women, the State, and Welfare*. Madison: University of Wisconsin Press, 1990.

Greenwood, Janette Thomas. *Bittersweet Legacy: The Black and White "Better Classes" in Charlotte, 1850–1910*. Chapel Hill: University of North Carolina Press, 1994.

Greenwood, Janette Thomas. *First Fruits of Freedom: The Migration of Former Slaves and Their Search for Equality in Worchester, Massachusetts, 1862–1900*. Chapel Hill: University of North Carolina Press, 2009.

Gross, Kali N. "African American Women, Mass Incarceration, and the Politics of Protection." *Journal of American History* 102 (June 2015): 25–33.

Gross, Kali N. *Colored Amazons: Crime, Violence, and Black Women in the City of Brotherly Love, 1880–1910*. Durham, NC: Duke University Press, 2006.

Grossberg, Michael. *Governing the Hearth: Law and the Family in Nineteenth-Century America*. Chapel Hill: University of North Carolina Press, 1985.

Gutman, Herbert. *The Black Family in Slavery and Freedom, 1750–1925*. New York: Vintage, 1976.

Hahn, Steven. *A Nation under Our Feet: Black Political Struggles in the Rural South from Slavery to the Great Migration*. Cambridge, MA: Belknap Press of Harvard University Press, 2003.

Hahn, Steven, Steven F. Miller, Susan E. O'Donovan, John C. Rodrigue, and Leslie Rowland, eds. *Land and Labor, 1865*. Ser. 3, vol. 1 of *Freedom: A Documentary*

History of Emancipation, 1861–1867. Chapel Hill: University of North Carolina Press, 2008.

Haines, Zenas. *Letters from the Forty-Fourth Regiment M.V.M.: A Record of the Experience of a Nine Months' Regiment in the Department of North Carolina in 1862–3*. Boston: Herald Job Office, 1863.

Haley, Sarah. *No Mercy Here: Gender, Punishment, and the Making of Jim Crow Modernity*. Chapel Hill: University of North Carolina Press, 2016.

Hall, Jacquelyn Dowd. "Ola Delight Smith's Progressive Era: Labor, Feminism, and Reform in the Urban South." In *Visible Women: New Essays on American Activism*, edited by Nancy A. Hewitt and Suzanne Lebsock, 166–98. Urbana: University of Illinois Press, 1993.

Hamilton, Joseph G. De Roulhac. "The Freedmen's Bureau in North Carolina." *South Atlantic Quarterly* 8 (1909): 53–67, 154–63.

Hannigan, Charles Francis. *New Bern: "The Athens of North Carolina."* New York: Whitehead, 1927.

Harley, Sharon. "For the Good of Family and Race: Gender, Work, and Domestic Roles in the Black Community, 1880–1930." *Signs* 15 (1990): 336–49.

Harris, Cheryl. "Whiteness as Property." *Harvard Law Review* 106 (1993): 1709–91.

Harris, M. Keith. "Slavery, Emancipation, and Veterans of the Union Cause: Commemorating Freedom in the Era of Reconciliation." *Civil War History* 53 (2007): 264–90.

Hartman, Saidiya. *Wayward Lives, Beautiful Experiments: Intimate Histories of Social Upheaval*. New York: Norton, 2019.

Hayden, René, Anthony E. Kaye, Kate Masur, Steven F. Miller, Susan E. O'Donovan, Leslie Rowland, and Stephen A. West. *Land and Labor, 1866–67*. Ser. 3., vol. 2 of *Freedom: A Documentary History of Emancipation, 1861–1867*. Chapel Hill: University of North Carolina Press, 2013.

Heinegg, Paul. *Free African Americans in North Carolina*. 2nd ed. Abqaiq, Saudi Arabia: Heinegg, 1991.

Hickel, K. Walter. "Justice and the Highest Kind of Equality Require Discrimination: Citizenship, Dependency, and Conscription in the South, 1917–1919." *Journal of Southern History* 66 (2000): 749–80.

Hickel, K. Walter. "War, Region, and Social Welfare: Federal Aid to Servicemen's Dependents in the South, 1917–1921." *Journal of American History* 87 (2001): 1362–91.

Hicks, Cheryl. *Talk with You Like a Woman: African American Women, Justice, and Reform in New York, 1890–1935*. Chapel Hill: University of North Carolina Press, 2010.

Higginbotham, Evelyn B. "African-American Women's History and the Metalanguage of Race." *Signs* 17 (1992): 251–74.

Higginbotham, Evelyn B. *Righteous Discontent: The Women's Movement in the Black Baptist Church, 1880–1920*. Cambridge, MA: Harvard University Press, 1993.

Hine, Darlene Clark. "Rape and the Inner Lives of Black Women in the Middle West." *Signs* 14 (1989): 912–20.

Hodes, Martha, ed. *Sex, Love, Race: Crossing Boundaries in North American History*. New York: New York University Press, 1999.

Hodes, Martha. *White Women, Black Men: Illicit Sex in the Nineteenth-Century South*. New Haven, CT: Yale University Press, 1997.

Holder, Anne. "What's Sex Got to Do with It: Race, Power, Citizenship, and 'Intermediate Identities' in the Post-Emancipation South." *Journal of African American History* 93 (2008): 153–73.

Holt, Thomas. "'An Empire over the Mind': Emancipation, Race, and Ideology in the British West Indies and the American South." In *Region, Race, and Reconstruction: Essays in Honor of C. Vann Woodward*, edited by J. Morgan Kousser and James M. McPherson, 283–313. New York: Oxford University Press, 1982.

Hood, James Walker. *One Hundred Years of the African Methodist Episcopal Zion Church; or, The Centennial of African Methodism*. New York: AME Zion Book Concern, 1895.

Hunter, Tera. *Bound in Wedlock: Slave and Free Black Marriage in the Nineteenth Century*. Cambridge, MA: Harvard University Press, 2017.

Hunter, Tera. *To 'Joy My Freedom: Southern Black Women's Lives and Labors after the Civil War*. Cambridge, MA: Harvard University Press, 1997.

Jackson, Ronald Vern. *1890 North Carolina Census Index: Special Schedule of the Eleventh Census (1890) Enumerating Union Veterans and of Union Veterans of the Civil War*. North Salt Lake, UT: Accelerated Indexing Systems, 1984.

James, Horace. *Freedman's Affairs, North Carolina, 1864–5: Annual Report of the Superintendent of Negro Affairs in North Carolina, 1864, with an Appendix Containing the History and Management of the Freedmen in This Department up to June 1st, 1865*. Boston: Brown, 1865.

Johnson, Guion Griffis. *Ante-Bellum North Carolina: A Social History*. Chapel Hill: University of North Carolina Press, 1937.

Jones, Jacqueline. *Labor of Love, Labor of Sorrow: Black Women, Work, and the Family, from Slavery to the Present*. New York: Vintage, 1984.

Jones, Martha. *Birthright Citizens: A History of Race and Rights in Antebellum America*. New York: Cambridge University Press, 2018.

Justesen, Benjamin R. *George Henry White: An Even Chance in the Race of Life*. Baton Rouge: Louisiana State University Press, 2001.

Kaiser, John James. "'Masters Determined to Be Masters': The 1821 Insurrectionary Scare in Eastern North Carolina." Master's thesis, North Carolina State University, 2006.

Katznelson, Ira. *When Affirmative Action Was White: An Untold History of Racial Inequality in Twentieth-Century America*. New York: Norton, 2005.

Kaye, Anthony. *Joining Places: Slave Neighborhoods in the Old South*. Chapel Hill: University of North Carolina Press, 2007.

Kelley, Robin D. G. *Freedom Dreams: The Black Radical Imagination*. New York: Beacon, 2002.

Kelley, Robin D. G. "'We Are Not What We Seem': Rethinking Black Working-Class Opposition in the Jim Crow South." *Journal of American History* 80 (1993): 75–112.

Kenzer, Robert C. "The Uncertainty of Life: A Profile of Virginia's Civil War Widows." In *The War Was You and Me: Civilians in the American Civil War*, edited by Joan E. Cashin, 112–35. Princeton, NJ: Princeton University Press, 2002.

Kerber, Linda K. *No Constitutional Right to Be Ladies: Women and the Obligations of Citizenship*. New York: Hill and Wang, 1998.

Kessler-Harris, Alice. "Designing Women and Old Fools: The Construction of the Social Security Amendments of 1939." In *U.S. History as Women's History: New Feminist Essays*, edited by Linda K. Kerber, Alice Kessler-Harris, and Kathryn Kish Sklar, 87–106. Chapel Hill: University of North Carolina Press, 1995.

Kessler-Harris, Alice. *In Pursuit of Equity: Women, Men, and the Quest for Economic Citizenship in 20th-Century America*. New York: Oxford University Press, 2001.

Kornbluh, Felicia Ann. *The Battle for Welfare Rights*. Philadelphia: University of Pennsylvania Press, 2007.

Kornbluh, Felicia Ann. "To Fulfill Their 'Rightly Needs': Consumerism and the National Welfare Rights Movement." *Radical History Review* 69 (1997): 76–113.

Kretz, Dale. "Pensions and Protest: Former Slaves and the Reconstructed American State." *Journal of the Civil War Era* 7 (2017): 425–45.

Krowl, Michelle A. "African American Women and the United States Military in Civil War Virginia." In *Afro-Virginian History and Culture*, edited by John Saillant, 173–210. New York: Garland, 1999.

Lebsock, Suzanne. *The Free Women of Petersburg: Status and Culture in a Southern Town, 1784–1860*. New York: Norton, 1985.

Lee, Chana Kai. *For Freedom's Sake: The Life of Fannie Lou Hamer*. Urbana: University of Illinois Press, 1999.

LeFlouria, Talitha. *Chained in Silence: Black Women and Convict Labor in the New South*. Chapel Hill: University of North Carolina Press, 2015.

Lemke-Santangelo, Gretchen. *Abiding Courage: African American Migrant Women and the East Bay*. Chapel Hill: University of North Carolina Press, 1996.

Levenstein, Lisa. *A Movement without Marches: African American Women and the Politics of Poverty in Postwar Philadelphia*. Chapel Hill: University of North Carolina Press, 2009.

Lindsey, Treva B. *Colored No More: Reinventing Black Womanhood in Washington, D.C.* Urbana: University of Illinois Press, 2017.

Litwack, Leon. *Been in the Storm So Long: The Aftermath of Slavery*. New York: Knopf, 1979.

Logan, Frenise A. *The Negro in North Carolina, 1876–1894*. Chapel Hill: University of North Carolina Press, 1964.

Logan, Rayford. *The Betrayal of the Negro: From Rutherford B. Hayes to Woodrow Wilson*. New York: Collier, 1965.

Long, Gretchen. *Doctoring Freedom: The Politics of African American Medical Care in Slavery and Emancipation*. Chapel Hill: University of North Carolina Press, 2012.

Lowry, Thomas. *Sexual Misbehavior in the Civil War: A Compendium*. Bloomington, IN: Xlibris, 2006.

Magdol, Edward. *A Right to the Land: Essays on the Freedmen's Community*. Westport, CT: Greenwood, 1977.

Manning, Chandra. *Troubled Refuge: Struggling for Freedom in the Civil War*. New York: Knopf, 2016.

Martin, Jonathan. "Craven County (1705)." *North Carolina History Project*. Raleigh, NC: John Locke Foundation, 2016. http://northcarolinahistory.org/encyclopedia/craven-county-1705/.

Martin, Michael T., and Marilyn Yaquinto, eds. *Redress for Historical Injustices in the United States: On Reparations for Slavery, Jim Crow, and Their Legacies*. Durham, NC: Duke University Press, 2007.

Masur, Kate. "'A Rare Phenomenon of Philological Vegetation': The Word 'Contraband' and the Meanings of Emancipation in the United States." *Journal of American History* 93 (2007): 1050–84.

McClintock, Megan. "Binding Up the Nation's Wounds: Nationalism, Civil War Pensions, and American Families, 1861–1890." Ph.D. diss., Rutgers University, 1994.

McClintock, Megan. "Civil War Pensions and the Reconstruction of Union Families." *Journal of American History* 83 (1996): 456–80.

McClintock, Megan. "The Impact of the Civil War on 19th Century Marriages." In *Union Soldiers and the Northern Homefront: Wartime Experiences, Postwar Adjustments*, edited by Paul Cimbala and Randall M. Miller, 395–416. New York: Fordham University Press, 2002.

McCrady, Edward, Jr., and Samuel Ashe. *Cyclopedia of Eminent and Representative Men of the Carolinas*. Vol. 2. Madison, WI: Brant and Fuller, 1892.

McCurry, Stephanie. *Confederate Reckoning: Power and Politics in the Civil War South*. Cambridge, MA: Harvard University Press, 2010.

McGuire, Danielle. *At the Dark End of the Street: Black Women, Rape, and Resistance—A New History of the Civil Rights Movement from Rosa Parks to the Rise of Black Power*. New York: Vintage Books, 2010.

Mills, Quincy T. *Cutting across the Color Line: Black Barbers and Barber Shops in America*. Philadelphia: University of Pennsylvania Press, 2013.

Mink, Gwendolyn. "The Lady and the Tramp: Gender, Race, and the Origins of the American Welfare State." In *Women, the State, and Welfare*, edited by Linda Gordon, 92–122. Madison: University of Wisconsin Press, 1990.

Mink, Gwendolyn. *The Wages of Motherhood: Inequality in the Welfare State, 1917–1942*. Ithaca, NY: Cornell University Press, 1995.

Mitchell, Michelle. "Silences Broken, Silences Kept: Gender and Sexuality in African American History." *Gender and History* 11, no. 3 (1999): 433–44.

Mobley, Joe A. *James City: A Black Community in North Carolina, 1863–1900*. Raleigh: North Carolina State Archives, 1981.

Morrison, Toni, ed. *Racing Justice, Engendering Power: Essays on Anita Hill, Clarence Thomas, and the Construction of Social Reality*. New York: Pantheon, 1992.

New Bern, N.C. Directory, 1880 and 1881. Richmond, VA: Hill Directory Company, 1881.

New England Freedmen's Aid Society. *Second Annual Report of the New England Freedmen's Aid Society*. Boston: New England Freedmen's Aid Society, 1864.

North Carolina. *Journal of the House of Representatives of the General Assembly of the State of North Carolina, at Its Session of 1870–71*. Raleigh, NC: Moore, 1871.

North Carolina. *Public Laws of the State of North Carolina, Passed by the General Assembly at the Sessions of 1866 '67*. Raleigh, NC: Pell, 1867.

North Carolina. *Revised Code of North Carolina, Enacted by the General Assembly at the Session of 1854; Together with Other Acts of Public and General Nature, Passed at the Same Session*. Boston: Little, Brown, 1855.

North Carolina, Constitutional Convention. *Executive Documents: Convention, Session 1865: Constitution of North Carolina, with Amendments, and Ordinances and Resolutions Passed by the Convention, Session, 1865*. Raleigh, NC: Cannon and Holden, 1865.

Norwood, Arlisha. "Single Women without Men: Single African-American Women in Civil War and Post Civil War Virginia." Ph.D. diss., Howard University, 2019.

O'Brien, Gail Williams. *The Color of the Law: Race, Violence, and Justice in the Post–World War II South*. Chapel Hill: University of North Carolina Press, 1999.

O'Donovan, Susan. *Becoming Free in the Cotton South*. Cambridge, MA: Harvard University Press, 2007.

O'Leary, Cecilia Elizabeth. *To Die For: The Paradox of American Patriotism*. Princeton, NJ: Princeton University Press, 1999.

Oliver, John William. *History of the Civil War Military Pensions, 1861–1885*. Madison: University of Wisconsin Press, 1917.

Orleck, Annelise. *Storming Caesar's Palace: How Black Mothers Fought Their Own War on Poverty*. Boston: Beacon, 2006.

Outland, Robert B., III. "Slavery, Work, and Geography of North Carolina Naval Stores Industry, 1835–1860." *Journal of Southern History* 62 (1996): 27–56.

Parramore, T. C. "Foster, Charles Henry." In *Dictionary of North Carolina Biography*, edited by William S. Powell, 2:227. Chapel Hill: University of North Carolina Press, 2000.

Patterson Green, John. *Fact Stranger than Fiction: Seventy-Five Years of a Busy Life with Reminiscences of Many Great and Good Men and Women*. Cleveland, OH: Riehl, 1920.

Penningroth, Dylan C. *The Claims of Kinfolk: African American Property and Community in the Nineteenth-Century South*. Chapel Hill: University of North Carolina Press, 2003.

Plant, Rebecca Jo, and Frances M. Clarke. "'The Crowning Insult': Federal Segregation and the Gold Star Mother and Widow Pilgrimages of the Early 1930s." *Journal of American History* 102 (2015): 406–32.

Prather, H. Leon. *We Have Taken a City: Wilmington Racial Massacre and Coup of 1898*. Cranbury, NJ: Associated University Presses, 1984.
Quadagno, Jill. *The Color of Welfare: How Racism Undermined the War on Poverty*. New York: Oxford University Press, 1994.
Quarles, Benjamin. *The Negro in the Civil War*. Introduction by William McFeely. Cambridge, MA: Da Capo, 1989.
Randolph, Sherie M. "Evelyn Brooks Higginbotham, the Metalanguage of Race, and the Genealogy of Black Feminist Legal Theory." *Signs* 42 (2017): 621–28.
Randolph, Thomas P., and Edward Hall, comps. *The Pension Attorney's Guide: A Ready Reference to the Laws of States Relating to Pensions, the Standard Decisions upon All Matters*. Washington, DC: Sheiry, 1892.
Redkey, Edwin S., ed. *A Grand Army of Black Men: Letters from African American Soldiers in the Union Army, 1861–1865*. New York: Cambridge University Press, 1992.
Regosin, Elizabeth A. *Freedom's Promise: Ex-Slave Families and Citizenship in the Age of Emancipation*. Charlottesville: University Press of Virginia, 2002.
Regosin, Elizabeth A., and Donald Shaffer, eds. *Voices of Emancipation: Understanding Slavery, the Civil War, and Reconstruction through the U.S. Pension Bureau Files*. New York: New York University Press, 2008.
Reid, George W. "Four in Black: North Carolina's Black Congressmen, 1874–1901." *Journal of Negro History* 64 (1979): 229–43.
Reid, Richard. *Freedom for Themselves: North Carolina's Black Soldiers in the Civil War Era*. Chapel Hill: University of North Carolina Press, 2008.
Reid, Richard. "Government Policy, Prejudice, and the Experience of Black Civil War Soldiers and Their Families." *Journal of Family History* 27 (2002): 374–98.
Reid, Richard. "Raising the African Brigade: Early Black Recruitment in Civil War North Carolina." *North Carolina Historical Review* 70 (1993): 266–301.
Reiff, Janice L., Michel R. Dahlin, and Daniel Scott Smith. "Rural Push and Urban Pull: Work and Family Experiences of Older Black Women in Southern Cities, 1880–1900." *Journal of Social History* 16 (1983): 39–48.
Roberts, Dorothy. *Killing the Black Body: Race, Reproduction, and the Meaning of Liberty*. New York: Pantheon, 1997.
Robinson, Armstead L. "Plans Dat Comed from God: Institution Building and the Emergence of Black Leadership in Reconstruction Memphis." In *Toward a New South? Studies in Post–Civil War Southern Communities*, edited by Orville Vernon Burton and Robert C. McMath Jr., 71–102. Westport, CT: Greenwood, 1982.
Rodrigue, John C. "Black Agency after Slavery." In *Reconstructions: New Perspectives on the Postbellum United States*, edited by Thomas Brown, 40–65. New York: Oxford University Press, 2006.
Romeo, Sharon. *Gender and Jubilee: Black Freedom and the Reconstruction of Citizenship in Civil War Missouri*. Athens: University of Georgia Press, 2016.
Rose, Nancy E. "Gender, Race, and the Welfare State: Government Work Programs from the 1930s to the Present." *Feminist Studies* 19 (1993): 318–42.

Rosen, Hannah. "'Not that Sort of Woman': Race, Gender, and Sexual Violence in the Memphis Riots of 1866." In *Sex, Love, Race: Crossing Boundaries in North American History*, edited by Martha Hodes, 267–93. New York: New York University Press, 1999.

Rosen, Hannah. *Terror in the Heart of Freedom: Citizenship, Sexual Violence, and the Meaning of Race in the Postemancipation South*. Chapel Hill: University of North Carolina Press, 2008.

Rothman, Joshua D. *Notorious in the Neighborhood: Sex and Families across the Color Line in Virginia, 1787–1861*. Chapel Hill: University of North Carolina Press, 2003.

Sapiro, Virginia. "The Gender Basis of American Social Policy." In *Women, the State, and Welfare*, edited by Linda Gordon, 36–54. Madison: University of Wisconsin Press, 1990.

Scarborough, William Kauffman. *Masters of the Big House: Elite Slaveholders of the Mid-Nineteenth-Century South*. Baton Rouge: Louisiana State University Press, 2003.

Schecter, Patricia A. "'All the Intensity of My Nature': Ida B. Wells, Anger, and Politics." *Radical History Review* 70 (1998): 48–77.

Schultz, Jane E. "Race, Gender, and Bureaucracy: Civil War Army Nurses and the Pension Bureau." *Journal of Women's History* 6 (1994): 45–69.

Schwalm, Leslie. *A Hard Fight for We: Women's Transitions from Slavery to Freedom in South Carolina*. Urbana: University of Illinois Press, 1997.

Schwartzberg, Beverly. "'Lots of Them Did That': Desertion, Bigamy, and Marital Fluidity in Late-Nineteenth-Century America." *Journal of Social History* 37 (2004): 573–600.

Schweninger, Loren. "Black-Owned Businesses in the South, 1790–1880." *Business History Review* 63 (1989): 22–60.

Schweninger, Loren. "John Carruthers Stanly and the Anomaly of Black Slaveholding." *North Carolina Historical Review* 67 (1990): 159–92.

Schweninger, Loren. "Property Owning Free African-American Women in the South, 1800–1870." *Journal of Women's History* 1 (1990): 13–44.

Scott, Rebecca J. "The Battle over the Child: Child Apprenticeship and the Freedman's Bureau in North Carolina." *Prologue* 10 (1978): 101–13.

Sefton, James. *The United States Army and Reconstruction, 1865–1877*. Baton Rouge: Louisiana State University Press, 1967.

Shaffer, Donald. *After the Glory: The Struggles of Black Civil War Veterans*. Lawrence: University Press of Kansas, 2004.

Shaffer, Donald. "'I Do Not Suppose that Uncle Sam Looks at the Skin': African Americans and the Civil War Pension System, 1865–1934." *Civil War History* 46 (2000): 132–47.

Shaw, Stephanie. "Black Club Women and the Creation of the National Association of Colored Women." *Journal of Women's History* 3 (1991): 10–25.

Shotwell, R. A. *New Bern Mercantile and Manufacturer's Business Directory and North Carolina Farmers Reference Book*. New Bern, NC: W. E. Vestal, 1866.

Silkenat, David. *Driven from Home: North Carolina's Civil War Refugee Crisis*. Athens: University of Georgia Press, 2016.

Simpson, Brooks D., LeRoy P. Graf, and John Muldowny eds. *Advice after Appomattox: Letters to Andrew Johnson, 1865–1866*. Knoxville: University of Tennessee Press, 1987.

Sims, Anastatia. *The Power of Femininity in the New South*. Columbia: University of South Carolina Press, 1997.

Singleton, William Henry. *Recollection of the Slavery Days*. Introduction and annotations by Katherine Mellen Charron and David Cecelski. Chapel Hill: University of North Carolina Press, 2007.

Skocpol, Theda. "America's First Social Security System: The Expansion of Benefits for Civil War Veterans." *Political Science Quarterly* 108 (1993): 85–116.

Skocpol, Theda. *Protecting Soldiers and Mothers: The Political Origins of Social Policy in the United States*. Cambridge, MA: Harvard University Press, 1992.

Slap, Andrew L. "'No Regular Marriage': African American Veterans and Marriage Practices during Reconstruction." In *This Distracted and Anarchical People: New Answers for Old Questions about the Civil War Era North*, edited by Andrew L. Slap and Michael T. Smith, 171–83. New York: Fordham University Press, 2013.

Smith, Jessie Carnie, ed. *Encyclopedia of African American Popular Culture*. Vols. 1–4. Westport, CT: Greenwood, 2011.

Smith, Suzanne E., *To Serve the Living: Funeral Directors and the African American Way of Death*. Cambridge, MA: Harvard University Press, 2010.

Sommerville, Dianne. "The Rape Myth in the Old South Reconsidered." *Journal of Southern History* 61 (1995): 481–518.

Stanley, Amy Dru. "Conjugal Bonds and Wage Labor: Rights of Contract in the Age of Emancipation." *Journal of American History* 75 (1988): 471–500.

Stansell, Christine. *City of Women: Sex and Class in New York, 1789–1860*. New York: Knopf, 1986.

Stevenson, Brenda. *Life in Black and White: Family and Community in the Slave South*. New York: Oxford University Press, 1996.

Stevenson, Brenda. "What's Love Got to Do with It?: Concubinage and Enslaved Black Women and Girls in the Antebellum South." *Journal of African American History* 98 (2013): 99–124.

Stoler, Ann Laura. *Carnal Knowledge and Imperial Power: Race and the Intimate Colonial Rule*. Berkeley: University of California Press, 2010.

Stowell, Daniel W. *Rebuilding Zion: The Religious Reconstruction of the South*. New York: Oxford University Press, 1998.

Taylor, Amy Murrell. *Embattled Freedom: Journeys through the Civil War's Slave Refugee Camps*. Chapel Hill: University of North Carolina Press, 2018.

Taylor, Keenga-Yamahtta. *From #BlackLivesMatter to Black Liberation*. Chicago: Haymarket Books, 2016.

Taylor, Susie King. *Reminiscences of My Life in Camp: An African American Woman's Civil War Memoir*. Introduction by Catherine Clinton. Athens: University of Georgia Press, 2006.

Thompson, E. P. *The Making of the English Working Class*. New York: Vintage, 1990.
Turner's North Carolina Almanac. Raleigh, NC: Edwards and Broughton, 1873.
U.S. Congress. *Report of the Joint Committee on Reconstruction*. 39th Cong., 1st sess., 1865–66. House Report no. 30. Washington, DC: Government Printing Office, 1866.
U.S. Congress. House. *House Documents, Otherwise Publ. as Executive Documents: 13th Congress, 2nd Session–49th Congress, 1st Session*. U.S. Congressional Serials Set. Washington, DC: Government Printing Office, 1871.
U.S. Department of the Interior. *Annual Report of the Commissioner of Pensions to the Secretary of the Interior, for the Fiscal Year Ended June 30, 1898*. Washington DC: Government Printing Office, 1898.
U.S. Department of the Interior. *Annual Reports of the Department of the Interior for the Fiscal Year Ended June 30, 1901*. Washington, DC: Government Printing Office, 1901.
U.S. Department of the Interior. *Annual Reports of the Department of the Interior for the Fiscal Year Ended June 30, 1910*. Vol. 1. Washington, DC: Government Printing Office, 1911.
U.S. Department of the Interior. *Decisions of the Department of the Interior, Pensions and Bounty-Land Claims, 1887–1930*. 22 vols. Washington, DC: Government Printing Office, n.d.
U.S. Department of the Interior. *Laws of the United States Governing the Granting of Army and Navy Pensions Together with Regulations Relating Thereto*. Washington, DC: Government Printing Office, 1916.
U.S. Pension Bureau. *Annual Report of the Commissioner of Pensions to the Secretary of the Interior, for the Fiscal Year Ended June 30, 1898*. Washington, DC: Government Printing Office, 1898.
U.S. Pension Bureau. *General Instructions to Special Examiners of the United States Pension Office, August 16, 1881*. Washington, DC: Government Printing Office, 1881.
U.S. Pension Bureau. *List of Pensioners on the Roll January 1, 1883; Giving the Names of Each Pensioner, the Cause for Which Pensioned, the Post-Office Address, the Rate of Pension per Month, and the Date of Original Allowance, as Called for by Senate Resolution of December 8, 1882*. 1883. Baltimore, MD: Genealogical Publishing, 1970.
U.S. Pension Bureau. *A Treatise on the Practice of the Pension Bureau, Governing the Adjudication of Army and Navy Pensions: Being the Unwritten Practice Formulated by Calvin B. Walker*. Washington, DC: Government Printing Office, 1882.
U.S. War Department. *The War of the Rebellion: A Compilation of the Official Records of the Union and Confederate Armies*. 128 vols. Washington, DC: Government Printing Office, 1880–1901.
Vass, Lachlan Cumming. *History of the Presbyterian Church in New Bern, N.C., with a Resumé of Early Ecclesiastical Affairs in Eastern North Carolina and a Sketch of the Early Days of New Bern, N.C.* Richmond, VA: Whittet and Shepperson, 1886.

Vinovskis, Maris, ed. *Toward a Social History of the American Civil War: Exploratory Essays*. Cambridge: Cambridge University Press, 1990.
Vogel, Jeffrey E. "Redefining Reconciliation: Confederate Veterans and the Southern Reponses to Federal Civil War Pensions." *Civil War History* 51 (2005): 67–93.
Walbert, David. "Distribution of Land and Slaves." In *Antebellum North Carolina*, North Carolina Digital History. Chapel Hill: Learn NC, University of North Carolina, 2009. http://www.learnnc.org/lp/editions/nchist-antebellum/5347.
Walker, Juliet E. K. *The History of Black Business in America: Capitalism, Race, Entrepreneurship*. Chapel Hill: University of North Carolina Press, 2009.
Walkowitz, Judith R. *City of Dreadful Delight: Narratives of Sexual Danger in Late Victorian London*. Chicago: University of Chicago Press, 1992.
Watson, Alan. *History of New Bern and Craven County*. New Bern, NC: Tryon Palace Commission, 1987.
Watson, Irving A., ed. and comp. *Physicians and Surgeons of America*. Concord, NH: Republican Press Association, 1896.
Weber, Gustavus Adolphus. *The Bureau of Pensions: Its History, Activities and Organization*. Baltimore, MD: Johns Hopkins University Press, 1923.
Welke, Barbara Y. "When All Women Were White, and All Blacks Were Men: Gender, Class, Race, and the Road to Plessy, 1855–1914." *Law and History Review* 13 (1995): 261–316.
White, Deborah Gray. *Arn't I A Woman: Female Slaves in the Plantation South*. New York: Norton, 2011.
White, Deborah Gray. "Mining the Forgotten: Manuscript Sources for Black Women's History." *Journal of American History* 74 (1987): 237–42.
White, George H. *Defense of the Negro Race—Charges Answered: Speech of Hon. George H. White, of North Carolina, in the House of Representatives, January 29, 1901*. Washington, DC: Government Printing Office, 1901.
Whitted, Rev. J. A. *A History of Negro Baptist in Eastern North Carolina*. Raleigh, NC: Edwards and Broughton, 1908.
Williams, Heather. *Help Me Find My People: The African American Search for Family Lost in Slavery*. Chapel Hill: University of North Carolina Press, 2012.
Williams, Heather. *Self-Taught: African American Education in Slavery and Freedom*. Chapel Hill: University of North Carolina Press, 2007.
Williams, Linda. *Constraint of Race: Legacies of White Skin Privilege in America*. University Park: Pennsylvania State University Press, 2004.
Wilson, James Grant, and John Fiske. *Appleton's Cyclopaedia of American Biography*. 6 vols. New York: Appleton, 1900.
Wolfram, Walt, and Erik Thomas. *The Development of African American English*. Hoboken, NJ: Wiley-Blackwell, 2002.
Wood, Kirsten. *Masterful Women: Slaveholding Widows from the American Revolution through the Civil War*. Chapel Hill: University of North Carolina Press, 2004.

Woodward, C Vann. *The Strange Career of Jim Crow.* 3rd rev. ed. New York: Oxford University Press, 1974.
Works Projects Administration. *Slave Narratives: A Folk History of Slavery in the United States from Interviews with Former Slaves.* Vol. 11, part 2. Washington, DC: Library of Congress, 1941.
Wright, Richard. *Black Boy: A Recollection of Childhood and Youth.* New York: Harper and Row, 1945.
Zipf, Karin. *Labor of Innocents: Forced Apprenticeship in North Carolina, 1715–1919.* Baton Rouge: Louisiana State University Press, 2005.
Zipf, Karin. "Promises of Opportunity: The Freedmen's Savings and Trust Company Bank in New Bern, North Carolina." Master's thesis, University of Georgia, 1994.

Index

Page numbers in italics indicate figures.

Act of July 14, 1862, general law pension system, 9, 61. *See also* general law pension system
Act of June 6, 1866, 9, 18, 62–63, 65, 77, 259n15
Act of July 27, 1868, 238n123
Act of June 15, 1873, 65
Act of August 7, 1882: children's pensions under, 127, 156, 172; claims under, 19, 69–70, 124, 129; and cohabitation/remarriage, 100, 145, 163–68, 173, 178–79, 181, 183; fraud investigations, 184, 268n3; Latham and, 194; Lee and, 195; Little and, 197; Powers and, 135, 137–38, 140, 169, 171; Rodman and, 193; and slave marriage, 145; widows and, 128, 182–83, 188–89
Act of March 3, 1899, 66, 160, 263n79
Act of March 3, 1901, pension restoration, 64, 155, 201, 261n58, 273n81
African Methodist Episcopal Zion (AMEZ) Church, 51, 105; Andrew Chapel, 109; Clinton Chapel, 59, 68, 79, 113–14; New Bern, 46; Piney Grove AMEZ Church, 103; St. Peter's AMEZ Church, 109
Alexander, Roberta Sue, 58
Alexander, Sophia and Spencer, 51–52, 57, 191, 195–97, 203, 268n3
American Missionary Society, 58
Anders, Israel, 60, 103
Anderson, Edith, 176
apprenticeship, 247n31; children and, 28; in North Carolina, 57–58, 77, 85, 107–8, 135, 235n84, 236nn86–87; slavery and, 239n1
Archibald, Gracy, 103
Arnell, S. M., 130
Arrears Act (1879), 66, 125, 151, 238n125, 243n53
Askew, Elsia and Isaac, 148–49, 225n87
Aycock, Charles B., 174, 186
Aycock, W. F., 131

Bailey, Alfred, 133
banking, 58–59
Banks, Caesar, 77, 89, 151–52, 200–201
Banks, Charlotte, 5, 43, *90*; appeals by, 150–51, 201, 260n38, 272n74; economic survival, 154–55, 162, 205; and marriage, 86, 88–89, 101, 150–52, 161, 200, 239n3, 242n49; in New Bern, 6, 40, 50, 79, *118*; and pension benefits, 4, 16, 19, 77–78, 91, 94–95, 145, 204, 215
Banks, Eliza and Jacob, 96–97, 238n128
barbers, 242n42
Barfield, David, 196
Barlow, Harriet, 43, 260n41
Bates, Henry G., 52, 114, 141–42, 192, 251n82
Beaufort, 24, 29–31, 45
Beecher, James, 41
Bell, James, 110, 170–71
Bell, Nancy Ann, 160
Bentley, James A., 96, 125
Bercaw, Nancy, 47, 119
Berlin, Ira, 62
Bickford, Nathan, 174–75, 265n46
Biddle, William P., and Biddle plantation, 26, 56, 222n31
Biggs, Herman, 30
Biggs, York and Maria (mother), 44, 88
Bishir, Catherine, 25
Bishop, Elsie, 191
Black Codes, 85–86, 247n40
Blackley, Ann, 91–92, 98, 239n3
Black Reconstruction (Du Bois), 2

black soldiers: enlistment and recruitment, 35–39, 226nn93–94, 228n117; Fort Pillow massacre, 9, 61; numbers, 225n86; support for families, 44; as veterans, 53–56, 59–60, 66; widows of, 9, 56–57, 61–64, 108–9, 191–92, 220n50; wives of, 39–42, 66, 104–6. *See also* U.S. Colored Troops (USCT)
Blackwell, Judy, 37
Blango, Giles, 179
Boris, Eileen, 11
Boyd, Ambrose, 135
Boyd, Harriet, 150
Boyd, Peter and Annie, 103–4
Bragg, Mary and Henry, 147
Bray, Nicholas, 224n69
Brown, Caroline, 202, 268n3, 273n88
Brown, Charrity, 163, 172, 193, 202, 208, 263n5, 265n46
Brown, Easter, 39, 44, 85, 156, 227n108, 261–62n62
Brown, Elsa Barkley, 6, 183
Browning, Judkin, 29
Bryan, James Christopher, 112, 249n66
Bryant, Fannie, 157–59
Bureau of Refugees, Freedmen, and Abandoned Lands. *See* Freedmen's Bureau
Burney, Larry and Lana, 104, 121–22, 150
Burnside, Ambrose E., 30
Bussey, Cyrus, 2, 140
Butler, Benjamin F., 30, 36, 42, 223n54
Butler, Caroline, 146

Caphart, Charlotte. *See* Banks, Charlotte
Carpenter, Edward W.: Biggs and, 88; as claims agent, 37, 52, 67, 82–83, 185; criminal investigation of, 65, 68, 97–98, 141–42, 175, 184, 190, 266n54; Douglass and, 102, 111, 114; interracial relationship, 177, 258n90; Marshall and, 116; Oxly and, 53, 82, 130; as pension attorney, 79, 81; Powers and, 106; Proctor and, 87, 93; rape defense, 81, 240n6; suspension of, 99, 110; Whitely and, 117
Carpenter, Seth, 67, 81–82, 240n11
Cartwright, Charlotte. *See* Banks, Charlotte
Cecelski, David, 39
Charlotte News and Observer, 176
Cheatham, Henry P., 71, 176
Chicago Tribune, 68, 124
children: Aid to Dependent Children, 208, 210–11, 274n9; mothers' pensions, 208; pension benefits of, 172; poor black women's views of, 57. *See also* apprenticeship
Chip, Rodney, 130
churches and religion, 59, 89, 258n89. *See also* African Methodist Episcopal Zion (AMEZ) Church
citizenship: black disfranchisement, 19, 59, 71–72, 174, 184–85, 192–93, 199; colored conventions, 46, 231nn3–4; *Dred Scott v. Sandford* (1857), 13; entitlement to benefits, 2, 12; Joint Select Committee on Klan Violence, 13; pension appeals, 197–98, 206; Radical Mass Meeting, 47; Union widowhood and, 1; voting rights, 47, 219n45, 231n4, 231n7
Civil Rights Act of 1875, 69, 124
Civil Rights Cases of 1883, 69
claims agents, 254n21; black, 72, 82–83, 101–2, 115, 124–25, 141, 172, 218n15; and fraud and exploitation, 97–99, 124–25, 253n2; misconduct by, 72, 141, 172, 191–92; role of, 6–7, 68–69, 78, 218n16; white, 67, 83
Clark, Amelia, 89
Clark, David, 91
Clark, Isabella, 97
Clarke, Frances M., 210
class and racial tensions, 35, 193–94
Click, Patricia, 50
Cole, John, 131
Coleman, Eda and Isaac, 129, 241n25
Coleman, Phillip, 82
Colored Ladies' Relief Association, 38–39, 227n102
Colyer, Vincent, 30, 34, 223n55, 224n69
Conega, Edward and Tena, 65
Confiscation Acts of 1861 and 1862, 35, 38
contraband of war, 30, 32, 34, 223n54
Cooper, Abigail, 50
Copes, Sarah, 28–29, 108, 223n44
Cotton, Ann M., 131
Cotton, Lawrence, 194
Council, Harriet, 208
Counts, Maria, 121, 253n110
Counts (Simmons), Mary and Caesar, 93–94, 97, 128–29, 244n70
Cox, Charles, 116
Cox, Christopher C., 64
Cradle, Rebecca Ann, 39, 81, 240n7
Craven County: elections in, 47, 59, 71, 99, 184. *See also* New Bern
Crocker, Lucy and Henry, 41
Cuthrell, Celia, 81, 84, 190, 240n9

Davis, Henry G., 127
Davis, Webster, 176
DeCree, Mary Ann, 153
Democratic Party, 29, 70, 101; and black disfranchisement, 72, 184, 199; and pension agents, 174, 175; and white supremacy, 175–76, 188, 190
Dempsey, Elizabeth, 37, 43
Dependent Pension Law of 1890, 9–10, 19, 66, 121–22, 144–47, 149, 153, 159–61
Dickerson, Isaiah H., 214
disease: black women's nursing skills, 42–43; pension denials and, 138–39; yellow fever, 42
domestic violence. *See* intimate partner violence
Donald, Gatsey, 239n3
Donnell, John R., and Donnell plantation, 25, 27, 37, 50, 95, 221n16
Donnell ex-slave community, 34–35, 41
Douglass, Charlotte (Bryant), 114
Douglass, Frederick (abolitionist leader), 35
Douglass, Frederick C. (claims agent), 17, 112–14, 117, 249–50n73, 250–51n81, 251n86; Banks and, 150–51; Bryant and, 158; Carpenter and, 110–11, 114, 190; as claims agent, 16, 68, 114, 116, 121–22, 155; Gallion and, 138, 172–73, 265nn37–38; Gardner and, 157; Gatlin and, 199; investigations of, 72, 141, 165, 183–84, 188, 197, 250n79, 257n80; Lee and, 115; and licensure, 174–77, 185–86, 266n54, 268n85; Marshall and, 116; Powers and, 102, 134–35, 138–40; Wendly and, 120, 191–92
Douglass, Mamie, 114, 176, 250–51n81
Dove, Mary Elizabeth, 28
Dred Scott v. Sandford (1857), 13
Drew, William T., 65
Du Bois, W. E. B., 2, 5, 209
Dudley, Margaret, 87, 89, 91, 203
Dudley, William W., 125–26
Duggins, Harriet, 53, 193, 199, 233n42, 270n37
Dunkin, Joseph, 119
Dunn, Isaac B., 141–42, 188

education and schools, 58, 236n89
Edwards, Laura F., 62, 85, 237n110, 254n22, 255n27
Ellison, Harriet and Mathew, 152
Emancipation Proclamation, 35–36, 40
enslaved people, 18, 26–29, 112, 148, 222n. *See also* slave marriage
Evans, H. Clay, 178–79, 181, 186, 188, 193
Ex-Slave Mutual Relief, Bounty and Pension Association, 214

Farnham, Thomas J., 42
Feimster, Crystal, 190, 227n109
Flowers, James, 38
Flowers, Presilla, 148
Foner, Eric, 5
Fonville, Fanny. *See* Whitney, Fanny
Fonville, William F., 176
Fosgate, Rosanna, 121–22, 239n3
Foster, Charles Henry, 79
Foster, John G., 224n73
Fourteenth Amendment, 2, 12, 124
Foy, Dinah, 188
Foy, Enoch, and family, 26
Foy, Julia Ann, 26, 32, 83, 87, 92, 121, 203, 273n84
Foy, Nelson, 92
Foy, William, 32
Frankel, Noralee, 3, 85
Franklin, Mary, 131, 268n3
Fraser, Nancy, 14
Freedmen's Bureau, 2; and apprenticeship, 236nn86–87; and claims 65–66, 238n128; closure of, 99, 121; Hassell and, 58; and marriage, 3, 85; and mothers, 137; in North Carolina, 44, 47–51, 231n13
Freedmen's Savings and Trust Company Bank, 58
Fulford, W. H., 170

Galbraith, F. W., 132–33
Gallion, Emmett D.: Brown and, 164; charges against, 265n26; as criminal investigator, 141–42; Douglass and, 172–75, 186; and fusion politics, 181; Lee and, 139, 164, 169, 194–95, 263–64n6; Moore and, 168; Neel and, 173–74; as pension examiner, 130, 254n21; Powers and, 134–38, 140, 163, 170–71, 175, 263n1, 265n38
Galloway, Abraham, 36, 46–47
Gardner, Harriet (Woodus), 61, 156, 158–59
Gardner, Laura (Stott) and William, 61, 156–59, 262n65
Gatlin, Mary Ann and Riley, 152–53, 199–200, 264n9
General Instructions to Special Examiners of the United States Pension Office, 126, 128–29, 166, 178

general law pension system, 121, 132, 134, 144, 146, 151, 156, 182. *See also* Act of July 14, 1862, general law pension system
Gilmore, Glenda, 151, 192
Gilpin, Charles, 130, 163, 167, 170–71, 174, 178–80
Glymph, Thavolia, 38, 203, 224n78
Goddett family, 103, 246n4
Goethe, Thomas, 72, 130, 187–90, 200
Goodwin, Joanne, 211
Gordon, Linda, 11, 14, 108, 219n28
Grand Army of the Republic (GAR), 71, 148, 174, 177
grassroots pension networks: building of, 18; churches and, 119; claims agents and, 17; communities and, 120, 253n2; in New Bern, 5–6, 102, 114–17; postmaster and, 119; and witnesses, 120–21, 131
Green, Jamsey and Robert, 150, 160–61
Green, W. H., 176
Green, William A., 43, 229n139
Green, William Henry, 95–96
Grimes, Hull, 89
Gross, Kali, 196
Gutman, Herbert, 43

Hahn, Steven, 6, 51, 245n98
Haley, Sarah, 55, 190, 219n33
Hammond, Martha and Wright, 55, 84, 87
Hanehan, Betsey, 55
Hannel, Eugene, 81, 240nn6–7
Hargett, Dumar, 112–13, 249n71
Harris, Sarah (Richardson), 42
Harris, W. L., 130
Harris, W. O., 42
Harrison, L. F., 188
Harrison, William Frederick, 105
Harvey, Philis and Joseph, 53, 83, 121
Hassell, Mariah F. and Benjamin, 57–58, 120
Hassell, Mary, 91–92, 239n3
Heinegg, Paul, 28
Hendrick, Benjamin S., 79
Henson, Rosanna, 62, 237n107
Hicks, Cheryl, 15
Higginbotham, Evelyn Brooks, 10
Hill, E. G., 163, 170
Hill, Jane, 175, 177, 203, 266n54, 267n70
Hilton, Laura, 190, 264n9
Hine, Darlene Clark, 82, 167
Holloway, David, 88–89, 101, 151–52, 200–201
Holloway, Frances, 83
Holt, Thomas, 2, 8
Hood, James Walker, 46, 59
House, Callie D., 214
Howard, Oliver Otis, 2, 48–49, 51, 241n25
Hubbs, Ethelbert, 52–53, 83, 114
Huggins, Hardy (Stalp), 111
Hughes, Isaac W., 28
Hunter, Tera, 4, 10, 47, 94, 154
Hyman, John A., 71

interracial relationships, 8, 106–7, 142, 156–59
intimate partner violence, 7, 12–13, 112, 117, 135, 214, 246n22. *See also* Moore, Mary Jane (Sears) and Jacob
Ives, Penelope and Joseph, 55, 154–55, 234n69, 237n100, 264n9

Jackson, Louisa. *See* Powers, Louisa
Jackson, Lucy, 53
James, Hagar, 89
James, Horace, 32, 34, 44, 53, 224n73, 226n89, 227n101, 230n152
James City: blacks in, 52, 77, 117, 147, 193; church and school in, 53; Douglass in, 114, 120, 175; Freedmen's Bureau in, 51; land disputes, 199; property heirs and, 51; special examiners in, 68, 130; temporary settlement, 6, 16, 32; white missionaries in, 198–99. *See also* Trent River settlement
Jarmon, Dilcy, 87, 92, 121–22, 239n3, 243n60
Jenks, Michael E., 93
Johnson, Andrew, 48, 51, 54, 231n5
Johnson, Delia, 55
Johnson, James Weldon, 209
Johnson, John S., 79, 89, 119
Johnson, Lyndon B., 212
Joint Committee on Reconstruction, 50
Jones, Anna, 271–72nn64–65
Jones, Hansey, 147
Jones, Henry, 25, 35
Jones, Lanner, 38
Jones, Martha, 13
Jones, Mattie, 248n44
Jones, W. H., 176
Jones, Walter, 56
justice: economic, 5–6, 15, 182; pensions and, 18, 69–70, 72, 214

Kaye, Anthony, 5
Kelley, Lavinia and Thomas, 187–88
Kelley, Robin D. G., 214, 275n23

Kent, Mary E. and Henry, 28, 132–33, 191, 204, 255n41, 268n3
Kessler-Harris, Alice, 11
Ketter, Don, 106–7
Kincaid, D. H., 179–80
King, Francis P., 42
Kinsley, Edward, 36
Ku Klux Klan, 71

Larkins, Eliza, 56
Latham, Sarah and Jesse, 106, 120
Latham, Tammer, 193–94, 268n3, 270n41
Lavender, Ellis, 122
Lavenhouse, Judith and George (son), 44, 60, 150
Lee, Mary, 57, 114–15, 150, 257n71; appeals by, 139, 169, 182; Douglass and, 115, 137, 186; Gallion and, 138–39, 164, 169, 174, 263–64n6; grassroots pension network and, 120–21; investigations of, 72, 268n3; Mattie Jones and, 248n44; in New Bern, 79, 101; and pension benefits, 16, 18, 19, 145, 159, 166, 204–5, 262n76; and worthiness, 172, 194–95, 197
Lee, Phillip J., 59, 115
Lee, Simeon, 114, 138–39
Lemon, George E., 190
Levenstein, Lisa, 14, 214
Lewis, Frederick H., 156
Lincoln, Abraham, 29–30, 34–35, 237n107
Little, Louisa and James, 178, 196–98, 201, 203, 268n3, 272n65
Little, Maria and Benjamin, 131, 148, 268n3
Lochren, William, 163, 172
Long, Lila, 93, 239n3
Louisiana "employable mother" rule, 212
Lucas, Flora, 43

Manly, Mathias, 176, 257n80, 266n63
Manor, Edny, 27
Marcy, Henry Orlando, 37
marriage, 3, 105, 147: black women and, 3; and economic dependence, 92–94; legal, 4, 9, 12, 15, 84–86, 100, 144–45, 200; Pension Bureau and, 62–63, 84, 261n49; soldiers and, 43, 228n120, 230n140; and women's citizenship, 4, 38, 54. *See also* remarriage; slave marriage
Marriage Act of 1866 (North Carolina), 84–87, 103, 122
Marshall, Andrew J., 59, 116
Martin, Benjamin and Mary Ann, 106, 136
Martin, John A., 110
Mason, Charles, 132
Maxwell, H. P., 130, 179
McCabe, Thomas, 159
McClain, Dow, 129–30
McClintock, Megan, 13–14, 152
McCoy, Sarah, 55
McGuire, Danielle, 214
McSorley, Charles D., 72, 130, 194
Meigs, Montgomery C., 30, 32
Memphis riots (1866), 54–55
Mercer, Lewis, 55
Merrick, Emanuel, 79, 116, 251n90
Militia Act of 1862, 35, 38, 224n78
Mills, Quincy, 87
Mink, Gwendolyn, 11
Moles, Violet, 55
Moore, Charity, 98, 239n3
Moore, Leonidas J., 174, 177, 198
Moore, Liddia, 193
Moore, Mary Jane (Sears) and Jacob, 104–5, 109–10, 168–69, 203, 248n50, 264n23
Moore, Queen Audley, 214–15
Moore, Susan, 55
Morris, Brevett, 47, 57–58, 231n8, 235n82
Morris, Harriet and Caesar, 91–92, 261n51
Mosley, Robert G., 172

National Freedmen's Relief Society, 58
National Welfare Rights Organization, 212–13
Neel, Julia, 44, 83–84, 155–56, 173–74, 186, 241n28
Nelson, Charles Alexander, 53, 98, 233n40
New Bern, 16, 42, 52, 55, 220n1; antebellum, 18, 23–25, 29, 221n27, 223n49; blacks in, 27–30, 34, 46, 101, 230n152, 231n1, 245n3; black women in, 26, 39, 165, 222n30, 227n109; during Civil War, 29, 37–38, 223n49, Fifth Ward, 6, 16, 46–47, 50–52, 79; post–Civil War, 44–45; sanitary conditions, 42, 229n132; special examiners in, 129; whites in, 52, 165, 264n9. *See also* Craven County
New Berne Committee on Correspondence, 54
New Berne Journal, 177
New Berne Times, 53, 67, 84
Newbernian, 53, 81
Newbern Journal of Commerce, 82
Newbern Weekly Journal of Commerce, 47

New York Times, 68, 124, 175
New York Tribune, 79
Norman, Mary E. and Turner, 26, 53, 60, 111–13, 208, 249n63, 249n72, 250n77; Douglass and, 79, 102, 111, 153, 250–51n81; and pension claims, 120, 122, 144–45, 250n77
North Carolina Sentinel (New Bern), 27
nursing, 42–43, 228n124, 229n136

Oats, Charles, 38
Oden, Dicy and Allen G., 51–52, 146, 191, 257n80, 269n29
O'Hara, James, 58, 71, 116, 122, 129, 157, 236n89, 254n20
O'Leary, Cecilia, 71
Oliver, Cloie, 28
Oxley, John B., 82, 142
Oxly, Frances, 53, 233n44
Oxly, Sarah, 240n15, 241n17, 241n20, 254n20, 258n89; Carpenter and, 142, 177, 258n90; "The Colored Quakeress," 227n103; as entrepreneur, 39, 53, 82, 129

Palmer, Curtis, 169
Palmer, William L., 42, 52, 55, 83–84, 114, 141, 232n36
Peldon, Dianna, 199, 201, 233n42, 268n3
Penningroth, Dylan, 195
pension benefits, 18: and cohabitation/remarriage, 78, 91–92, 96–97, 99; eligibility, 146, 187; evidentiary requirements, 64–65, 142–43; and fraud and exploitation, 65, 67–68, 82, 86–87, 95, 147, 238n119; levels of, 159–60, 262n76; and marriage and widowhood, 9–10, 152–53, 158–59, 188, 260nn41–42, 269n21; means test, 146, 259n7; mothers and, 155–56; as rights, 7, 9, 19, 88, 102, 152–53, 155–56, 183, 188, 206, 260nn41–42; suspended, 93; survivors' benefits, 77; veterans and, 66, 160–61, 263n78
Pension Bureau (Pension Office), 65–66; and families, 10, 136; history, 8–9; and invalids, 253n1; and investigations, 127–29; and rights and equality, 123–24; rules, 125–26; Special Examination Division, 67–68, 70, 93, 124–26, 164–65, 167, 182, 194–95, 207
Perry, Caroline, 150
Pettiford, Allen, 55
Pickett, Violett, 268n3, 270n43
Pierson, Clinton D., 47
Pierson, Lydia, 53, 194, 197, 268n3
Plant, Rebecca Jo, 210
Platt, Thomas C., 127
Poole, Julia A., 55
Porter, William, 130, 141, 163, 265n37
poverty, 261n51
Powers, Louisa, 41, 101–4, 108–10, 228n124, 229n136; appeals by, 140, 201, 204, 257n66; and children, 106, 108, 172, 246n7, 247n28, 247n43, 265n34; Douglass and, 138; investigations of, 134–38, 140, 163, 169–71, 175; and pension claims, 16, 18, 19, 134–38, 145, 181–83, 205, 215, 268n85; and rape claim, 135, 139
Powers, Samuel, 36–37, 41–42, 101–3, 106–9, 135, 137, 163, 225n88
Powers, Siddy, 106, 136, 170–71
Prigden, Elizabeth, 71
Pritchard, Jeter C., 122, 175
Proctor, Caroline (Shine), 87
Proctor, David, 67, 82–83, 86–87, 92–93, 98–99, 188, 240n13
Proctor, Margaret, 188, 269n21
Proctor, Marinda (Dudley), 87

race: and class, 35, 193–94; and gender, 5, 11–12, 15, 73, 165, 208, 212–13
Ragsdale, George H.: Banks and, 89, 91, 150; Brown and, 156; Carpenter and, 68, 88, 97–98, 141; Proctor and, 87; as special examiner, 67, 78, 86, 92, 93, 95, 122
rape and sexual violence: black women and, 55, 253n3; concubinage, 82, 241n19; congressional hearings on, 13; pension claims and, 135, 139; Union soldiers and, 227n109; white supremacy and, 175–76, 266n57. *See also* Cradle, Rebecca Ann; intimate partner violence
Reconstruction (Foner), 5
Reconstruction, 4–5
refugees: Duplin county prisoners, 36–37, 225n88; migration to Union-occupied areas, 223n52; re-enslavement, 33–34, 224n69; temporary settlements, 226n89; Union Army employment, 32–35
Reidy, Joseph, 62
remarriage: pensions and, 63, 67, 78, 84, 86–89, 93–94, 96, 126–27, 154–55, 165, 256n45, 261n58; poverty and, 154–55, 166; sexual immorality and, 100, 164. *See also* marriage

reparations, 214–15, 275n23
Republican Party, 71–72, 181, 245n98, 267n83
respectability, 15, 70, 81–82, 105, 151, 192–97, 208, 220n48, 260n37, 270n37
Revised Pension Statutes amendment, 127, 256–57n65
Reynolds, Thomas, 56
Rhem, Joseph L., 26
Richardson, Hezekiah, 28, 54
Richardson, Jane and Henry, 26, 56, 97, 235n77
Richardson, Sarah. *See* Oxly, Sarah
Riggs, Lafayette, 27
Roanoke Colony, 34–35, 48–51, 224nn73–74
Roberts, J. O'C., 130
Rodman, Mary Ellison, 167–70, 193
Romeo, Sharon, 13, 40
Rosen, Hannah, 13, 55, 60
Rouse, Rebecca, 106–7
Rouse, Sam. *See* Powers, Samuel
Rowland, Leslie, 62
Rue, George, 59
runaways. *See* refugees

Schwalm, Leslie, 2–3
Schwartzberg, Beverly, 152
Scott, Rebecca J., 57
Selective Service Act, 209, 211
Selective Service Readjustment Act (GI Bill), 211–12
service law of 1890. *See* Dependent Pension Law of 1890
Settle, Thomas, 122
Sewall, Frederick D., 45
Seymour, Augustus Sherrill, 52–53, 67, 81, 240n10
Shaffer, Donald, 15
Sherman Act, 47, 231n5
Shontz, H. F., 130
Simmons, Arthur, 186
Simmons, Furnifold M., 157, 174, 199–200, 273n84
Simmons, Mary Ann, 133, 256n45
Simmons, Mathew, 94
Simmons, Matilda, 93, 121, 243n67
Simmons, William, 25
Singleton, William Henry, 36
Skinner, Amanda, 121
Skinner, Winney, 179
Skocpol, Theda, 13, 66, 144
Slade, Peggy and Miles, 148
Slaughter-House Cases (1873), 69
slave marriage: legal status, 112; meaning of, 145, 151–52, 200; retroactive recognition, 4, 9, 62, 78, 84, 187; scrutiny, 69–70, 152, 187–88
Sleight, Mary Ann, 65, 121
Small, Hannah and Alfred, 59, 116, 227n102
Smith, J. Speed, 133
Smith, Nicy and James, 153–54, 260nn47–48, 268n3
Social Security Act, 210–12
social welfare reform, 13–14
Southern Claims Commission, 83
Sparrow, Clarissa and Spencer, 147
Special Examination Division, Pension Bureau. *See* Pension Bureau, Special Examination Division
Spellman, Fannie, 179
Spellman, Rebecca, 88, 239n3
Spencer, Lucy, 191
Spicer, Benjamin B., 51, 232n29
Spivey, Washington, 57, 119
Squires, Amy, 79
Stamp, Ann, 32
Stanly, Catherine, 26, 222n30
Stanly, Edward, 33–35
Stanly, John C., 25, 221n19, 221nn21–22, 224n69
Starkey, Mary Ann, 32, 36, 38–39
Stevenson, Brenda, 82
Stevenson, Peter, 187
Stevenson, Rosannah, 108
Stockton, I. C., 130
Stott, Laura. *See* Gardner, Laura (Stott) and William
Sumner, Charles, 34, 224n70
Supplementary Pension Act (1864), 9, 61, 65

Thomas, Lorenzo, 40
Tinker, George, 52, 233n38
Titterton, Ritty, 140
Trent River settlement, 32, 40–41, 44, 48, 51, 226n89, 232n17, 232n29. *See also* James City
Tripp, Shadrick, 175, 266n52
Tubman, Harriet, 207, 274n1
Tucker, Richard, 60, 96, 230n140, 231n8
Tyler, Grafton, 130, 257n78

unworthiness. *See* worthiness
U.S. Colored Heavy Artillery (USCHA), 28, 42, 104

U.S. Colored Troops (USCT): chaplain, 229n139; disbandment, 54–55; flag ceremony, 38, 227n101; 135th Regiment, 54, 234n55; Thirty-Fifth Regiment, 37, 91, 102, 104, 189; U.S. Colored Infantry, 38
U.S. Department of the Interior, 138–40
U.S. Pension Bureau. *See* Pension Bureau (Pension Office)

Vonveil, Mary, 167–70

Walden, Mathew, 38
Wallace, Hetty and Benjamin, 161
Wallace, Maria, 54
Wallace, Violet Ann, 194, 197
Washington, David, 55
Washington Post, 68
Waters, Sarah and Isaac, 161, 170
Watson, Jim, 109, 134–35, 137–38, 170
Watterson, Harvey M., 45
Waugh, Carrie, 53, 199, 233n42
welfare state, 11, 207, 212–13, 215
Wells, Matilda, 40, 43, 121, 146, 179–81, 252–53n109, 268n3
Wendly, Hettie and George, 105, 195, 203, 247n26; Douglass and, 120–21, 191–92, 199; examiner interviews, 131–32, 188
Whitby, Mary, 108, 187
White, Charlotte, 109
White, George Henry, 58, 71–72, 110, 115, 177, 182, 184–85
Whiteley, Merritt, 116–17
Whitfield, Benjamin, 115–16
Whitney, Fanny, 5, 25, 35, 40, 48, 50, 79, 108, 189; Green and, 244n79; investigations of, 72, 95–96, 268n3; marriage laws and, 84, 162, 269n24; pension claims, 1, 6, 12, 16, 19, 77–78, *80*, 101, 205, 209
Whitney, Harry, 25, 37, 96, 175
Whittlesey, Eliphalet, 49–50
Wiggins, Philip, 36, 59–60, 116, 196
Wiggins, Violet, 154
Williams, Abner, 28–29
Williams, Clara and Silas, 189, 204, 268n3
Williams, Frank, 133
Williams, James, 180
Williams, Mary. *See* Lee, Mary
Williams, R. Amelia, 53, 199, 233n42
Williams, Sarah. *See* Copes, Sarah
Wilson, Jesse, 201
Windsor, Mattie C., 202, 273n88
Winn, Baily, 85, 156, 261–62n62
Woman's American Baptist Home Mission Society of Chicago, 53, 199
Woodard, Carolina, 55
Woodworth, Caroline, 55
World War I, 209–10
World War II, 211
worthiness 18–19, 124; black communities and, 6, 8, 12, 14, 47–48, 88–89, 91, 96, 110, 117, 128–29, 131–34, 136–37, 145, 147–50, 153–54, 168–69, 178–80, 183, 195–97, 206, 255n41, 258n4, 271n61; and morality, 69–70, 129–31, 147, 173, 178–80, 182–84, 189, 254n22, 256–57n65, 269n24; Pension Bureau officials and, 72–73, 78, 84–86, 95, 124–25, 127, 145, 147–48, 167–68, 184, 188–89, 194, 196, 253–54n11, 257n78, 259n15, 261n58; and surveillance, 7, 11, 165, 172, 184, 214; white supremacy and, 188–90, 237n115, 255n27; white women and, 15, 189–91
worthy widowhood, 9, 13, 172, 202–3, 219n28; black women and, 149, 166–68; and marriage, 10, 19, 92, 110, 124, 161–62, 183; and sexual immorality, 131

York, Amos, 122

Zipf, Karen, 59, 106–7, 247n31

CPSIA information can be obtained
at www.ICGtesting.com
Printed in the USA
LVHW080502300122
709678LV00014B/489